SHOW DOGS

Their Points and Characteristics.
How to Breed for Prizes and Profit.

Copyright © 2017 Read Books Ltd.
This book is copyright and may not be
reproduced or copied in any way without
the express permission of the publisher in writing

British Library Cataloguing-in-Publication Data
A catalogue record for this book is available from the
British Library

Photo., Elliot and Fry, Baker Street, W.

Yours faithfully,
Theo. Marples

SHOW DOGS

THEIR POINTS AND CHARACTERISTICS.
HOW TO BREED FOR PRIZES AND PROFIT.

WITH CHAPTERS ON THE ORIGIN OF THE
DOG, HIS INTELLIGENCE AND UTILITY, AND
HINTS UPON HOW TO SELECT PUPPIES

THIRD EDITION.
(REVISED.)

By THEO: MARPLES, F.Z.S.,
Editor of "OUR DOGS"
(Author of "Prize Dogs," "How to Choose a Dog," etc.)

Assisted in the Revision by
ARTHUR F. MARPLES,
Sub-Editor of "OUR DOGS"

TO MY ESTEEMED FRIEND,

THE LATE

J. SIDNEY TURNER, Esq., J.P., M.R.C.S., F.L.S., F.R.S. (Medicine),

FORMERLY CHAIRMAN OF

THE KENNEL CLUB,

AND A

DISTINGUISHED WRITER AND AUTHORITY ON DOGS,

THIS WORK

IS

MOST RESPECTFULLY DEDICATED.

PREFACE TO FIRST EDITION.

The great and growing interest which the British fancier everywhere nowadays takes in show dogs and their breeding and propagation must be the apology, if apology be needed, for one of their number having the temerity to place at their disposal in book form the result of a life's experience and observation in a pursuit which in many cases has developed into a profession.

The chapters of this work have already run through the pages of " Our Dogs," and the result of their incorporation and publication in book form is partly at the request of many fanciers, interested in one or other of the breeds treated upon, who have perused them, but more particularly from a desire on the part of the author to assist struggling breeders and exhibitors up the ladder of fame, by, in however small a degree, endeavouring to throw light upon the cult of the show dog and his successful breeding, and of imparting the result of his own knowledge and experience, gained from a long and close association with the pursuit. The work, while in no way claiming to be a pretentious one, is still practical, comprehensive, up to date, and, the author hopes, reliable, all the latest standard descriptions of the various breeds, which have been formulated by specialist clubs, being furnished, together with other information and data which it is hoped may be found interesting and of some benefit to the aspiring philokuon; and possibly the more experienced showman and expert may also glean something from its pages which may add to his knowledge of prize and pedigree dogs and their culture on scientific lines.

The treatment of dogs in health and sickness and their preparation for the show bench have been purposely omitted from this work, since that subject is dealt with in the author's other little work, entitled " Prize Dogs," etc., which now becomes an indispensable companion volume to " Show Dogs," the two works furnishing the average student in classic canine lore with a complete curriculum of the more salient features and requirements in connection with the breeding and exhibition of dogs.

THE AUTHOR.

PREFACE TO SECOND EDITION.

The interest which is taken in "dogs of high degree" by dog lovers the world over, referred to in the preface to the first edition of this work, has happily not only continued since its publication, but has, in the interim, grown to a great extent. Several new breeds have either been evolved or unearthed and established on fixed lines, and older ones brought to greater perfection; many pillars of the kennel world have during that period, alas! paid the inevitable debt, and new ones have sprung up, which, with other innovations, serve to punctuate the changes that have taken place, rendering necessary a revised edition of "Show Dogs" in order to bring everything connected with the classic dog bang up to date.

In this new edition a different method of illustration has, it will be seen, been adopted, which the author hopes will meet with the approval of its readers. Instead of photographs of more or less celebrated dogs which have adorned the British show bench, the author has selected the series of sketches of "Ideal" dogs of the different breeds, which that very clever canine artist, Arthur Wardle, contributed to and which ran through the pages of "Our Dogs" (which are reproduced by the special permission of "Our Dogs" Publishing Company, Limited). The essence of the change of illustration lies in the fact of these "ideal" drawings forming correct models for breeders to breed up to, and a guide to all persons who desire to possess the best specimens of the breed they severally affect.

The author has no apology to offer for the publication of this revised edition of "Show Dogs," since the many eulogiums the first edition received from the most eminent experts in the country and the unprecedented sale of the work together are indisputable testimony to its great appreciation by those in whose interest it is issued, and for which the author takes this opportunity of expressing his sincere gratitude and appreciation.

THE AUTHOR.

PREFACE TO THIRD EDITION.

The continued growth of the interest taken in pedigree prize dogs, the further development of their breeding to type, and general expansion of the operation of breeders and exhibitors, and the advent of several new breeds to the show bench, to be specialised in and placed upon the Kennel Club's register, must be my apology, if apology be needed, for the publication of this third and thoroughly revised edition of "Show Dogs," which is now brought right up to date and which has had the widest sale, probably, of any book on dogs ever published.

In this latest revision I have called in the services of my son, Mr. Arthur F. Marples, sub-editor of "Our Dogs," who, like his father, has made a study of and association with the canine cult, including kennel journalism, his sole occupation or profession, to which he has assiduously devoted himself from leaving school right up to the present.

The sketches of the newest breeds of dogs have been drawn by R. Ward Binks, whose beautiful canine portraiture is now so popular.

THE AUTHOR.

INDEX TO CHAPTERS.

	PAGE
Preface to First Edition	vii
" to Second Edition	viii
" to Third Edition	ix
Origin, History, Evolution, Utility, and Virtues of the Dog	xv
Kennel Club Classification of Breeds	xxiii
Airedale Terriers	137
Afghan Hounds	275
Alsatian Wolfdogs	153
Bassethounds	15
Beagles	12
Bearded Collies	199
Bedlington Terriers	140
Black-and-Tan Terriers (Min.)	219
Bloodhounds	1
Border Terriers	143
Borzois	34
Bulldogs	160
" (Miniature)	166
Bull-mastiffs	272
Bull Terriers	99
Cairn Terriers	150
Chow Chows	244
Clydesdale Terriers	238
Collies	192
Corgi	271
Dachshunds	20
Dalmatians	204
Dandie Dinmont Terriers	128
Deerhounds	30
Eastern Greyhounds	273
Elkhounds	42
Foreign Dogs	278
Foxhounds	9
Fox Terriers	103
French Bulldogs	167
Glossary of Technical Terms .... Facing Page	304
Great Danes	176
Greyhounds	26
Griffon Bruxellois	268
Harriers	11
Irish Terriers	109
Irish Wolfhounds	38
Italian Greyhounds	242
Japanese	225
Kennel Club Rules	283
Kerry Blue Terriers	113
King Charles Spaniels	220
Maltese	240
Manchester Terriers	215
Mastiffs	171
Miniature Trawler Toy Spaniels	232
Newfoundlands	181

	PAGE
Old English Broken-haired Terriers	127
Old English Sheepdogs	200
Otterhounds	7
Papillons	257
Pekingese	228
Pointers	50
Pomeranians	249
Poodles	207
Pugs	254
Retrievers (Flat-coated)	66
,, (Curly)	68
,, (Labrador)	71
,, (Russian Yellow)	73
,, (Golden)	75
Salukis	273
Samoyeds	247
Schipperkes	260
Scottish Terriers	120
Sealyham Terriers	116
Setters (English)	54
,, (Irish)	59
,, (Gordon)	62
Shetland Sheepdogs	264
Skye Terriers	133
Spaniels, Sporting (Irish Water)	78
,, (English Water)	81
,, (Clumber)	82
,, (Sussex)	85
,, (Field)	87
,, (English Springers)	90
,, (Welsh Springers)	93
,, (Cockers)	95
St. Bernards	186
Truffle Hunters	271
Turnspits	271
Unclassified British Breeds	271
Welsh Terriers	124
West Highland White Terriers	146
Whippets	47
White English Terriers	212
Yorkshire Terriers	234

INDEX TO ILLUSTRATIONS.

The Author		Frontispiece
Ancient Toy Dog	Facing Page	xviii
Australian Dingo	,,	281
Belgian Draught Dog	,,	xviii
Field Trials (Pointers at Work)	,,	xx
Græco-Roman Group of Prehistoric Dogs	,,	xvi
Miss Caselli with her Chihuahuas	,,	281
Mummy Heads of Egyptian Dogs	,,	xvi
Sheepdog Trials (Penning)	,,	xx

	PAGE
Airedale Terrier	137
Alsatian Wolfdog	154
Bassethound (Smooth)	15
,, (Rough)	17
Beagle	12
Bedlington Terrier	140
Black-and-tan Terrier (Miniature)	219
Bloodhound	1
Border Terrier	143
Borzoi	34
Bulldog	160
,, (Miniature)	166
Bull Terrier	99
Cairn Terrier	150
Chow Chow (Rough)	244
,, (Smooth)	245
Clydesdale Terrier	238
Collie (Rough)	193
,, (Smooth)	198
,, Scottish Bearded	199
Dachshund	20
Dalmatian	204
Dandie Dinmont Terrier	128
Deerhound	30
Elkhound	43
Foreign Dogs (Afghan Hound)	276
,, (Eskimo)	278
,, (Lhassa Terrier)	279
,, (Pyrenean Sheepdog)	282
,, (Tibet Mastiff)	280
Foxhound	9
Fox Terrier (Smooth)	103
,, (Wire-haired)	106
French Bulldogs	168
Great Dane	177
Greyhound	27
Griffon Bruxellois	268
Harrier	11
Irish Terrier	109
Irish Wolfhound	39
Italian Greyhound	242
Japanese	225
Kerry Blue Terrier	113

	PAGE
King Charles Spaniel (Black-and-tan)	220
,, (Blenheim)	221
,, (Ruby or Red)	222
,, (Tricolour or Prince Charles)	223
Maltese	240
Manchester Terrier	215
Mastiff	172
Newfoundland (Black)	182
,, (White-and-black)	184
Old English Sheepdog	201
Otterhound	7
Papillon	257
Pekingese	228
Pointer	50
Pomeranian	249
Poodle (Corded)	207
,, (Curly-coated)	209
Pug (Fawn)	254
,, (Black)	255
Retriever (Flat-coated)	67
,, (Curly)	70
,, (Labrador)	72
,, (Golden)	76
Saluki	274
Samoyed	247
Schipperke	260
Scottish Terrier	120
Sealyham Terrier	116
Setter (English)	55
,, (Irish)	60
,, (Gordon)	63
Shetland Sheepdog	265
Skye Terrier (Drop-eared)	133
,, (Prick-eared)	135
Spaniel (Irish Water)	79
,, (Clumber)	83
,, (Sussex)	85
,, (Field, coloured)	88
,, (English Springer)	91
,, (Welsh Springer)	93
,, (Cocker)	96
St. Bernard (Rough)	186
,, (Smooth)	188
Welsh Terrier	124
West Highland White Terrier	146
Whippet	47
White English Terrier	213
Yorkshire Terrier	234

The Origin, History, Evolution, Utility, and Virtues of the Dog.

The origin of species, so far as it relates to dogs, seems to be a subject which has never been thoroughly solved and which is probably insolvable. Scientists and students of natural history have for a long period of years endeavoured to penetrate the opaque atmosphere of the distant past, and although their historical and geological researches have given us a fund of the most interesting information and data, we are still left in great measure to conjecture in fixing the precise origin of the domesticated dog.

This being the position of things, it would be presumption on my part to attempt in this little work to traverse a region which has baffled some of the greatest scientists, or in other words to "rush in where angels fear to tread." Nor is the origin of the dog really very pertinent to this work, although, of course, it would be somewhat incomplete without some reference to the subject. That reference, however, will be brief, and the opinion of the author offered for what it is worth.

The most generally accepted theory is that the dog is descended from the wolf or jackal, one or both. It is quite true that he is closely allied to the former animal in structural anatomy, physical features, in his habits, such as the gyratory movements before lying down, the voiding of urine, and (leaving out the bark, which is, of course, an acquired habit, the result of domestication) the period of gestation is the same. It is a fact, too, that the domestic dog may be successfully crossed with the wolf, and from this fact it is assumed by some that the former is his original ancestor. Some writers include also the fox, but the physical differences between this vulpine and the dog are such as to prevent successful alliance, and I believe that whilst undoubted crosses between the dog and wolf have taken place, no really reliable and authentic case of a dog-fox or dog-jackal alliance having been successful is on record.

Mr. R. I. Pocock, author of a very able article on the ancestry of the dog, which appears in the first volume of *The Kennel Encyclopædia*, writing to me from the Zoological Society's Gardens, London, in answer to an enquiry, says :—

> Neither Dr. Chalmers Mitchell, the secretary, nor myself have any personal knowledge and experience of hybridism between dogs and jackals and dogs and foxes.

The foregoing, coming from two such eminent zoological authorities, reduces the hypothesis of the dog's origin to this single animal—the wolf—at most.

In the October number of *The Contemporary Review* appears an interesting article on the origin of the dog by Woods Hutchinson, who himself leans to the theory also of the wolf origin, but propounds the new one that instead of the dog having allied himself to man, man allied himself to the dog, which, however, is really one and the same thing.

The following are a few extracts from this article :—

> While the method of capture and rearing has played an important part in the domestication of the dog, there is a considerable and increasing body of evidence which points in another and rather unexpected direction. This is, to put it briefly, that instead of man adopting the dog into his family, *the dog adopted man into his pack !* This sounds at first distinctly improbable, and may even raise the cry of Nature Faker !

Yet those who have watched the ways of wild men and wild animals together most closely are the most inclined to regard it as not merely possible, but probable.

The mechanism of the process would appear to have been that a certain number of the more intelligent of the wolves or wild dogs of the region found that it was more profitable to follow man in his hunting expeditions and let him do the killing, for their share of the entrails and waste parts of the animal, than it was to kill for themselves. From following him on his hunting expeditions, they gradually came to following him home; and finding that bones and offal, and occasionally human bodies, were to be picked up around these encampments, they became a sort of permanent hangers-on of the tribe. In a little time, doubtless, man took the hint, and after he had wounded an animal found it was more profitable to sit down (savages always have plenty of time) and let his canine followers run in upon the quarry and chase it down, endeavouring to get in at the death himself, than to track it on his own account.

The writer, however, is, like all other writers, bound to confess himself beaten in his attempt to discover the precise origin of the dog. On this point he says:—

> The precise origin and pedigree of the dog is still "wropt in mystery." Long and keenly as it has been studied, we are no nearer a conclusion than in Darwin's day. Like his illustrious co-partner, ourselves we hardly are sure whether he is of single or of multiple origin. Whether each particular race or tribe of man domesticated or entered into an alliance with their particular variety of *Canis*, wolf, jackal, fox, dhole, which happened to range the same hunting grounds with them, and from this complex mixture grew up the modern dog in his innumerable varieties; or whether some single tribe happened to domesticate some now extinct form of wild canine which was so peculiarly adapted and suited to the purposes of the chase and of the sheepfold that he spread from hand to hand, and gradually supplanted all other rival breeds.

There are several facts which in my opinion tend to disprove the wolf descent theory, the most fatal being that hybrids generally are sterile and will not reproduce themselves. Then again, whilst wild dogs are easily reclaimed, the wolf remains a savage, and practically untamable. He has certainly been, on occasions, when born in captivity, tamed to a certain extent, but never to the extent that it would be safe, when grown up, to allow him his full liberty. Other alliances with animals and with birds of a kindred species somewhat disprove the wolf-dog theory. Alliances have been effected between the lion and tiger, but the hybrid offspring were sterile. Also between the horse and ass, but here again further reproduction stops, as it does in the case of the hybrids from crosses between other animals, and also between birds, notably the canary and linnet.

So much for the negative theory of the wolf origin, and now let me give one or two illustrations, which to my mind are further, if not conclusive, evidence of the dog having descended from a wild example of his own particular species.

Darwin, in his researches into the origin of the species, made several practical experiments. One of these was the collecting together of a large number of fancy pigeons of totally different sizes, varieties, and types, and allowing them to breed together. And what was the result? They all reverted back to one uniform type of pigeon—viz., the common wild wood pigeon, but still a pigeon and not any other bird. I contend that if the several divergent varieties of the horse were so bred together—from the shire horse to the Shetland—they would revert back to one uniform variety, and that the wild horse. So with the dog. If all the present-day varieties of the domestic dog were to be bred together, it is my firm conviction that the result would give us the wild dog pure and simple, many of which still inhabit different parts of the wilds of the world, the Dingo, or wild dog of Australia, probably

Specially photographed for the Author by Fradelle & Young, 283, Regent St., W.

BRACE OF GRÆCO-ROMAN DOGS OF GREYHOUND TYPE FOUND NEAR THE ANCIENT LANUVIUM AT MONTE CAGNOLO.

(*British Museum.*)

Specially photographed for the Author by Fradelle & Young, 283, Regent St., W.

MUMMY HEADS OF EGYPTIAN DOGS.

(*British Museum.*)

being a fair example of the original. If further evidence is necessary to support my theory, it is the fact that these wild animals, closely allied in type and character, such as wolves, jackals, foxes, hyenas, etc., on the one hand, and lions, tigers, leopards, wild cats, etc., on the other, do not, in their natural wild state, intermix, although, of course, they have many opportunities of doing so.

It seems scarcely feasible to assume that the "Great Architect of the Universe," whose handiwork in the animal kingdom is so perfect, the mechanism of which, to the minutest detail, is as perfect as the mainspring of all life is perplexing, would create a world of animals, birds, etc., the natural propensity of many of which is to feed upon one another, and leave man, the climax of His work, and who it is said He " made in His own image," practically defenceless among the savage beasts of the earth. There would, of course, be no repeating rifles in those days, no implements of war, or appliances of defence, except what the ingenuity of man in his most primitive state might invent; and unless he was a vegetarian, it seems most difficult to understand how he could procure flesh, or fowl, how he could protect his flocks or himself from the marauding propensity of wild beasts, without the aid of an animal of some sort.

With such a vast array of animals of every conceivable kind, many closely allied in physical structure and habits, yet really quite distinct, it seems unnecessary and indeed superfluous to search for the origin of the dog in a wolf ancestry. It would surely be little more trouble, while the Creator was at it, to create a species of wild dog, possessed probably of more intelligence and sagacity than a wolf, or jackal, which would lend itself more readily to subjugation by man, for which it was primarily intended, and with whom he would readily form an alliance, an offensive and defensive alliance as a companion, and to aid him in his pastoral pursuits, and the chase, which, we must assume, would constitute his sole and entire occupation.

In my opinion, the origin of the domestic dog is co-existent with the origin of man himself, and he will, in all likelihood, become extinct only with the extinction of the human race. My opinion is based, not upon learning, but upon logic and the facts to which I have already referred.

Historical records show that many varieties of the domestic dog have existed for thousands of years. Egyptian monuments and Roman sculpture depict dogs of many different and distinct breeds, such as a sort of Greyhound, Mastiff, Toys, etc., which were used for hunting, as guards, pastoral duties, for other purposes, and as pets. His evolution, therefore, is no new thing, but I think it will be quite safe to assert that in no other period of history has the same attention been given to the dog's culture and development on scientific lines as at the present time, or anything approaching it. The march of civilisation seems to have extended to the "friend of man," and with it a desire on the human's part not only to develop all the dog's innate faculties, but to improve his outward appearance. The aim of modern devotees has been to obtain a combination of utility with beauty, which is a process distinctly to be encouraged. And in no country has this process of canine evolution and development been carried to such an extent, nor reached such a pitch of perfection, as in the United Kingdom, the fancier instincts of whose inhabitants, their love of livestock and faculty for bringing breeds to perfection, are proverbial and known the world over. It is probably during the last half century more than during any other period, that the most progress has been made in the culture of the dog, during which England has become practically the market of the world for prize and pedigree stock in the way of horses, cattle, poultry, dogs, etc.

There are in the United Kingdom at the present time over 1,000 dog clubs and societies specially devoted to the culture of prize and pedigree dogs on arbitrary lines, conceived by the promoters to enable the different varieties of sporting or working dogs to fulfil their avocation to the best advantage, and in the case of purely fancy breeds to differentiate types and impart a distinctive feature of beauty to each, according to the ideas of the respective experts. Moreover, in no other period of history can it be shown that ladies ever took such a deep interest in dogs and their breeding and exhibition. In 1894 the ladies of the United Kingdom under the patronage of Her Majesty Queen Alexandra, a devoted dog lover and successful breeder and exhibitor of several varieties of the dog, notably Borzois, Japanese Spaniels, Bassethounds, etc., formed themselves into an Association—The Ladies' Kennel Association, since Incorporated, for the purpose of promoting and encouraging the breeding and culture of prize and pedigree dogs, and of instituting a competitive show, which is successfully held annually.

Under the beneficent influence of the Kennel Club—which was established in 1873, which has grown with the fancy, and contains in its ranks many of the most reputable and eminent experts in the doggy world, with the result that it has become the recognised kennel authority and has assumed governmental functions—the pursuit has been fostered and has grown to enormous proportions. Whereas in the old days association with dogs and dog shows was looked upon with a certain amount of reproach, the tables are now entirely turned, and not only do all classes of the community from the King (who is Patron) and H.R.H. the Duke of Connaught (who is President of the Kennel Club) down freely support and patronise these institutions, but it is felt to be a great honour to be associated, officially or otherwise, with dogs and dog shows, which is accentuated in the case of patrons of the sport who are fortunate enough to carry off prizes.

Most of the dog clubs and associations of foreign countries and our colonies are now affiliated to the Kennel Club, which gives to our ruling authority a wide and altogether unique international influence in the kennel world.

As showing the progress of public dog shows since their institution in 1859, by Mr. Pape at Newcastle-on-Tyne, when the entries all told numbered 60, I give the following table containing the number of classes provided and number of entries made at some of the leading shows in Great Britain and Ireland during 1924, the total number held in that year amounting to 1,219.

Show.	Classes.	Entries.
Cruft's	906	6,690
Manchester	529	3,957
Dublin	202	1,393
Ladies' Kennel Association	735	3,533
Cardiff	403	2,307
Kensington	794	4,878
Kennel Club	741	5,083
Edinburgh	530	3,431
Birmingham	773	4,651

In the olden time the dog was doubtless used for many purposes, which in these days of higher canine cultivation have been multiplied. In England, besides being an indispensable adjunct to the gun, he was used to track criminals, to guard property, and as a beast of burden. About the middle of the last century, immediately preceding the dawn of dog shows, the sentiment of the nation became so strong against his use for this last-named purpose that an Act of Parliament was passed abolishing it. The practice still survives in many countries, from those in the Arctic circle, where he is used to draw sledges, etc., down to those so contiguous to England even as Holland and Belgium, where the dog is largely used to draw milk carts, vegetable carts, carts on farms, and for many other purposes for which the horse and ass are ordinarily used in England.

Owing to many terrible murders in recent years in England, the ancient custom of the employment of the dog in the tracking of criminals has been revived, Bloodhounds having upon more than one occasion been so employed, in one case, that of the Blackburn murder, in 1878, with complete success, the dog in that instance being a half-bred Bloodhound.

Specially photographed for the Author by Fradelle & Young, 283, Regent St., W.
ANCIENT TOY DOG.
(*British Museum.*)

BELGIAN DRAUGHT DOG, EXHIBITED AT THE AMSTERDAM SHOW.
THE PROPERTY OF BARON VAN TUYLL.

Although dogs were used for war purposes both in England and other countries hundreds of years back, this country has only lately revived the custom. In Germany and France dogs are officially attached to their armies and specially trained as scouts and for ambulance work with the greatest success.

The fields of utility in which the dog is most largely employed in England are as the herdsman's and sportsman's assistant, for which peaceful pursuits he has been trained to very great perfection, and in which he shows marvellous prowess. Field Trials have been instituted for Sheepdogs all over the country, and there is no more interesting spectacle than to see a well-trained dog, by the mere wave of the hand or the whistle of his owner, gather semi-wild sheep together over vast tracts of country, put them through various obstacles and evolutions, and unaided fold in a small pen, in the space of a few minutes. Many stories of the marvellous sagacity of some farmers' dogs are told, which seem almost incredible. It is a common practice for dogs to single out particular sheep from a flock and bring them to a given point. But it is on record that a certain cattle dog, who was in the habit of accompanying its master, a butcher, to a market town to assist in bringing the beasts he purchased home, a distance of a dozen miles, on one occasion, when his master got helplessly drunk, the faithful dog took the cattle safely home himself, and then returned in quest of his master, whom he found by going from public-house to public-house which the sagacious dog knew he was in the habit of frequenting.

Hunting without the services of the dog would be an impossibility, and shooting would be bereft of a great deal of its charm. There is no finer sight than to see a well-trained Pointer or Setter hunt for, locate game, and then, instead of trying to catch and kill it, which is the dog's natural instinct to do, "pointing" or "setting" it, until his owner comes up, flushes and brings the birds down, which even then are left untouched by the faithful animal, whose education and training have eradicated his natural propensity and substituted this marvellous power of restraint. In this connection it is a most interesting sign of the times that in the many field trials for sporting dogs instituted by the Kennel Club, The International Gun Dog League, Spaniel Club, Labrador Retriever Club, Pointer and Setter Clubs, etc., the rather nondescript type of dog which characterised the competitions in the earlier trials is now finding many rivals in pure bred pedigree dogs which have distinguished themselves on the show bench. Doubtless the latter will increase as time goes on, and the nondescript gradually become altogether eliminated. All good show dogs of the sporting varieties are built on such lines as should enable them to fulfil their avocation in the field to the best possible advantage. Whether they are able to do so or not is all a question of natural aptitude (which no anatomy, however perfect, can supply) and training. There are, of course, different degrees of intelligence and sagacity in dogs, whether they be cross-bred or pure-bred, just the same as in human beings.

Then we have the performing dogs, the intelligence of many specimens of which is almost human. Lord Avebury, I think it was, entered upon a system of tuition of his dogs, with a view of fathoming the extent of their intellectual capabilities. He taught them by degrees to ask for food, water, to go out, go to their kennel, etc., by means of a set of cards with these requirements inscribed thereon, which proves the reasoning power of the dog to a certain extent.

Remarkable instances might be given of the wonderful homing instinct of the dog, and his rare sagacity in many directions, especially in that of rescuing human life from a watery grave, or from perishing on the snow-capped mountains of Switzerland, for which deeds he has earned imperishable fame.

Some owners of dogs are so imbued with a sense of admiration for the great intelligence and sagacity of their dogs, that they have brought themselves to believe they can talk, actually utter distinct words, but this theory is, of course, purely Utopian.

Of the dog's great fidelity and devotion to his master or mistress under all circumstances, favourable and adverse, everyone who has kept a well-reared dog will readily bear testimony. Whether his master be a prince or a poor man, his faithfulness and devoted attachment are just the same. He is just as contented to share the company, uncertain food and shelter of the latter, as he is to enjoy the association and luxuries of the former, and equally eager to protect and serve one as the other. In this connection the two finest of the many tributes paid to the innate worth of the dog are probably those of Lord Byron, in the famous verses and epitaph on his dog "Boatswain," and Senator Vest's not less famous panegyric on the dog.

The following inscription and epitaph are to be seen on Boatswain's tomb in Newstead Abbey, where the body was interred in 1808 :—

"Near this spot
Are deposited the Remains of one
Who possessed Beauty without Vanity,
Strength without Insolence,
Courage without Ferocity,
And all the Virtues of Man without his Vices.
This Praise, which would be unmeaning Flattery
If inscribed over human ashes,
Is but a just tribute to the Memory of
BOATSWAIN, a Dog,
Who was born at Newfoundland, May, 1803,
And died at Newstead Abbey, Nov. 18, 1808."

EPITAPH.

"When some proud son of man returns to earth,
Unknown to glory, but upheld by birth,
The sculptor's art exhausts the pomp of woe,
And storied urn records who rests below ;
When all is done, upon the tomb is seen,
Not what he was, but what he should have been :
But the poor dog, in life the firmest friend,
The first to welcome, foremost to defend,
Whose honest heart is still his master's own,
Who labours, fights, lives, breathes for him alone,
Unhonour'd falls, unnoticed all his worth,
Denied in Heaven the soul he held on earth :
While man, vain insect ! hopes to be forgiv'n,
And claims himself a sole exclusive heaven.
Oh, man ! thou feeble tenant of an hour,
Debas'd by slavery or corrupt by power,
Who knows thee well must quit thee with disgust ;
Degraded mass of animated dust !
Thy love is lust, thy friendship all a cheat,
Thy smiles hypocrisy, thy words deceit !
By nature vile, ennobled but by name,
Each kindred brute might bid thee blush for shame.
Ye ! who perchance behold this simple urn,
Pass on—it honours none you wish to mourn :
To mark a friend's remains these stones arise ;
I never knew but one,—and here he lies."

Shortly after the Civil War, when Senator Vest was a young man, just beginning the practice of law, and without the fame which afterwards became his, he happened to be in attendance upon a term of the Johnson County Circuit Court, at Warrensburg, Missouri. A suit for damages for the killing of a dog was on the docket, and was in due time called. Voluminous evidence was introduced to show that the defendant had shot the dog in malice, while other evidence tended to show the dog had attacked the man. There were attorneys engaged in this case who, if not then, have since

FIELD TRIAL POINTERS. CH. MISS SENSATION AND GARRYOWEN POINTING GROUSE. A BEAUTIFUL POINT AND BACKING.

SHEEPDOG TRIALS: PENNING.

become famous. Senator F. M. Cockrell and Ex-Gov. T. T. Crittenden defended, while Judge John Phillips, of the United States District Court, and Col. Wells H. Blodgett represented the owner. Senator Vest was not employed in the case, but was invited to speak for the plaintiff. The occasion is said to have been a rare one, and his speech has been highly praised, and has gone the rounds of the Press for forty years.

It is stated by those who were present at the trial that at the outset he took no apparent interest in the case, made no notes, and seemed preoccupied throughout the hearing of the testimony. Certainly he made no reference to any testimony introduced, but arose in his always quiet and dignified manner, deliberately scanned the face of each juror, and in a soft, low tone, unaccompanied by gesture of any kind, began his address :—

> Gentlemen of the Jury,—The best friend a man has in the world may turn against him, and become his enemy. His son or daughter that he has reared with loving care may prove ungrateful. Those who are nearest and dearest to us, those whom we trust with our happiness and our good name, may become traitors to their faith. The money that a man has he may lose. It flies away from him, perhaps when he needs it most. A man's reputation may be sacrificed in a moment of ill-considered action. The people who are prone to fall on their knees to do us honour when success is with us, may be the first to throw the stone of malice when failure settles its cloud upon our heads.
>
> The one absolutely unselfish friend that man can have in this selfish world, the one that never deserts him, the one that never proves ungrateful or treacherous, is his dog. A man's dog stands by him in prosperity and in poverty, in health and in sickness. He will sleep on the cold ground, where the wintry winds blow and the snow drives fiercely, if only he may be near his master's side. He will kiss the hand that has no food to offer ; he will lick the wounds and sores that come in encounter with the roughness of the world. He guards the sleep of his pauper master as if he were a prince. When all other friends desert he remains. When riches take wings, and reputation falls to pieces, he is as constant in his love as the sun in its journeys through the heavens.
>
> If fortune drives the master forth an outcast in the world, friendless and homeless, the faithful dog asks no higher privilege than that of accompanying him, to guard him against danger, to fight against his enemies. And when the last scene of all comes, and death takes his master in its embrace, and his body is laid away in the cold ground, no matter if all other friends pursue their way, there by the graveside will the noble dog be found, his head between his paws, his eyes sad, but open in alert watchfulness, faithful and true even in death.

The effect of the speech is said to have held the court room audience spellbound, and when Senator Vest concluded his remarks there was not a dry eye in the house. The case was submitted to the jury without further argument, and in a very few moments they returned a verdict in favour of the owner of the dog for the full amount sued for. The case finally reached the Supreme Court, where it was affirmed, and is set forth in detail in the 50th Missouri Reports.

Such is the account of this most touching tribute.

A YORKSHIRE POET'S TRIBUTE TO THE DOG.

One of the most touching tributes of the poor to the house-dog of the family circle is that written by a Yorkshire poet named Darbyshire, in the local vernacular, entitled—

"AHR PINCHER."

Seven-and-sixpence a year, dus ta 'ear?
    Fur a good-for-nowt dog like thee;
Thah kno's very well thah't not worth it,
    Er why dus ta blink so at me?
Come, lift up them ears o' thine, wil'ta
    And 'eer what thi gaffer's to say,
Thah's been a good useful servant,
    But, for aw that, thi time's up to-day;
Thah's fowt for thi friends like a tiger,
    Thah's play'd wi' these bairns like a lamb—
But we can't find brass for thi licence,
    Thah'll a' ta be thrown in t' dam.
Why, thah's whinin'! Thi tail's stop'd waggin'—
    Thah must understand what ah say;
Very well, then, thah shan't go i't watter,
    We'll tak' thee and gi' thee away;
Else loise thee—but thah's owt but a beauty:
    Foaks al' say thah wur best lost ner fun;
But we, that have reared thee and kno' thee,
    Al' loise a good friend when thah't gone.
When we come dahnstairs in a mornin'
    We s'll miss thi owd friendly wag;
And at neet, when we come fro't factory,
    Thah'll not meet us, so fussy and glad.
And these childer, how they'll miss thee,
    When they haven't thi long ears to pull;
Here, come and lay dahn upo' t' arston—
    Can't ta see that me heart is full?
But thah't not gone yet, and thah kno's it,
    Er, why ar' ta' waggin' thi tail?
Can't ta see what ah've just been thinkin',
    To do wi' less bacca and ale?
Ay, thah't an owd un! Where's me hat?
    Thah's helped me to get ah't o' t' fix.
Stop here; tak' care o' these childer,
    Ah'll go and get Seven-and-six.

THE KENNEL CLUB'S CLASSIFICATION OF BREEDS.

SPORTING BREEDS.

SPORTING.

AFGHAN HOUNDS.
BASSET HOUNDS.
BEAGLES.
BLOODHOUNDS.
BORZOIS.
DACHSHUNDS.
DEERHOUNDS.
ELKHOUNDS.
FOXHOUNDS.
GREYHOUNDS.
HARRIERS.
IRISH WOLFHOUNDS.
OTTERHOUNDS.
SALUKIS.
WHIPPETS.

GUNDOGS.

ENGLISH SETTERS.
GORDON SETTERS.
IRISH SETTERS.
POINTERS.
RETRIEVERS (Curly-coated).
,, (Flat-coated).
,, (Golden).
,, (Labrador).
,, (Interbred).
,, (Crossbred).

SPANIELS (Clumber).
,, (Cocker).
,, (Field).
,, (Irish Water).
,, (Springer, English).
,, (Springer, Welsh).
,, (Sussex).

TERRIERS.

AIREDALE TERRIERS.
BEDLINGTON TERRIERS.
BORDER TERRIERS.
BULL TERRIERS.
CAIRN TERRIERS.
DANDIE DINMONT TERRIERS.
FOX TERRIERS (Smooth).
,, (Wire).
IRISH TERRIERS.
KERRY BLUE TERRIERS.
MANCHESTER TERRIERS.
SCOTTISH TERRIERS.
SEALYHAM TERRIERS.
SKYE TERRIERS.
WELSH TERRIERS.
WEST HIGHLAND WHITE TERRIERS.

NON-SPORTING BREEDS.

NON-SPORTING.

ALSATIAN WOLFDOGS.
BULLDOGS.
CHOW CHOWS.
COLLIES (Rough).
,, (Smooth).
DALMATIANS.
FRENCH BULLDOGS.
GREAT DANES.
MASTIFFS.
NEWFOUNDLANDS.
OLD ENGLISH SHEEPDOGS.
POODLES.
POODLES (Miniature, under 15 in.).
ST. BERNARDS.
SAMOYEDES.
SCHIPPERKES.
SHETLAND SHEEPDOGS.

TOY DOGS.

BLACK-AND-TAN TERRIERS (Miniature).
GRIFFONS BRUXELLOIS.
ITALIAN GREYHOUNDS.
JAPANESE.
KING CHARLES SPANIELS.
MALTESE.
PAPILLONS.
PEKINGESE.
POMERANIANS.
PUGS.
YORKSHIRE TERRIERS.

Any other Breed or Variety not Classified above.
(Breed or Variety to be Specified).

CROSS-BREEDS.

CHAPTER I.

The Bloodhound.

This imposing specimen of the canine tribe, by its phenomenal features, its sage appearance, and historical tradition, excites more interest and curiosity probably than any other of the species. Its origin, like that of many other breeds which have been handed down to us, is " wropt in mystery." When so many of our historians, ancient and modern writers, and latter-day experts, including such authorities as Mr. Edwin Brough and Dr. Sidney Turner, have failed to fix the Bloodhound's exact origin and evolution, it is useless for me

BLOODHOUND.

to attempt to do so. I will, therefore, content myself by giving the most authentic data on the subject which are at present available.

The following appears in " British Dogs," published in 1903, the author of which is A. W. Drury :—

The first printed book touching on dogs that we have is the " Book of Huntynge," by Juliana Berners. The list of dogs given by her does not include Bloodhounds, but it does the Lemor and Raches, both of which were dogs that ran their game by scent, and the former was probably the nearest approach to our notions of a Hound, and was used to trace the wounded deer, etc., the name Lymer being taken from the fact of his being led in a leash, or lyam. In more ancient times, the Lyme-hound, under the name of Inductor, appears to have been employed to lead up to the harbour of the game sought, being selected for that work on account of the superiority of his scenting powers. Xenophon (500 B.C.) describes a Lymehound as a dog that follows up by scent the quarry in quest, and then, calling others together, rouses the game by barking. The principles of breeding were sufficiently well known to the hunting men of Greece and Italy to assure us that this special superiority of nose would be propagated and improved by mating the animals most distinguished in that quality; in fact, the first principle in breeding, and one that lies on the surface, staring the most unobservant in the face, that like produces like, would certainly be acted on, and so the earliest steps be taken in fixing a special type of Hound, the particular quality of which we see inherited now by many allied breeds.

No doubt at the date at which the " Book of Huntynge " was written, and for a long time previous, English Hounds were being modified by crosses from imported dogs brought in by the Norman conquerors from France, some varieties of them having originally come from the East, and the slow hunting Hounds of that day have, by various commixture, produced for us the varieties we now recognise.

Dr. Caius mentions the Bloodhound as " the greatest sort which serves to hunt, having lips of a large size, and ears of no small length." In Turberville's " Book of Hunting " there are a number of dogs portrayed, all of a Hound type, and with true Hound ears; whereas, in the " Book of St Albans," printed a century earlier, the dogs represented have much smaller ears, and thrown back, as the dogs are seen straining on the slips, Greyhound-like. Turberville has a good deal to say about Hounds. If he could be credited, the progenitors of our modern dogs originally came from Greece, and the first of them that reached this country were landed at Totnes.

It was the custom in Turberville's time to range the dogs according to colour; of these, white and fallow, white spotted with red, and black, were most esteemed. White-spotted with black or dun was not so very much valued. The best of the fallow dogs were held to be those with their hair lively red, with white spots on the forehead, or a white ring round the neck; and of these it is said : " Those which are well joynted and dew-clawed are best to make Bloodhounds," clearly showing, as passages from all the old writers could be quoted to do, that the term Bloodhound was applied to the dog because of the work set him, and that, in fact, where Hounds are spoken of the Bloodhound is included. That the work of this Hound was varied—that he was used as a Lymehound, as well as in tracking wounded deer and deer-stealers, sheep-stealers, and other felons, even so late as two centuries ago, is clear from Blome's instructions in his work, " The Gentleman's Recreation " (1868) : " To find out the Hart or Stag, where his harbour or lare is, you must be provided with a Bloodhound, Draughthound, or Sluithound, which must be led in aliam; and, for the quickening his scent, it is good to rub his nose with vinegar."

Blackhounds, called St. Huberts, are described as mighty of body, with legs low and short, not swift in work, but of good scent. The following couplet shows that the St. Hubert Hounds were highly thought of—

My name came first from holy Hubert's race;
Soygllard my sire, a Hound of singular grace.

The Count le Couteulx de Canteleu, in his work, " Les Races des Chiens Courans Francais," says : " The Hounds of St. Hubert, famous since the eighth century, under the name of Flemish Hounds, were divided into two varieties, the black and the white. The most esteemed was the black variety, and the abbots of the St. Hubert Monastery preserved the breed in memory of their founder. They were generally black, running into tan, tan markings over the eye, and feet the same colour; long ears."

Descendants of the white St. Huberts existed in the Duke of Lorraine's Hounds, spoken of by Ligniville ; Salno also mentions the existence of the black and the white St. Huberts in their native country, the Ardennes.

In 1620 we have an account of two packs of the black-and-tan St. Huberts belonging to the Cardinal de Guise and the Marquis of Souvray. The St. Huberts were transported to England at the time of the Conquest, and Henry IV. presented a team to James I. From about 1200 to the year 1789, the abbots of the St. Hubert Monastery annually supplied the royal kennels of France with three couples of black-and-tan St. Hubert Hounds, which were used as limiers, and were very greatly prized. At the end of Louis XIV.'s reign, according to Gaffet de la Briffardiere, they were preserved by gentlemen in the North of France for their all-round hunting capacities. By the time of D'Yauville the breed had become rare.

There is no higher living authority on the question than the Count, and he has no doubt that the Bloodhound was derived from the St. Hubert. He considers that at the time when fox hunting in something like its present form was first instituted, the Sleuthound, or hound of the country, was not found fast enough, and crosses were made with the Greyhound and other breeds, and gradually the present Foxhound was evolved. During this transition it became customary, when speaking of the hound of the country (as distinct from the Foxhound), to allude to him as the Bloodhound, meaning the Hound of pure blood, just as we speak of a blood horse.

"Stonehenge" has the following on the origin and antecedents of the breed in his work written in 1887 : This breed is so named because it is supposed to possess peculiar powers of scenting the blood flowing from the wounds made in its quarry. Before the invention of the rifle, the arrow was used to give the first wound, and this was sufficient to enable the forester to make his pick from the herd, because, though the arrow would seldom cause immediate death, yet it would lead to a flow of blood sufficient to induce the Bloodhound to hunt that one deer in preference to the rest of the herd. He was also employed to track the sheep-stealer, in which occupation his tendency to follow blood was developed in a similar manner. At present the deadly rifle has taken one occupation from him, and the law, by preventing sheep-stealing, has deprived him of the other. Hence it has come to pass that the Bloodhound is now kept for ornamental purposes only. Many breeders of this dog, however, still contend that he might be made useful in tracking criminals if laid on the trail of one shortly after a crime is committed. In Cuba, no doubt, a dog of more or less pure breed was used to hunt slaves, and as the African is well known to emit a strong scent, it is probable that this was taken advantage of by the white slave-owner. But it seems impossible that any dog can be taught to hunt a white man (supposing him to be a stranger) without exciting him to hunt all of the same colour. The matter was publicly tested at Warwick this year, but in a most imperfect manner, and it still remains unsettled.

From the foregoing, it will be seen that not only is the origin of the Bloodhound somewhat obscure, but even its name, one authority ascribing it to the incident of this Hound originally tracking his quarry from the stains of blood let fall, another putting it down to the fact of the dog being a sort of thoroughbred—a Hound of pure blood, hence the word. That the breed is of great antiquity goes without saying, and that its scenting powers are, by reason of its enormous nasal development, more acute than any other breed, is beyond dispute. It is this fact which impelled the authorities of olden times to use the Bloodhound for tracking criminals. Even in our own time the dog has been so used. It was a Bloodhound, it will be remembered, that unearthed the Blackburn barber, Fish, the murderer of the little girl, Emily Holland, 50 years ago, after the efforts of the police were completely baffled. The dog winded the scalp of the poor little victim, concealed in the chimney of the murderer's shop. Later, in 1889, when the London police were baffled in their attempts to discover the author of the series of Whitechapel murders, supposed to have been perpetrated by a person boldly signing himself "Jack the Ripper," the then chief of the Metropolitan Police, Sir Charles Warren, sent for Mr. Edwin Brough, of Scarborough, who at the time owned the largest kennel of the breed in England, and who, without doubt, is the most capable judge and greatest living authority on the breed, authorising this gentleman to put some of his Hounds on the trail of the arch-criminal. And although Mr. Brough put one or two of his cleverest Hounds, practised in hunting the clean boot, on the track of this fiend, his efforts were futile in running the criminal to earth. The labyrinth of footprints which in the late and early hours characterise the pavements of busy London, with its surging millions of population, proved to be too intricate for the subtle powers of smell of Hounds with the most refined olfactory organs, and so the Whitechapel murders remain a mystery to this day.

This experiment was not lost to the world, however, for although a failure, it focussed public opinion to the possible utility of the Bloodhound in such cases, although, of course, a large section of the community look with repugnance upon the practice of hunting men down by the aid of Bloodhounds, which savours of a return to the dark ages—to the days of serfdom and slavery.

From that date, breeders began to turn their attention more to a cultivation of the well-attested olfactory powers of their Hounds, which were being bred almost exclusively for the show bench, and whose powerful organs of smell were lying comparatively dormant. Soon the Association of Bloodhound Breeders was formed, which instituted field trials, several of which have been held, and some of them very successfully. Various stakes, single, in couples, and teams, were offered to the hounds showing most prowess in hunting the clean boot on a course which was secured and carefully protected, as far as possible, from human tread for some time before the trials. The services of judges of eminence in the hunting field were secured, and altogether the innovation proved to be as popular with the public as it has been beneficial to the Hounds in developing their great qualities, which previously had rarely been called into requisition. Following this Association, the Bloodhound Hunt Club was instituted, whose aim and objects were much the same, the latest development in this direction being the formation by the late Mr. Henry P. East, of the Holmleigh (Devon) Bloodhound Hunt, which regularly met and hunted the clean boot, just like Foxhounds do the fox, and which was the only club ever formed for such a purpose. This hunt was discontinued with the almost tragic death of its master, but, of course, may be revived. There is also the Northern Bloodhound Club and a Bloodhound Club of America, which was founded in 1894. The latter's name is the English Bloodhound Club, and one of its objects, which are set out in the preamble of its constitution, is as follows:—

> To improve and to encourage the Bloodhound breed of dogs in America, and to assist in establishing their more general use in connection with the detective service of the country.

The chief points to look for in the selection of Bloodhound puppies at from two to four months old, and even afterwards, are : Great length of head, narrowness of skull, great depth and squareness of foreface, big nostrils, long ears, set low, great bone, and short back.

The following description of the Bloodhound, or Sleuthhound, was drawn up by Dr. J. Sidney Turner and Mr. Edwin Brough, and has been adopted by the Association of Bloodhound Breeders :—

GENERAL CHARACTER.—The Bloodhound possesses in a most marked degree every point and characteristic of those dogs which hunt together by scent (Sagaces). He is very powerful, and stands over more ground than is usual with Hounds of other breeds. The skin is thin to the touch, and extremely loose, this being more especially noticeable about the head and neck, where it hangs in deep folds.

HEIGHT.—The mean average height of adult dogs is 26in., and of adult bitches 24in. Dogs usually vary from 25in. to 27in., and bitches from 23in. to 25in.; but, in either case, the greater height is to be preferred, provided that character and quality are also combined.

WEIGHT.—The mean average weight of adult dogs, in fair condition, is 90lb., and of adult bitches 80lb. Dogs attain the weight of 110lb., bitches 100lb. The greater weights are to be preferred, provided (as in the case of height) that quality and proportion are also combined.

EXPRESSION.—The expression is noble and dignified, and characterised by solemnity, wisdom, and power.

TEMPERAMENT.—In temperament he is extremely affectionate, neither quarrelsome with companions nor with other dogs. His nature is somewhat shy, and equally sensitive to kindness or correction by his master.

HEAD.—The head is narrow in proportion to its length, and long in proportion to the body, tapering but slightly from the temples to the end of the muzzle, thus (when viewed from above and in front) having the appearance of being flattened at the sides, and of being nearly equal in width throughout its entire length. In profile, the upper outline of the skull is nearly in the same plane as that of the foreface. The length from end of nose to stop (midway between the eyes) should be not less than that from stop to back of occipital protuberance (peak). The entire length of head from the posterior part of the occipital protuberance to the end of the muzzle should be 12in., or more, in dogs, and 11in. or more, in bitches.

SKULL.—The skull is long and narrow, with the occipital peak very pronounced. The brows are not prominent, although, owing to the deep-set eyes, they may have that appearance.

FOREFACE.—The foreface is long, deep, and of even width throughout, with square outline when seen in profile.

EYES.—The eyes are deeply sunk in the orbits, the lids assuming a lozenge or diamond shape, in consequence of the lower lids being dragged down and everted by the heavy flews. The eyes correspond with the general tone of colour of the animal, varying from deep hazel to yellow. The hazel colour is, however, to be preferred, although very seldom seen in red-and-tan Hounds.

EARS.—The ears are thin and soft to the touch, extremely long, set very low, and fall in graceful folds, the lower parts curling inwards and backwards.

WRINKLE.—The head is furnished with an amount of loose skin, which in nearly every position appears superabundant, but more particularly so when the head is carried low; the skin then falls into loose pendulous ridges and folds, especially over the forehead and sides of the face.

NOSTRILS.—The nostrils are large and open.

LIPS, FLEWS, AND DEWLAP.—In front the lips fall squarely, making a right angle with the upper line of the foreface; whilst behind they form deep, hanging flews, and being continued into the pendant folds of loose skin about the neck, constitute the dewlap, which is very pronounced. These characters are found, though in a less degree, in the bitch.

NECK, SHOULDERS, AND CHEST.—The neck is long; the shoulders are muscular and well sloped backwards; the ribs are well sprung, and the chest well let down between the forelegs, forming a deep keel.

LEGS AND FEET.—The forelegs are straight and large in bone, with elbows squarely set; the feet strong and well knuckled up; the thighs and second thighs (gaskins) are very muscular; the hocks well bent and let down and squarely set.

BACK AND LOIN.—The back and loins are strong, the latter deep and slightly arched.

STERN.—The stern is long and tapering, and set on rather high, with a moderate amount of hair underneath.

GAIT.—The gait is elastic, swinging, and free, the stern being carried high, but not too much curled over the back.

COLOUR.—The colours are black-and-tan, red-and-tan, and tawny; the darker colours being sometimes interspersed with lighter or badger-coloured hair, and sometimes flecked with white. A small amount of white is permissible on chest, feet, and tip of stern.

CHAPTER II.

The Otterhound.

This is an ancient British sporting breed, a number of packs of which are kept in different parts of the country, which are regularly hunted. They are very naturally located where rivers are well stocked with fish, for those may be said to be the natural preserves and haunts of the carnivorous aquatic, the otter, who is exceedingly hard bitten when cornered.

The sport of otter hunting is a very old one, records of which can be found as far back as the twelfth century. There are probably from 15 to 20

OTTERHOUND.

packs kept in Great Britain and Ireland at the present time, which is not a large number, the principal being the Dumfriesshire, Carlisle, and the Culmstock. A pack consists of anything from 9 to 14 couples.

[1] The earlier Otterhounds were of much smaller size than the present-day animal, having been produced probably by a cross between a large rough Terrier and Water Spaniel. The increased size has no doubt been obtained by later crosses with the Scottish Deerhound and English Bloodhound, of which the most typical exhibition specimens of to-day show unmistakable traces. The weight of one of these will be anything between 85lb. and 100lb., height at shoulder 25 or 26 inches, length of head from occiput to tip of nose 11 to 12 inches. These rough measurements indicate the size of the dog, who is well balanced in his proportions, with a deep chest, straight

7

forelegs, short back, and powerful quarters. He has a long, narrow head, with deep flews, and big nose, rather small deep set eyes, well protected by thick eyebrows, but with very little stop. His ears are low set and long, folding like those of a Bloodhound. The coat should be rough and wiry, grizzle in colour, skin thick, which together offer the best resistance to the water. In general appearance he is a large, rugged-looking, symmetrical dog, full of Hound character, with a look of great hardihood and determination.

It is possible that the Otterhound may have been imported from France, for he is an almost exact replica of the famous Vendee Hounds, and about the same size.

Whatever the origin of the Otterhound may have been, or its component parts are, its type and features are now well established and understood. As an exhibition animal, the breed has never been very popular, having altogether escaped the attentions of the fancier. Classes are provided at only the Crystal Palace, Birmingham, and one or two of the larger shows, the entries invariably coming from the hunts mentioned. There is no specialist club for the Otterhound, and consequently no standard of points laid down.

The chief points to look for in the selection of Otterhound puppies, at from two to four months old, are those detailed in the selection of Bloodhound puppies, added to which is a dense coat.

CHAPTER III.

The Foxhound.

This is undoubtedly the king of British Hunting Hounds. His origin again has never been clearly traced, but a consensus of authoritative opinion ascribes the old Talbot Hound as his foundation. No doubt as time went on, huntsmen might desire that the Foxhound should be made a little speedier, and for this purpose a Greyhound cross may have been obtained. Again, in order to maintain or improve his tenacity, an infusion of Bulldog blood may at some time have been resorted to, but that was before Bulldogs were brought

FOXHOUND.

to their present pitch of perfection. It would be the blood of the old, long-faced, leggy, fighting, and bull-baiting type. We, however, owe, without doubt, the beautifully balanced, graceful, and clean-cut Hound of to-day more to careful selection in his breeding than to any out-crosses. The English Foxhound is the hackney and the gamecock of the canine tribe. There are high breeding, pluck, and endurance stamped in every line of his anatomy. The beautiful straight forelegs, like gun-barrels, and short strong feet are one of the great features of the breed. In describing the virtues of any other breed in which straight forelegs and good strong feet are a *sine qua non*, it is quite a common thing for a person to sum these good points up by saying the dog has " legs and feet like a Foxhound," such an established virtue has this part of the dog's anatomy become. So is it with his oblique and well-laid

9

back shoulders, his gracefully arched neck, enormous spring of rib, strong loins, and powerful hindquarters—all prominent features in the breed, and properties that give to the dog pace and endurance, paramount qualities in the hunting field. The head of the Foxhound should be equally well balanced, the skull flat and of medium width, the muzzle long, rather narrow and deep, and square at the end, with large nostrils. The head should be level throughout, and almost free from "stop," the "flew" being only moderately developed. Ears close to the head, eye hazel colour and medium in size. The colour of the Foxhound is not of great moment, so long as it is not black or wholly white. The favourite colour is black and hare tan, distributed in large patches on a white body, but hare-tan patches are quite admissible. The ears of Foxhounds are surgically rounded in order to avoid their being lacerated in forcing their way through bramble or hawthorn. The English Foxhound is smooth-coated, but there is a wire-haired variety indigenous to Wales, which is called the Welsh Foxhound, but which is sometimes used in the Principality for hunting the hare. These dogs are of lighter build, and do not possess the substance or squareness of muzzle of their English prototype. The types of English Foxhound vary little in consequence of the varying nature of the country over which they are hunted. In a mountainous district a rather lighter Hound is used, and in a flat country a sturdier type of dog, but taken altogether their type and character are very uniform.

Fox-hunting, the sport of kings, is greatly cherished in the British Isles, and has been a favourite pursuit of the nobility and aristocracy from feudal times. The strains of different hunts are preserved with the greatest care, the Foxhound Stud Book, which contains authenticated pedigrees of dogs for hundreds of years back, being held in the greatest reverence by hunting men—it is their Bible. The aggregate amount of money expended in Fox-hunting in this country annually must be very considerable—amounting probably to millions.

We, however, are not treating in this little work upon the national sport in which the Foxhound is used, but merely as an exhibition specimen. Classes for Foxhounds are provided at several of our principal shows, whilst a really good specimen is almost a "dead snip" for first prize in a mixed "Sporting Variety" or "Any Variety" class, which invariably appear in the schedule of all shows. The Peterborough Hound Show is devoted entirely to English hunting Hounds, and is the most unique and interesting show in the world. Here may be seen the pick of most of the packs of Foxhounds, Harriers, and Beagles in the three kingdoms—a show that furnishes an object-lesson in Hound lore.

There is no hard-and-fast rule as to the weight of a Foxhound, but the best weight is from 75lb. to 85lb. for dogs, and 2lb. or 3lb. less for bitches. Height at shoulder from 23in. to 25in. Snipiness, coarse skull, cow hocks, flat sides, unstraight forelegs, and open feet are unpardonable faults in a Foxhound, and coarseness in coat should heavily discount a dog's other good properties.

The chief points to look for in the selection of Foxhound puppies, at from two to four months old and after, are: A long, level head, big nostrils, square muzzle, great bone, deep chest, short back.

CHAPTER IV.

The Harrier.

This comes second in importance from a hunting point of view to the Foxhound, of which he is a smaller edition to a great extent. There is, however, less uniformity in size and type in the Harrier than the Foxhound, some packs of Harriers averaging 50lb. to 55lb., and others reaching 70lb. to 75lb. Some are of a low-set, sturdy type, and others of a much more racy build, these varieties being due to the difference in the nature of the country over which they are hunted. Some packs of Harriers partake more of the

HARRIER.

Beagle in type and character, whilst others show marked Bloodhound characteristics, notably the Penistone Harriers, one of the oldest hunts in the country. The Southern Hounds are quite different, being far smaller, and for the most part lower set in build. It is therefore most difficult to lay down a code of points for the Harrier as an exhibition specimen, in view of the existence of this variation in size and character. There are, however, several leading features in common in all Harriers, and these are : Long heads, free from stop, square muzzles, sloping shoulders, straight forelegs, round, cat-like feet, short backs, well-sprung ribs, strong loins, and sound hindquarters with well-bent stifles. These are indispensable properties in all hunting Hounds, whose caudal appendages should be of sickle shape when carried in full cry, and all of whom should possess true Hound character, free from any alien tinge, and move with the greatest liberty and freedom.

The chief points to look for in the selection of Harrier puppies at two to four months old and after are those detailed in connection with the Foxhound.

CHAPTER V.

The Beagle.

The Beagle is so seldom exhibited that his claim to be considered "a show dog" may be open to question, but it is at least as strong as the Foxhound, Harrier, and Otterhound already described. The friends of the merry little Beagle would prefer to describe him as "the smallest variety of Hound." Still, specimens are from time to time exhibited; a few of our leading shows provide classes, and three or four times a year we may be sure of seeing a grand turnout of the little Hounds, at the Summer Show of the Beagle Club,

BEAGLE.

at Peterborough, which is confined to hare-hunting packs, and at one or two other well-known fixtures.

The Beagle is without doubt one of the oldest distinct breeds we have; the poet Appian, who wrote about the year 200, is made by translators to refer to the Beagle, and so are the forest laws of King Canute, but if we skip these and come to modern times, it is certain that Queen Elizabeth had a favourite pack of "Pocket" Beagles, then called the "Glove" or "Singing" Beagle. George IV. revived them, but does not seem to have been able to get them so small, and Prince Albert continued the attempt with more or less success, since which time Beagles have not basked in royal favour. The following excellent description was published over sixty years ago in the "Sportsman's Library," by Mr. Mills:—

"Beagles to be very choice can scarcely be bred too small. The standard of perfection is considered to be from 10 to 11 inches, and the latter should be the maximum height. Although far inferior in speed to the Harrier, the sense of smelling is equally if not more exquisite in the Beagle. In pursuing the hare, he exercises indefatigable vigilance, energy, and perseverance, every winding and double is traced with a

12

degree of exactness which must be seen to be enjoyed and justly estimated, and his cry loads the air with unequalled music. Nothing can be more melodious and beautiful than to hear the pigmy pack open at a hare, and if slow, comparatively speaking, in running her, should the scent be good she stands but little chance of escape from them in the end."

It should always be remembered that the Beagle is as distinct as a breed can be ; and is not a small Foxhound or a small Bloodhound ; still, he is a Hound, and in consequence has many points in common with all good Hounds, the short back, compact body, straight legs, round feet, powerful loin, and nicely placed shoulders ; but the true Beagle head is a beautiful thing to look at, and is seldom seen in absolute perfection, a skull free from coarseness, but with plenty of room, a full, soft, almost pleading eye, a nostril wide and large, a deep pendulous lip, and thin, long, low-set ears. The great difficulty is to get such a head on a perfect body and legs. In colour, the beautiful blue mottle is very typical of the breed, and usually greatly admired, but black, tan and white, black and tan, hare pie, lemon and white, or any other Hound colour is equally allowable.

There is a rough or wire-haired variety, now very scarce, but a few are occasionally seen at shows ; they are said to be hardy and useful in a rough country. The extreme limit of height allowable is 16 inches, and the Pocket Beagle must not exceed 10 inches, but individual specimens of 8 inches have been exhibited at the Crystal Palace and elsewhere. These are greatly valued for rabbit shooting, as they can follow wherever bunny leads, and drive him out to face the guns. In a suitable country they are capable of affording much sport in connection with hare hunting, for although the actual kills may be few, those who find keen enjoyment in seeing Hounds hunt can watch every yard of run, even if they have passed the best milestones on life's journey, and will find these miniature Hounds at least as keen and as full of music as their larger brethren.

At shows, judges who understand the variety have to watch for two opposite faults, both of which are common. (1) " Toyishness " ; generally pretty little pets for a lady, but with round skulls, no power below the eye, thin coats, and legs like pencils, all of which mean loss of Hound character, for the perfect Pocket Beagle must still be a Hound. (2) " Coarseness " ; the general impression being that you are looking at a stunted dwarf Hound ; these often have great bone and powerful heads, but altogether lack quality and that thoroughbred look so characteristic of the true Pocket Beagle ; usually they have been bred from full-sized Hounds, but from accident or ill-health have failed to grow as nature intended. There is just the same difference in human beings between the man of fine stature and physique and a dwarf and a pigmy race of mankind.

When judging the larger variety the real Beagle lover considers first if he has a true Beagle before him or merely a small Hound, and at a large show his task is never easy, the best of legs and feet being often seen under a head which is not that of a Beagle, and a beautiful and typical head too often appears above bad shoulders, legs and feet. The poor judge must be left to solve the difficulty, which is obvious. Let us hope he may find a fair Beagle head on good legs, or a perfect type of head on legs and feet which are passable. " Plenty of bone " is usually highly valued, but excess of bone or anything else is useless, and not to be encouraged ; it makes the little Hound appear coarse, and is of no practical utility to him. It is even open to question if a light-boned Hound does not get through a long day equally as well as his heavy-boned brother, provided his loin, back, and shoulders are all right.

Beagle interests are looked after by the Beagle Club, which opens its doors to all interested in the Beagle as a breed, regardless of the purpose for which it may be kept, and by the " Association of Masters of Harriers and Beagles," which is confined to those who keep or have kept hare-hunting packs.

The chief points to look for in the selection of Beagle puppies at from two to four months old and after, are : A well-balanced head, showing stop, square muzzle, compact body, straight forelegs.

The following is the standard of points laid down by the Beagle Club :—

HEAD of fair length, powerful without being coarse, skull domed, moderately wide, with an indication of peak; stop well defined, muzzle not snipy, and lips well flewed.

NOSE black, broad, and nostrils well expanded.

EYES brown, dark hazel or hazel, not deep set or bulgy, and with a mild expression.

EARS long, set on low, fine in texture, and hanging in a graceful fold close to the cheek.

NECK moderately long, slightly arched, and throat showing some dewlap.

SHOULDERS clean and slightly sloping.

BODY short between the couplings, well let down in chest, ribs fairly well sprung and well ribbed up, with powerful and not tucked-up loins.

HINDQUARTERS very muscular about the thighs, stifles and hocks well bent, and hocks well let down.

FORELEGS quite straight, well under the dog, of good substance, and round in bone.

FEET round, well knuckled up, and strongly padded.

STERN of moderate length, set on high, and carried gaily, but not curled over the back.

COLOUR, any recognised Hound colour.

COAT.—Smooth variety : Smooth, very dense, and not too fine or short. Rough variety : Very dense and wiry.

HEIGHT not exceeding 16 inches.

GENERAL APPEARANCE.—A compactly built Hound, without coarseness, conveying the impression of great stamina and activity.

CLASSIFICATION.—It is recommended that Beagles should be divided at shows into rough and smooth, with classes for "not exceeding 16 inches and over 12 inches," "not exceeding 12 inches and over 10 inches," and "not exceeding 10 inches."

STANDARD OF POINTS.

Skull	6
Ears	10
Eyes	3
Expression	5
Muzzle, jaws, and lip	10
Coat	5
Legs and feet	15
Neck and shoulders	10
Chest	5
Back, loin, and ribs	15
Hindquarters	10
Stern	6
	100

Pocket Beagles must not exceed 10 inches in height. Although ordinary Beagles in miniature, no point, however good in itself, should be encouraged if it tends to give a coarse appearance to such minute specimens of the breed. They should be compact and symmetrical throughout, of true Beagle type, and show great quality and breeding.

DISQUALIFYING POINT.—Any kind of mutilation. (It is permissible to remove the dew claws.)

CHAPTER VI.

The Bassethound.

We owe the introduction of the Bassethound, a dwarfed French hunting Hound, into this country as an exhibition dog. to my old friends, the late Sir Everett Millais, Bt.. and the late Mr. George R. Krehl, somewhere about the 'seventies, although I believe Lord Onslow possessed one or two specimens given to him by Lord Galway anterior to that date, which he used for hunting. The two former gentlemen were the first breeders and exhibitors of Bassethounds in England, and were among the founders of the Bassethound Club.

BASSETHOUND (Smooth-coated).

The breed was at one time very popular, being kept for the most part by the well-to-do classes. I believe Mr. Millais' (as he was then known) Model was the first Bassethound to be exhibited in England. This was at Wolverhampton Show in 1875. Later Lord Onslow imported Fino and Finette from the Comte le Conteulx, the breeder of Model, which was the means of calling public attention to the breed. About this time, Mr. Krehl imported the famous dog, Fino de Paris, who exercised an extensive influence on the breed. This dog gave us Ch. Bourbon, and later Champions Forrester, Merlin, etc. The late Sir Everett Millais wrote a small book on the breed : " Bassets : Their Use and Breeding"; but before this " Wildfowler " (an Anglicised Frenchman) contributed a most exhaustive and interesting article on the various races of French dwarfed Hounds to the earliest edition of " British Dogs," the author of which was my esteemed friend, the late Mr. Hugh Dalziel. I cannot do better than make an extract from this article, which gave the breed a great impetus in England, where it had now obtained a firm footing. It is as follows :—

Any Hound which stands lower than 16 inches (no matter his " provincial " breed) is called in France and in Belgium a Basset. The derivation of the expression Basset is clear: *bas* means low; and, therefore, Basset means low-set, a very appropriate denomination as applied to these diminutive Hounds.

The vast army of French and Belgium Bassets may be divided into three grand classes—viz., Bassets *à jambes droites* (straight-legged), ditto *à jambes demi-torses* (with forelegs half crooked), and *à jambes torses* (forelegs fully crooked). And in each of these classes will be found three varieties of coats—viz., the Bassets *à poil ras* (smooth-coated), those *à poil dur* (rough-coated), and a class half rough, half smooth-coated, which is called half griffon.

The types vary for almost each province, but the general characteristics remain throughout pretty well the same. All well-bred Bassets have long, pendulous ears, and Hounds' heads; but the crooked-legged breed show always better points in these respects than the straight-legged ones, simply because, when a man wishes to breed a good Basset *à jambes torses*, he is obliged to be very careful in selecting the stock to breed from, if he does not wish his experiment to end in failure; for, should there be the slightest admixture of foreign blood, the 'bar sinister' will be at once shown in the forelegs. Hence the Bassets *à jambes torses* show, as a rule, far better properties than their congeners.

In build the Basset *à jambes torses* is long in the barrel, and is very low on his pins; so much so that, when hunting, he literally drags his long ears on the ground. He is the slowest of Hounds, and his value as such cannot be over-estimated. His style of hunting is peculiar, inasmuch that he will have his own way, and each one tries for himself; and if one of them finds, and 'says' so, the others will not blindly follow him and give tongue simply because he does (as some Hounds, accustomed to work in packs, are apt to do); but, on the contrary, they are slow to acknowledge the alarm given, and will investigate the matter for themselves. Thus, under covert, Bassets *à jambes torses* following a scent go in Indian file, and each one speaks to the line according to his own sentiments on the point, irrespective of what the others may think about it. In this manner, it is not uncommon to see the little Hounds, when following a mazy track, crossing each other's route without paying any attention to one another; and, in short, each of them works as if he were alone. This style I attribute to their slowness, to their extremely delicate powers of scent, and to their innate stubborn confidence in their own powers. Nevertheless, it is a fashion which has its drawbacks; for, should the individual Hounds hit on separate tracks of different animals, unless at once stopped, and put together on the same one, each will follow its own find, and let the shooter or shooters do his or their best. That is why a shooter who is fond of that sort of sport rarely owns more than one or two of these Hounds. One is enough, two may be handy in difficult cases, but more would certainly entail confusion, precisely because each one of them will rely only on the evidence of his own senses.

I have now several clever Bassets *à jambes torses* in my mind's eye, and their general description would be about as follows: Height, between 10 inches and 15 inches at shoulder; longish barrels; very crooked forelegs, with little more than an inch or two of daylight between the knees; stout thighs; gay sterns; conical heads; long faces; ears long enough to overlap each other by an inch or two (and more sometimes) when both were drawn over the nose; heavy-headed rather, with square muzzles; plenty of flews and dewlap; eyes deep set, under heavy wrinkles; fore paws wide, and well turned out; markings, hare-pied and white, black tan and white, tan and white, black with tan eyebrows, and tan legs and belly, etc.—in short, all the varieties of Hound markings will be found among them. They have excellent tongues for their size, and when in good training and good condition they will hunt every day, and seem to thrive on it. They are very fond of the gun, and many are cunning enough to "ring" the game, if missed when breaking covert, back again to the guns until it is shot. Some of these Bassets are so highly prized that no amount of money will buy them; and, as a breed, it may safely be asserted that it is probably the purest now in existence in France. They hunt readily deer, roebuck, wild boars, wolves, foxes, hares, rabbits, etc., but if entered exclusively to one species of quarry, and kept to it, they never leave it to run riot after anything else. I have seen one, when hunting a hare in a park, running through fifty rabbits and never noticing them. They go slowly, and give you plenty of time to take your station for a shot—hence their great value in the estimation of shooters. They are chiefly used for smallish woods, furze fields, and the like, because, if uncoupled in a forest, they do not drive their game fast enough; and though eventually they are bound to bring it out, yet the long time they would take in so doing would tell against the sport. Moreover, large forests are cut about by ditches, and here and there streamlets, boulders, and rocks intervene with difficulty the short, crooked-legged Hound would be slow in surmounting. He is, therefore, not so often used there as for smaller coverts, where his voice can throughout the hunt be heard, and thereby direct the shooters which posts of vantage to take.

BASSETHOUND (Rough-coated).

The Bassethound Club was founded in 1883, the devotees of the breed at the time evolving a standard of points and description, later establishing a stud book, compiled by Mr. Millais, who was the club's first hon. secretary. Later, Mr. Millais made some interesting experiments in the crossing of his Bassethounds with Bloodhounds, which experiments he embodied in another book called "Rational Breeding." His lead in this direction was never followed; instead, further importations were made to counteract the injurious effects consanguinity was having upon the breed. When the breed was at the zenith of its popularity, a decade or so before the close of the 19th century, big prices were realised for individual Hounds of superlative merit. Mr. Krehl, we believe, obtained £500 for his kennel of some six Hounds, while Mrs. Tottie claimed Wantage at Cruft's Show in 1900 at her catalogue price of £150. She belonged to Mr. A. Croxton Smith, a well-known breeder and admirer of the Bassethound then and now. Then, I believe, Mr. John Stark once refused a similar or even bigger price for his beautiful smooth bitch, Ch. Queen of the Geisha, later owned by the late Mr. John W. Proctor, and which was regarded by experts to be the most perfect Bassethound of all time in England.

The earliest importations were all of the smooth variety, the first rough Bassethound to be exhibited in England being the Rev. J. C. Macdona's **Romano**.

The only actual difference between the two varieties is the coat; the one being smooth-coated, and the other, broken or wire-haired. The great features to be aimed at in the Bassethound are length and narrowness of head, squareness of muzzle, length and quality of ears, length of body, shortness and soundness of limb. The tendency in breeding is thickness and coarseness of skull, snipiness and lightness of bone and legginess. The nearer the head approaches to that of the Bloodhound the better.

It is ordained that the forelegs should show a certain amount of "crook," but by what process of logic this is considered necessary in a dog that has to run after and track his quarry is not clear. He is, of course, required to be slow, but crook is not necessary for that, and renders the dog liable to risks of being or becoming unsound.

The chief points to look for in the selection of Bassethound puppies at two to four months old and after, are :—Very long head, narrow skull, showing occipital bone well developed, deep square foreface, long loose ears, set on low, great bone, long body, big quarters, deep chest.

The following description and points were drawn up by the late Sir Everett Millais, and adopted by the now defunct Bassethound Club :—

POINTS OF THE BASSETHOUND (SMOOTH).

	Value.
Head, skull, eyes, muzzle, and flews	15
Ears	15
Neck, dewlap, chest, and shoulders	10
Forelegs and feet	15
Back, loins, and hindquarters	10
Stern	5
Coat and skin	10
Colour and markings	15
"Basset character" and symmetry	5
Total	100

GENERAL APPEARANCE.

1. To begin with the head as the most distinguishing part of all breeds. The head of the Bassethound is most perfect when it closest resembles a Bloodhound's. It is long and narrow, with heavy flews, occiput prominent, *la bosse de la chasse*, and forehead wrinkled to the eyes, which should be kind, and show the haw. The general appearance of the head must present high breeding and reposeful dignity; the teeth are small, and the upper jaw sometimes protrudes. This is not a fault, and is called the *bec de lievre*.

2. The ears are very long, and when drawn forward folding well over the nose—so long, that in hunting they will often actually tread on them; they are set on low, and hang loose in folds like drapery, the ends inward curling, in texture thin and velvety.

3. The neck is powerful, with heavy dewlaps. Elbows must not turn out. The chest is deep, full, and framed like a "man-of-war." Body long and low.

4. Forelegs short, about four inches, and close-fitting to the chest till the crooked knee, from where the wrinkled ankle ends in a massive paw, each toe standing out distinctly

5. The stifles are bent, and the quarters full of muscle, which stands out, so that when one looks at the dog from behind it gives him a round barrel-like effect. This, with their peculiar waddling gait, goes a long way towards Basset character—a quality easily recognised by the judge, and as desirable as Terrier character in a Terrier.

6. The stern is coarse underneath, and carried hound-fashion.

7. The coat is short, smooth, and fine, and has a gloss on it like that of a racehorse. (To get this appearance, they should be hound-gloved, never brushed.) Skin loose and elastic.

8. The colour should be black, white, and tan; the head, shoulders, and quarters a rich tan, and black patches on the back. They are also sometimes hare-pied.

9. Weight for dogs from 40lb. to 50lb.; bitches from 35lb. to 45lb.

POINTS OF THE BASSETHOUND (ROUGH).

	Value.
Head and ears	20
Body, including hindquarters	35
Legs and feet	20
Coat	15
Basset character, etc.	10
Total	100

GENERAL APPEARANCE.

1. The head should be large, the skull narrow but of good length, the peak well developed. The muzzle should be strong, and the jaws long and powerful: a snipy muzzle and weakness of jaw are objectionable. The eyes should be dark, and not prominent. The ears should be set on low, of good length and fine texture.

2. The neck should be strong, of good length, and muscular, set on sloping shoulders.

3. The body should be massive, of good length, and well ribbed up, any weakness or slackness of loin being a bad fault. The chest should be large and very deep, the sternum prominent.

4. The forelegs should be short and very powerful, very heavy in bone, either half-crooked or nearly straight. The elbows should lie against the sides of the chest, and should not turn out.

5. Hindquarters should be powerful and muscular, the hind legs should be rather longer than the forelegs, and should be well bent at the stifles.

6. Stern of moderate length, and carried gaily; should be set on high.

7. Coat: An extremely important point. It should be profuse, thick and harsh to the touch, with a dense undercoat. The coat may be wavy.

8. Colour: Any recognised hound colour.

9. Weight: Dogs from 40-50lb., bitches rather less.

The Rough Basset should appear a very powerful hound for his size, on short, strong legs. Body massive and good length, without slackness of loin. The feet should be thick, well padded, and not open. The expression should be kindly and intelligent. Any unsoundness should disqualify the hound.

CHAPTER VII.

The Dachshund.

The word **Dachshund** does not mean, as was at one time popularly supposed, "Badger-hound" (by which name they erroneously appear in the first volume of the K.C.S.B.), but Badger-dog, "Dachs" being German for badger, and "hund" meaning dog. The breed is a purely Teutonic one, being indigenous to Germany, where they have been employed to hunt and unearth the badger for many generations back. The exact origin of the Dachshund, like that of many English breeds, is wrapt in some obscurity. He may, and which is very probable, derive his ancestry from the dwarfed Hounds of southern and western France, from whence he may have drifted into Germany, and have been bred down, and there employed for the specific

DACHSHUND.

purpose stated. In Germany there are two sizes, which are determined by weight, viz., under 15lb. and over 15lb. There are also two varieties, the smooth-haired and rough-haired. The colours of the smooth variety are several, black and tan, liver, liver and tan, red, and dappled.

It was probably this early misconception (if it was a misconception) which led to the framing of the English standard description and points on distinctly Hound lines, more particularly in head.

In the earlier history of the breed in England, certainly a more houndy dog prevailed than is the case to-day, and indeed some few owners hunted the hare with their Dachshunds. Still, it must be remembered that in 1885 and 1886, Mr Harry Jones had the temerity to "beard the lion in his den," by taking over to Brussels his beautiful bitch, Wagtail, dam of the famous Ch. Jackdaw, where she won at each of the shows of the Royal St. Hubert Society, not only firsts in her class, but the "prix d'honneur" for best Dachshund in the show, and this under a recognised German Dachshund judge.

In the course of time the earlier Hound characteristics have been somewhat modified, with the result that there is now, as I contend in the article quoted, little or no real difference between the best bench specimens of Germany and England.

It is a singular fact that the English Dachshund Club, formed in 1881, preceded the establishment of the German " Teckel Klub " by ten years, and Dachshunds were exhibited in England five or six years before they made their appearance on the show bench in Germany. This was at the Birmingham Show of 1872.

In these latter days there has been a tendency in England to moderate the crook in the forelegs of the Dachshund, an excess of which is certainly very objectionable, since it is the cause of " knuckling over," which means unsoundness, and all unsoundness, either of limb or mouth, in this breed should incur absolute disqualification. I cannot, however, go so far in this craze for sound fronts as to accept a straight-legged Dachshund, as some judges do. If ever a fashion or fad sets in for any particular point, it is almost sure to be carried to extremes, and so " ridden to death." Still, if the wild animal whose habitat is underground is taken as a model in the matter of arch of loin in the Dachshund, it may with much force be urged that his limbs should, by the same rule, be regarded as a pattern for his foe. It is a significant fact that, unlike the Dachshund, the forelegs of all such wild animals are perfectly straight, but—and it is an important but—it can with great logic be urged in favour of the big, broad, turned-out forefeet of the Dachshund that with such weapons he can the more easily and quickly get at his quarry, just as the broad blade of a big shovel would remove more earth than a narrow one.

The whole thing hangs upon a rational interpretation of the functions of the animal under notice.

The things to be avoided, therefore, in breeding Dachshunds are unsoundness, snipiness (which is invariably found in the Terrier-like Teckel of Germany, with his goggle eyes and tight skin), coarseness, and abnormal long flat backs. It is equally necessary to avoid the present-day tendency to Toyishness, to which some of our kennels seem to be drifting. The Dachshund is, or should be, a workman, and not a drawing-room pet.

In later years other clubs have been founded in different parts of the country.

The chief points to look for in the selection of Dachshund puppies at from two to four months old and after are : A long, level head, small eye, ears set rather low, long body, showing distinct arch in loin, deep chest, great bone, short legs.

The following are the standard of points of the English and German Dachshund Clubs side by side.

ENGLISH AND GERMAN DACHSHUND CLUBS.
Code of Points.

ENGLISH.

General Appearance (10 points).—Long and low, but with compact and well-muscled body, neither crippled, cloddy, nor clumsy, with bold defiant carriage of head and intelligent expression.

Head and Skull (9 points).—Long, and appearing conical when seen from above, and from a side view tapering to the point of the muzzle. Stop not pronounced, and skull should be slightly arched in profile and appearing neither too broad nor too narrow.

Eyes (3 points).—Medium in size, oval, and set obliquely. Dark in colour, except in the case of Chocolates, which may be lighter, and in Dapples one or both wall eyes are permissible.

Ears (5 points).—Broad, of moderate length, and well rounded (not narrow, pointed, or folded), relatively well back, high, and well set on, lying close to the cheek, very mobile as in all intelligent dogs; when at attention the back of the ear directed forward and outward.

Jaw (5 points).—Neither too square nor snipy, but strong, lips lightly stretched, fairly covering the lower jaw.

Neck (3 points).—Sufficiently long, muscular, clean, no dewlap, slightly arched in the nape, running in graceful lines into the shoulders, carried well up and forward.

GERMAN.

General Appearance.—Gnome-like, short-legged, elongated, but stiff figure, muscular. Notwithstanding the short limbs and long body, neither appearing stunted, awkward, incapable of movement, nor yet lean and weasel-like; with pert, saucy pose of the head and intelligent expression.

Head.—Elongated, and, as seen from above and from the side, tapering towards the point of the nose, sharply outlined and finely modelled, particularly in profile.

Skull.—Neither too wide nor too narrow, only slightly arched, and running gradually without break (stop) (the less the break (stop) the better the type), into a well-defined and slightly arched nasal bone.

Eyes.—Medium sized, oval, set obliquely, clear and energetical expression. Except the silver colour of the grey and spotted dogs and the yellow eyes of the brown dogs, the colour is a transparent brown.

Ears.—Relatively well back, high and well set on, with forward edge lying close to the cheeks; very broad and long, beautifully rounded (not narrow, pointed, or folded), very movable, as in all intelligent dogs; when at attention the back of the ear directed forwards and upwards.

Jaws.—Capable of opening wide, extending to behind the eyes.

Teeth.—Well developed, particularly the corner teeth; these latter fitting exactly. Incisors fitting each other or the inner side of the upper incisors touching the outer side of the lower.

Nose.—Point and root long and slender, very finely formed.

Lips.—Tightly stretched, well covering the lower jaw, neither deep nor snipy, with corner of mouth slightly marked.

Neck.—Sufficiently long, muscular, lean, no dewlap, slightly arched in the nape, running in graceful lines between the shoulders, usually carried high and forward.

English.

FOREQUARTERS (10 points).—Shoulder blades long, broad, and set on sloping, lying firmly on fully developed ribs or thorax, muscles hard and plastic. Chest very oval, with ample room for heart and lungs, deep and well-sprung-out ribs towards the loins, breast bone prominent.

LEGS AND FEET (25 points).—Forelegs very short and in proportion to size, strong in bone. Upper arm of equal length with, and at right angles to, shoulder blade; elbows lying close to ribs, but moving freely up to shoulder blades. Lower arm short as compared with other animals, slightly inclined inwards (crook), seen in profile moderately straight, not bending forward or knucking over (unsoundness), feet large, round, and strong, with thick pads; toes compact and with distinct arch in each toe; nails strong. The dogs must stand true—*i.e.*, equally on all parts of the foot.

BODY TRUNK (9 points).—Long and muscular, the line of back slightly depressed at shoulders and slightly arched over loin, which should be short and strong; outline of belly moderately tucked up.

HINDQUARTERS (10 points).—Rump round, full, broad; muscles hard and plastic; hip bone or pelvis bone not too short, broad and strongly developed, set moderately sloping; thigh bones strong, of good length, and joined to pelvis at right angles; lower thighs short in comparison with other animals; hocks well developed and seen from behind the legs should be straight (not cow-hocked); hind feet smaller in bone and narrower than forefeet. The dog should not appear higher at quarters than at shoulders.

German.

SHOULDERS.—Long, broad, and set sloping, lying firmly on fully developed thorax; muscles hard and plastic.

CHEST.—Corresponding with his work underground, muscular, compact; the region of the chest and shoulders deep, long, and wide; breast bone strong and so prominent as to show a hollow on each side.

FORELEGS.—Upper arm of equal length with and at right angles to shoulders, strong-boned, and well muscled lying close to ribs, but moving freely up to shoulder blade. Lower arm short as compared with other animals, slightly inclined inwards; strongly muscled and plastic towards front and outside, inside and back parts stretched by hard tendons.

FEET.—Forefeet broad and sloping outwards; hind feet smaller and narrower; toes always close together, with distinct bend in each toe; nails strong and regularly pointed outwards; thick soles.

BACK.—In the case of sloping shoulders and hindquarters, short and firm; if steep (straight) shoulders and hindquarters, long and weak; line of back behind shoulders only slightly sunk and only slightly arched near the loins.

TRUNK.—Ribs full, oval, with ample width for heart and lungs, deep and hanging low between forelegs, well sprung out towards loins, loins short and tight and broad, line of belly moderately drawn up, and joined to hindquarters with loosely stretched skin.

HINDQUARTERS.—Rump round, full, broad, muscles hard and plastic; pelvis bone not too short, broad and strongly developed, set moderately sloping.

HIND LEGS.—Thigh bone strong, of good length, and joined to pelvis at right angles; thighs strong and with hard muscles; buttocks well rounded out; knee-joint developed in length; lower leg short in comparison with other animals, at right angles to thigh bone, and firmly muscled; ankle bones well apart, with strong, well-sprung heel and broad Achilles tendons.

| ENGLISH. | GERMAN. |

STERN (5 points).—Set on fairly high, strong and tapering, but not too long and not too much curved nor carried too high.

COAT AND SKIN (3 points).— Short, dense, and smooth, but strong. The hair on the underside of tail coarse in texture; skin loose and supple.

COLOUR (3 points).—Any colour. No white except spot on breast. Nose and nails should be black. In red dogs a red nose is permissible, but not desirable. In Chocolates and Dapples the nose may be brown or flesh-coloured. In Dapples large spots of colour are undesirable, and the dog should be evenly dappled all over.

TAIL.—Set on at medium height and firmly; not too long, tapering without too great curvature, not carried too high, well (but not too much) haired. (A brush tail is, however, better than one without, or with too little, hair, for to breed a weather-proof coat must always be the aim.)

COAT.—Short, thick as possible, glossy, greasy (not harsh and dry), equally covering entire body (never showing bare spots).

COLOUR.—(*a*) Single-coloured: Red, yellowish-red, yellow, or red or yellow with black points, but one colour only is preferable, and red is better than yellowish red, and yellow. White is also allowed. Nose and nails black; red also permitted, but not desirable.

(*b*) Two-coloured: Deep black, or brown, or grey, each with yellow or reddish-brown spots over the eyes, on the sides of the jaws and lower lips, on the inner rim of ear, on the breast, on the inside and back of legs, under the tail, and from there down one-third to one-half of the under-side of the tail. Nose and nails black in black dogs, brown in brown dogs, grey in grey dogs, and also flesh colour.

In one and two-coloured dogs white is permissible, but only to the smallest possible extent, as spot or small streaks on breast

(*c*) Spotted: Ground is a shining silver-grey, or even white, with dark, irregular spots (large spots are undesirable), of dark grey, brown, yellowish red or black.

Neither the light nor the dark colours should predominate. The main factor is such a general appearance that at some distance the dog shall show an indefinite and varied colour which renders him particularly useful as a hunting dog. The russet-brown marks are darker in darker-spotted dogs, and yellower in the lighter ones, and there may be an indication of these in the case of a white foundation. Light eyes are permitted; when the ground colour is white a flesh-coloured or spotted nose is not a fault. White marks are not desirable in dark dogs, but are not to be regarded as faults which disqualify.

English.

WEIGHT.—Heavyweight dogs, not exceeding 25lb.; heavyweight bitches, not exceeding 23lb. Lightweight dogs, not exceeding 21lb.; lightweight bitches, not exceeding 19lb.

FAULTS.—In general appearance weak or deformed, too high or too low to the ground; ears set on too high or too low; eyes too prominent; muzzle too short or pinched, neither undershot nor overshot; forelegs too much crooked or with hare or terrier feet, or flat spread toes (flat-footed); out at elbows; body too much dip behind the shoulders; loins weak or too much arched; chest too flat or too short; hindquarters weak or cow-hocked, and hips higher than shoulders. It is recommended that in judging Dachshunds the negative points (faults) should only be penalised to the extent of the values allotted to such positive points.

German.

HEIGHT AT SHOULDER.—$7\frac{1}{8}$ to $8\frac{5}{8}$ inches.

WEIGHT.—Divided into three classes: Light-weight: Dog under $16\frac{1}{2}$lb.; bitches under $15\frac{1}{2}$lb. Medium-weight: Dogs from $16\frac{1}{2}$ to 22lb.; bitches, $15\frac{1}{2}$ to 22lb. Heavyweight: Dogs and bitches over 22lb.

DEFECTS.—Too weak or crippled, too high or too low on legs; skull too wide, too narrow, or too much arched; ears set on too high, too heavy, or too short, also set on too low and narrow, or long or slack; stop too pronounced and goggle-eyes; nasal bone too short or pressed in; lips too pointed or too deep; over-shot; short developed neck; forelegs badly developed, twisted, or poorly muscled, hare-footed or flat-spread toes; too deeply sunk behind shoulders—*i.e.*, hollow-backed; loins too much arched and weak; ribs too flat or too short; rump higher than shoulders; chest too short or too flat; loins arched like a Greyhound; hindquarters too narrow and poor in muscle; cow-hocked; tail set on high and carried too high or too much curled; too thin, long, or hairless (rat-tailed); coat too thick, too coarse, too fine, or too thin; colour dead, dull, or too much mixed. In black dogs with russet-brown marks (tan), these latter should not extend too far, particularly on the ears.

CHAPTER VIII.

The Greyhound

Is among the few breeds which can lay claim to great antiquity, and one of a fewer number still which has in the evolution of the canine species preserved its original form and character. The Greyhound must have existed long before the Christian era. We can find it depicted in Egyptian sculpture, and later we read of it in King Canute's time, when great restrictions were placed upon the keeping of a Greyhound by the Forest Laws, doubtless owing to the dog's great prowess in the field of sport. The Greyhound has always been used as a sporting dog from the earliest times, and is invariably associated with the rich. A Welsh proverb says : " You may know a gentleman by his horse, his hawk, and his Greyhound."

In earlier times the Greyhound was doubtless a sturdier animal than the dog of to-day, because he was used for hunting other and larger animals than the hare—deer, wild boar, and probably the wolf. Still, his anatomy, if not a replica of the modern dog, was practically on the same lines. The Greyhound, without doubt, is the progenitor of the Scottish Deerhound, the Irish Wolfhound, and other kindred species. The march of civilisation has materially modified the conditions of British sport in many directions, and whilst boar and wolf hunting have become extinct in these isles, coursing, which was indulged in in the first century, still survives, but very much modified from what it was in the early days. The growth of the population and the gradual absorption of much of the rural districts of our little sea-girt isles by manufactures and commerce have put further restrictions upon the sports and pastimes of the people. Coursing is conducted upon more scientific lines than it used to be, but is still the sport of the rich. Greyhounds are bred now purely for this particular sport, under its altered conditions, the chief features aimed at being speed, cleverness, endurance, and gameness. The Greyhound of to-day is a very highly bred animal—the thoroughbred of the canine species. He is one of the few dogs who hunt their quarry by sight, his power of smell, as a result, having become obliterated almost by its continued disuse. He is, also, about the only variety who has practically escaped the attentions of the fancier. There are, of course, very many coursing clubs, but the sport seems to be not nearly so popular as it used to be, say, half a century ago. This is greatly to be regretted, for there is no higher form of British sport, none more humane, and none more free from corruption.

As, however, coursing does not quite come within the scope of this work, being a subject which in itself could only be treated adequately in a work of similar magnitude, I must leave it with the remark that the show Greyhound should be built on such lines, anatomically, as shall enable him to fulfil its most strenuous requirements. Coursing clubs have not thought it necessary to lay down any code of points or standard description of the Greyhound, the breeding of which is conducted much on the "rule-of-thumb" lines. The chief, if not only, consideration that enters into the philosophy of the breeder of coursing Greyhounds is merit on the course. Bitches are mated to dogs who have shown great prowess in the field, altogether irrespective of their make and shape ; although, of course, no Greyhound can ever be successful on the course unless he is built on galloping lines, any more than a railway engine could ever make the journey from Manchester to London in three and a half hours unless it possessed the latest and most improved mechanism. There is, however, this difference between the

GREYHOUND.

construction of an engine and a Greyhound. Assuming the latter to be built on the speediest lines of canine architecture possible, much of his powers will be futile unless he possesses gameness—a big heart; whereas the former will always respond to the invitation of the driver, who it is that requires the heart. That gameness and grit so essential to success on the course are qualities that can never be ascertained or appraised in the show ring, where only the make and shape of the dog can enter into the calculations of the judge. All an adjudicator can provide for in that direction is heart room— that is, well-sprung ribs, which is one of the many cardinal points in the grand and graceful outline and beautiful symmetry of this classic canine.

There can be little doubt that many and varied crosses have from time to time been resorted to in order to preserve the stamina of the Greyhound. It is on record that the services of the Bulldog have been requisitioned for the purpose of infusing more gameness into the Greyhound, all traces of which may be obliterated outwardly in the fifth generation. And doubtless other breeds have been similarly employed.

Coursers have not even such an elementary guide as weight in their breeding curriculum, but practice has proved that the medium-sized dog is the most capable. This is a dog of about 65lb. to 70lb. weight. Head is a part of the dog's anatomy of little or no account, since he has no particular use for it except to kill with his jaws. For this purpose, the longer and stronger they are the better. Ears again count for nothing, but a small eye is objectionable, since it is with his eyes that the Greyhound sights the hare, and a rather large eye, set in not too close, enables him the better to see puss's many turns. A long and muscular neck is a great essential, set well into obliquely placed shoulders. The forelegs should be as straight as gun-barrels, but the elbows should not be turned in, which prevents the dog from getting down to his work. Rather should they be turned out a trifle. The chest should be deep, the ribs gradually widening as they reach their terminus. The loins should be slightly arched, very broad and thick, like two big Atlantic cables traversing the dog's back, and merging into broad and big hindquarters, the muscles of which should resemble two big round loaves of bread stuck on the dog, as my esteemed and venerable friend, Mr. Berry, president of the Bulldog Club, used to say. The thighs should be wide, and very muscular, both first and second thighs, the stifles well bent, and the hocks well let down, being formed so as to appear from behind perfectly parallel, and free from the slightest taint of what is called " cow-hocks."

Flat or long loins are very objectionable, by which the dog loses the control over his hindquarters. The dog should be well " cut-up " under his loins, in order that he may have greater freedom for the working of his hind limbs. Briefly, the dog should be comparatively short coupled on the top, but should, when standing, cover a lot of ground below, and he should neither be too long on the leg nor too short.

Colour is an altogether immaterial point; a good Greyhound, like a good horse, cannot be a bad colour. The tail should be long and strong, since it is to the dog what the rudder is to the ship.

The chief points to look for in the selection of Greyhound puppies at from two to four months old and after are: A long neck, well-placed shoulders, great bone, deep chest, well-sprung ribs, and big hindquarters.

The following is the standard description adopted by the Greyhound Club of Great Britain :—

GENERAL DESCRIPTION.—In judging Greyhounds it is essential that the judge should bear in mind that the beautiful lines of the breed are one of its biggest assets. This breed is essentially built for speed, ability to bend and turn with his game, and possess the build (or formation) which will fit him for his work in the field in combination with the graceful lines of a thoroughbred. It is absolutely essential that he should be well balanced throughout.

HEAD AND NECK.—The head should be long, well chiselled, without stop and not too narrow between the ears. Eye large, clear, with keen expression and free from any defect; teeth level and strong, pig-jawed, or undershot a grave disqualifying fault. The neck should be long and muscular, but not throaty, and well let into the shoulders.

FOREQUARTERS.—The shoulders should be obliquely placed, showing muscle without any bossiness, muscles starting just above elbow and fining off towards the tops of the blade bones, which should not be too far apart.

LEGS.—The legs should be perfectly straight, good bone, and good length from the elbow to knee, elbows turning neither in or out, fairly short pasterns which should not be bent back too much. The feet should be well formed, with thick pads, toes well knuckled up, but the feet must not be too short or too long.

HINDQUARTERS—Should be powerful, of a fair length, carrying plenty of muscle, with a good second thigh, great length between the hip and stifle joint, which should be well bent, hocks powerful, well let down, turning neither in nor out.

BODY.—Fairly long, but any length should preferably be from the top of shoulder to last rib, and not from last rib to hip bone. Brisket deep, ribs well sprung, loin slightly higher than top of shoulder, giving that slightly arched look which, with a good cut up under loin, gives that general racy appearance so desirable. Tail long, fine, and carried under the hindquarters.

WEIGHT AND HEIGHT.—All dogs should be 50 to 55lb.; bitches, 45 to 55lb. minimum. The desirable height at shoulder for dogs is 27 inches, and for bitches 26 inches.

CONDITION.—The condition of a Greyhound should be firm and well muscled; the muscles should be elastic as a race-horse and rippling under the skin when the dog is in motion; the Greyhound should not carry too much flesh and not too little. The fit Greyhound with sufficient amount of flesh firm and clean is the ideal.

CHAPTER IX.

The Deerhound.

The exact origin of the Deerhound has never been ascertained, but one thing is certain—viz., that he is an offshoot of the Greyhound, by which name he is still known in some parts of the Highlands of Scotland. Some writers allege that he is descended from the Irish Wolfhound, whose great antiquity is beyond dispute; and it may be that in the earlier days crosses with the breed were resorted to, in order to obtain or improve the rough coat and hardihood of the Scottish dog, necessary for the more trying and Arctic-like

DEERHOUND.

climate of North Britain. The Deerhound, like all Scottish breeds, is a shaggy-coated dog, but, unlike some, is not, and may never have been, indigenous to Scotland. In the olden time a similar dog was used for deerstalking in England, but as the sport gradually became practically extinct, owing to the growth of the towns and villages and the increase of commerce, which made such an inroad upon pastoral pursuits, there was, of course, no use for the Deerhound, who has developed into a purely exhibition specimen, except in a few of the more remote parts of Scotland, where he is still used in his natural avocation. The Deerhound must not be confounded with the Staghound, which still survives in England, and which is more on the lines of a Foxhound, to which family he undoubtedly belongs, since, like this Hound, he hunts his quarry by scent. Devonshire is the only county in which stag hunting survives, except, of course, the Royal Buckhounds, which are occasionally hunted in Windsor Great Park. The days of this kingly sport in the United Kingdom are numbered, there being a strong public feeling against the pursuit of what are practically tame deer. Speaking of the origin of the Scottish Deerhound, in a very interesting and well-written treatise on the breed by Mr. G. W. Hickman, a well-known authority, in "British Dogs," this gentleman quotes from Pitscottie's "History of Scotland," published about 1600, to prove the dog's great antiquity under its present nomenclature. The passage referred to is as follows:—"The King (A.D. 1528) desired all gentlemen that had dogges that war guid to bring thame to hunt in the saidis boundis, quhilk the most pairt of the noblemen of the Highlands did, sick as the Earles of Huntlie, Argyle, and Athol, who brought their deir houndis with thame, and hunted with his majestie."

The cutting up of the large forests in Scotland into smaller shootings, and the introduction of the quick-firing rifle, have together rendered less necessary the uses of the Deerhound, or Highland Greyhound, as he is called in some parts of "Bonnie Scotland," where also the show bench has become his greatest field of fame, leaving him with but the symbol of a great name as a purely sporting dog.

The Scottish Deerhound, rich in historical tradition, with his legitimate occupation, like that of the martial Moor, gone, is still a great public favourite in both England and Scotland, and boasts of a large number of enthusiastic devotees. A club was established a quarter of a century ago to look after his interests, which has done much to popularise the breed. This club laid down a standard of points at the instance of Mr. G. W. Hickman and Mr. R. Hood-Wright, in 1892, who formulated most of its clauses, which has resulted in the development of the dog from the material existing upon recognised and uniform lines, and the production of an animal at once graceful and imposing and in every way fitted, outwardly, to fulfil the function of his specific avocation.

In practice, a medium-sized dog has been found to be the speediest, and this principle has obviously guided the authors of this standard, in which elephantine proportions and coarseness are deprecated, just as weediness and want of stamina must be avoided in breeding these fine dogs, which, as a rule, make excellent companions and guards, in both of which spheres of life they have been immortalised by Sir Walter Scott and other great writers.

In addition to the Irish Wolfhound cross, the Borzoi has been utilised as an outcross for the Deerhound, and with good effect. Mr. Hood-Wright resorted to this outcross, the result of which has been an accentuation of the graceful outline the Deerhound should possess, as well as a retention of the powerful jaw and big hindquarters so necessary in the breed. Probably the coat of the Deerhound would suffer to some extent by this alien alliance, but that could be remedied in a few generations by judicious mating.

The main features of the breed are a combination of speed or galloping properties, with power and endurance, pluck being a paramount quality requisite in the breed, but one that can only be ascertained in actual practice, and therefore one that cannot be provided for in discussing the dog's anatomy, except so far as is furnished by well-sprung ribs, which denote heart room.

Straight forelegs, and short, cat-like feet, a deep chest, broad, powerful, and slightly arched loins, and big, powerful hindquarters, with well-bent stifles and well-let-down hocks, are the chief points to obtain. Many Deerhounds are straight in stifles, which gives them a stilty appearance and materially handicaps them in the matter of grace and movement. Thick shoulders, again, are a great blemish, which, with very heavy bone, often mean a thick skull, another objectionable feature in the breed.

The chief points to look for in the selection of Deerhound puppies at from two to four months old and after are: A long, level head, dark eye, long neck, well-placed shoulders, great bone, deep chest, well-sprung ribs, big hindquarters, short body.

Below is the standard description of the Deerhound Club referred to:—

HEAD.—The head should be broadest at the ears, tapering slightly to the eyes, with the muzzle tapering more decidedly to the nose. The muzzle should be pointed, but the teeth and lips level. The head should be long, the skull flat, rather than round, with a very slight rise over the eyes, but with nothing approaching a stop. The skull should be coated with moderately long hair, which is softer than the rest of the coat. The nose should be black (though in some blue-fawns the colour is blue), and slightly aquiline. In the lighter coloured dogs a black muzzle is preferred. There should be a good moustache of rather silky hair, and a fair beard.

EARS.—The ears should be set on high, and, in repose, folded back like the Greyhound's, though raised above the head in excitement without losing the fold, and even, in some cases, semi-erect. A prick ear is bad. A big thick ear, hanging flat to the head, or heavily coated with long hair, is the worst of faults. The ear should be soft, glossy, and like a mouse's coat to the touch, and the smaller it is, the better. It should have no long coat or long fringe, but there is often a silky, silvery coat on the body of the ear and the tip. Whatever the general colour, the ears should be black or dark-coloured.

NECK AND SHOULDERS.—The neck should be long—that is, of the length that befits the Greyhound character of the dog. An over-long neck is not necessary, nor desirable, for the dog is not required to stoop to his work like a Greyhound, and it must be remembered that the mane which every good specimen should have detracts from the apparent length of neck. Moreover, a Deerhound requires a very strong neck to hold a stag. The nape of the neck should be very prominent where the head is set on, and the throat should be clean-cut at the angle and prominent. The shoulders should be well sloped, the blades well back, and not too much width between them. Loaded and straight shoulders are very bad faults.

TAIL.—The tail should be tolerably long, tapering, and reaching to within 1½in. of the ground, and about 1½in. below the hocks. When the dog is still, dropped perfectly straight down, or curved. When in motion it should be curved when excited, in no case to be lifted out of the line of the back. It should be well covered with hair, on the inside thick and wiry, underside longer, and towards the end a slight fringe not objectionable. A curl or ring tail very undesirable.

EYES.—The eyes should be dark; generally they are dark brown or hazel. A very light eye is not liked. The eye is moderately full, with a soft look in repose, but a keen, far-away look when the dog is roused. The rims of the eyelids should be black.

BODY.—The body and general formation is that of a Greyhound of larger size and bone. Chest deep rather than broad, but not too narrow and flat-sided. The loin well arched and drooping to the tail. A straight back is not desirable, this formation being unsuitable for going up-hill, and very unsightly.

LEGS AND FEET.—The legs should be broad and flat, a good broad forearm and elbow being desirable. Forelegs, of course, as straight as possible. Feet close and compact, with well-arranged toes. The hindquarters drooping, and as broad and powerful as possible, the hips being set wide apart. The hind legs should be well bent at the stifle, with great length from the hip to the hock, which should be broad and flat. Cowhocks, weak pasterns, straight stifles, and splay feet very bad faults.

COAT.—The hair on the body, neck, and quarters should be harsh and wiry, and about 3in. or 4in. long; that on the head, breast, and belly is much softer. There should be a slight hairy fringe on the inside of the fore and hind legs, but nothing approaching "the feather" of a Collie. The Deerhound should be a shaggy dog, but not overcoated. A woolly coat is bad. Some good strains have a slight mixture of silky coat with the hard, which is preferable to a woolly coat, but the proper coat is a thick, close-lying, ragged coat, harsh or crisp to the touch.

COLOUR.—Colour is much a matter of fancy. But there is no manner of doubt that the dark-blue grey is the most preferred. Next come the darker and lighter greys or brindles, the darkest being generally preferred. Yellow and sandy-red or red-fawn, especially with black points—*i.e.*, ears and muzzles—are also in equal estimation, this being the colour of the oldest known strains, the McNeil and the Chesthill Menzies. White is condemned by all the old authorities, but a white chest and white toes, occurring as they do in a great many of the darkest-coloured dogs, are not so greatly objected to, but the less the better, as the Deerhound is a self-coloured dog. A white blaze on the head or a white collar should entirely disqualify. In other cases, though passable, an attempt should be made to get rid of white markings. The less white the better, but a slight white tip to the stern occurs in the best strains.

HEIGHT OF DOGS.—From 28in. to 30in., or even more if there be symmetry without coarseness, but which is rare.

HEIGHT OF BITCHES.—From 26in. upwards. There can be no objection to a bitch being large, unless too coarse, as even at her greatest height she does not approach that of the dog, and therefore could not have been too big for work, as over-big dogs are. Besides, a big bitch is good for breeding and keeping up the size.

WEIGHT.—From 85lb. to 105lb. in dogs; from 65lb. to 80lb. in bitches.

NOTE.—The average height of Deerhounds has increased since the foregoing standard was drawn up, and although Hounds of the heights mentioned are quite eligible for competition, it is desirable that dogs should be not less than 30in. and bitches 28in. at the shoulder respectively.

POINTS, ARRANGED IN ORDER OF IMPORTANCE.

1. TYPICAL: A Deerhound should resemble a rough-coated Greyhound of larger size and bone.

2. MOVEMENTS: Easy, active, and true.

3. HEIGHT: As tall as possible consistent with quality.

4. HEAD: Long, level, well balanced, carried high.

5. BODY: Long, very deep in brisket, well-sprung ribs, and great breadth across hips.

6. FORELEGS: Strong and quite straight, with elbows neither in nor out.

7. THIGHS: Long and muscular; second thighs well muscled stifles nicely bent.

8. LOINS: Well arched and belly well drawn up.

9. COAT: Rough and hard, longer and softer beard and brows.

10. FEET: Close and compact, with well-knuckled toes.

11. EARS: Small, with Greyhound-like carriage.

12. EYES: Dark, moderately full.

13. NECK: Long, well arched, and very strong, with prominent nape.

14. SHOULDERS: Clean, set sloping.

15. CHEST: Very deep, but not too narrow.

16. TAIL: Long and slightly curved; carried low.

17. TEETH: Strong and level.

18. NAILS: Strong and curved.

CHAPTER X.

The Borzoi,

Or Russian Wolfhound, is among the most popular of our foreign importations. As no wolves now exist in the British Isles, his introduction into this country has not been prompted by and on account of his great sporting proclivities. It is, no doubt, to his imposing appearance, his elegance and refinement, that his popularity among the moneyed classes must be attributed, for the Borzoi is by no means a working-man's dog. At the Crystal Palace Show in 1872 three Borzois were entered, and there was a brace exhibited by Lady Emily Peel at an earlier Crystal Palace show. A dog was shown by the then well

BORZOI.

known firm of Messrs. Hill and Ashton, of the Meersbrook Kennels, Sheffield. This was in the 'eighties, and it was shown as a Siberian Wolfhound. Some years later the Duchess of Newcastle created a stir in the English kennel world by the importation of several fine specimens from the kennels of the Czar at Gatchina. From this stock Her Grace founded the finest kennel in England, and the Duchess's keen interest in the breed at once gave it an impetus. Later still Her Majesty Queen Alexandra, then the Princess of Wales, was presented by the Czar with a couple of these courtly Hounds, one of which was Alex, who soon became a champion on the show bench.

The breed may now be said to have thoroughly "caught on." A club was formed (in 1892), of which the Duchess of Newcastle was elected president, and a few years later a show of Borzois was promoted at Southport, at which Her Grace acted as judge. This show, however, has not been continued by the club, which has been content to support the Kennel Club's Show and the more prominent fixtures in the country.

The breed was imported into the United States a little later than in England, where it has become in equal favour as a companion and for exhibition. The leading kennel in that country was the Valley Farm Kennels, Hartford County, Conn., which was owned by a syndicate consisting of Messrs. Joseph B. Thomas jun. Ralph H. Thomas, A. Douglass Dodge, Howard H. Mossman, and Chauncey J. Hamlin. This firm on two occasions sent Mr. Thomas, jun., to Russia, for the purpose of procuring Hounds for their kennel, and a number of important importations were made from the kennel of the Grand Duke Nicholas, at Perchina, near Moscow, which was said to be the largest and best kennel in Russia, excelling even that of the Czar, from which dogs could not be bought, but obtained only by Court favour. This firm published an illustrated catalogue, which contained, in addition to particulars of the inmates of the kennels, an interesting account of the breed as it was kept and used in its native land, from the pens of the late Mr. James Watson (taken from "Country Life in America") and Mr. Thomas, the latter of whom recounted his interesting experiences in Russia.

Wolf-hunting is the great national sport of Russia, corresponding with fox-hunting in England. Wolves were coursed in those vast dominions much in the same way that hares are coursed in England. Young Hounds are taught hunting by the aid of captive wolves in enclosed grounds, the wolf being given a certain amount of law, and then two Borzois are slipped at him. I have often regretted that when I visited the Russian capital in 1903 to judge at the dog show, indisposition prevented me from visiting the Imperial kennels, and not only viewing the Czar's team of Borzois, but of witnessing a wolf coursed. I. however, saw the best collection of Borzois the country can produce outside the Imperial kennel, at the St. Petersburg Show, which were judged by the Czar's chief huntsman, with whom I had a conversation upon the breed, and from whom I gathered much information.

The Borzoi is one of the most ancient breeds in Russia, in which country the varieties of the dog are very limited. In earlier times it was an exclusive breed, being kept only by the Czar and Grand Ducal families. This exclusiveness tended to deterioration for want of an outcross, and various outcrosses have been resorted to with a Siberian Hound and English Greyhound. Such crosses very naturally, for a time, affected the type of the Borzoi, which, however, was restored by the Grand Duke Nicholas and other breeders.

Although the dog is not used for his legitimate avocation in England, yet the standard formulated by the English Borzoi Club has been framed with the dog's sporting proclivities clearly in view, and the "points" therein laid down are such as should enable him to fulfil his natural calling to the very best advantage.

The Borzoi (or Barzoi, as the breed is termed on the Continent, and Psovoi in Russia) is of the Greyhound species, but he is a bigger and more powerful Hound, and longer-coated. Like the latter, he hunts more by sight than scent, and is a very game dog.

The chief requirements of the Borzoi may be summed up in four words, all beginning with "s"—viz., size, speed, strength, symmetry. Although built very much on the lines of the Greyhound, the Borzoi differs from his English prototype very materially in many particulars besides size and coat. His head is altogether different. In the Greyhound, the head, either for coursing or for exhibition, is of little or no account. In the Borzoi it is a most important feature, and its formation is unique. The muzzle should be of extraordinary length, and the jaws exceedingly strong and powerful, whilst the skull should be comparatively short and very narrow. There should be no "stop" whatever, but, on the contrary, the nasal bone should be filled up to the level of the temples, and the skull, instead of being level with the nose (which should be slightly Roman), should run at a slight angle or declivity, the occiput being clearly developed. Extraordinary depth of chest is required in the Borzoi. This often means flat sides, which are admissible in the Russian Wolfhound, but unpardonable in a Greyhound. Sloping shoulders, well-laid back and straight forelegs, with hare feet, are, with an arched, strong loin, well-bent stifles, and hocks well let down, all attributes of speed, whilst the necessity of a strong, muscular neck is obvious. The eyes should be small and dark, and showing great determination in their expression. The ears should be small, their carriage being immaterial, but the rose ear is the most pleasing to the eye. A ring tail is very objectionable, and so is a short tail, since the tail, which should be long, strong, and well feathered, forms the rudder to the canine ship.

The coat is not an important point, except that it should be rough and silky. The same may be said of the colour of the Borzoi, except that self-coloured specimens and black-marked specimens are objectionable. The prevailing and admissible colours are white, or white with fawn, grey, blue, or brindled markings.

The Borzoi in his build and architecture seems to be an exaggeration of everything, and this is what should be aimed at—great size, with great elegance, and a total absence of coarseness.

Borzois kept purely for sport, like English Foxhounds living under similar conditions, would make very poor companions. And although the innate sporting virtues of the Borzoi in England are but lying dormant, yet their lack of development and long course of domesticity combined have rendered the Borzoi of to-day a charming companion.

The chief points to look for in the selection of Borzoi puppies at from two to four months old and after are :—A phenomenally long head, rather Roman in shape of muzzle, very well filled up under the eyes, small eyes, set in obliquely, very narrow skull, with occipital bone well developed, powerful neck, very narrow shoulders, long straight forelegs, very deep chest, loin arched, graceful outline.

The following is the Borzoi Club's standard of points, the height at shoulder being fixed at a low minimum. In my opinion it could be raised, for a dog of even 30 inches and a bitch 28 inches at shoulder are rather undersized specimens. An inch put on to that would make each only a fair average.

HEAD.—Long and lean. Skull very slightly domed and narrow, stop not perceptible, inclining to Roman nose. Head so fine that the direction of the bones and principal veins can be clearly seen. Bitches' heads should be finer than the dogs'. Jaws long, deep, and powerful ; teeth even, neither pig jawed nor undershot, nose large and black, never pink or brown.

EARS.—Small and fine in quality ; not too far apart, and when in repose the occiput touching or nearly so.

EYES.—Dark, intelligent, expressive, set somewhat obliquely, placed well back but not too far apart ; eyelids dark—eyes should not be light or staring.

NECK.—Clean, slightly arched, continuing the line of back, powerful, and well set on, free from throatiness.

SHOULDERS.—Clean, sloping well back, fine at withers, free from lumpiness.

CHEST.—Great depth of brisket, rather narrow.

RIBS.—Nicely sprung, very deep, giving heart room and lung play.

BACK.—Rising in a nice arch, the arch being more marked in the dogs, rather bony and free from any cavity.

LOINS.—Broad, and very powerful, with plenty of muscular development.

THIGHS.—Long, well developed, with good second thigh.

FORE-LEGS.—Lean and straight. Seen from the front narrow like blades, from the side wide at shoulder, narrowing down to foot; elbows neither turned in nor out, pasterns strong.

HIND-LEGS.—Long, muscular, stifles well bent, hocks broad, clean and well let down.

MUSCLES.—Highly developed and well distributed.

FEET.—Rather long, toes close together and well arched, never flat.

COAT.—Long and silky (never woolly), either flat, wavy, or rather curly. Short and smooth on head, ears, and front of legs, on neck the frill profuse and rather curly, fore-legs and chest well feathered, on hind-quarters and tail feathering long and profuse.

TAIL.—Long, well feathered, carried low, not gaily.

HEIGHT.—At shoulder—Dogs from 29in. upwards; bitches from 27in. upwards.

GENERAL APPEARANCE.—Very graceful, aristocratic, and elegan combining courage, muscular power, and great speed.

Points decided on at the Club's general meeting in 1922 :—

Head complete (eyes and ears included)	15
Neck	10
Shoulders and chest	15
Ribs, back, and loin	15
Hind-quarters, stifles, and hocks	15
Legs and feet	15
Coat, tail, and feather	10
General appearance	5
Total	100

CHAPTER XI.

The Irish Wolfhound.

This is without doubt one of the oldest breeds known to the British Isles, but as to its exact origin no sufficiently reliable data exist that will fix it. One thing is certain—viz., that 100 years or so ago the breed was very nearly extinct, since which it has been resuscitated—some will probably say manufactured—by crosses with the Great Dane and Deerhound, which were undoubtedly resorted to. The original Wolfhound was, according to ancient writings—some of them legendary—and illustrations, shown to be a veritable giant—a huge, grizzly, shaggy-coated, long-groined, powerful, yet fleet-looking Hound. Reinagle's picture, however, corrects this idea, and gives us the outline of a dog more in keeping with our modern example.

Doubtless when wolves became extinct in Ireland, early in the 18th century, the breed would degenerate, until, as I have already pointed out, it became either wholly or all but extinct.

It was not until the advent of dog shows that breeders turned their attention to the once famous Irish Wolf-dog, and probably Captain Graham's monograph on the breed gave a fillip to the desire for its resuscitation and cultivation. Ultimately a club in the interests of the breed was formed, and still exists, and to the efforts of its devotees do we owe the magnificent Hounds England possesses to-day. In fact, at no period in the history of the breed, as it has been ascertained from research into kennel archives, from family paintings, books, and other data, did more imposing and typical specimens exist than are to be found in England to-day. Singularly, these efforts to revive the ancient Hibernian breed have been confined almost exclusively to Englishmen, who own all the best dogs, and in my opinion the largest, the soundest, and most typical representative of the breed was Major and Mrs. Shewell's young dog, Champion Cotswold, which, I believe, held an unbeaten record on the show bench.

With all the efforts that have been put forth, the Irish Wolfhound has not "caught on" with the general public, doubtless owing to the invasion of England by so many foreign breeds, such as the Great Dane, Borzoi, St. Bernard, etc., his breeding and propagation being confined to a comparatively limited number of enthusiasts.

As in the case of most big dogs, the great difficulty in breeding the Irish Wolfhound is to ensure straight forelegs and sound hindquarters. Of course, a great deal depends upon the rearing of the dogs in this particular connection. A puppy may be born sound and straight in limb, and become incurably defective by his faulty bringing up. Still, that is the tendency, and such faults as cow-hocks (which are very prevalent in the breed), crooked forelegs, or splay feet, once established, become hereditary, and should be carefully avoided. There is a certain amount of similarity between the Scottish Deerhound and Irish Wolfhound, some of the blood of each of which no doubt courses through the veins of the other, but the Irish dog is bigger, less elegant in outline, and a heavier and more powerful dog. He has, too, or should have, a harder texture of coat and more powerful jaw. A little white on the chest or feet is perfectly immaterial, and colour is of but secondary importance, the most favourite colour being grizzle or wheaten.

The chief points to look for in the selection of Irish Wolfhound puppies at from two to four months old and after are:—A long, level head, great strength of muzzle, big nostrils, enormous bone, big body, deep chest, big hindquarters, moderately short body.

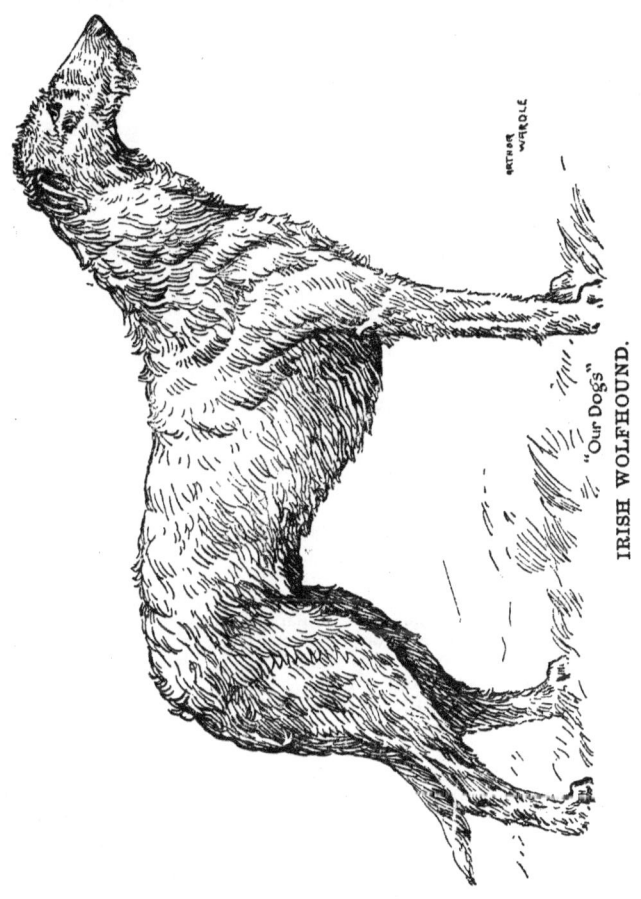
IRISH WOLFHOUND.

Some time ago a correspondence raged in *Our Dogs* on the breed, and a writer (who is a reliable authority) over the *nom de plume* of "Breeder" gave his views in the following very succinct description and scale of points :—

Height, 34in.; weight, 140lb.; girth, 38in.; head, 14in.; avoiding the broad forehead, and with strong muzzle. Eyes small and dark. Ears neatly tucked and cocked. Body long, deep, and supple. Tail long and lashing. Neck clean and arched. Hocks well let down, and without a suspicion of "cow." Legs like parallel rulers. Coat rough and wiry. Beard and eyebrows plentiful. Colour, any met with in the Deerhound. Muscular all over, of course.

The following scale of point-values has been suggested by "Breeder" in the paper above named :—

HEAD ..		25
Length and shape of	10	
Ears	8	
Beard and eyebrows	5	
Eyes	2	
BODY ..		25
Height at shoulder	12	
Substance and girth	7	
Length and symmetry of body	6	
LIMBS ..		25
Loins and hocks	10	
Forelegs	8	
Feet	7	
THE REST		25
Coat	12	
Neck	6	
Tail	3	
Nails	2	
Teeth	2	
Total		100

The Irish Wolfhound's standard description is as follows :—

GENERAL APPEARANCE.—The Irish Wolfhound should not be quite so heavy or massive as the Great Dane, but more so than the Deerhound, which in general type he should otherwise resemble. Of great size and commanding appearance, very muscular, strongly though gracefully built, movements easy and active; head and neck carried high; the tail carried with an upward sweep with a slight curve towards the extremity.

THE MINIMUM HEIGHT AND WEIGHT of dogs should be 31in. and 120lb.; of bitches 28in. and 90lb. Anything below this should be debarred from competition. Great size, including height at shoulder and proportionate length of body, is the desideratum to be aimed at, and it is desired to firmly establish a race that shall average from 32in. to 34in. in dogs, showing the requisite power, activity, courage, and symmetry.

HEAD.—Long, the frontal bones of the forehead *very* slightly raised, and *very* little indentation between the eyes. Skull not too broad. Muzzle long and moderately pointed. Ears small and Greyhound-like in carriage.

NECK.—Rather long, very strong and muscular, well arched, without dewlap, or loose skin about the throat.

CHEST.—Very deep. Breast wide.

BACK.—Rather long than short. Loins arched.

TAIL.—Long and slightly curved, of moderate thickness, and well covered with hair.

BELLY.—Well drawn up.

FOREQUARTERS.—Shoulders muscular, giving breadth of chest, set sloping. Elbows well under, neither turned inwards nor outwards.

LEG.—Forearm muscular, and the whole leg strong and quite straight.

HINDQUARTERS.—Muscular thighs and second thigh long and strong as in the Greyhound, and hocks well let down and turning neither in nor out.

FEET.—Moderately large and round, neither turned inwards nor outwards. Toes well arched and closed. Nails very strong and curved.

HAIR.—Rough and hard on body, legs, and head; especially wiry and long over eyes and underjaw.

COLOUR AND MARKINGS.—The recognised colours are grey, brindle, red, *black*, pure white, fawn, or any colour that appears in the Deerhound.

FAULTS.—Too light *or* heavy a head, too highly arched frontal bone, large ears and hanging flat to the face; short neck; full dewlap; too narrow or too broad a chest; sunken or hollow or quite straight back; bent forelegs; overbent fetlocks; twisted feet; spreading toes; too curly a tail; weak hindquarters and a general want of muscle; too short in body.

CHAPTER XII.

The Norwegian Elkhound.

This beautiful variety of Scandinavian hunting dog is one of the most intelligent, docile, interesting, and rationally-built of all the foreign dogs introduced into this country. Individual specimens have been seen at our shows for many years back, which perforce had to be exhibited in the Foreign Dog or Variety classes. It has been left to the incident of a post-war enthusiasm for some of the European varieties, to bring to the front in this country this charming variety of the canine species.

Like all the varieties of the dog bordering on the Arctic circle, the Norwegian Elkhound possesses the fur-like coat, prick ears, and curled tail of his compatriots. He is, however, possessed of a milder and more docile disposition than some of these hardy dogs of the nothern regions, and beams with intelligence. The natural virtues of the Elkhound have only to be known to be loved and admired, and no wonder that when his traits did become generally known in this country he should quickly gather round him quite a galaxy of admirers and devotees.

The Elkhound, as his name implies, is used in his native country for hunting the elk, in connection with which sport he furnishes his owners with a most invigorating and enjoyable pastime with the gun in the forests of Norway and Sweden. The dog's fur-like coat furnishes a fine protection for him in these cold regions, and his sturdy build and stout limbs aid him greatly in negotiating the snow-clad woodlands of his native country, whilst his quick intelligence, hearing, and sight, and unerring olfactory organs, never fail him in beating his quarry.

In the matter of the working qualities of the Norwegian Elkhound, I cannot do better than quote from notes contributed to *Our Dogs* by that well known Elkhound authority, my old and esteemed friend and literary confrere, Mr. Will Hally; and also from the Christmas Number of *Our Dogs*, n which a very interesting article on "Elkhounds and Elk-hunting in Norway," by that familiar sporting writer R. Clapham, appears.

Mr. Will Hally says :—

A considerable part of my Elkhound correspondence during the past six months has been the answering of questions as to the uses of Elkhounds—what they are used for and not used for in Norway. As these queries are still coming in, I shall gladly avail myself of extracts from a letter which Colonel Scovell has had from the chairman of the Norwegian Elkhound Club, and which will publicly, and once and for all, answer some at least of the questions. In the first place, the chairman of the Norsk Dyrehundklub says that, as far as he knows, Elkhounds are never used in Norway for drawing carts. He has heard of one Elkhound—a dog which belonged to Mr. Anker, of Fredrikshald—which taught itself to catch fish in the rivers ; that feat was mentioned in the Norwegian Kennel Club's publication, and no doubt accounted for the story that Elkhounds are used for catching fish.

In Elk hunting, the hounds are kept on a leash all the time for tracking, until the hunter can get sight of the elk, and then to hold the elk at bay until the hunter can get within reach to shoot. The first method is mostly used where the forests are very open—in the northern districts, such as Namdalen, etc. Elkhounds are often used for hunting the bear, and for such smaller beasts of prey as stoats and martens,

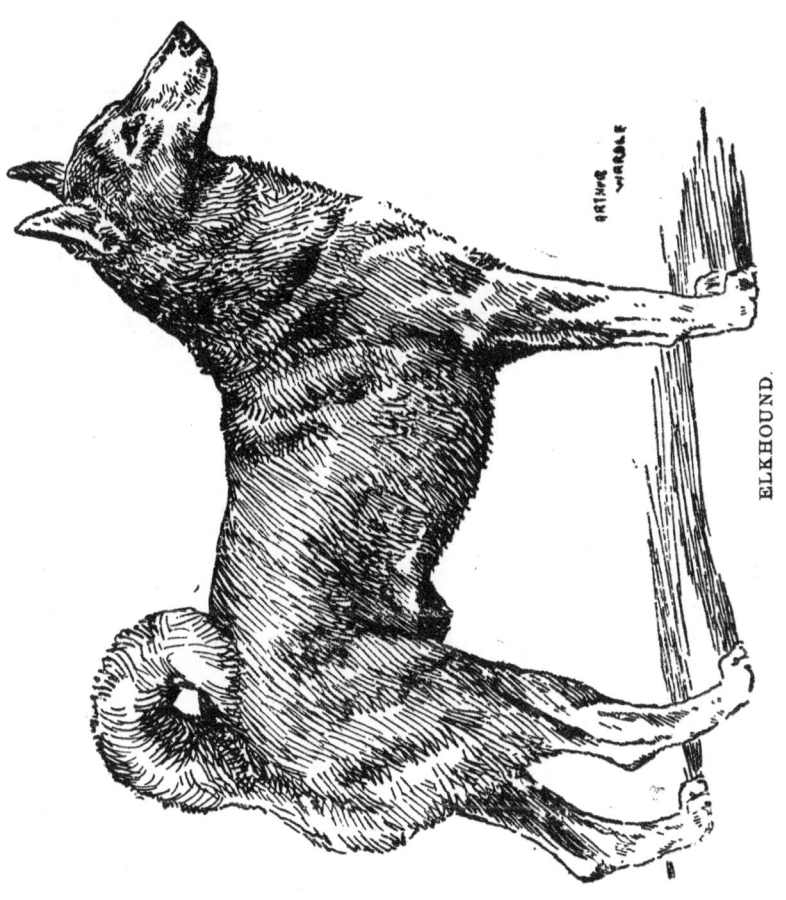

ELKHOUND.

while they are also utilised in the shooting of such birds as woodgrouse. Occasionally, too, they are trained to drive hares and foxes, and to "stand for birds" like a Pointer. As a guard, of course, the Elkhound is in general use, and for that purpose he has no superior, while the breed's mental ability may be summed up in this sentence : " Elkhounds are very quick to learn."

Mr. R. Clapham says :—

The Scandinavian elk and the American moose belong to the same family, and are alike in appearance, but the palmated antlers of the former do not reach the dimensions and weight attained by the magnificent head of the latter. Still, for all that, the elk is a worthy quarry for the sportsman, and his pursuit calls for energy and determination as well as stamina on the part of one who would add a Norwegian elk head to his trophy collection. Like other members of the cervidæ, the elk is a woodland animal by nature, making his home in the spruce and hardwood forests, where he browses on the leaves and young shoots of the deciduous trees. One's first sight of an elk carries one back in mind to prehistoric times, for the great beast which in Canada may weigh well over a thousand pounds, has a most antediluvian appearance. He is decidedly Roman-nosed, and his great shoulders are abnormally high, while his long legs carry him over the ground at a swift trot when danger threatens. He leaves an enormous footprint in mud or snow, that quite dwarfs the track of the very largest Scottish stag. Being an animal of such curious bodily conformation, there is no wonder that the ancients held queer ideas about the elk. Pliny the Younger tells us that " Moreover, in the island Scandinavia there is a beast called Macklis. Common he is there and much talk we have heard of him."

* * * * *

Elk, like moose, are hunted in various ways, but so far as I am aware the Scandinavian method of finding them with a dog, or dogs, applies solely to that country. In America moose are still hunted or more usually called during the rutting season. The instrument used in "calling" is a cone made of birch bark, and is known as a moose horn. In Norway the elk hunter relies on his dog to locate the quarry, and he keeps the animal on the leash, just as the old-time harbourer did with his lyme hound when out in search of a warrantable stag. In Sweden the dog, or often a couple of dogs, are worked loose, their job being to beat a fairly wide area of forest, and after finding elk to bring them to bay until the hunter can reach the spot armed with his rifle. In the vernacular a Hound on leash is a "bind-hund," while a free-ranging dog is a "lös-hund." When using the latter the elk, or elks, may stand to bay and then break it on the approach of the hunter, in consequence of which the man with the rifle often has to travel fast and far in order to keep in touch with his dog when it rounds up the quarry again.

When I judged at Oslo, the capital of Norway (then called Christiania), many years ago, I saw the finest collection of Elkhounds that it was possible to behold, and my admiration for the breed led me to make as close an acquaintance with it as was possible.

Although, of course, the Norwegian Elkhound is a hound, and strongly imbued with the hunting traits required in a hound, there are probably few other hounds which possess the domestic traits to the extent to which the Norwegian Elkhound possesses them. This hound makes one of the finest companions possible, and he has few superiors as a house dog. By reason of his great intelligence and docility he can be taught almost anything.

In 1923 the increased number of admirers of the Elkhound formed themselves into a club to promote the best interests of the breed in this country under the title of "The British Elkhound Society," the first president of which was Lady Dorothy Wood, with Commander R. F. Eyre, R.N., her vice, and a strong committee of zealots which included Lady Kitty Vincent and Lord Alington, with Lieut.-Col. G. J. Scovell, C.B.E., as the first honorary secretary-treasurer.

The Society formulated a carefully drawn-up standard description and points, and first list of judges whom the Society considered competent to judge the breed. No fewer than 55 members were enrolled the first year, and with the breed now recognised by the Kennel Club and placed upon its register the Norwegian Elkhound was given a great send-off and new status, which should form the basis of greater progress and popularity than it has ever enjoyed previously in this country.

The standard description and points are as follows :—

GENERAL APPEARANCE.—That of a very handsome, virile sporting dog of compact build, with medium-size, erect, pointed ears, a tightly curled tail, and heavy weather-resisting coat. He must not be long in back, but muscular, elastic and sinuous in movement, with a deep chest, well-sprung ribs, strong neck, and sturdy limbs.

HEAD.—Capacious, deep, and wedge-shaped; moderately broad between the ears, and bevelled, but the skull not domed; the " stop " well defined, but not too pronounced; well filled out under the eyes, the muzzle of medium length, tapering nicely to the nose, yet not sharply. The nostrils well developed, showing scenting power, and should project slightly over the upper lip. The lips meeting closely, without overlapping. The jaws strong, with level teeth and strong canines.

EARS.—Very mobile at the base and of medium size, erect, and graduating to a point. They should be carried erect, though capable of being lowered backward when expressing affection and during sleep.

EYES.—Of medium size, bright and full of energy, the iris preferably dark and not prominent. They should not be set too far apart, but have a keen forward outlook. The oblique position, which gives a wolfish expression, is not desirable.

NECK.—Powerful, full throated, proportionate in length, and well set up.

BODY.—Short in the couplings, the back wide and straight from neck to stern; the chest rather wide and deep, with well-rounded ribs. The loins muscular, the shoulders sloping.

LEGS AND FEET.—The forelegs of medium length, set well back at the elbow, strong, straight, and of good bone. Hind legs well rounded at the stifle, the sinewy hocks somewhat high rather than much let down, and not greatly bent. The feet compact, oval in shape, and well padded; the toe nails firm, hard, and prominent. The retention of dew claws is optional.

TAIL.—Of medium length (*i.e.*, when untwisted should reach to hock), curling tightly over the back, not carried too much to one side or the other, and furnished with an abundant growth of bristling outstanding hair, but without " brush."

COAT.—Short, close, and smooth on head and legs; on the body deep, of medium length, and crisp, made of thick, woolly undercoat with harsh hair growing through it, forming the outer coat, which should stand straight away from the body with an even surface and be quite free from curl. About the neck and front part of the chest the coat is longer, forming a sort of frill which, with the ears pricked up, the energetic eyes, and the curled tail, gives the animal its unique and alert appearance.

COLOUR.—Grey of various shades, with black ends to longer covering hair; light grey, wolf grey, elk grey, and brownish grey. A grey with definite black markings is objectionable. A wholly black, brown, or white dog is not permissible. On the back and haunches the surface tips of the long hair are usually darker than at the root, and the ears may be black. The chest, underparts, and legs should be light in colour, inclining to silver white. Pronounced dark markings on legs and paws from the knee downwards will be considered as being a blemish.

CHARACTER.—Hardy, courageous, intelligent, and sensible, with great independence of character, and with no sign of undue nervousness.

BITCHES.—Are usually smaller in size, lighter in weight, with rather more refined features and finer in general characteristics.

FAULTS.—Undershot or overshot jaw, cow hocks, oblique eyes, and undue nervousness.

The chief points to look for in a puppy are:—A longish head, small ears, great bone, a very dense coat, and compact body.

CHAPTER XIII.

The Whippet,

Or Race Dog, is one of the most graceful, and to-day one of the most popular, of the canine species. In conformation he is neither more nor less than a Greyhound in miniature. In character he is as keen a little sportsman as ever drew breath, whilst in disposition he is most companionable, and he is easily kept in condition. Originally he was called the "Snap" Dog (no doubt because these dogs have a habit of "snapping" at each other when they meet strange companions, and sometimes when running on the track), and was used in the North of England mostly by the colliers and other working men to course rabbits. He was, in fact, the working-man's Greyhound. Enclosed coursing gradually came into disrepute, and has now become extinct. Racing, however, is still a popular pastime with the working classes, being

WHIPPET.

carried on mostly in the Northern counties and the South of Scotland. It is termed straight running, and takes place at grounds attached to hotels, where a track is formed. The Whippets are trained to run at a rag or handkerchief. They are held in leash at a given mark, being handicapped according to weight or previous performances, and are liberated at the shot of a pistol by a man who is called the starter, the owner or other person being stationed at the other end of the track, and who shakes the handkerchief, at the same time shouting to the respective dogs, and egging them on to the best of his ability. The dogs become very excited and strain every nerve to get at this handkerchief, for which they make a dash on completing the course, shaking it savagely. The judge is stationed at a point which completes the track, usually one of 200 yards, and which is defined by a white chalk mark across the cindered path. For rabbit coursing, Whippets are run by height at shoulder; in racing, by weight.

The weights of the racing Whippet vary from 10lb. to 22lb. or 23lb., the best running weight being about 15lb. or 16lb. This is the best weight for the show bench, a 12lb. dog being looked upon as being under-sized, and a 20lb. dog as too big.

The sport of Whippet racing has been in existence probably about 70 years, but it is only within the last 50 years that the Whippet has come to be recognised as a distinct breed, and classes provided for him at shows. The Kennel Club placed the Whippet on its register even more recently still. About 35 years ago the Whippet was honoured by a work being published on the breed and the sport to which it is devoted, by Mr. Freeman Lloyd, then a canine journalist of repute in this country, and who is still following the same calling in America. Mr. Lloyd gathered his information from experts in the North, in the various centres of the sport in Lancashire, Durham, and Northumberland. He was, in conjunction with Mr. John Tatham, also mainly instrumental in the sport being introduced into London, about 25 years ago. About this time a handicap was first introduced at a dog show, the occasion being the show of the Ladies' Kennel Association, the first or second, which was held in the Ranelagh Club grounds at Barn Elms, and the sport was for the first time witnessed by King Edward and Queen Alexandra (then the Prince and Princess of Wales). Whippet races were included in the repertoire of several subsequent shows, but did not " catch on," and the sport ended in a " fizzle " in the London district.

Mr. Lloyd's work deals fully with the sporting side of the Whippet, this article being intended to treat upon the breed more as an exhibition specimen, in which connection he has come into great favour.

The origin of the Whippet is somewhat uncertain, but sure it is that he is an offshoot of the Greyhound. He was probably first obtained by a cross with a small Greyhound and Italian Greyhound, or a White English Terrier may have been used in his manufacture. Darlington was one of the first shows at which a class was made for the Whippet, when he was designated " Snap " Dog. At the present time, classes are provided at every important show, at some shows as many as six or eight being given. The institution some years ago of a Whippet Club doubtless gave the breed an impetus, and helped to popularise it. As a result, a first-class show specimen is now worth well on to £100. Sixty or seventy pounds is quite a common price to pay for a tip-top specimen. Many cast-off runners, dogs or bitches, who " snap " at their opponents while running on their track, which renders such dogs useless, or worse, as race dogs, find their way into the show ring. These are, of course, the more shapely and well formed specimens, which terms cannot always be applied to champions of the track.

There are two varieties of the Whippet, the Smooth and the Rough coated, the latter suggesting a cross with the Bedlington Terrier in the original manufacture of the breed. Only the Smooth-coated are exhibited, the prevailing and favourite colour being fawn, although black, brindled, brindled-and-white, blue, and fawn-and-white are plentiful enough. Colour is of no consequence whatever in the breed.

Whippets are now well established, and are easily bred to type. They are, too, dogs easily kept in show condition, and can be kept very cheaply, much more so than when kept for running. As in the case of the coursing Greyhound, so with the race Whippet, he must be kept at a high pitch of muscular training to be of any use. It has been said, in the case of working-men keeping these dogs for sport, that cases are on record of their Whippets being fed on the choicest mutton chops, while the fare of the wives and families was bread and butter.

The points of the Whippet may be briefly summed up, as pointed out at the beginning of this article, by saying he should be an exact duplicate in miniature of the Greyhound, and I therefore refer readers to the description of the " long tail," which applies to the Whippet in every detail.

The following is the description of the Whippet as formulated by the Whippet Club :—

HEAD.—Long and lean, rather wide between the eyes, and flat at the top ; the jaw powerful, yet clearly cut ; teeth level and white.

EYES.—Bright and fiery.

EARS.—Small, fine in texture, and rose shape.
NECK.—Long and muscular, elegantly arched, and free from throatiness.
SHOULDERS.—Oblique and muscular.
CHEST.—Deep and capacious.
BACK.—Broad and square, rather long, and slightly arched over loin, which should be strong and powerful.
FORELEGS.—Rather long, well set under dog, possessing fair amount of bone.
HINDQUARTERS.—Strong, and broad across, stifles well bent, thighs broad and muscular, hocks well let down.
FEET.—Round, well split up, with strong soles.
TAIL.—Long, tapering, and nicely carried.
COAT.—Fine and close.
COLOUR.—Black, red, white, brindle, fawn, blue, and the various mixtures of each.
WEIGHT.—The ideal weight for bitches, $17\frac{1}{2}$in. height, 20lb.; for dogs, $18\frac{1}{2}$in. height, 21lb.

In selecting a Whippet puppy at from two to four months old and after, the points to look for are almost identical with those of the Greyhound, of which it is a miniature, except that less bone is required and probably a little more arch of loin, both of which variations are calculated to give the Whippet a little more speed, if less "staying" power, speed only being the great desideratum in the Whippet.

CHAPTER XIV.

The Pointer.

There is more than one theory as to the exact origin of the Pointer, but a concensus of opinion points to that which makes him of Spanish origin, and date of his advent in England as somewhere in the beginning of the eighteenth century. It is said by one authority that in all likelihood the first Pointers imported into this country were brought from Spain by our army at the conclusion of peace at Utrecht in 1712, as indicated by the name, which is taken from the Spanish *punta*. The earlier specimens, judging from old

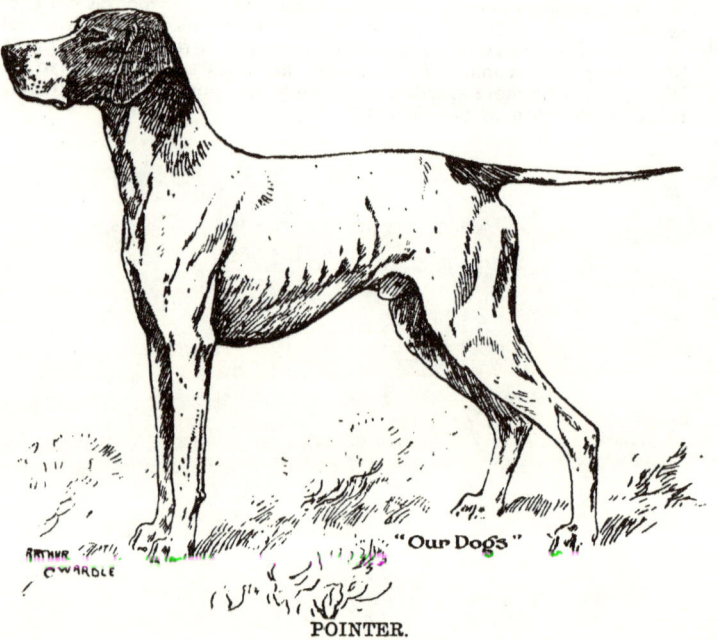

POINTER.

prints, were very similar to the Spanish dogs, even to those existing in Spain to-day. These are lemon-marked dogs for the most part, very dish-faced and full-eyed, and of racy architecture, showing high breeding and great dash. Many of them have split noses, the result, no doubt, of the close inbreeding from particular Spanish strains, which were noted for their great prowess in the field. This type of dog has come to be spoken of, and generally recognised, as the "old-fashioned Spanish Pointer."

The crossing of the Pointer with the Foxhound, which was resorted to after the advent of dog shows, in order to give stamina to the breed and improve his outline and symmetry, it is contended by some authorities, has had a deleterious effect upon the correct sporting qualities of the breed, since the bent and instinct of these two breeds are in many respects quite opposite. Both hunt by scent, it is true, but the one hunts by ground scent and the other " winds " his game more ; the one hunts to kill, and the other not even to touch. An infusion of Foxhound blood, it is said, is calculated to destroy, for the time being, those fine traits of hunting in the first place, and natural restraint in the Pointer which it has taken generations upon generations to cultivate. One of the stoutest advocates of the Spanish type, and greatest enemies of the Foxhound or other alien crosses, was the late Mr. Wm. Arkwright, who wrote a very splendid work on the Pointer as a sporting dog, in which he gave the result of great research on his part into his history and antecedents, and produced the most valuable information and data on the subject.

Other authorities are of opinion that the Foxhound cross has been beneficial in the way indicated—viz., by imparting stamina and constitution to a breed which had become delicate by its consanguinity, and that the Pointer's specific working qualities have been restored in their entirety by subsequent inbreeding to its own species or variety, whose impaired constitution and intelligence have even been benefited by the cross.

The Pointer is one of the most prized and elegant of the sporting varieties, showing the lineament of high breeding in every muscle and movement. He is to the ordinary dog what the thoroughbred horse is to the hackney or roadster. In this work I am dealing with him mostly as a show specimen, although the lines I shall lay down for what I conceive to be his correct anatomy are those which should enable him to fulfil his avocation in the field to the best advantage.

Four leading features of the Pointer are pace, endurance, intelligence, and powers of smell. To ensure these, the dog should be built on galloping lines, with narrow and obliquely set shoulders, straight forelegs, and firm, short, powerful feet, and strong pasterns. He should be comparatively short in the back, with strong and very slightly arched loin, and well-sprung ribs, strong hindquarters, with well-bent stifles and hocks well let down. Coming to head, about which so many opinions differ, there can be no question that the foreface—as in all dogs which hunt by scent—should be long and the muzzle square, showing a little flew. There should be a well-defined stop and flat skull, not too wide, and entirely free from cheekiness, which, with a small eye, is an indication of a headstrong disposition. The eyes should not be full or globular, but moderate in size, and the ears set on below the level of the skull, but not pendulous, rather short comparatively, and to lie close to the head. The tail should be moderate in length, free from feather, strong at the root, tapering to a fine point, and carried straight out from the root.

I publish the description furnished by Mr. Arkwright to " British Dogs," which, it will be seen, differs from the foregoing in many details, and is descriptive more of the "old Spanish Pointer," which had a warm corner in the heart of this distinguished sportsman and authority. Such a dog, however, I venture to submit as an old associate of the show ring, would not meet with favour by the majority of judges.

The colours of the Pointer are liver-and-white and lemon-and-white, whole black, and black-and-white, the two first-named being those most favoured in the show ring, although a good Pointer, like a good horse, cannot well be a bad colour.

There was about 35 years ago a Pointer Club, but it had only a brief existence, being supplanted by the Pointer and Setter Society, which is purely a shooting dog club, and which conducts field trials annually, and in this way ensures a cultivation and development of all that is best and good in this grand gundog, with his great sporting traditions in three continents.

Ch. Coronation was one of the most successful and typical modern show specimens of her day and generation, under many, or I may say most, judges, except Mr. Arkwright, Mr. Smale, and one or two others, who did not like her type, and yet Ch. Sandbank, who illustrates the breed in " British Dogs " in connection with Mr. Arkwright's able article, was of the modern show-bench pattern, and won many of his bench spurs while in the possession of

Mr. Arkwright. He was also a well-broken dog, and clever in the field, and that is what should be aimed at—viz. to produce a Pointer good-looking from an anatomical point of view, and as good in the field.

The following is the description referred to :—

HEAD.—This should be lengthy ; the eye being just half-way between occiput and nostril. There should be a well-pronounced stop between the eyes, and a good drop from skull to set-on of the well-dished muzzle. At the junction between skull and muzzle the head should be cleanly cut : this seems to give character to the face ; when this part is filled up, it makes the head look what is called " gummy." The skull should be wide between the ears : dogs with wide and full temples are the most intelligent and have the best noses ; they should not, however, have large or prominent cheek-bones. The lips, thin yet ample, should not hang down like the Bloodhound's, nor yet taper up to nostrils so much as the Foxhound's.

EYES.—These should not be sunken like the Hound's, but large and full of animation and intelligence. A sullen, hard-looking eye is to be avoided : it is frequently the indication of a headstrong, ungovernable animal, almost worthless in the field.

EARS.—These should be thin and silky, and of medium length. They should be set high on the skull, and hang flat on the cheeks.

NECK.—This should be long and muscular, spring out cleanly from the shoulders, and joined to the skull in the same way. It should be slightly arched.

FORELEGS.—These should be straight and strong ; the arms muscular ; the elbows well let down, and coming down well under the body —not out at elbow, or pigeon-toed. The pastern should be slanting and of fair length.

FEET.—These should be of proportionate size to the dog, and pointed like those of the hare.

SHOULDERS.—These should be long, fine, and sloping backwards. Great attention should be given to them, as a dog with a thick, loaded, straight shoulder will have a cramped, stilty, laboured gallop.

CHEST.—This should be deep, but not too wide ; the ribs well sprung from the backbone, and massive.

BODY.—This should be well developed and powerful ; a weak, tucked-up body is a great defect, indicating lack of constitution, and a dog without that will not be capable of enduring consecutive days of hard work. The back ribs should be deep, the loin appearing to spring from them, as excessive length from last rib to hip and a concave loin form a very objectionable combination.

LOIN.—This should be slightly arched, very wide, strong, and muscular.

HIND LEGS AND THIGHS.—It is upon these that a dog chiefly depends for his propelling leverage. If they are weak and ill-formed the dog is a poor " stayer." The thighs should be very long and muscular, well developed, with a prominent second thigh ; the stifle long and well bent ; the hocks large and strong and parallel—not turned in, often called " cow-hocked " ; the hip-bones wide apart and placed as high as the line of the back. The dogs with wide, ragged hip-bones are generally endowed with speed and endurance.

TAIL.—This should be rather short, fine at tip, and strong at root. It should be set on just below the line of back, but not too low down to make the dog look " goose-rumped." It must not be curled over the back like the Hound's, nor yet must it droop like the Clumber's. It should be carried in a lively manner just about level.

SYMMETRY.—This may be defined as a perfect unity of proportion in all the points before enumerated, so as to present the beautiful outline that is so pleasing to the eye—a perfect adaptation of each part of the dog for the exercise of all his powers to the greatest advantage. For instance, some dogs possess several points in a very marked degree of excellence, and still, because other parts are deficient, their symmetry will be said to be at fault. Unless all parts are considered collectively, no estimate can be formed of symmetry ; and then it is very difficult to estimate correctly.

COLOUR.—A predominance of white has been thought to be best, because it assists the sportsman in detecting the whereabouts of his dogs in high cover ; but as to the colour of the markings on this white ground, it may be urged that no importance attaches ; and, in support of this opinion, equally good specimens of different colours are frequently seen. Some time back the lemon or orange and whites were most fashionable, but latterly the liver-and-whites have been the most successful prize winners. Black and white, and the whole colours—black, liver, and various shades of yellow—are also quite correct for Pointers, but any tricolour is very suspicious. Still, in olden times the Pointer might be of almost any colour—even brindle being admissible, according to John Mayer (1814).

The chief points to look for in the selection of Pointer puppies at from two to four months old and after are :—Great length of head, square muzzle, decided " stop," rather narrow skull, short round body, short straight tail, deep chest, great bone, and straight forelegs, and short strong feet.

CHAPTER XV.

The English Setter

Holds a foremost place in the affections of all sportsmen, as well as show men. Besides being a most useful, intelligent, and hardy dog in the field, he is withal a handsome animal, appealing to all dog lovers of whatever class or creed. He is, too, a very ancient English variety. There is some difference of opinion as to whether he sprang from the Springer Spaniel, or the latter from him, but certain it is that he existed and was used and prized for his sporting proclivities as early as the fifteenth century. In the early days the dog was, of course, bred purely for sport, and few sportsmen, whether of the "old-English-gentleman" class—a race, unhappily, fast disappearing from our midst—or of the farming class, were without their brace of Setters. Judging from old prints and other records, the ancient Setters were mostly lemon-and-white in colour, and a bigger and stronger dog than those which grace our game preserves and the show bench of to-day. The Setter, it is recorded, was the dog that was first used for hawking, and has been a constant companion of the gun for centuries. I am not, however, dealing with the dog as a sportsman, his fascinating association in connection with which, and his long and illustrious history, would form a most interesting volume in itself.

The era of dog shows naturally effected a reformation of most breeds and the creation of others. The Setter was one of the first to come under the show man's hand. About this time the late Mr. Laverack came upon the scene; he was a gentleman who took up the breeding of Setters, not, however, for the show bench, but for the field, and who established a strain to which has been given his own cognomen, and are to-day known as the Laverack Setters. They are, for the most part, black-white-and-tan in colour, and heavily ticked. Mr. W. D. Drury, author of "British Dogs," gives in this well-written and very authentic work a short history of Mr. Laverack, but adds his own opinion that the part this breeder played in connection with Setter breeding has done the breed great, if not irreparable, harm.

A native of some Westmorland village, he appears in his youth to have been a shoemaker's apprentice. Early in life, however, he came into possession of a legacy bequeathed to him by some distant relative. On this he appears to have been able to gratify the exceeding love for sport which was doubtless in his blood from some remote ancestor. In those days, which would be about 1825, there was any amount of grouse shooting to be got for nothing by anyone who was not afraid of roughing it, and Laverack appears to have led a nomadic life devoted to Setters and shooting for at least forty years. He was a good sportsman, and undoubtedly a most marvellous judge of dogs, and for that reason a most successful breeder of beauty and of some excellence.

It always seemed a great pity that he "gave himself away" to the public by publishing his miraculous in-and-in pedigrees, which can be seen in the Kennel Club Stud Book. He probably believed them to some extent himself, but whether he ever succeeded in inducing others to do so, with the exception, perhaps, of a very few, is far more dubious. To any man of common-sense, not to speak of any practical experience, they are simply an impossibility. One thing is, however, certain—that his talent for selection enabled him to breed very closely, and so to preserve and increase the beauty of his type, and that his inherent canineness, as well as his perfect judgment, enabled him to select occasional fresh strains of blood, which improved, instead of destroying, the excellence of the progeny.

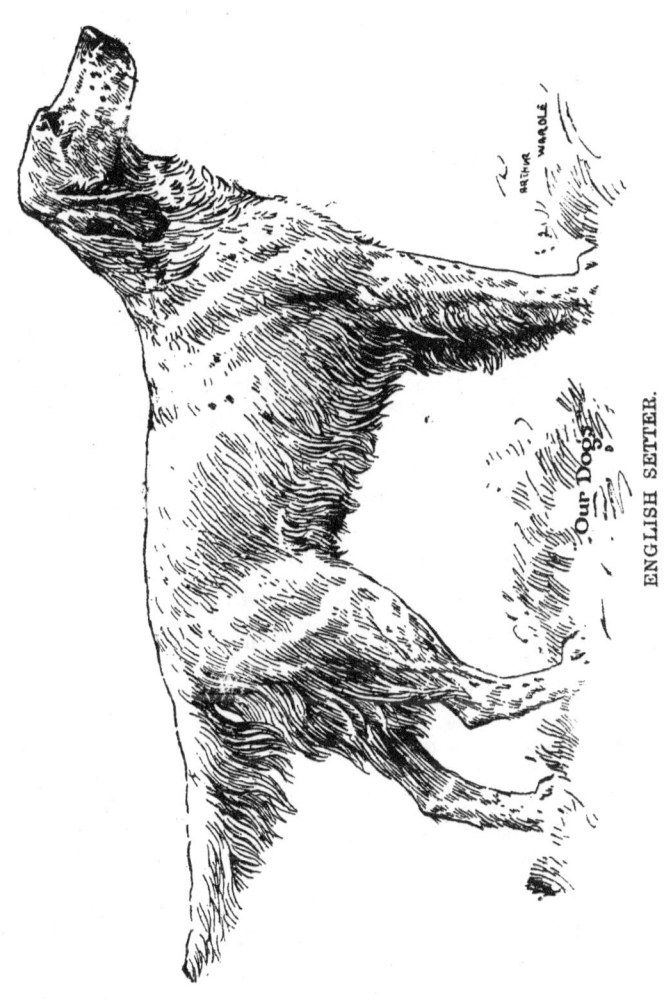
ENGLISH SETTER.

Sometimes also he, in the soothing atmosphere of a winter evening's fire, combined with the seductive effects of some good old port, disclosed a few faint shadows of his dark secrets. One of them is here related.

Once on a time there was a tract of country on the Borders called "the Debatable Land," nominally belonging to the Earls of Carlisle. Now, this country swarmed with gipsies, and that strange people had from time immemorial claimed the right to shoot over this tract at their own sweet will, so on August 12th in each year they were accustomed to form a band of thirty or more, and, with a large army of Setters, and probably Pointers as well, make a regular raid on the said moors, and it is not surprising that the keepers gave them a wide berth.

Well, on one Twelfth, Laverack accompanied this mob, and he had with him one of his best dogs. Among all the Setters which were ranging far and wide, Laverack's keen eyes noted one animal, liver-and-white, which was *facile princeps*, and beat the whole lot in both nose and pace, though by no means a good-looking one. "Well, sir," the old man said, "I hunted up those gipsies. I found that dog, I bought him, and I bred from him!"

There is some reason to suspect that in much later times a judicious cross was effected with the Pointer; but there seems to be very little doubt at all that the Irish Setter also was called in to refresh the blood. The writer feels sure that the old man, in his later days, having sold all his best dogs at temptingly high prices, was *obliged*, in order to save his strain from utter extinction, to resort to some outside agency to preserve it, and there are some good judges who fancy that they can even now trace some of these crosses in the world-wide progeny that has resulted from the (in many cases) injudicious and indiscriminate use of the Laverack Setter with the old English strains.

Now, it is commonly said among Setter men that Laverack was a great benefactor to the Setter and the Setter lover. The writer's opinion is that this idea admits of very grave doubt. One thing seems certain, viz., that the Laverack and its crosses caused a great number of men to give up shooting over dogs altogether, and that for one simple reason only, viz., that they could not break either the original or its offspring. The ancient Laverack excelled in beauty; it also had surpassing good field qualities, a very high head, a wonderful nose, great pace, endurance, pluck, and a marvellous "sporting instinct." By this last is meant such a love for game-finding that it would go on for ever, even though never a bird was shot to it; but to all these qualities it added an almost invincible headstrongness and obstinacy, and this rendered it an impossible object of training to nine men out of ten, of that day at all events. So things happened thus: everyone sought to cross his breed with a Laverack, of some sort or another, and everybody did it; and so a headstrong breed arose which no one could manage, and therefore men went out shooting without their dogs. The writer recollects Laverack himself being once asked on the moors with respect to a dog of his, which was endued with perpetual motion, entire self-hunting, and utter regardlessness of whistle, "However do you get that dog home at night?" "Why, sir, I just waits till he points, and then I put a collar and chain on him and lead him home."

Mr. Laverack never called his dogs by his own name—that was the doing of the British public; indeed, he never claimed to have *invented* his strain, only to have *continued* it. Here are his own words, copied from a letter written by himself: "The breed of Setters that I have found most useful and valuable, combining the essential qualities of a setting dog—viz., innate point, speed, nose, method of range or carriage, with powers of endurance—has been known in the northern counties of Cumberland, Northumberland, and the southern counties of Scotland as the old original black or silver grey, and in Scotland as the old blue Beltons. How they originated I can't say; but I can state with confidence that I can trace back this breed for a period of seventy-five years or more, having had them in my own possession forty years, and the late Rev. A. Harrison, of Carlisle, from whom I originally obtained them, had them thirty-five years previously."

In contrast to the late Mr. Laverack, the efforts of another well-known Setter enthusiast, in Mr. R. Purcell Llewellin, stand in bold relief. Mr. Llewellin, by more judicious crossing, established another strain, known by his name also, which will long survive him. "British Dogs" has the following interesting particulars of Mr. Llewellin and the origin of the strain of Setters known by his name :—

And now we come to the most celebrated strain of the modern Setter —indeed, we may safely call it the only English Setter now existing that deserves the name of a distinct strain. This was originally evolved, and has been continued up to the present time, by the judgment and devotion of its founder, Mr. Richard Purcell Llewellin. Mr. Llewellin, the descendant of a noted old Welsh sportsman of that name, commenced Setter breeding very soon after the first inauguration of field trials, nearly forty years ago. He began with black-and-tans and with some of the old-fashioned English Setters. He entered these at trials and was badly beaten. He then purchased some of the finest and best Irish Setters that could be procured, and with them and their progeny he won extensively at dog shows and sometimes at trials. Not yet satisfied, he tried crossing the Irish with the Laverack, and obtained thereby some exceedingly handsome specimens, which at shows were well-nigh invincible. Among these he bred a bitch called Flame, a perfectly formed red-and-white of wonderful quality. This bitch, it is worthy of note, after being sold by him, became the ancestress of the fashionable show winners of past and present days, and perhaps there are very few of these winners now which do not contain some of her blood.

His experience of the English and Irish cross was that although, as stated, the progeny was invariably most handsome, yet it did not possess the sporting instincts and capacities of either parent. Mr. Llewellin, therefore, made further search for his ideal, and at last found it.

In 1871 he purchased, at a very high figure, the brace winners at the Shrewsbury Trials, Dick and Dan. This splendid brace of dogs was the property of Mr. Statter, Lord Derby's agent, and had been bred by him by Armstrong Duke, of Sir V. Corbet's strain, out of Rhæbe, who was nearly pure Gordon (by Gordon I do not mean black-and-tan). Mr. Llewellin discarded Dick as vastly inferior to his brother Dan, and then crossed Dan with the best pure Laverack bitches; and thus originated the celebrated breed, individuals of which speedily eclipsed, both at shows and trials, every other strain, and which still remains in its owner's hands, pure, unstained, and as good and handsome as ever.

Mr. Llewellin's strain embraces and includes all the celebrated blood of the old kennels that we have noted, and it has only been by the most careful and scientific selection—which, of course, called for a judgment of which few men are possessed—that he has so notably succeeded. The more perfectly shaped animals were selected, and this with the greatest rigour, while all that was at all faulty was discarded. The character also and the innate proclivities of each individual were most carefully studied, and the minor faults and infirmities in one individual were corrected by selecting a mate which in those special particulars he considered calculated to do so. In this manner Mr. Llewellin may be said to have attained the object for which he had worked for many years—viz., the combining of great beauty with surpassing field excellence. And this was abundantly proved by the practical invincibility of his strain, both in the field and on the show bench.

Whilst the "Laverack" strain has practically become lost, the "Llewellin" survives, and is amongst the handsomest on the show bench, as well as most remarkable in the field, except that many of them have somewhat degenerated in size. They, however, show the beautiful chiselling of head, high intelligence, gracefulness of outline, and dash. The Llewellin Setters are mostly blue Belton in colour—that is, blue ticked,—although lemon marked dogs still crop up in breeding.

An English Setter Club is in existence, whose object is to encourage and foster the breeding of the English Setter on lines which should enable him to fulfil his avocation in the field to the best advantage. The Club holds field trials, and occasionally offers prizes at dog shows, with a view to encouraging the propagation of Setters of the correct type and conformation. The Club has also formulated a code of points for the guidance of breeders and owners, which may be said, taken as a whole, to be a desirable and correct code.

Description of the English Setter.

HEAD.—Should be long and lean, with a well-defined stop. The skull oval from ear to ear, showing plenty of brain room, and with a well-defined occipital protuberance. The muzzle moderately deep and fairly square; from the stop to the point of the nose should be long, the nostrils wide, and the jaws of nearly equal length; flews not to be pendulous. The colour of the nose should be black, or dark, or light liver, according to the colour of the coat. The eyes should be bright, mild, and intelligent, and of a dark-hazel colour—darker the better. The ears of moderate length, set on low, and hanging in neat folds close to the cheek; the tip should be velvety, the upper part clothed with fine silky hair.

NECK.—Should be rather long, muscular, and lean, slightly arched at the crest, and clean cut where it joins the head; towards the shoulder it should be larger, and very muscular; not throaty or any pendulosity below the throat, but elegant and bloodlike in appearance.

BODY.—Should be of moderate length, with shoulders well set back, or oblique; back short and level; loins wide, slightly arched, strong and muscular.

Chest deep in the brisket, with good, round, widely sprung ribs, deep in the back ribs—that is, well-ribbed up.

LEGS AND FEET.—Stifles well bent and ragged, thighs long from hip to hock. The forearm big and very muscular, the elbow well let down. Pasterns short, muscular, and straight. The feet very close and compact, and well protected by hair between the toes.

TAIL.—The tail should be set on almost in a line with the back; medium length, not curly or ropey; to be slightly curved or scimitar-shaped, but with no tendency to turn upwards; the flag or feather hanging in long pendant flakes. The feathers should not commence at the root, but slightly below, and increase in length to the middle, then gradually taper off towards the end; and the hair long, bright, soft, and silky; wavy, but not curly.

COAT AND FEATHERING.—The coat from the back of the head in a line with the ears ought to be slightly wavy, long, and silky, which should be the case with the coat generally; the breeches and forelegs, nearly down to the feet, should be well feathered.

COLOUR AND MARKINGS.—The colour may be either black and white, lemon and white, liver and white, or tricolour—that is, black, white, and tan; those without heavy patches of colour on the body, but flecked all over, preferred.

Briefly, the English Setter is throughout a symmetrically built dog. He should have a long, telescopic head, with but little " stop," square muzzle, rather narrow skull, showing a distinct occipital development, yet not too pronounced. Ears small and set on low; eyes medium in size and full of intelligence, with a nice soft expression. The neck should be slightly arched, of good length, finishing in obliquely set and well-laid-back shoulders. The body should be comparatively short, and ribs well sprung. Two common defects in the English Setter are flat sides and loosely placed elbows. The former is always an indication of want of heart room, and cannot be tolerated, but the latter does not always imply want of galloping power. The out-at-elbows formation in the breed is no doubt hereditary, and may in some degree have been brought about in the dog's ancestors, by his natural crouching habit in the field. Indeed, for actual work, and this mode of prosecuting it, which is natural in the Setter, it is a moot question whether an out-at-elbows formation is not a distinct advantage. It is a requisite in the Bulldog to enable him to get down to *his* " game," and why should not the Setter be so facilitated, since it is the dog's natural mode of approaching and " setting " *his* game? On the show bench such a formation, however, in both cases is discouraged, but straight forelegs are indispensable in a good specimen. The stifles should be well bent, and hocks well let down. Standing broadside, an English Setter should appear a little taller at the shoulder than at the rump, or slightly giraffe-like in architecture. His high poise of head, like that of the Pointer, is peculiar to these two breeds, and so is the pose of his hindquarters, another characteristic peculiar to the breed. He should stand in a slightly crouching attitude behind, something like a cat does when it is about to spring upon its prey.

The coat of the English Setter should be flat, and the legs and tail well feathered. The latter should be short and carried straight out from its root. The eyes should be hazel in colour, a light or gooseberry eye in any sporting breed being objectionable.

In breeding, the main points to guard against are long backs, flat sides, and snipy muzzles, which always heavily handicap a dog in the show ring, and denote want of pace and scenting power in the field.

For his size the Setter is rather low in stature, more so than the Pointer, and averages in weight from 45lb. to 6olb., bitches invariably being a few pounds smaller than dogs.

The chief points to look for in the selection of English Setter puppies at from two to four months old and after are :—Great length of head and squareness of muzzle, rather narrow skull, showing an occipital development, short body, short, straight tail, deep chest, straight forelegs.

THE IRISH SETTER.

As to the origin of the Irish Setter, little authentic information is available, except that it is a breed, like all " Ireland's reds," indigenous to the Emerald Isle, and one that has been in existence for some centuries at least. Originally the Irish Setter was purely a sporting dog, and well adapted to the work alike in the mountainous and boggy districts of Ireland, owing to its great dash and powers of endurance. The Irish Setter, like the thoroughbred, is an example of high breeding, being, like most Irish horses, an animal of great quality—the thoroughbred of the Setter species. Before the era of dog shows the dog was valued alone for his splendid sporting attributes, for his fine nose, great determination and dash, and wonderful powers of endurance, which he undoubtedly possesses. Little attention was paid to type—a term unknown in the breeding kennel,—and colour was of no consequence. The Irish Setters of those days were, however, all red or red-and-white. The advent of dog shows and the establishment of a club for the breed in Ireland inspired breeders to aim at a greater fixity of type, and out of the raw material available the beautiful red Irish Setter of to-day was evolved. Whilst a consensus of opinion decided that the true Irish Setter should be a red dog, vested interests insisted that the red-and-white specimens which existed should not be altogether discarded, and although the whole-coloured red is the more popular and predominating colour, the red-and-whites are still recognised, and at some shows classes are made for them.

A red-and-white dog is, of course, just as good in the field as a whole red, and there is therefore no rational reason why the colour should not be recognised, and especially as it provides a place in the field and on the show bench for what I may term mismarked reds, and is thus an economic of canine nature.

At some shows in Ireland classes are still provided for the red-and-white, and some breeders (who, of course, own dogs of this colour) declare that they possess greater sporting virtues than the reds. This I should very much dispute.

Whilst the Irish Setter is about the same size as the English Setter, and in most essentials is built on similar lines, in others, and notably in head, he greatly differs from his Anglo-Saxon brother. The head of the Hibernian is not quite so long in proportion, the lips are not so square at the muzzle, and the occipital bone is not so well developed. The eyes of the Irishman are lighter —a rich hazel colour—and are set in differently, showing less " haw," or, in fact, none at all, and they exhibit a totally different expression, just as the expression of the red Irish Water Spaniel and red Irish Terrier differs from that of any English variety—an expression peculiarly Irish, and one that is more easily detected than explained. A little stop is required.

Since pace is one of the leading essentials in an Irish Setter, the dog must be built on galloping lines, embodied in sloping and well-laid-back shoulders, straight forelegs, and strong pasterns, deep chest, well-sprung ribs,

IRISH SETTER.

short couplings, and strong loin, well-bent stifles, and well-let-down hocks. These are his main features and requirements, the rest of his anatomy being mere details and embellishments. Any departure from these cardinal virtues should be carefully avoided in breeding, and all coarse or weedy specimens scrupulously discarded, or, what is better, destroyed.

No more graceful or classic canine enters a show field or field-trial course than the Irish Red Setter, which I venture to think, however, has made but little progress during the last decade or so. Many of our best specimens have been exported to the United States, where so many Irishmen themselves have migrated, for which country the breed seems to be well adapted, and where are to-day to be found better specimens than exist in Great Britain or in their native country. There is, however, plenty of the raw material left in " Ould Oireland," and all that is required is more enterprise among our English and Celtic friends to husband the resources of the two countries, and again place this beautiful breed upon the pinnacle of eminence its great merit and many charms deserve.

The chief points to look for in the selection of Irish Setter puppies at from two to four months old and after are almost identical with those of the English Setter, with colour added, which should, of course, be a deep red.

The following is the published description and standard of points of the Irish Red Setter Club :—

HEAD.—Should be long and lean. The skull oval (from ear to ear), having plenty of brain room, and with well-defined occipital protuberance. Brows raised, showing stop. The muzzle moderately deep, and fairly square at end. From the stop to the point of the nose should be long, the nostrils wide, and the jaws of nearly equal length, flews not to be pendulous. The colour of the nose dark mahogany or dark walnut, and that of the eyes (which ought not to be too large) rich hazel or brown. The ears to be of moderate size, fine in texture, set on low, well back, and hanging in a neat fold close to head.

NECK.—Should be moderately long, very muscular, but not too thick, slightly arched, free from all tendency to throatiness.

BODY.—Should be long. Shoulders fine at the points, deep, and sloping well back. The chest as deep as possible, rather narrow in front. The ribs well sprung, leaving plenty of lung room. Loins muscular and slightly arched. The hindquarters wide and powerful.

LEGS AND FEET.—The hind legs from hip to hock should be long and muscular ; from hock to heel, short and strong. The stifle and hock joints well bent, and not inclined either in or out. The forelegs should be straight and sinewy, having plenty of bone, with elbows free, well let down, and, like the hocks, not inclined either in or out. The feet small, very firm ; toes strong, close together, and arched.

TAIL.—Should be of moderate length, set on rather low, strong at root, and tapering to a fine point ; to be carried as nearly as possible on a level with or below the back.

COAT.—On the head, front of legs, and tips of ears, should be short and fine ; but on all other parts of the body and legs it ought to be of moderate length, flat, and as free as possible from curl or wave.

FEATHERING.—The feather on the upper portion of the ears should be long and silky ; on the back of the fore and hind legs long and fine ; a fair amount of hair on the belly, forming a nice fringe, which may extend on chest and throat. Feet to be well feathered between toes. Tail to have a nice fringe of moderately long hair, decreasing in length as it approaches the point. All feathering to be as straight and as flat as possible.

COLOUR AND MARKINGS.—The colour should be a rich golden chestnut, with no trace whatever of black ; white on chest, throat, or toes, or a small star on the forehead, or a narrow streak or blaze on the nose or face not to disqualify.

STANDARD OF POINTS.

Head	10
Eyes	6
Ears	4
Neck	4
Body	20
Hind legs and feet	10
Forelegs and feet	10
Tail	4
Coat and feather	10
Colour	8
Size, style, and general appearance	14
Total	100

THE GORDON SETTER.

The Gordon or Black-and-tan Setter is popularly supposed to be a Scottish product, and indigenous to Scotland. There is, however, some doubt about that, although the dog's precise origin is enveloped in some mystery. The name is taken from the Duke of Richmond and Gordon, who kept the breed largely at Gordon Castle in the early part of last century, and about whose kennel a theory exists that a Scottish Black-and-tan Collie on an adjacent farmstead accidentally crossed one of the Duke's tricolour Setter bitches (the prevailing colour of His Grace's Setters) and that from this alien alliance the present pure (?) Black-and-tan Setter sprang. This may be true or it may be legendary, but be that as it may, from a kennel of Setters somewhat varied in colour was ultimately founded a famous strain—now recognised as a distinct variety.

A more reasonable theory, however, would be a cross with a leggy black Springing Spaniel, because there is much in common in the physiognomy of the Gordon Setter and the Field Spaniel, which in those days was a leggy, Settery type of dog. This transition would be very easily accomplished without the loss of any of the working characteristics of the Setter, and seems a more likely explanation of the dog's origin. There is another theory—viz., that the Black-and-tan Setter has been produced by a cross with the Irish Setter and the black Pointer, which latter is a Scotch product. This seems a more feasible theory than the Collie story, if somewhat less romantic. At the same time, each of the explanations presented is more or less mere conjecture, as there is absolutely no definite information on the point available. Nor does it much matter for the purpose of this article, since the variety is now thoroughly acknowledged and firmly established.

When judging at the show of the Norwegian Kennel Club at Christiania in 1914, I was struck by the large collection of Gordon Setters, amongst them many very good ones, with a specialist judge to award the prizes, that were benched at that show. We could not raise a collection half so good in the whole of the United Kingdom. Doubtless they are the result of a few importations from England (and maybe Holland, which possesses several good kennels), from which this collection has been raised by in-breeding. Most of the winners were quite correct in type, but there was one marked feature which ran through almost the whole collection, and that was prevailing top-knots, very narrow fronts, and turned-in toes, all marked characteristics of the Irish Water Spaniel, proving, to my mind, an undoubted admixture of Irish Water Spaniel in the Irish Setter, and through the latter to the Gordon Setter.

Black-and-tan Setters were exhibited at the first Birmingham Dog Show, in 1860, at which show classes were provided for them and have been ever since, as well as at all leading dog shows in Great Britain and Ireland and on the Continent.

The Gordon Setter is a slightly bigger and stronger made dog than either the English or Irish Setter, and better adapted to the mountainous districts of Scotland, being a splendid dog in the field, showing great endurance.

As a show dog, under which category we must consider him more specifically, he is hardly so popular as either of his kinsmen, and is in fewer hands. In fact, the leading exhibitors in this country at the present time may be counted nearly on the fingers of the two hands. In general features there is a great similarity, the lines of the body and the shape and set-on of the limbs being much the same, except, as I have already stated, the dog in his architecture is somewhat stronger throughout. It is in the head where, as the index to all breeds, the greatest difference is found. The Gordon Setter's skull is a little stronger than that of his Anglo-Saxon or Celtic relative, and the occipital bone is less developed. He is, and should be, deeper in the "stop," and his eyes are more sunken and show more haw. As in all sporting breeds where dogs hunt by scent, the muzzle should be long and square and the nostrils large. The ears should be small rather, and carried flat to the side of the head, and the coat flat. The Gordon Setter usually

BLACK-AND-TAN OR GORDON SETTER.

shows a great amount of feathering, and often white hairs are intermixed with the tan of the feather. Although this is objectionable in these days of fine points, it is not fatal, since it cannot affect the dog's working capabilities in the least, and is only a slight blemish pointing to his ancestry. Great stress, however, is laid by experts upon the necessity for rich tan markings, which certainly give the dog the appearance of great quality, but pale tan is no great fault. The first desideratum is make and shape, a good head, flat, dense coat, and great symmetry. A snipy muzzle, sour expression, thick, chubby head, crooked forelegs, and a curly coat are defects to be scrupulously avoided by the breeder.

The chief points to look for in the selection of Black-and-tan or Gordon Setter puppies at from two to four months old and after are almost identical with those of the English Setter, except colour, which should, of course, be black-and-tan, the tan requiring to be of a rich mahogany.

The following are the description and scale of points adopted by the Gordon Setter Club :—

There seems to be little authentic information as to the Gordon Setter. Authorities, however, agree that originally the colour was black, white, and tan. . . . . . Of late years, no doubt, the breed has been tampered with for show purposes, and crosses, more particularly with the Irish Setter, with the idea of improving the colour, have been resorted to, to the detriment of the dog for both show-bench and field purposes. Probably the pale buff in the place of the tan, frequently verging on stone colour, and the diffusion over the body, instead of being developed on the recognised points, is mainly due to this cause ; if so, it will require careful breeding through many generations to eradicate.

The head of the Gordon Setter is much heavier than that of the English Setter ; broad at the top between the ears, the skull being slightly rounded, the occiput well developed, and the depth from the occiput to the bottom of the lower jaw much greater than in the English Setter. The width between the eyes should perhaps not be too great, speaking with caution. The nose should be moderately long and broad across the top, giving room for the nerves of scent (in fact, the opposite to snipiness), the nostrils well distended, making this the widest part of the nose. The shape of the underjaw is perhaps a matter of fancy : Old Kent had a very heavy muzzle and underjaw, with remarkably bright and penetrating eyes ; in these his likeness has been transmitted to many of his descendants in a remarkable degree. Many Gordon Setters show slight " haw " and " dewlap " ; a proper development of these is probably the true type. The ears vary considerably, some being long, silky, and hanging close to the face ; others are much shorter. These are also matters of fancy, and therefore of minor importance. The body of the Gordon Setter is also heavier than that of the English Setter, but may be judged on the same lines. The tail is often long, giving a bad carriage ; this does not interfere with good work. The great beauty of this dog is his lovely colour, and as this in perfection is in no way antagonistic to his working qualities, great prominence should be given to it in judging. Formerly, without doubt, the prevailing colours were black, white, and tan. The black should be a jet, not brown or rusty ; the tan should be a rich dark mahogany, and should be exhibited on the inside of the thighs, showing down the front of the stifle to the ground, and on the forelegs to the knees. The muzzle also should be tan, the spots over the eyes well defined, not blurred, and on the points of the shoulders also. Blurring and diffusion over the belly and other parts of the dog probably indicate contamination with other blood. It is of the highest importance, if we are to get back the real hunting qualities of this breed and the show qualities also, that purity of blood should be the chief aim in breeding. A first cross may sometimes *appear* to answer, but succeeding generations will certainly show the cross, and will deteriorate in all the qualities we prize.

A splendid intelligence, fine scenting powers, and great endurance are the main characteristics of the Gordon Setter. If purity of blood is maintained we may not only recover the qualities that some fear we have partly lost, but also develop their natural powers to an extent hitherto unknown. A well-formed head is of the first importance if we are to develop and maintain that intelligence which is the great charm and usefulness of the dog.

SCALE OF POINTS.

Head and neck	35
Shoulders and chest	12
Loin and quarter	12
Feet and legs	16
Colour	10
Coat, feather, and quality	10
Tail	5
Total	100

CHAPTER XVI.

The Retriever.

There are five varieties of the Retriever—the Curly-coated, the Flat-coated (formerly described as the Wavy-coated), the Labrador, the Golden, and the Russian Yellow. The first and third named are the two oldest varieties, the flat-coated dog being of modern manufacture—in all likelihood the product of the two, with a splash of Spaniel, Newfoundland, or Setter, whilst the two last named are even more recent productions or introductions.

THE FLAT-COATED RETRIEVER

Was used as a shooting dog long before he became known on the show bench, but he was not then nearly so uniform in type and character as we now see him. It is to Mr. Thorpe-Bartram and the late Mr. S. F. Shirley, founder and for a quarter of a century President of the Kennel Club, and one or two others, that we owe the beautiful type of flat-coated Retriever, which is now so universally popular, both as a workman and show dog. Many specimens of the day combine the two qualities, which disproves the theory held by some fossilised sportsmen that the average show dog has no brains, and is useless for work in the field. Did not two champion flat-coated Retrievers figure high in the stakes for flat-coated Retrievers at the trials in 1906 promoted by the Kennel Club, and often since? In fact, most of the large and prominent exhibitors regularly shoot over their show dogs.

The enormous classification now provided at the Kennel Club's and all the larger and more important shows is evidence of the great and growing popularity of the flat-coated Retriever, whilst the calibre of the breeders and exhibitors of this variety, almost without exception, is a guarantee that gun-shy and indifferent workers will find no abiding place in their kennels.

The variety was first known as "wavy-coated" Retrievers, since the dogs in vogue anterior to their being introduced to the show bench were for the most part wavy in coat. This waviness of coat was held to be a drawback to the dog in the field, first, because it indicated a soft coat, and, secondly because such a coat has a tendency to hold water. It was therefore ordained by a consensus of expert opinion that the coat of the dog should be flat, and by degrees the name "wavy" was substituted by "flat," until the former has become an obsolete nomenclature.

In size, head, and general conformation, the flat-coated variety differs but little from the curly-coat. The points and features are all practically the same, the only real difference being in coat. This, as already stated, should be flat, the outer coat rather harsh to the touch, there being an undercoat for warmth, the outer one being for weather resistance. The legs, both before and aft, and the tail, should be feathered, and the feet protected by well-feathered pads.

In breeding flat-coated Retrievers the object to aim at is to produce a strong, well-made, useful dog, showing quality—a workman in architecture, with the finish of the gentleman. Length of head, good shoulders, a strong loin and quarters, with straight forelegs and a flat coat, are the chief points to aim at and preserve. The flat-coats have rarely the same spring of rib as the curly-coats, in which they reveal their unmistakable Setter ancestry; but this should be cultivated. Light eyes are a prevailing defect in the flat-coats, and should be avoided as much as possible, as it is invariably an indication of uncertain temper or a headstrong disposition.

FLAT-COATED RETRIEVER.

The chief points to look for in the selection of flat-coated Retriever puppies at from two to four months old and after are :—A long level head free from lippiness, dark eye, nicely balanced skull, small ears set close to side of head, short back, short straight tail, deep chest, well sprung ribs, straight forelegs well boned, and a flat, close, dense coat.

The following is the description and scale of points adopted by the Flat-coated Retriever Association :—

GENERAL APPEARANCE.—A bright active dog of medium size (weighing from 6olb. to 7olb.), with an intelligent expression, showing power without lumber and raciness without weediness.

HEAD.—This should be long and nicely moulded. The skull flat and moderately broad. There should be a depression or stop between the eyes, slight and in no way accentuated so as to avoid giving either a down or a dish-faced appearance. The nose of good size with open nostrils. The eyes, of medium size, should be dark brown or hazel, with a very intelligent expression (a round prominent eye is a disfigurement), and they should not be obliquely placed. The jaws should be long and strong, with a capacity of carrying a hare or pheasant. The ears small and well set on close to the side of the head.

NECK, SHOULDERS, AND CHEST.—The head should be well set in the neck, which latter should be long and free from throatiness, symmetrically set and obliquely placed in shoulders running well into the back to allow of easily seeking for the trail. The chest should be deep and fairly broad with a well-defined brisket, on which the elbows should work cleanly and evenly. The fore ribs should be fairly flat, showing a gradual spring, and well arched in the centre of the body, but rather lighter towards the quarters. Open couplings are to be ruthlessly condemned.

BACK AND QUARTERS.—The back should be short, square, and well ribbed up, with muscular quarters. The stern short, straight, and well set on, carried gaily, but never much above the level of the back.

LEGS AND FEET.—These are of the greatest importance. The forelegs should be perfectly straight, with bone of good quality carried right down to the feet, which should be round and strong. The stifle should not be too straight or too bent, and the dog must neither be cowhocked or move too wide behind, in fact he must stand and move true all round on legs and feet, with toes close and well arched, the soles being thick and strong, and, when the dog is in full coat, the limbs should be well feathered.

COAT.—Should be dense, of fine quality and texture, flat as possible. Colour, black or liver.

THE CURLY-COATED RETRIEVER.

As the prototype, in all likelihood, of the flat-coat, I will deal with the curly-coated variety first, and at once declare that a really sound and typical curly-coated Retriever is one of the most useful sportsmen that ever entered a cover, and one of the handsomest sporting dogs ever seen on a show bench. Useful as a sporting dog, because he combines pace with endurance, intelligence with a good nose, and is, on account of his size and strength, able to retrieve almost anything shot to him. Some individual specimens are said to be headstrong, but that is often the result of neglected or defective training.

As to the real origin of the curly-coated Retriever there is no authentic information, but there can be little doubt that he has been manufactured by a cross with the Poodle, the Irish Water Spaniel, and the Newfoundland, Labrador, or Setter. When and by whom he was first evolved, however, it is impossible to say, beyond pointing to the fact of his existence at the end of the eighteenth and beginning of the nineteenth century, as shown by old prints and paintings, which was certainly before the advent of the flat-coated variety, either as a sporting or show bench dog.

Be that as it may, we have the dog before us whose features are quite distinct from any other variety, and which have long been thoroughly recognised. Indeed, at one time the curly-coated Retriever was by far the most popular of the varieties, but he has been somewhat supplanted in the affection of the devotees of this breed by the flat-coat. Still, a large number of shooting as well as show men hang tenaciously to the curly-coat, and declare that in all that goes to constitute an all-round sporting dog he stands without his equal in the field.

The main reason the dog has lost favour somewhat with sportsmen is, first, because of the trouble involved in keeping his coat in order, more particularly for the show bench, which has resulted in his having been to a great extent supplanted by his flat-coated relative.

The coat is, of course, the great characteristic of the curly variety, and should consist of a small, tight curl from the occiput to the tip of the tail, much resembling the astrachan. The colour is black, although, as in all black breeds, red or brown specimens will sometimes crop up, and occasionally odd white specimens, which are, of course, "sports." The best size for a curly-coated Retriever dog is a dog standing about twenty-four inches at the shoulder, and weighing 65lb. to 75lb. Any deviation from that size is undesirable, and should be discouraged, except for an allowance of a few pounds in weight and an inch or so in height in the case of a bitch.

As the curl is the leading characteristic, so is it the most difficult to obtain in breeding; that is to say, to secure the close, tight, short curl so desirable. An open or long coat is very undesirable, and indeed almost a disqualification. In general formation a curly-coated Retriever presents the appearance of a proportionate, well-balanced, powerful, active-looking, and symmetrical dog, with a graceful contour. He should, in fact, be built much on the lines of a hackney or finely-bred cob. The head should be long, level, with clean-cut lips, a small, dark eye, and small, closely set ears. The neck should be moderately long, and shoulders well laid back, free from bossiness, with well-sprung ribs, a thick loin, and big, powerful hindquarters. The forelegs should be as straight as a gun barrel, and the feet short, strong, and cat-like; the hind legs wide in the thighs, with well-bent stifles and nicely let-down hocks. The tail should be short, carried straight out, and covered with short curls from root to tip. The body of the Retriever should be short and compact, but not so short as to lose liberty, which should be possessed by all the varieties.

The treatment of the coat in the curly variety is an important matter. The coat should never be combed or brushed. If the dog, whether a young puppy or an older specimen, does not shed the coat properly, the old coat should be carefully pulled out. If the coat has a tendency to grow long, some owners clip the dog all over with fine horse clippers, or coarse barbers' clippers, which induces the coat to grow the desired short, crisp curl, although, of course, a really bad-coated dog can never be made into a good one. The curls on the head shou'd finish in a straight line across the occiput, the hair on the face only being short and smooth:

The chief points to look for in the selection of curly-coated Retriever puppies at from two to four months old and after are identical with those of the flat-coated variety, except the coat, which should be short and crisp at the age given. This discription of coat is most likely to develop into the small tight curls so desirable.

The Curly-Coated Retriever Club, founded in 1890, publishes the following scale of points and standard description:—

HEAD.—Long and narrow for the length, with jaws long and strong, free from lippiness, with good teeth; wide open nostrils, moist and black.

EYES.—Cannot be too dark, rather large, showing great intelligence and splendid temper; a full, Pug's eye an objection.

EARS.—Rather small, set on low, lying close to the head, and covered with short curls.

COAT.—Should be one mass of short, crisp curls from the occiput bone to the point of tail; a saddle back, or patch of uncurled hair behind

CURLY-COATED RETRIEVER.

shoulders, and white patch on breast, should be penalised, but few white hairs allowed in an otherwise good dog. Colour, black or liver.

SHOULDERS.—Very deep, muscular, and obliquely placed.

CHEST.—Not too wide, but decidedly deep.

BODY.—Rather short, muscular, and well ribbed up.

LOIN.—Powerful, deep, and firm to the grasp.

LEGS.—Forelegs straight, with plenty of bone, and set well under body.

FEET.—Round and compact, with toes well arched.

TAIL.—Should be short, carried pretty straight, and covered with short crisp curls, tapering towards the point.

GENERAL APPEARANCE.—A strong, smart dog, with long graceful neck, muscular and well placed, free from throatiness (such as in a Bloodhound); moderately low on leg, active, lively, and beaming with intelligence and expression.

SCALE OF POINTS.	Value.
Head	15
Eyes	5
Ears	5
Coat	25
Shoulders, chest, body, and loin	15
Legs and feet	20
Tail	5
General appearance	10
Total	100

THE LABRADOR,

Whose origin his name indicates, is in type and character a modified edition of the flat-coat, the two breeds possessing almost all points in common, except that the coat is smooth but dense, and the dog is somewhat smaller and lower on leg, also a little squarer in muzzle. Most of these dogs are thicker in head than the flat-coated Retriever, and light eyes are more the rule than the exception. The variety has the reputation of possessing excellent working properties, an unapproached hardihood, and a good nose, doubtless the result of generations of tuition. It has recently been used by some breeders as an out-cross for the flat-coats, which are becoming terribly inbred, but first crosses, at least, have not and do not, as a rule, turn out very favourably. Still, one cannot imagine a more likely source from which to arrest the too close consanguinity which at present characterises the flat-coated family. For some years now classes have been provided at all the leading shows in the country, and, as showing the rapid progress of the breed, large entries are more the rule than the exception. In fact, Labradors now quite overshadow all the other varieties of Retrievers in numbers both at shows and field trials.

The Labrador Retriever Club publishes the following description :—

GENERAL DESCRIPTION.—The general appearance of the Labrador should be that of a strongly built, short-coupled, very active dog. Compared with the wavy or flat-coated Retriever he should be wider in the head, wider through the chest and ribs, wider and stronger over the loins and hindquarters. The coat should be close, short, dense, and free from feather.

HEAD.—The skull should be wide, giving brain room; there should be a slight "stop," i.e., the brow should be slightly pronounced, so that the skull is not absolutely in a straight line with the nose. The head should be clean-cut and free from fleshy cheeks. The jaws should be long and powerful, and quite free from snipiness or exaggeration in length; the nose should be wide and the nostrils well developed. The ears should hang moderately close to the head, rather far back, should be set somewhat low, and not be large and heavy. The eyes should be of a medium size, expressing great intelligence and good temper, and can be brown, yellow, or black.

"Our Dogs"
LABRADOR RETRIEVER.

NECK AND CHEST.—The neck should be long and powerful, and the shoulders long and sloping. The chest must be of a good width and depth, the ribs well sprung, and the loins wide and strong, stifles well turned, and the hindquarters well developed and of great power.

LEGS AND FEET.—The legs must be straight from the shoulder to ground and the feet compact with toes well arched and pads well developed; the hocks should be well bent, and the dog must neither be cowhocked nor move too wide behind; in fact, he must stand and move true all round on legs and feet.

TAIL.—The tail is a distinctive feature of the breed; it should be very thick towards the base, gradually tapering towards the tip, of medium length, should be practically free from any feathering, but should be clothed thickly all round with the Labrador's short, thick, dense coat, thus giving that peculiar " rounded " appearance which has been described as the " otter " tail. The tail may be carried gaily, but should not curl too far over the back.

COAT.—The coat is another very distinctive feature; it should be short, very dense and without wave, and should give a fairly hard feeling to the hand.

COLOUR.—The colour is generally black, free from any rustiness, and any white marking, except possibly a small spot on the chest. Other whole colours are permissible.

The chief points to look for in the selection of Labrador puppies at from two to four months old and after are identical with those of the flat-coated Retriever, except that the coat is required even more dense and is shorter, and the dog is somewhat shorter in both head and legs.

THE RUSSIAN YELLOW AND GOLDEN RETRIEVER.

These two varieties of Retriever sprang from the same source. As to their origin, I cannot do better than reprint an article which appeared in *Our Dogs* of March 1st, 1912, for the particulars of which I was indebted to my friend, Col. the Hon. Le Poer Trench. It is as follows:—

YELLOW RUSSIAN RETRIEVERS.

An interesting feature of Cruft's late Show, as we pointed out at the time, was the introduction to public notice by Col. the Hon. Le Poer Trench of that fascinating breed of dog, " The Marjoribanks and Ilchester breed of yellow Russian Retrievers and Trackers."

This breed was originally imported by that fine old sportsman, Mr. Dudley Marjoribanks, shortly after the Crimean War. This gentleman (who was subsequently created Lord Tweedmouth) first saw them in the year 1858 in a circus at Brighton, where there was a troop of them performing under a Russian keeper. They were splendid upstanding dogs of the Retriever stamp, and of a rich cream or yellow colour. So fascinated was Mr. Marjoribanks with them that he bought the lot, and sent them up to his forest in Inverness-shire. Here they were found to fully realise his expectations, and to be not only well able to retrieve, but also to possess the most wonderful noses and powers of " tracking "— so useful in a deer forest,—and he retained them exclusively for his own family's use; the only other person allowed to breed from them being his nephew, the late Earl of Ilchester, and bitches were not parted with.

For the first quarter of a century after their advent an occasional sportsman of good position might be seen followed by a handsome yellow dog, which was known as the " Marjoribank " breed of yellow Russian Retriever.

The inbreeding consequent on the foregoing arrangement resulted, after a lapse of time, in a deterioration of the physique of the breed— so much so that their original importer, who bought them as Russian dogs, made efforts to get fresh blood from Russia, but without success. In consequence, he felt himself obliged to approve of " a cross " being introduced to fortify the breed. The cross selected was with the

Bloodhound—possibly in consequence of the breed being possessed of almost the same tracking qualities as the Bloodhound. But, be that as it may, the result was that, though excellent dogs were at first produced, the pure strain of the original yellow Retriever became practically lost, as the *new blood* took the command both in type and colour, with occasional variations.

Early in the 'eighties, Colonel Trench (to whom we are indebted for the specimens of the resuscitated breed shown at Cruft's) became possessed of one of these dogs bred by the late Earl of Ilchester, and a beautiful specimen of the breed. This dog was seen by the late Lord Tweedmouth (who had lost his true breed by the introduction of the cross), who was greatly pleased with it, and after a careful inspection pronounced him to be a perfect type of the dogs acquired by him in 1858.

Colonel Trench, finding this dog so good for sporting purposes and such a good companion, and being aware that bitches were not disposed of, had a picture made of him, and sent it to various parts of Russia in Europe in the hope of getting a pure bitch of the breed for breeding purposes, but he was as unsuccessful as Lord Tweedmouth had been. His Lordship, sympathising with the efforts made by Colonel Trench, made him a present of a bitch, but it was a cross. She was subsequently poisoned by a gang of poachers.

A little later, through the influence of Colonel Trench (who was subsequently elected on the Committee of the Club for the second time), Russian Yellow Retrievers were placed upon the Club's register, and Mr. Harding Cox drew up a standard description and code of points, of which the following is a copy:—

Drawn up by Major Harding Cox, with the concurrence of Lord Tweedmouth, the Earl of Ilchester, and Col. Hon. Le Poer Trench.

DESCRIPTION OF THE YELLOW RUSSIAN RETRIEVER AND TRACKER. (Descended from the Caucasian yellow sheepdog. First imported into this country by Dudley Marjoribanks, Esq., in 1858, and since known as the Marjoribanks and Ilchester Breed.)

1. THE GENERAL APPEARANCE of the Yellow Retriever is a large, somewhat massive and dignified-looking dog, very sturdily built, with big bone, and a suggestion of power throughout his structure.

2. HEAD long and rather massive, the skull flat and rather broader than that of the flat-coated Retriever. The face long and the jaws strong and level, with some depth. The nose and flews black and large, the nostrils wide. The eye rather full but not prominent, of a rich brown colour, and the lids darkly pencilled, not pendulous.

3. BODY of powerful build and symmetrical withal.

4. SHOULDERS very long and laid flat and well back. Neck rather shorter than is the case with the flat-coated or coloured Retriever, and more in conformity with that of the Labrador.

5. FORELEGS straight, with very big bone carried well down to the feet, which are large, close, and well knuckled up.

6. CHEST moderately broad and very deep, with plenty of heart room; ribs well sprung, deep, and showing no falling-off in their extremity; stifles well bent and bony.

7. BACK AND LOINS broad and powerful.

8. QUARTERS high and broad.

9. HIND LEGS showing muscle and power in first and second thighs. HOCKS (not so well et down as in some breeds) are bony and absolutely true in movement.

10. THE HEIGHT of this breed ranges from 23 to 27 inches in dogs, and 21 to 25 in the case of bitches.

11. COAT rather long, fine and dense, with a decided crimp or loose curl on the back, which is more pronounced on the quarters and rump. The legs are well feathered, and the stern, which extends to the poin of the hock, is well bushed and carried low or on a level with the back.

12. THE COLOUR is of a rich tawny yellow tinge darkening on the back and showing lighter creamy tints on the flanks, legs, and belly. Any admixture of pure white is to be deprecated, but very often the colour shades off in the feet to a very light tint. The warmer red shadings which are observable in dogs where a cross of the Irish Setter or Bloodhound has been admitted are detrimental as a clear index of such a cross having been resorted to.

NEGATIVE POINTS.

Light yellow eye or "Dudley" nose.
Flat feet, weak pasterns, and cow hocks.
Crooked forelegs.
Colour other than as described.

SCALE OF POINTS.	Value.
General appearance and type	15
Head properties	15
Colour	20
Feet and legs	10
Shoulders, chest, and ribs	10
Action	5
Quarters, hind legs, and hocks	10
Stern	5
Size	5
Back and loins	5
Total	100

It would be audacious for me to attempt to criticise the findings of such great authorities in connection with this breed; but, if I may be allowed, I would respectfully suggest that the description of the dog's "stifles" would have been more appropriately inserted under the description of "Hind Legs" rather than in that of "Chest," in which it appears.

THE GOLDEN RETRIEVER

Admittedly springs from the same origin, but while Colonel Trench's Russian Yellow Retrievers presumably are descended from the dogs of Mr. Dudley Marjoribanks *before* he crossed them with the Bloodhound, the Golden Retriever descends from Mr. Marjoribank's dogs *after* that cross. These are my conclusions from the facts deduced from the foregoing particulars coupled with other information and the important fact of Colonel Trench's dogs in colour, conformation, and character being of the type of Sandy, the dog he obtained from Mr. Marjoribanks, whilst the majority of the "Golden" Retrievers exhibited were of a different type and much deeper in colour.

The following is the Golden Retriever Club's standard of points for Golden Retrievers :—

HEAD.—Broad in skull, well set on a clean and muscular neck, muzzle powerful and wide, not weak jawed, good stop. EYES.—Dark and set well apart, very kindly in expression, with dark rims. TEETH.—Even, neither under or over-shot	20
COLOUR.—Rich golden, must not be as dark as an Irish Red Setter or cream colour. The presence of a few white hairs on chest or toes permissible. But white collar, feet, or blaze to be penalised	20
COAT.—Must be flat or wavy, good undercoat, dense, and water-resisting	5
EARS.—Small and well set on	5

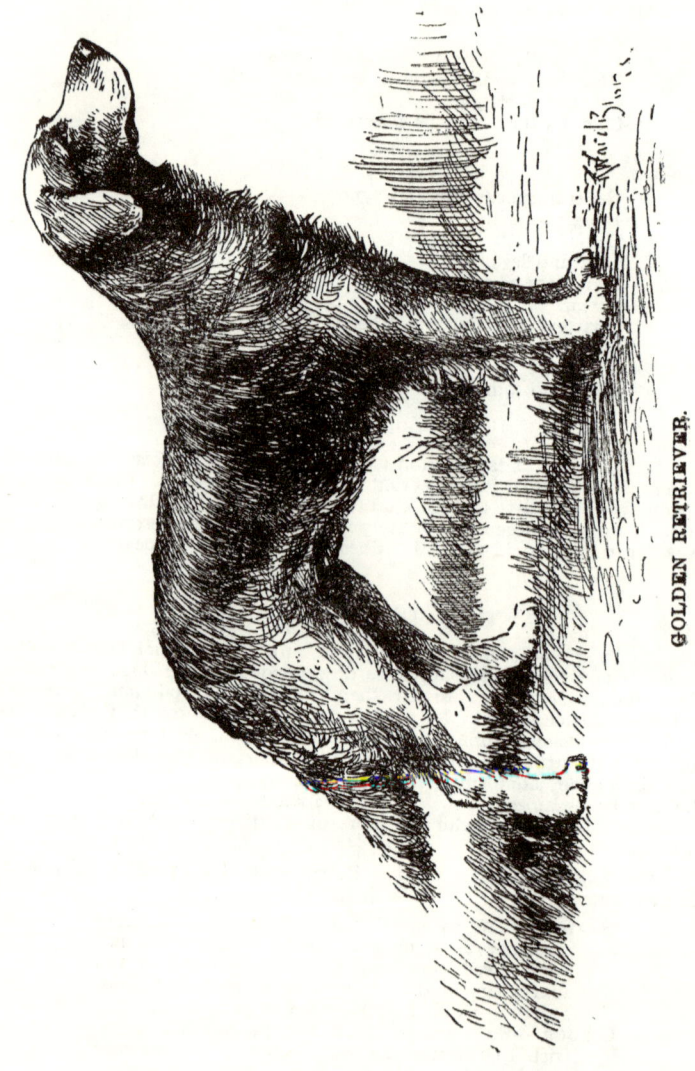

GOLDEN RETRIEVER.

FEET.—Round and cat-like, must not be open or splay 10
FORELEGS.—Straight, with good bone 10
HIND LEGS.—Strong and muscular, well-bent stifle.
    HOCKS.—Well let down, not cowhocked 10
NOSE.—Should be black, but a light-coloured nose should not debar a dog from honours who is good in all other respects 5
TAIL.—Should be straight, not curled at tip or carried over the back 5
BODY.—Well balanced, short coupled, and deep through the heart. LOINS.—*Must* be strong. BACK RIBS.—*Must* be deep and strong, with good second thighs. SHOULDERS.—*Must* be well laid back and long in the blade 25

                            Total 115

GENERAL APPEARANCE.—Should be of a symmetrical, active, powerful dog, a good level mover, sound and well put together, with a kindly expression, not clumsy or long in the leg.

A Golden Retriever Club was established to promote the welfare of this branch of the " Marjoribanks and Ilchester" Retrievers, which has also formulated a standard description and code of points, as given above.

Mrs. Charlesworth, who is a great enthusiast in connection with the Golden Retriever, speaks in high praise of their working qualities in the field, the result of, I should say, an Irish Setter and not a Bloodhound cross.

The Kennel Club has recognised the Golden Retriever as a distinct variety by placing it upon the register; but I think in both cases " flat or wavy coat" should have been added to the description of these two varieties, since there are both brown or golden and yellow *curly-coated Retrievers*, although they are not very numerous.

The chief points to look for in the selection of Golden or Russian Yellow Retriever puppies are :—Long head, square foreface, great bone, short body dense coat.

CHAPTER XVII.

Sporting Spaniels.

The Spaniel family of to-day is divided into seven varieties—viz., Irish Water, Clumber, Sussex, Field and Cocker (which are subdivided by colour), Springer, and Welsh Springer.

These are the only varieties of the Sporting Spaniel now recognised by the Kennel Club, and which have been given a place upon the Club's register.

The Sporting Spaniel is exceedingly well provided for in the way of specialist clubs to look after his interests. The first that was founded, thirty or fifty years ago, is the Spaniel Club, which takes under its special care the whole of the varieties of the Sporting Spaniel. So does the Sporting Spaniel Society, which is an offshoot of the parent Spaniel Club. Both these clubs have in late years—the latter initiated them—instituted Spaniel Trials, for the purpose of developing and preserving the working propensity of the Spaniel. These trials, in connection with both clubs, have been an unqualified success, and have demonstrated that the show Spaniel has not lost the wonderful natural instinct for sport, since many show dogs have, from time to time, figured in the prize list at Field Trials. It cannot be expected that dogs which are kept for exhibition purposes purely, and have never been broken to the gun or employed in field work, should be much use in the field. But this is a stigma to which they are often subjected by some sporting men. It would be just as rational to expect a boy who had never been to school, or seen figures, to do a rule-of-three or other sum. The instinct and capability are there in both cases, and only want bringing out. In the case of the Spaniel it has been proved that after lying dormant for several successive generations, the sporting instinct has been brought out, by tuition and practice, to a remarkable degree. Doubtless, in-breeding to a great extent affects dogs mentally as well as physically, and renders them less fit to fulfil the functions of field work. This applies, of course, not to Spaniels alone, but to all dogs.

We are, however, concerned here with the Spaniel more from an exhibition than sporting point of view.

In addition to the Spaniel Club and Sporting Spaniel Society, there exist the Cocker Spaniel Club, the Clumber Spaniel Club, the Northern and Midlands Spaniel Club, English Springer Club, Field Spaniel Society, and other minor clubs.

Taking the

IRISH WATER SPANIEL

first, we find him a quaint, but very useful, Spaniel, and very distinct in type and features from any other of the Spaniel family, which latter may be said to be more or less developments one from the other, for specific purposes in the field.

An old friend of ours, Mr. J. S. Skidmore, J.P., of Nantwich, once famous as a successful breeder and exhibitor of the Irish Water Spaniel, pays the dog a tribute, both as a workman and as a companion, in a contribution he made to the first edition of " British Dogs," from which we make the following excerpt :—

To a sportsman of limited means, or one who has not accommodation to keep a team, the Irish Water Spaniel is the most useful dog he can have, inasmuch as he can be made to perform the duties of Pointer, Setter, Retriever, and Spaniel ; but, as his name implies, he is peculiarly fitted by temperament and by a water-resisting coat for the arduous duties required by a sportsman whose proclivities lie in the direction of wildfowl shooting. In this branch of sporting these dogs have no equal, being able to stand any amount of hardship; this, combined with an indomitable spirit, leads them into deeds of daring from which many dogs would shrink. Many are the feats recorded of their pluck, sagacity, and intelligence. To a well-bred and trained specimen no sea is too rough, no pier too high, and no water too cold—even if they have to break the ice at every step they are not daunted, and day after day they will follow up such work, being of the "cut-and-come-again" sort. As companions for a lady or a gentleman they have no equal, whilst a well-behaved dog of the breed is worth a whole kennel of Toys to the children; he will allow the little ones to pull him about by the ears, will roll over and over with them, fetch their balls as often as thrown for him, and act as their guard in times of danger.

As to the origin of the Irish Water Spaniel there is very little authentic information. Mr. McCarthy seems to have been one of if not the first exhibitor of the breed, and a successful one, although the Irish Water Spaniel

IRISH WATER SPANIEL.

was previously kept largely in Ireland for sporting purposes, and a valued member of "Ireland's" Reds—Red Setter, Red Spaniel, Red Terrier, Red Wolfhound, and Red Horse may be added.

The most likely and feasible theory of his origin is a cross between the Poodle and the Irish Setter. There is much in common in type and character between the Poodle and Irish Water Spaniel—viz., in coat, conformation, head, and general character, while in disposition the dog inherits all the dash and determination of the Irish Setter, and partakes of his colour, which we can quite understand would be deepened by crossing in again to the Poodle. The Irish Water Spaniel exhibits, too, the great intelligence of the Poodle, who, although regarded as a trick and fancy dog, will hunt and retrieve on land or water with most Spaniels.

Whatever his origin, his type now is thoroughly fixed and recognised by all experts and judges, among whom there is an almost unanimous consensus of opinion upon his "points."

In the scale of points and description of the Irish Water Spaniel Club, the height of the dog is given, but not his weight. The latter should be from 50lb. to 60lb., dogs, of course, being a little heavier than bitches.

The difficulty in breeding is to get the correct coat and colour and a good head and topknot, with a smooth tail. Those are the chief features of the breed. The topknot can, of course, be cultivated, and the coat can be much improved by careful treatment, whilst the tail can easily be *made* smooth. However, it is always advisable to breed from dogs whose foregoing points are very pronounced, and avoid breeding particularly from short-headed, thick-skulled, or light-eyed specimens. The head should be long, level, and wedge-shaped, the occiput pronounced, and ears set low and carried close to the head. Muzzle long and square, but not lippy, with large nose. The Club's description furnishes the rest.

The breed, notwithstanding its encouragement by clubdom, does not make the progress and enjoy the popularity its merit, beauty, and utility deserve. This is doubtless owing to the difficulty encountered in breeding characteristic specimens, and to coat troubles.

The chief points to look for in the selection of Irish Water Spaniel puppies at from two to four months old and after are :—A long head, dark eye, long ears, short back, short whip tail, good size and bone, straight forelegs, and a dark, close coat.

DESCRIPTIVE PARTICULARS.

HEAD.—Capacious skull, rather raised in the dome and fairly wide, showing large brain capacity. The dome appears higher than it really is, from its being surmounted by the crest or top-knot, which should grow down to a point between the eyes, leaving the temple smooth.

EYES.—Comparatively small, hazel or dark brown, and very intelligent-looking.

NOSE.—Dark liver coloured, rather large and well developed.

EARS.—Set on rather low. In a full-sized specimen the leather should not be less than 18in., and with feather about 24in. The feather on the ear should be long, abundant, and wavy.

NECK.—Should be " Pointer-like," *i.e.*, muscular, slightly arched, and not too long. It should be strongly set on the shoulders.

BODY (INCLUDING SIZE AND SYMMETRY).—Height at shoulder from 20 to 23in., according to sex and strain; body fair-sized, round, barrel-shaped, and well ribbed up.

SHOULDERS AND CHEST.—Chest deep and not too narrow. Shoulders strong, rather sloping, and well covered with hard muscle.

BACK AND LOIN.—Back strong. Loins trifle arched and powerful.

HINDQUARTERS.—Round and muscular, and slightly drooping towards the set on of the stern.

STERN.—A "whip tail," thick at the base and tapering to a " sting." The hair on it should be short, straight, and close lying, excepting for a few inches from its root, where it gradually merges into the body coat in some short curls.

FEET AND LEGS.—" Forelegs " straight and well boned. They should be well furnished with wavy hair all round and down to the feet, which should be large and round. " Hind legs " stifle long and hocks set low; they should be well furnished, except from the hock down the front.

COAT.—Neither woolly nor lank, but should consist of short crisp curls right up to the stern.

COLOUR.—A dark rich liver-puce (to be judged by its original colour). A sandy light coat is a defect.

GENERAL APPEARANCE.—That of a strong, compact dog, with a quaint and very intelligent aspect. They should not be leggy, as power and endurance are required of them in their work.

SCALE OF POINTS FOR JUDGING IRISH WATER SPANIELS.

POSITIVE POINTS.

Head and jaw	10
Eyes	5
Topknot	5
Ears	10
Neck	7½
Body	7½
Forelegs	5
Hind legs	5
Feet	5
Stern	10
Coat	15
General appearance	15
Total positive points	**100**

NEGATIVE POINTS.

Light yellow or gooseberry eye	10
Cording, or tags of matted dead hair	12
Moustache, or poodle hair on the cheek	5
Lank, open, or woolly coat	7½
A natural sandy light coat	8
Furnishing of tail more than half-way down to sting	7½
Setter-feathering on legs	10
White patch on chest	5
Total negative points	**65**

DISQUALIFICATIONS.—Total absence of topknot; a fully feathered tail; and white patch on any part of the dog, except a small one on the chest or toe.

THE ENGLISH WATER SPANIEL

Is really the principal member of the family of Water Spaniels. He is for the most part a liver-and-white, liver-roan, or blue-roan dog, on the lines of a leggy Field Spaniel, with a curly coat. The type of this dog is not nearly so well fixed as are the other varieties of the Spaniel, simply because it has not received so much attention at the hands of the showman. He is in the condition in which most of its ancestors existed over half a century ago, although he probably boasts of greater antiquity than any other member of the Spaniel family. We read of the English Water Spaniel so far back as the beginning of the sixteenth century. There can be little doubt that for centuries before the advent of shows in England, a Water Spaniel, much after the type of dog depicted and portrayed in this article, was used for wildfowling in England, and which had the reputation of being a most useful all-round sportsman, and who was, without doubt, the only Spaniel in the country at one time. It is from the English Water Spaniel that all the other varieties have been evolved, excepting the Irish Water. As to how he has been bred there is no evidence whatever. It is, however, admitted that our Spaniel originated from Spain, which accounts for the name, and no doubt he is the result of importations crossed with dogs already existing in England.

There are few shows that provide classes for English Water Spaniels, and very few specimens are exhibited. At the same time, a standard description and code of points have now been evolved, and which represent the features of the variety, which has been ousted from, or, rather, never allowed to obtain a footing in, the show ring by its various offshoots, which have appealed with greater force to the public taste.

The chief points to look for in the selection of English or other than Irish Water Spaniel puppies at from two to four months old and after are: A long head, square muzzle, short back, great bone, and straight forelegs.

The following is the standard formulated by the Spaniel Club:—

HEAD.—Long, somewhat straight, and rather narrow; muzzle rather long.

EYES.—Small for the size of the dog.

EARS.—Well set on, and thickly clothed with hair inside and out.

NECK.—Straight and long.

BODY (INCLUDING SIZE AND SYMMETRY).—Large and very deep throughout, back ribs well developed, not quite so long as in Field Spaniels.

NOSE.—Large.

SHOULDERS AND CHEST.—Shoulders low, and chest rather narrow, but deep.

BACK AND LOIN.—Strong, but not clumsy.

HINDQUARTERS.—Long and straight; rather rising toward the stern than drooping, which, combined with the low shoulder, gives him the appearance of standing higher behind than in front.

STERN.—Docked from 7 to 10in., according to the size of the dog carried a little above the level of the back, but by no means high.

FEET AND LEGS.—Feet well spread, large, and strong; well clothed with hair, especially between the pads. Legs long and strong; the stifles well bent.

COAT.—Covered with crisp curls; no top-knot, but the close curl should cease on the top of the head, leaving the face perfectly smooth and lean-looking.

COLOUR.—Black-and-white, liver-and-white, or self-coloured black or liver. The pied for choice.

GENERAL APPEARANCE.—Sober looking, with an independent manner.

SCALE OF POINTS FOR JUDGING ENGLISH WATER SPANIELS.

POSITIVE POINTS.

Head, jaw, and eye	20
Ears	5
Neck	5
Body	10
Forelegs	10
Hindlegs	10
Feet	5
Stern	10
Coat	15
General appearance	10
Total Positive Points	100

NEGATIVE POINTS.

Feather on stern	10
Top-knot	10
Total Negative Points	20

THE CLUMBER SPANIEL.

This is one of the most useful and popular of the several varieties of the Sporting Spaniel, and also one of the oldest. He is at once the most dignified and yet most docile, most daring and yet most tractable. He differs from all other varieties in that he is a heavier and entirely more massive dog, and therefore less active, or, to put it more correctly, a slower dog in the field. In this way he is often described as the old man's sporting dog, in which there is much truth, although as an all-round sportsman the Clumber is probably without his equal—he is excellent alike as a field and water dog.

There is very little information available concerning the origin of the Clumber, but there is little doubt that he was evolved by one of the Dukes of Newcastle, at his Nottinghamshire seat, Clumber, from which the dog takes his name, and where the breed is still kept in all its purity. In all likelihood this Duke was getting on in years, and found the Spaniels of his time too fast for him. He therefore conceived the idea of weighting the Spaniel, in order to reduce his pace, by crossing him with some heavier dog, without losing the Spaniel's sporting instincts. What the cross or crosses were are now mere conjecture, as there is no authentic record. Judging from the dog's general type, the St. Bernard might be suggested, but this was before the dog's advent into England, at least as an exhibition specimen. Other breeds may be suggested, but, as I have already stated, it is all conjecture. We shall have to deal with the breed, therefore, as we find it. The Clumber Spaniel of to-day, in type and character, is not quite what he was a quarter of a century ago. At that time we had better specimens, if fewer of them, and the dog was always a favourite with the nobility and aristocracy, which, with his dignified bearing and classic lineage, caused him to be dubbed the aristocrat of the Spaniel family.

CLUMBER SPANIEL.

The leading features of the Clumber are—a massive head, with rather short, deep, and square muzzle, on a massive body, moderately long, with great bone, rather short legs, and a dense, flat coat. The colour should be white, with slight lemon markings. Some experts are very strong in their views as to colour in a Clumber, denouncing the mahogany-marked specimens —why is never very clear. It is an old saying that "a good horse cannot be a bad colour," and what drawback mahogany or dark-tan markings in a Clumber can be to a dog in fulfilling his avocation it is impossible, of course, to show. It is alleged that it denotes impure breeding, but this has never been shown, and therefore the theory seems to be altogether irrational.

Probably the worst fault in a Clumber from a show-bench point of view is a snipy foreface, and weedy, light build. In breeding, these two disqualifying defects should be carefully avoided. A cock-tail is a defect in all Sporting Spaniels. The leading points to aim at are those before-enumerated, to which I may add a nicely defined stop, hazel-coloured eye (the shade of which will vary with the colour of the markings), and a medium-sized ear, set on rather low and carried close to the cheek. The forelegs, of course, should be perfectly straight, the bone big and round, and the stifles of the hind legs well bent. The back should be level and the ribs well sprung.

Clumbers require roomy kennels, and are great drinkers; they should have a constant supply of fresh water.

The chief points to look for in the selection of Clumber Spaniel puppies at from two to four months old and after are:—A short, massive head, square muzzle, well-defined stop, massive body, low set and of moderate length, enormous bone, and light pale orange or lemon markings, flat, dense coat, and down-carried tail.

The following are the official description and standard of points formulated by the Spaniel Club:—

HEAD.—Large, square, and massive, of medium length, broad on top, with a decided occiput; heavy brows, with a deep stop; heavy muzzle, with well-developed flew.

EYES.—Dark amber, slightly sunk, and showing haw.

EARS.—Vine-leaf shaped, and well covered with straight hair, and hanging slightly forward; the feather not to extend below the leather.

NECK.—Very thick and powerful, and well feathered underneath.

BODY (including size and symmetry).—Long and heavy, and near the ground. Weight of dogs, about 60 to 75 lb.; bitches, 50 to 60 lb.

NOSE.—Square and flesh-coloured.

SHOULDERS AND CHEST.—Wide and deep, shoulders strong and muscular.

BACK AND LOIN.—Back straight, broad, and long; loin powerful, well let down in flank.

HINDQUARTERS.—Very powerful and well developed.

STERN.—Set low, well feathered, and carried about level with the back.

FEET AND LEGS.—Feet large and round, well covered with hair; legs short, thick, and strong; hocks low.

COAT.—Abundant, short, and straight.

COLOUR.—Plain white, with lemon markings; orange permissible but not desirable; slight head markings, with white body preferred.

GENERAL APPEARANCE.—Should be that of a heavy, square, massive dog, with a thoughtful expression.

SCALE OF POINTS FOR JUDGING CLUMBER SPANIELS.

POSITIVE POINTS.

Head and jaw	15
Eyes	5
Ears	5
Neck	5
Body	15
Forelegs	10
Hind legs	5
Feet	5
Stern	5
Colour of markings	10
Coat and feather	10
General appearance	10
Total positive points	100

NEGATIVE POINTS.

Curled coat on ears	10
Curled coat	20
Bad carriage of tail	10
Snipy face	15
Legginess	10
Light eyes	5
Crooked forelegs	15
Total negative points	85

THE SUSSEX SPANIEL

Has probably made less headway than any of the sub-varieties of the Sporting Spaniel, and to-day its leading devotees may be counted almost on the fingers of one hand. Originally emanating from the County of Sussex, from which it takes its name, and doubtless evolved from the common liver-and-white Spaniel which formerly abounded in the southern counties, and which was at one time called the Norfolk Spaniel, the Sussex, a golden-liver Field Spaniel, has now been given a very distinct type. A long and low dog, with a flat coat, its head is shorter and stronger than that of the other varieties of the Field Spaniel, with which it has in recent years been largely crossed. The peculiar golden tinge at the extremities of the liver-coloured hair is one of the characteristics of the Sussex Spaniel, and much marked in the "Rosehill" strain, possessed by Mr. Campbell Newington, a great enthusiast in the breed, who both shot over and exhibited his Spaniels. An even greater name in the Sussex Spaniel world, and one to conjure with, at one time was that of Mr. Moses Woolland, who for nearly a quarter of a century was invulnerable on the show bench with his Sussex Spaniels, until

SUSSEX SPANIEL.

he dispersed his kennel in 1905. The "Woolland" strain, originating from Mr. T. Jacobs and the late Mr. Holley, are still pre-eminent wherever they are kept in their purity.

The great length of body, shortness of legs, and short, thick head, are all exaggerations from the original which modern fashion has ordained, but which from reasons of utility seem undesirable. Already a tendency to moderate the thick head (which always denotes stupidity in a dog) has set in, and no doubt a modification of the lengthy bodies and extremely short legs will follow. The colour is both attractive and pleasing, and doubtless will be retained, but in all probability with difficulty in its present purity. It is a notorious fact that the Sussex Spaniels which leave the southern counties for more northern latitudes invariably lose, in a smaller or greater degree, the rich golden-liver colour which characterised them on their native heath. This metamorphosis is doubtless due to the difference in the subsoil. The rich golden colour of the Sussex Spaniel as kept in the south is no doubt in a great measure due to the red subsoil of the southern counties, which gives us the red cattle, and red or bay horses.

For sporting purposes the Sussex Spaniel is an unfortunate colour, being often indistinguishable at a distance from some of the game he is required to hunt, as well as from the cover itself in the fall, when the autumnal tints prevail. In this way the whole-coloured Sussex Spaniel is rarely used as a sporting dog, being relegated almost exclusively to the show bench. It is only at the larger shows, too, that classes are provided for him, although he is invariably eligible for the Spaniel class, Any Other Variety, where he is not specifically provided for.

Probably no variety of the Sporting Spaniel has been a greater victim to in-breeding in order to fix the dog's type, and this, again, has militated against his intelligence and utility as a worker.

It was to correct these defects and the exaggerations referred to that the Sporting Spaniel Society came into existence, and which has evolved a description and standard of points in some details diametrically opposed to those of the Spaniel Club. In this particular variety, however, the former club seems to have jumped to the other extreme in the matter of length of leg and one or two other points.

The chief points to look for in the selection of Sussex Spaniel puppies at from two to four months old and after are :—A short, massive head, square muzzle, well-defined stop, lengthy body, on short, straight forelegs, great bone, flat coat of a deep golden colour, down-carried tail.

The type as laid down by the Spaniel Club is still that which is in vogue for the show bench, and is as follows :—

Positive Points.

Head	10
Eyes	5
Nose	5
Ears	10
Neck	5
Chest and shoulders	5
Back and back ribs	10
Legs and feet	10
Tail	5
Coat	5
Colour	15
General appearance	15
Total positive points	100

Negative Points.

Light eyes	5
Narrow head	10
Weak muzzle	10
Curled ears or high set-on	5
Curled coat	15
Carriage of stern	5
Topknot	10
White on chest	5
Colour (too light or too dark)	15
Legginess, or light of bone	5
Shortness of body or flat-sided	5
General appearance, sour or crouching.	10
Total negative points	100

DESCRIPTIVE PARTICULARS.

HEAD.—The skull should be moderately long, and also wide, with an indentation in the middle, and a decided stop; brows fairly heavy; occiput full but not pointed, the whole giving an appearance of heaviness without dulness.

EYES.—Hazel colour, fairly large, soft and languishing, not showing the haw overmuch.

NOSE.—The muzzle should be fairly long and square, and the lips somewhat pendulous; the nostrils well developed and liver colour.

EARS.—Thick, fairly large, and lobe-shaped; set moderately low, but relatively not so low as in the Black Field Spaniel; carried close to the head, and furnished with soft, wavy hair.

NECK.—Long, strong, and slightly arched, but not carrying the head much above the level of the back. There should not be much throatiness, but well-marked frill in the coat.

SHOULDERS AND CHEST.—Former sloping and free; latter deep and well developed, but not too round and wide.

BACK AND BACK RIBS.—The back and loin are long, and should be very muscular, both in width and depth; for this development the back ribs must be deep. The whole body is characterised as low, long, level, and strong.

LEGS AND FEET.—The arms and thighs must be bony, as well as muscular, knees and hocks large and strong; pasterns very short and bony; feet large and round. The legs rather short and strong, with great bone, and moderately well feathered. The hind legs should not be apparently shorter than the forelegs, or be too much bent at the hocks, but should not have much hair below this point.

TAIL.—Should be docked from five to seven inches, set low, and not carried above the level of the back; thickly clothed, with moderately long feather.

COAT.—Body coat abundant, flat, and with no tendency to curl moderately well feathered on legs and stern.

COLOUR.—Rich golden-liver. This is a certain sign of the purity of the breed, dark liver or puce denoting unmistakably a recent cross with the black or other variety Field Spaniels.

GENERAL APPEARANCE.—Rather massive and muscular, but with free movements and nice tail action. Weight from 40lb. to 50lb.

THE FIELD SPANIEL.

This is one of the most popular varieties of the Sporting Spaniel, and to all intents and purposes is, in its present form, a modern creation, dating from somewhere about the advent of dog shows. The Field Spaniel is somewhat lower on leg and longer in body in proportion than any other Spaniel. This anatomical formation, in the first place, had its origin in the introduction of a Spaniel better adapted for getting under gorse and brushwood than was the Springer, and a dog that was less active than the Cocker. It is from these two older varieties, with an admixture of the Sussex, that the beautiful Field Spaniels of to-day, in all their pretty colours, were first evolved. The colours are black, black-and-tan, liver, liver-and-tan, black-and-white, black-tan-and-white, liver-roan, blue-roan, etc. The blacks at one time were the most popular, but the craze for great length of body and lowness on leg was carried to such extremes that the variety at once degenerated into little less than elongated monstrosities. It lost the beautiful chiselling of head—at least, in many of the specimens exhibited—and straightness of forelegs, and the activity which all Sporting Spaniels should possess, more or less. A reaction among sporting men set in, and, owing to their efforts and those of the Sporting Spaniel Club, happily the heavy-headed, crooked-fronted, and sluggish, crocodile-like pattern are now almost obsolete.

We have to-day, too, a more rational type of dog, one that possesses all the features of an animal well fitted to perform the work originally prescribed for him, and yet free from the abnormalities which so disfigured the dog at one stage of his career. At that period it used to be frequently remarked that if breeders did not retrace their steps they would be producing Spaniels with no legs at all; they were so low on leg and so long in body that six legs would be required to ensure locomotion. The Sporting Spaniel Society, doubtless alive to this danger and disgusted with the distortions, divined a type of Field Spaniel, as far as length of leg and body goes, the very antithesis of those in vogue. Their type was much ridiculed at the time, and, although it never became recognised, the onslaught upon the deformities of the day had the effect of starting a reaction against them, with the result that they soon became unpopular, and to-day, as I have stated, the Field Spaniel is a fairly well-balanced dog, free from exaggerations, with a beautifully chiselled and intelligent head, and in every way fitted to fulfil his particular vocation to the best advantage, so far as make and shape go. It has been a case of extremes meeting, and it is to be hoped that we have seen the last of caricatures, in either the one or the other direction, and that the Field

FIELD SPANIEL (Coloured).

Spaniel may remain in all essentials what he is to-day, with the exception of improvement in a few minor defects noticeable in individual specimens, such as snipiness, light eyes, gay carriage of tail, and, in some cases, faulty front. These defects, however, are now the exception, and not the rule.

The type and conformation of the Field Spaniel should be the same in all his variegated colours—viz., a moderately low and long dog, straight on his forelegs, and sound in his hind limbs, with well-sprung ribs and strong loins and quarters. The head should be long, more level on the top than in any of the other varieties, excepting the English Springer, between which and the Field there is much in common in their chiselling. There should be some "stop," and the skull should be narrow, nicely bevelled at the back, with a slight occipital development. The muzzle should be deep and square at the end, showing a little "flew," and the ears set on low and moderately long, but not so as to impede the work of the dog in the field. The eye should, in all cases, be dark, especially so in the black variety, its shade being somewhat lighter in the lighter-coloured varieties. The coat should be flat, dense, glossy, and showing a fair amount of feathering, but excessive feathering is objectionable since it partakes more of the ornamental than the useful, which latter should be the guiding principle in the architecture of the animal. The best size for a Field Spaniel is between 40lb. and 50lb., dogs usually being two or three pounds heavier than bitches.

In breeding, the defects to be avoided are: Snipiness of foreface, light eyes, light bone, curl or waviness in coat, and " cock tails," which are very good as an American liqueur, but not as indicating the correct formation of the rudder of any sporting Spaniel.

The chief points to look for in the selection of puppies at from two to four months old and after, of all the varieties of Field Spaniels—black and coloured—are practically identical, and are: A long head, narrow skull, distinct stop, square muzzle, long body, flat back, short legs, the forelegs being straight and showing great bone, with a flat coat and down-carried tail.

The following are the standard description and points of the Field Spaniel Society :—

THE FIELD SPANIEL SOCIETY'S OFFICIAL STANDARD OF POINTS.

" A rationally built Field Spaniel—that is to say, a dog of medium height on leg, a little lower on the leg than a Springer and a little longer in the body, with his long and beautifully chiselled head, square foreface, and intelligent expression—a well-balanced dog throughout active and alert—is a most beautiful example of the Spaniel family, whose architecture, head (beaming with intelligence), substance, coat, and contour, all spell ' Utility.' "—THEO MARPLES, Esq., F.Z.S., in " Our Dogs."

HEAD.—Should be quite characteristic of this grand sporting dog, as that of the Bulldog, or the Bloodhound; its very stamp and countenance should at once convey the conviction of high breeding character, and nobility; skull well developed, with a distinctly elevated occipital tuberosity, which, above all, gives the character alluded to; not too wide across the muzzle, long and lean, never snipy nor squarely cut, and in profile curving gradually from nose to throat; lean beneath the eyes, a thickness here gives coarseness to the whole head. The great length of muzzle gives surface for the free development of the olfactory nerve, and thus secures the highest possible scenting powers.

EYES.—Not too full, but not small, receding or overhung; colour dark hazel or brown or nearly black, according to the colour of the dog. Grave in expression and showing no haw.

EARS.—Moderately long and wide, sufficiently clad with nice Setter-like feather, and set low. They should fall in graceful folds, the lower parts curling inwards and backwards.

NECK.—Long, strong, and muscular, so as to enable the dog to retrieve his game without undue fatigue.

BODY.—Should be of moderate length, well-ribbed up to a good strong loin, straight or slightly arched, never slack.

NOSE.—Well developed, with good open nostrils.

SHOULDERS AND CHEST.—Former long, sloping, and well set back, thus giving great activity and speed; latter deep and well developed, but not too round and wide.

BACK AND LOIN.—Very strong and muscular.

HINDQUARTERS.—Strong and muscular. The stifles should be moderately bent and not twisted either in or out.

STERN.—Well set on and carried low, if possible below the level of the back. in a straight line or with a slight downward inclination, never elevated above the back, and in action always kept low, nicely fringed with wavy feather of silky texture.

FORELEGS.—Should be of fairly good length, with straight, clean, flat bone, and nicely feathered. Immense bone is no longer desirable.

FEET.—Not too small; round, with short soft hair between the toes; good, strong pads.

COAT.—Flat or slightly waved, and never curled. Sufficiently dense to resist the weather, and not too short. Silky in texture, glossy and refined in nature, with neither duffleness on the one hand nor curl or wiriness on the other. On the chest, under belly, and behind the legs there should be abundant feather, but never too much, especially below, the hocks, and that of the right sort, viz., Setter-like. The hindquarters should be similarly adorned.

COLOUR.—This Society maintains that the Field Spaniel should be a self-coloured dog, viz., a *black* (as he was originally some 60 years ago) or a "sport" from black, *i.e.*, liver, golden liver, mahogany red, roans ; or any one of these colours with tan over the eyes, on the cheeks, feet, and pasterns. Other colours, such as black and white, liver and white, red or orange and white, etc., while not disqualifying a dog (provided the architecture is correct), will not be considered so desirable, since it is the aim of the Society to make a clear distinction between the Field and the Springer Spaniel.

HEIGHT.—About 18in. to shoulder.

WEIGHT.—From about 35lb. to 50lb.

GENERAL APPEARANCE.—That of a well-balanced, noble, upstanding sporting dog ; built for activity and endurance. A grand combination of beauty and utility, and bespeaking of unusual docility and instinct.

THE SOCIETY'S DESCRIPTION AND POINTS OF THE FIELD SPANIEL ARE AS FOLLOWS.

Head and jaw	15
Eyes	5
Ears	5
Neck	5
Body	10
Forelegs	10
Hind legs	10
Feet	10
Stern	10
Coat and feather	10
General appearance	10
Total	100

THE ENGLISH SPRINGER

Is probably the prototype of the whole of the sporting Spaniel family. Some of the earliest records speak of the "springing Spaniel," and he is no doubt a contemporary of the "setting Spaniel," the two varieties being the only Spaniels in existence at one period. They were probably much the same in type and conformation, the former being taught to "spring" at his quarry in flushing it, and the other to "set" it—hence the distinction. From the latter the Setter was doubtless evolved, and from the "springing Spaniel" the whole of the beautiful varieties we now possess have emanated, leaving the original a derelict on the sands of time. It is probably incorrect to say that the old English Springer has ever become extinct, for although he never gained a footing on the English show bench until very recently, when, through the instrumentality of Mr. W. Arkwright and the Sporting Spaniel Society, the Kennel Club were induced to place him on the register, yet he has been kept in his purity in many shooting kennels in different parts of the country, the owners of which have preferred utility to beauty, ignoring what they have termed the "elongated monstrosities" of the show ring.

The Sporting Spaniel Society was the first to come to the rescue of the old English Springer, guaranteeing classes for the variety at several of the more important shows. The entries in the English Springer classes at the earlier shows were a somewhat heterogeneous and motley group, embracing as they did all sizes and shapes from a half-bred Setter to half Cockers and Clumbers, misfit Field and Sussex Spaniels, and what were then known as Norfolk Spaniels—that is, the liver-and-white, medium-sized, symmetrical, and well-balanced type of Spaniel, which was, and is still, greatly used and much valued as a working dog all over the country. I often think that of all Spaniels this dog (about whose origin there is no distinct record, some holding that he is indigenous to the county of the same name, and others that he is the product of one of the Dukes of Norfolk), whose size, colour, and conformation are so fixed and distinct, and whose intelligence, tractability, endurance and capability in the field are beyond dispute, has very great claims to recognition as a distinct variety of the sporting Spaniel, both by the Spaniel Club and the Kennel Club. It is held by others that the Norfolk Spaniel and the English Springer are identical, one and the same, but I do not hold with this theory, and I have a letter before me from Sir Hugo FitzHerbert, Bart., a great enthusiast in the cause of the English Springer, of which he is a successful breeder and exhibitor, who also negatives the idea. Sir Hugo says that

SPANIEL (English Springer).

whole colours, whether black, liver, or red, were never associated with the Norfolk Spaniel, in which he is quite right; but these colours, and, indeed, all colours, have been, and are, associated with the English Springer. This further confirms my view of the uniformity of type of the Norfolk Spaniel, which, with its indisputable beauty and utility, and the fact of his having preserved his individuality through all the Spaniel evolutions and metamorphoses, in my opinion, gives him one of the strongest possible claims to recognition as a distinct variety.

The English Springer is, with the Norfolk Spaniel, one of the most rational dogs in point of architecture of all the Spaniel varieties, viewed from the vantage point of utility. He may be any colour almost, and is a leggy dog in comparison to the Field Spaniels, with a short and more symmetrical body, straight front, flat coat, a long head, square muzzle, rather narrow skull, and low-set ears. His eyes and expression, gait and feathering, are all distinctly Spaniel. He combines strength with activity, courage with docility, and all the characteristics of a workman and gentleman combined, without his vices. He is a dog of from 40lb. to 50lb. weight.

The chief points to look for in the selection of English Springer puppies at from two to four months old and after are: A long head, lean skull, distinct stop, square muzzle, short, well-balanced body, straight forelegs, longer in proportion than the Field Spaniel, flat coat, down-carried tail.

The Spaniel Club's Standard of Points of the English Springer.

Positive Points.

Head and jaw	15
Eyes	5
Ears	5
Neck	5
Body	10
Forelegs	10
Hind legs	10
Feet	10
Stern	10
Coat and feather	10
General appearance	10
Total positive points	100

Negative Points.

Light eyes	20
Light nose	15
Curled ears	10
Curled coat	15
Bad carriage of tail	10
Topknot	15
Crooked forelegs	10
Total negative points	95

Descriptive Particulars.

HEAD.—Skull well developed. Clearly defined stop, muzzle long, lean, and square, with a powerful jaw; neither under nor over shot, and nicely chiselled below the eyes.

EYES.—Neither too full nor too small; colour dark hazel or dark brown or nearly black.

EARS.—Set low, moderately long and wide, and sufficiently clad with nice Setter-like feather.

NECK.—Long, strong, and muscular.

BODY (including size and symmetry).—Medium length, well ribbed up to a good strong loin, straight or slightly arched, never slack, and the whole appearance is that of a well-balanced dog. Excessive length and lowness, however, should be penalised, as interfering with the dog's activity.

SHOULDERS AND CHEST.—Former sloping and free, latter deep and well developed, but not too round and wide.

HINDQUARTERS.—Very powerful and muscular, wide and fully developed.

STERN.—Well set on and carried low, nicely fringed with wavy feather of silky texture.

FEET AND LEGS.—Feet not too small, with good strong pads, legs straight and strong, nicely feathered; over-much feathering objectionable.

COAT.—Flat or slightly waved, and never curly. Sufficiently dense to resist the weather, and not too short; silky in texture, and glossy and refined in nature.

COLOURS.—Various: Black-and-tan, liver-and-tan, black, liver, black-tan-and-white, liver-and-white, liver-tan-and-white, lemon-and-white, roans, etc.

GENERAL APPEARANCE.—A combination of beauty and utility. Weight about 40lb.

Although there is some diversity of opinion about the correct type of English Springer, the type of which is by no means fixed, yet the foregoing description will give the reader an idea of the main features of the dog. It is a pity more Spaniel men do not take up his cause, and give to the world examples of a dog who has such claims upon sporting men at least, since as an all-round workman his descent and anatomy together give him a pre-eminent position.

THE WELSH SPRINGER.

Coming to the Spaniel product of "gallant little Wales," we have a variety which excels any of the English varieties for size, colour, and fixity of type. His origin, with the other varieties, is no doubt a common one, but while the red-and-white Field Spaniels in England have almost died out, in Wales the variety has been preserved and bred in its purity for a long

SPANIEL (Welsh Springer).

period, probably for hundreds of years, according to the records. In 1902 the Kennel Club placed the variety on the register. The variety has, however, been kept in several leading sporting Spaniel families in the Principality for many generations, no shooting expedition at one time being complete that did not include a team of these merry red-and-white Spaniels. As workers they have no superior, no day being too long and no covert too strong for the endurance and pluck of these gay Cambrians.

The Welsh Springer is a dog of from 30lb. to 40lb. weight, proportionate in all his parts, with a well-balanced head, straight front, grand spring of rib, and powerful hindquarters. He may be described as an enlarged Cocker, but shows less feathering than is found in most of the other varieties, and the ears are also shorter. As in all Spaniels, snipiness and thick heads are common defects, and the Welsh Springer is no exception. This said, the breed is at once a rational one, and possesses all the traits of his English cousin, while the uniformity of colour and its irregular distribution give to a group of Welsh Springers quite a picturesque appearance. In this way the variety has made great headway on the show bench, and enlisted a number of enthusiasts within its ranks, who are much devoted to the breed, not only for its general beauty, but also for its wonderful prowess in the field.

The chief points to look for in the selection of Welsh Springer puppies at from two to four months old and after are almost the same as those of the English Springer, the recognised colour being, of course, red-and-white.

The Welsh Spaniel or Springer is also known and referred to in Wales as a "Starter." He is of very ancient and pure origin, and is a distinct variety which has been bred and preserved purely for working purposes.

The following is the description formulated by the Welsh Springer Spaniel Club :—

HEAD, SKULL.—Proportionate, of moderate length, slightly domed, clearly defined stop, well chiselled below the eyes.

MUZZLE.—Medium length, straight, fairly square; the nostrils well developed and flesh coloured or dark.

JAW.—Strong, neither under nor overshot.

EYES.—Hazel or dark, medium size, not prominent, not sunken, nor showing haw.

EARS.—Set moderately low and hanging close to the cheeks, comparatively small and gradually narrowing towards the tip, covered with nice Setter-like feathering. A short chubby head is objectionable.

NECK AND SHOULDERS.—Neck, long and muscular, clean in throat, neatly set into long and sloping shoulders.

FORELEGS.—Medium length, straight, well boned, moderately feathered.

BODY.—Not long; strong and muscular, with deep brisket, well-sprung ribs; length of body should be proportionate to length of leg, and very well balanced; with muscular loin slightly arched and well coupled up.

QUARTERS.—Strong and muscular, wide and fully developed, with deep second thighs.

HIND LEGS.—Hocks well let down; stifles moderately bent (neither twisted in nor out), moderately feathered.

FEET.—Round, with thick pads.

STERN.—Well set on and low, never carried above the level of the back; lightly feathered, and with lively action.

COAT.—Straight or flat and thick, of a nice silky texture, never wiry or wavy. A curly coat is most objectionable.

COLOUR.—Dark rich red and white.

GENERAL APPEARANCE.—A symmetrical, compact, strong, merry, very active dog; not stilty, obviously built for endurance and activity, and from 33 to 40lb. in weight.

The Welsh Cocker is to all intents and purposes a smaller edition of the Welsh Springer, there being no divergence to speak of in either character or conformation. They are used for the thick gorse where it would be difficult for a larger dog to get with ease. I cannot quite follow the paradoxical description in the standard in respect of the foreface and jaw. If it must " not be snipy " and " not square," I am at a loss to know what sort of foreface is required. All Spaniels, in my opinion, should be free from snipiness in muzzle, and to be free from snipiness they must be " square "—one being the opposite of the other.

POINTS OF THE WELSH COCKER.

HEAD.—Not heavy, medium light, with moderate stop; foreface lean, but not snipy; jaw should not be square; nostrils well developed, flesh-coloured or dark; skull sufficiently large for plenty of brain. A chubby head is objectionable.

EYES.—Medium size, but not prominent; hazel or dark; intelligent expression; not sunken nor showing haw.

EARS.—Small, set fairly low, well clothed with hair without positive curl.

NECK.—Strong and neatly set on sloping shoulders.

BODY.—Compact and firmly knit, not long, giving appearance of a combination of power and activity. Length of body should be in proportion to length of leg; chest not too wide, but fairly deep and well developed. Loin strong, well ribbed up, and well coupled. Hindquarters strong.

LEGS.—Straight, plenty of liberty, with good-quality bone, moderate feather; not too short, so as to interfere with activity in working and getting over a rough country; hocks well let down and not twisted in or out; not feathered below the hocks.

FEET.—Round and firm.

STERN.—Not carried above line of back, with plenty of action.

COAT.—Flat or wavy, not curly. Not too profuse.

WEIGHT.—Not exceeding 25lb.

COLOUR.—Red- or orange-and-white.

GENERAL APPEARANCE.—Symmetrical, merry, sagacious, good-tempered, and active. Giving impression of a worker, without any approach to the Toy.

THE COCKER SPANIEL

At the present moment is the most popular of all the varieties of Sporting Spaniels, especially the coloured variety, which has come into public favour in late years with a bound. The Cocker, unlike the Field varieties, is free from any abnormalities, being a rationally built and symmetrical little dog, full of buoyancy and beaming with intelligence, and of tireless energy. These features and characteristics in the dog no doubt account for his popularity.

As to his origin there is the same mystery, but little doubt exists that the Cocker is amongst the most ancient of the Spaniel family. He derives his name from the fact that he was first used as an aid to the gun in shooting woodcocks, being a handy little dog in getting through the dense thickets and bramble, whilst as a retriever he probably has not his equal for nose and cleverness. No breed that has ever been exported to America has "caught on" so much as the Cocker, who is to-day one of the most popular breeds in the United States. In America the breed has, in my opinion, somewhat degenerated as a sporting dog, having drifted into Toyishness on the one hand, and become too low on leg in many cases, although, to the credit of American breeders be it said, the true type of the dog has been retained. Indeed, in one or two important particulars—viz., squareness of muzzle and stop—American Cockers have an advantage over the English dogs, in connection with which the lack in these points is a common deficiency.

At one time in England there were a large number of so-called Cocker Spaniels exhibited which were simply Field Spaniels in miniature, being of the long and low persuasion, with nice long and level heads—very pretty little Spaniels, but not Cockers, according to the generally accepted type and that recognised by the Spaniel Club and Cocker Spaniel Club, which latter was founded in 1904 by the large and growing number of Cocker enthusiasts for the purpose of promoting the interests of the Cocker Spaniel exclusively.

At one show, Derby, many years ago, where I was judging Spaniels, I well remember the large classes being composed of these Field Spaniels in miniature and Cocker Spaniels proper, in about equal proportions. Had I judged the whole as Cockers it would have necessitated my leaving out the small Field Spaniels, most of which were Cocker-bred. I therefore made a proposal to exhibitors—which was accepted and confirmed by the society—that the class or classes be divided into Cockers and Field Spaniels in miniature, and the prizes divided equally. Of course, for all practical purposes these small Field Spaniels are as capable, anatomically, to perform the specific work of the Cocker in the field as the more orthodox type. This being so, it always has been a question with me whether Field Spaniels should not be divided by weight, in the same way as are Pointers and other breeds, in order to include these very pretty little Spaniels, which still abound.

Cockers even vary very much in size and type. We have the Devonshire Cockers and the Welsh Cockers, and others indigenous to different districts in the country to which they are more or less adapted; but happily there is only one type now recognised in the show ring, and that is the short-coupled, sturdy, well-balanced, good-fronted, flat-coated dog with a nicely chiselled head, dark eye, and square muzzle, a *multum in parvo*, who looks like and *is* a workman from stem to stern, a dog of from 23lb. to 27lb. There was at one time a fixed weight, according to the ordination of the Spaniel Club, of 25lb., but this was very sensibly modified a few years ago, and that weight given as the most desirable average, any serious deviation either way to be penalised by judges. Previous to this alteration, certain well-known dogs, and one notable dog in particular, who in normal condition just turned the scale at 25lb., was exhibited and won before his breakfast at a certain show, to wit Birmingham, and passed muster as to weight, but after being fed was

COCKER SPANIEL.

over-weight, whereupon he was objected to and disqualified. He was a good Cocker, a champion, and it was the ludicrousness of the incident—of a Cocker being a champion before his breakfast, and afterwards not eligible for competition—which impelled the Spaniel Club to modify their rule.

The chief points, therefore, to aim at in breeding Cocker Spaniels are compactness of body, straightness of forelegs, squareness of muzzle, dark eyes, and flat coats, with a down-carriage of stern. Common defects in the breed, especially the coloured variety, are crooked fronts, light eyes, and cock tails, which are an abomination alike to sporting men and to good judges.

It is inadvisable to cross the colours with the blacks, except as an occasional outcross, because the litters or first crosses from such alliances will invariably be mismarked blacks, and therefore unfit for exhibition in either blacks or coloured Cocker classes. Of course, colour may right itself in the next cross, or, at furthest, subsequent mating if judiciously made. The first favourite colour is blue-roan, the colour well distributed, and after this the liver-and-red roans, but as in a horse, so in a coloured Cocker Spaniel, a really good dog can hardly be a bad colour.

The chief points to look for in the selection of Cocker Spaniel puppies, any colour, from two to four months old and after, are: A nicely balanced head, distinct stop, square muzzle, dark eye, short, compact body, well-balanced in proportion to length of leg, down-carried tail, and flat coat.

The following are the points and description laid down by the Cocker Spaniel Club :—

Scale of Points for Judging Cocker Spaniels.

Positive Points.

Head and jaws	10
Eyes	5
Ears	5
Neck	10
Body	20
Forelegs	10
Hind legs	10
Feet	10
Stern	10
Coat and feather	10
Total positive points	100

Negative Points.

Light eyes	10
Light nose	15
Hair curled on ears (very undesirable)	15
Coat (curly, woolly, or wiry)	20
Carriage of stern	20
Topknot	20
Total negative points	100

Descriptive Particulars.

HEAD.—A nicely developed square muzzle and jaw; stop distinct Skull and forehead should be well developed, with plenty of room for brain power. Cleanly chiselled, and not cheeky.

EYES.—Full, but not prominent, hazel or brown coloured, harmonising with colour of coat, with a general expression of intelligence and gentleness, decidedly wideawake, bright and merry.

EARS.—Lobular, set on low, leather fine, and not extending beyond the nose; well clothed with long silky hair which should be straight no positive curls or ringlets.

NECK.—Long, strong, and muscular, and neatly set on to fine sloping shoulders.

BODY (including size and symmetry).—Compact and firmly knit together giving the impression of a concentration of power and untiring activity; the total weight should be about 25lb. to 28lb.

NOSE.—Sufficiently wide and well developed to ensure the exquisite scenting power of this breed.

SHOULDERS AND CHEST.—The former sloping and fine, chest deep and well developed, but not too wide and round to interfere with the free action of the forelegs.

BACK AND LOIN.—Short in back; immensely strong and compact in proportion to the size and weight of the dog; slightly drooping towards the tail.

HINDQUARTERS.—Wide, well rounded, and very muscular.

STERN.—That most characteristic of blue blood in all the Spaniel family may, in the lighter and more active Cocker, although set low down, be allowed a slightly higher carriage than in the other breeds, but never cocked up over, but rather in a line with the back, although the lower its carriage and action the better, and when at work its action should be incessant in this, the brightest and merriest of the whole Spaniel family. Not docked too short.

FEET AND LEGS.—The legs must be well boned, feathered, and straight, for the tremendous exertions expected from this grand little sporting dog, and should be sufficiently short for concentrated power, but not too short to interfere with its full activity. Feet firm, round, and cat-like; not too large or spreading or loose-jointed.

COAT.—Flat and silky in texture, never wiry or wavy, with sufficient feather, but not too profuse and never curly.

COLOURS.—Various; in self colours a white shirt frill should never disqualify; but white feet should not be allowed in any specimen of self-colour.

GENERAL APPEARANCE.—That of an active, merry, sporting dog. The Cocker Spaniel does not follow on the lines of the larger Field Spaniel either in lengthiness, lowness, or otherwise; but is shorter in back, and rather higher on the legs.

CHAPTER XVIII.

The Bull-terrier.

The Bull-terrier holds a very high position amongst the Terrier varieties by reason of its sterling worth as a companion and as a dog. He has no superior in the matter of pluck, gameness, and indomitable courage, of which virtues he may be said to be the very embodiment, whilst as a companion he is as harmless as a kitten, as docile and tractable as a child, and as staunch and true as steel. Then, again, there is an entire absence of the coat trouble which is involved in the Wire or broken-haired Terriers. This is not only an advantage in obviating any coat preparation for the show ring beyond the fining of the tail and cleaning of the ears, but is more cleanly for the house, a consideration in cases where Terriers are kept as house dogs and are given, with little restriction, free access to their masters' or mistresses' apartments.

BULL-TERRIER.

The misty records and data of the origin of most breeds of dogs apply to a great extent to the Bull-terrier, whose creation cannot be distinctly traced, but which was at least given an impetus when bull-baiting and dog-fighting were made illegal pastimes by the Legislature in 1835.

The appetite of the populace, and also the gentry—not forgetting the undergraduates of Oxford and Cambridge,—for a more vicious form of sport than obtains in these days was not, of course, extinguished with the abolition of bull-baiting, which sport was largely substituted by dog-fighting, badger-baiting, etc., the former of which was, of course, carried on clandestinely. For this description of sport a different type of dog was, of course, required to the Bulldog—viz., a dog with a longer and more punishing jaw, and more agility, yet game and powerful. For this purpose the Bulldog was crossed with the Terriers available in those days, which were more or less of a nondescript pattern. This assumption is proved by the colour and type of the early Bull-terriers, which were either brindled or fallow smut in colour —taking after the Bulldog—with strong and Terrier-like bodies and limbs, and heads of fair length and strength, but not the clean-cut long head of the modern Bull-terrier. Many of the coloured Bull-terriers survive to this day ; and here I may mention that there is at this moment dawning on the Bull-terrier horizon a distinct desire among coloured enthusiasts to bring the coloured Bull-terriers, and more particularly the brindles, up to the level and type of the whites, which, for half a century or more, have held undisputed sway in general public esteem and on the show bench. This is both a legitimate and laudable aspiration, for while I would not for one moment attempt to disparage the smart, clean-looking whites, yet, in view of his origin, his avocation and tradition, it seems but logical that there should be brindle and fawn Bull-terriers as well as whites, brindle being a colour that is always associated with hardihood, and which is certainly handsome. The cropping of Bull-terriers' ears, happily abolished on the initiative of King Edward (then Prince of Wales), in 1895, is a relic of the dog-fighting days and the Bill Sikes era, when it was considered low to keep a Bull-terrier by reason of his tap-room and pugilistic associations. The dog still retains his pugilistic propensities, which are bred in him and inherent to his nature. He is the gamecock of the canine species, and undoubtedly the finest exponent of the " noble art " as applied to dogs, which puritans would probably describe as the " ignoble " art.

The dog has not only survived his " evil associations " of the past, but also the cropping edict of the Kennel Club, which, however, gave him a severe shaking, owing to the difficulty in breeding small fine drop ears, necessary under the new K.C. regime and the then ordination of the Bull-terrier Club. For cropping, the very opposite form of ear was best—viz., a big thick ear, which lent itself best for cropping purposes because the sinews and cartilage were stronger and more likely to leave the remains of the aural appendage permanently pricked. Vicious and brutal as was and is professional dog-fighting, it is so far to the credit of those who indulged in it that they had some consideration for the punishment likely to be inflicted upon the canine combatants, in the very ordination of cropping, which, while in itself necessitating the infliction of punishment, had the paradoxical purpose in view of minimising the torture of the dogs in the arena of the fighting ring.

The ear difficulty did not, however, turn out to be as stubborn a problem as breeders anticipated. By a process of selection, smaller ears were soon obtained, and as the clubs made either semi-erect or rose ears not only admissible, but preferable, the ear trouble quickly disappeared from the platform of practical politics in Bull-terrier breeding.

The white Bull-terrier doubtless owes his colour largely to crossings with the White English Terrier, and possibly with the Pointer or the Dalmatian, and amongst the earlier pioneers of his evolution stand out those doyens of the breed in the " good old days," the late Mr. " Jim " Hinks, a " Brummagem " sport, and Bill George, a London contemporary, both of varied accomplishments and wide experience, who saw the Bull-terrier's development from its chrysalis state of variegated colours to one of spotlessness in both colour and character, if this somewhat converse butterfly simile may be pardoned.

Leaving behind a record which has its bright as well as its black side, I come to the breed as we know him to-day, fully emancipated from his past records, and standing out as one of the ornaments of the canine race, a dog that will not disgrace but do credit to his owner anywhere and under any circumstances. Not only is he one of the most popular varieties in England to-day, but also in the United States of America, where the breed is flourishing, and one of the most numerous on the show bench ; in Canada, where it has been selected as the national breed of this great British Colony ; in India, where it is found to withstand the severity of the Asiatic climate better than any other British breed ; in Australia, and in other countries.

Briefly, the main points to aim at in breeding Bull-terriers are two which are always difficult to obtain—viz., a long head and a short back. Generally a long head accompanies a long back, and *vice versa*, and, therefore, where the opposite is obtained its value should be emphasised. But a long head is not in itself enough. The chiselling of the head is of more importance than mere length. What is required is a flat skull, nicely levelled all round and free from cheekiness, but in no way effeminate, a long punishing foreface, well filled up under the eyes, which adds to its power, and strong to the muzzle, which should be free from lippiness. The object of this latter point is obvious — viz., to prevent the dog biting his own lips in his encounter with either dog or other animal. The eyes should be small, dark, slightly sunken below the temples, which should not show any " stop," the face being quite level from the occiput to the tip of the nose. Cheekiness, lippiness, and light eyes are all objectionable, as is either an overshot or an undershot mouth. These two latter points are and should be fatal in the show ring in the case of a Bull-terrier more than most breeds, since he is required to use his mouth in everything he has to negotiate. Heavy shoulders and crooked forelegs are equally objectionable; the former should be heavily penalised, and the latter are unpardonable. Straight forelegs and short, strong feet, with clean shoulders, are the desiderata; well-sprung ribs and strong, nicely turned quarters, the hocks well let down, and a short three-quarter tail, coming right out of the terminus of his back and carried in a straight line therewith, are all important features of the breed. The Bull-terrier should be a well-balanced dog, proportionate in all his parts, neither too low on leg nor leggy; neither light in build nor broad and Bulldoggy, but a very powerful dog in a comparatively little compass—a *multum in parvo*, who gives one the impression of endurance without coarseness, agility and determination without vulgarity. Indeed, a perfect Bull-terrier is a dog of polish—a gentleman in both disposition and appearance from the tip of his nose to the end of his tail.

The breed is divided into two main weights—viz., heavy and medium. Weight is altogether immaterial in the Bull-terrier so long as he excels in the cardinal points and great characteristics of the breed, which applies to any and every weight, whether heavyweight or middleweight.

The chief points to look for in the selection of Bull-terrier puppies at from two to four months old, whether large or medium, are:—Great length of head, straight foreface—that is, free from stop—small closely set dark eyes, clean lips, well balanced but not thick head, short back and tail, straight forelegs, big ribs, level mouth, small ears.

The following is the Bull-terrier Club's standard description and code of points:—

The Bull-terrier is the gladiator of the canine race, and should be a trongly built, muscular, active, symmetrical animal, with a keen, determined expression; full of fire, but of sweet disposition amenable to discipline.

Details of Desired Points.

HEAD.—(1) Appearance: Oval, almost egg-shaped; fairly long, but strength must not be sacrificed for length; of considerable depth; not too wide or coarse, and cheek muscles should not be prominent.

(2) Profile: Should be almost an arc from the occiput to the tip of the nose; the more down-faced the better; no stop or indentation.

(3) Forehead: Fairly flat and not domed between the ears; the occiput not prominent.

(4) Foreface: Longer than the forehead and filled right up to the eyes—*i.e.*, egg-like.

(5) Muzzle: Should show great strength, and though tapering, should not be "snipy."

(6) Underjaw: Deep and strong.

(7) Lips: Tight and clean.

(8) Teeth: Sound, strong, clean, and perfectly regular; an undershot or overhung mouth is objectionable.

(9) Ears: Small and thin, situated on top of the skull, fairly close together; erect, semi-erect, or rose.

(10) Eyes: Well sunken; as nearly black as possible, with a piercing glint giving a keen expression; small, almond-shaped, or riangular; nearer the ears than nose, set closely together, and obliquely placed.

(11) Nose: Black, with large well-developed nostrils; bent downwards at the tip.

NECK.—Moderately long, tapering from shoulders to head; very muscular, arched, and free from all traces of dewlap or throatiness.

SHOULDERS.—Strong and muscular, but without any heaviness or loading; shoulder blades wide, flat, and sloping well back; no slackness or dip at the withers.

CHEST.—Broad, viewed from the front; deep from withers to brisket.

BODY.—Ribs well sprung—*i.e.*, rounded, back ribs deep; intercostal muscles well developed; the back, short, strong and muscular; no dip at withers; only slightly arched at loin.

LEGS.—Should be big-boned, but not coarse. *Forelegs*: Moderately high, perfectly straight, and the dog must stand well on them; the elbows should not turn outwards; pasterns strong and upright. *Hind legs*: Straight, viewed from behind; thighs very muscular; hocks well let down, and the bone to the heels short and strong.

FEET.—Round and compact, with the toes well arched—resembling those of the cat, not the hare.

TAIL.—Short, fine, set on low, and carried horizontally; thick where it joins the body, and tapering to a fine point.

COAT.—Short, flat, rather harsh to the touch, and with a fine gloss; the skin should fit the dog tightly.

COLOUR.—For white: pure white coat. For coloured and Staffordshire: colour (preferably brindle), to predominate.

FAULTS.—Light bone; legginess; soft expression; badly placed eyes; light eyes; domed skull; butterfly nose; pronounced cheekiness; dished face; lippiness; throatiness; teeth not meeting evenly; long and slack back; long, thick, and gay tail; loose shoulders; loaded shoulders; crooked elbows; weak pasterns; cow hocks; big and splay feet; toes turning either in or out; soft coat; long coat; narrow chest; flat sides; ewe neck; markings on head; and ticked coat.

DISQUALIFICATIONS.—Deafness; wall eye; wholly flesh-coloured nose; markings behind the set-on of head.

PREPARATION FOR SHOW.—The smellers, long eyebrows, and other long hairs on the head may be removed; the hair inside the ears clipped or shaved down to the true coat, not beyond; the long hair under the tail trimmed, and the sides thereof to proportion.

SCALE OF POINTS.

Neck, shoulders, body, and tail ..	20
Legs and feet	20
Head, skull, jaws, lips, teeth	20
Eyes and expression	15
Movement	10
Condition and Pure white body	10
Ears	5
	100

CHAPTER XIX.

The Fox-terrier

Is probably the most popular of all the Terrier breeds, and has more followers than any other variety. Each of the Terrier breeds has its complement of zealots who swear by their own particular fancy, and hold that breed up as a paragon of the Terrier persuasion and the acme of perfection in all that goes to constitute a true Terrier—that is to say, a game, good-looking dog capable of going to earth and doing something when he gets there.

The word " Terrier " is taken from the Latin term *terra*, meaning earth, and indicating a specimen of the canine species capable of following his quarry to ground. It is not all the breeds of Terriers that are able to do this. For instance, the Airedale Terrier, a more modern creation, would have difficulty in following either a fox or an otter to ground, although it is the latter that he was originally bred specifically to unearth, when, *in extremis*, he takes

FOX-TERRIER (Smooth-coated).

to ground. Some of the larger Skye Terriers would have difficulty in pursuing their quarry underground. It is, however, one of the essentials of the Fox-terrier that he shall not be bred too big for this particular function in his avocation, in which he no doubt excels, and added to which he probably combines a more graceful form and smarter appearance than any of his Terrier confrères, which together have led to his sobriquet of the " gentleman " of the Terrier varieties.

In the evolution of this beautiful Terrier, it is difficult to punctuate the exact period at which he may be said to have emerged from his chrysalistic state into the form we find him to-day. Some enthusiasts maintain that the Fox-terrier in reality is the creation of the last sixty years. Doubtless that is true, so far as the present-day show Fox-terrier goes, but the records show that Fox-terriers have existed as long as fox-hunting. They were not always white or parti-coloured, but often black-and-tan, smooth, and broken-haired. There can be no doubt whatever that the Fox-terrier, in one form or another, is a dog of great antiquity. Like almost all manufactured varieties, he is the product or combination of more or less homogeneous species of the canine race, with admixtures and outcrosses from time to time to suit the requirements of different huntsmen and Masters of Foxhounds, including, no doubt, an infusion of Bull-terrier.

Before the advent of dog shows the sole merit of the Fox-terrier lay in his capability to bolt the fox, for which purpose Terriers were, and are still, kept, for convenience, at farmhouses in the district of the hunt, as well as at the kennels. In those days colour and conformation counted for nothing. Dog shows have produced an entire reformation in the form and features of the dog. His devotees in the early days of dog shows could see in the material bequeathed to them by posterity the making of a beautiful Terrier without the sacrifice of his innate virtues, and the dog's development on recognised lines for the first time began. This was somewhere in the 'sixties, some little time before the formation of the Fox-terrier Club, which was founded in 1876. This Club, which was composed of, and still embraces, all the most competent experts and authorities on the breed, has exercised an enormous influence in bringing the breed to its present state of perfection. Since its institution, many other local or district Fox-terrier Clubs have come into being, all with the same object in view—viz., the improvement and popularising of this now famous member of the Terrier family.

It is unnecessary to go very deep into the dog's past ; suffice it to say that there can be no two opinions about the dog being a vast improvement upon his early exhibition days, when there was no fixity of type, when many of the winners were thick-headed, or fine-coated, or with indifferent fronts. True, sound mouths were an essential, and so they are to-day, and short, sturdily made dogs, who looked like going to ground, were sure of notice at the hands of our earlier judges, who were, for the most part, drawn from the ranks of hunting men.

The hand of the fancier soon altered this state of things. The Fox-terrier Club formulated a standard description of what a perfect Fox-terrier ought to be, based upon the specific avocation of the dog, and, singular to record, most of the founders of the Club still survive, and, with their half a century's experience, still maintain that same standard of points, which has been but slightly altered in the interim. That standard, which is, and always has been, recognised, may be said to be responsible for the type of Fox-terrier in vogue to-day. Few specimens have ever reached the ideal, but never probably in the history of the breed were there more good ones and more so nearly approaching the ideal. The whole has been accomplished by careful selection in breeding from the crude originals, for no outcrosses of any kind have been resorted to in the process. These remarks apply to both the Smooth- and the Wire-haired varieties, which have in great measure been kept distinct until recent years, when the outcrossing of one variety with the other has been indulged in, and which had become a necessity, owing to the great consanguinity existing in the breed. This experiment has been found to have disadvantages, as well as advantages. Whilst the cross will assuredly give more stamina to both varieties, and tend to improve them intellectually as well as physically, it will doubtless also have the effect of improving the coat of the Smooths, and in many cases of the Wire-hairs also , but many first crosses will be, and are, semi-Wire-hairs, which, however, may be bred out in subsequent generations. The Wire cross should have the advantage of giving the Smooths the much-needed character in head and expression ; and the Smooth cross should, in time, correct the fluffy-coated Wire-hairs.

The original aim at the improvement of the existing Fox-terrier in the matter of coat, of character, of legs and feet and raciness, which has been attended with such marked success, has, however, not been achieved without its penalties. At one time during this process of evolution our Terriers drifted from a smaller race of dog to one of more elephantine proportions, from a too short legged dog to its antithesis. Then an outcry was raised against the big dogs, coupled by a fruitless attempt to limit the size by the fixing of a weight limit. Gradually a reduction in size took place, with the result that to-day Fox-terriers are probably more uniform in size than at any other period in their history, although there are some few winners who approach what common sense says must be a limit in both directions—viz., in regard to oversize as well as undersize.

The best weight is between 17lb. and 19lb. A hard and fast line cannot be drawn, because heavy boned and bodied dogs will weigh more and look less than a light-boned and rather leggy dog. Speaking generally, however, a dog much under or over the weights named is not desirable, nor should he be encouraged.

Fashion and faddism again have been responsible for other variations which have been witnessed. One breeder has set his mind upon improving the legs and feet, for which he has made many sacrifices in the way of heads and other features. Another has been a stickler for heads, which he has obtained, in many cases, at the cost of legs and feet. Another has made coat his speciality, and so on. The result of this has been that certain kennels have become noted for legs and feet, others for bodies and, maybe, coats, others for heads, etc. It is probably owing to the blending of these various strains that we owe the uniformity of the present-day exhibition Fox-terrier.

But a blending of opposites does not always produce the happy medium, as would seem to be the natural result. Breeding has not yet been reduced to such an exact science. If it had, we should long since have reached perfection. Such crosses will more often produce some puppies too small and others too large, some puppies taking after one parent and some after the other—there are so many influences at work in breeding, certain strains exercising more influence on the progeny than others, whether for good or ill, the cause of which subtleties of nature is in most cases unfathomed. Where a certain feature has been thoroughly established by a long series of breeding experiments, that feature is most likely to assert itself, and it is the prosecution of this hypothesis that has frequently crowned the efforts of the breeder, the student of form and pedigree, with success.

Breeding, however, is a vast subject, and one that cannot be exhaustively dealt with in an article relating to one particular breed.

Taking the principal features of the Fox-terrier seriatim, the first requisite is a good head, although many breeders and judges regard good legs and feet as a *sine qua non*. By a good head I do not mean a long head, although a comparatively long head is desirable—a head measuring, say, eight inches from nose to occiput on an 18lb. dog, although measurements are illusory, because so much depends upon proportion in determining the length of a dog's head. The jaw should be strong, the teeth level, and the skull flat and free from cheekiness. There should be but very little stop, but the eyes should be set in horizontally, and not obliquely; they should be comparatively small, round, and dark. The ears, rather small, V-shaped, should drop forward, pointing to the eyes. The forelegs should be perfectly straight—a stereotyped phrase in the fancy being "straight as gun-barrels." The bone round and not flat, the feet short and cat-like, shoulders set well back obliquely, back short, loin strong, with ribs well sprung, quarters big, thighs wide, and hocks well let down, with tail set on in hound-like fashion. Indeed, excepting in head, the architecture of the Fox-terrier should much resemble that of the Foxhound, of which he is to a great extent an example in miniature. The coat of the Smooth should be close, but thick and dense, with just the least bit of frill and feathering, which is more profuse on the underside of the tail. It should be harsh to the touch. Happily, the day of the Bull-terrier-coated dog is long since past. The only difference in the two varieties is in the coat, the Wire-hair being broken and more profuse in coat, and the coat even more wiry and crisp to the touch.

The chief defects to be scrupulously avoided in breeding are snipy muzzles, long backs, wide fronts, flat sides, cow-hocks, and soft coats. There are minor defects, of course, such as full eyes, faulty ear carriage, and large ears, short necks, straight stifles, and flat, thin, or open feet.

The trimming of the coats of Wire-hairs is an important factor in the show dog. Little success can be hoped for on the show bench unless trimming is practised, since probably 75 per cent. of Wire-haired Fox-terriers require their coats trimming to a greater or lesser degree. This shows that perfection in coat, notwithstanding the long years of careful breeding on scientific lines, is still a long way off. It is very often the case that the best dogs have the worst coats. Trimming certain specified Terriers was allowed by the Kennel Club after a plebiscite of specialist clubs interested in an edict which came into force on June 17th, 1913.

A free use of comb and brush is rarely sufficient to remove the superfluous hair, which mars an otherwise good Terrier, and the finger and thumb are often used, or a specially devised comb, for getting out the hair. Sometimes even clippers are resorted to, but this is risky, as if done badly it is more than likely that the judge would turn out a dog so barbered. Again, the use of any foreign substance such as resin, alum, etc., if left in the coat, may mean disqualification in the show ring.

FOX-TERRIER (Wire-haired).

A dog that requires trimming should have his toilet attended to regularly and not spasmodically. In the case of very bad coats, a good plan, when not exhibiting the dog for a time, is to clip the dog all over with clippers such as are used for the human hair. This strengthens and improves the coat.

Some purists set their faces dead against trimming in any and every form, however mild, but they are in a very small minority. All practical Terrier owners and breeders admit that the trimming of both Smooth and Wire-haired Fox-terriers is absolutely essential to success in the show ring. The suppression of trimming would assuredly mean the discontinuance of exhibiting, and whilst the practice is, and always will be, liable to abuse, yet few experts will attempt to deny its necessity, and these are the people who cannot be deceived by it. Whilst it is possible to hide defects by trimming, on the other hand it shows up the good points and true outline and anatomy of a good but indifferently coated dog, which would otherwise be obscured.

The chief points to look for in the selection of Fox-terrier puppies at from two to four months old and after are : A long, lean head, square muzzle, level mouth, small dark eye, narrow skull, small neat V-shaped drop ears, short back, deep chest, narrow shoulders, good bone, and straight forelegs, and short cat-like feet. The coat in the Smooths should be dense, and in the Wire-hairs a little more profuse, and harder to the touch.

The following is the standard description and points for the two varieties as laid down by the Fox-terrier Club:—

SMOOTH-HAIRED.

1. HEAD.—The SKULL should be flat and moderately narrow, and gradually decreasing in width to the eyes. Not much " stop " should be apparent, but there should be more dip in the profile between the forehead and top jaw than is seen in the case of a Greyhound.

The CHEEKS must not be full.

The EARS should be V-shaped and small, of moderate thickness, and dropping forward close to the cheek, not hanging by the side of the head like a Foxhound's.

The JAW, upper and under, should be strong and muscular; should be of fair punishing strength, but not so in any way to resemble the Greyhound or modern English Terrier. There should not be much falling away below the eyes. This part of the head should, however, be moderately chiselled out, so as not to go down in a straight line like a wedge.

The NOSE, towards which the muzzle must gradually taper, should be black.

The EYES should be dark in colour, small, and rather deep set, full of fire, life, and intelligence; as nearly as possible circular in shape.

The TEETH should be as nearly as possible level—*i.e.*, the upper teeth on the outside of the lower teeth.

2. NECK.—Should be clean and muscular, without throatiness, of fair length, and gradually widening to the shoulders.

3. SHOULDERS.—Should be long and sloping, well laid back, fine at the points, and clearly cut at the withers.

CHEST.—Deep and not broad.

4. BACK.—Should be short, straight, and strong, with no appearance of slackness.

LOIN.—Should be powerful and very slightly arched. The fore-ribs should be moderately arched, the back-ribs deep; and the dog should be well ribbed-up.

5. HINDQUARTERS.—Should be strong and muscular, quite free from droop or crouch; the thighs long and powerful; hocks near the ground, the dog standing well up on them like a Foxhound, and not straight in the stifle.

6. STERN.—Should be set on rather high, and carried gaily, but not over the back or curled. It should be of good strength, anything approaching a " pipe-stopper " tail being especially objectionable.

7. LEGS.—Viewed from any direction must be straight, showing little or no appearance of an ankle in front. They should be strong in bone throughout, short and straight to pastern. Both fore and hind legs should be carried straight forward in travelling, the stifles not turned outwards. The elbows should hang perpendicular to the body, working free of the side.

FEET.—Should be round, compact, and not large. The soles hard and tough. The toes moderately arched, and turned neither in nor out.

8. COAT.—Should be straight, flat, smooth, hard, dense, and abundant. The belly and underside of the thighs should not be bare.

COLOUR.—White should predominate; brindle, red, or liver markings are objectionable. Otherwise this point is of little or no importance.

9. SYMMETRY, SIZE, AND CHARACTER.—The dog must present a general gay, lively, and active appearance; bone and strength in a small compass are essentials; but this must not be taken to mean that a Fox-terrier should be cloggy, or in any way coarse—speed and endurance must be looked to as well as power, and the symmetry of the Foxhound taken as a model. The Terrier, like the Hound, must on no account be leggy, nor must he be too short in the leg. He should stand like a cleverly-made hunter, covering a lot of ground, yet with a short back,

as before stated. He will then attain the highest degree of propelling power, together with the greatest length of stride that is compatible with the length of his body. *Weight* is not a certain criterion of a Terrier's fitness for his work—general shape, size, and contour are the main points; and if a dog can gallop and stay, and follow his fox up a drain, it matters little what his weight is to a pound or so, though, roughly speaking, 15 to 17lb. for a bitch, and 16 to 18lb. for a dog, in show condition, are appropriate weights.

WIRE-HAIRED.

The Wire-haired variety should resemble the Smooth in every respect except the coat, which should be broken. The harder and more wiry the texture of the coat is, the better. On no account should the dog look or feel woolly; and there should be no silky hair about the poll or elsewhere. The coat should not be too long, so as to give the dog a shaggy appearance; but at the same time it should show a marked and distinct difference all over from the Smooth species.

SCALE OF POINTS.

		Smooth.	Wire-haired.
1.	Head and ears	15	15
2.	Neck	5	5
3.	Shoulders and chest	10	10
4.	Back and loin	10	10
5.	Hindquarters	15	15
6.	Stern	5	5
7.	Legs and feet	15	15
8.	Coat	10	15
9.	Symmetry, size, and character	15	10
	Total	100	100

DISQUALIFYING POINTS.

1. Nose, white, cherry, or spotted to a considerable extent with either of these colours.
2. Ears, prick, tulip, or rose.
3. Mouth much undershot or much overshot.

CHAPTER XX.

The Irish Terrier

Is one of the most popular of the Terrier varieties, and one of the most companionable, most game, and good looking. He is one of the four native breeds of dogs, all red in colour, and which are often dubbed "Ireland's Reds." The Irish Terrier in disposition partakes of much of the character of the Irish race itself, being somewhat excitable in temperament, yet very intelligent, imbued with great pluck and determination, yet exceedingly sociable and companionable and vivacious. The pluck of the Irish Terrier has earned for him the sobriquet " Dare Devil," and that he is a daring dog is beyond dispute. He will not be in canine society five minutes before he will issue a challenge, irrespective of size or breeding of his associates, which

IRISH TERRIER.

disposition forcibly reminds one of the well-known story of Pat in a row when he dared anyone to " thread on the tails of his coat."

A veil of mystery enshrouds the origin of the Irish Terrier, just the same as obscures that of most breeds of dogs which seem to have been evolved by man in the first instance, almost unconsciously, and, perhaps, to a great extent aimlessly. There can be little doubt, however, that he is an Irish product. Such a sporting country as Ireland must always have had its Terrier, and, although there is little doubt that in the ages that have passed the Terriers indigenous to the Emerald Isle differed from the modern example, yet they formed its groundwork. Old prints of sporting scenes often portray a rough-coated Terrier, very much on the lines of the dog of to-day, and which varies in colour, but is generally red or wheaten. Nor is this aboriginal Terrier peculiar to any particular part of Ireland, but to every sporting district—north, south, east, and west,—according to old records and data.

The dog was, and is still, used in Ireland for the same purpose as the Fox-terrier in England,—viz., for bolting the fox, for rabbiting, and for killing vermin generally.

The advent of dog shows, as in the case of all other breeds, was the means of Irish Terrier lovers turning their attention to their own native Terrier, and out of the crude material at hand they moulded an animal which represents the views and ideas of Irish experts.

This is a dog of 23lb. to 26lb., proportionate in build, with a long, punishing head, short back, good front, and a wiry, weather-resisting coat. It is not to be wondered at that the Irish Terrier was quickly taken up by English fanciers, for he filled a gap in the list of English Terriers, being in size between his English contemporary—the Fox-terrier—and the later Airedale Terrier.

The breed was first exhibited at Dublin in the early 'seventies. Soon afterwards the Irish Terrier Club was formed, and a standard laid down, which has been slightly revised since, and which appears in connection with this article. Some of the earlier pioneers of the breed include such well-known zealots as Mr. George Jameson, Mr. E. F. Despard, Mr. Erwin, Dr. Carey, the late Mr. William Graham, and others, whilst to-day the breed boasts of a great army of admirers, with many clubs, besides the parent club, devoted to its promotion and welfare. Indeed, the Irish Terrier is one of the most popular and profitable of the many Terrier varieties, such a favourite that the contagion of his popularity has extended to America, Australia, South Africa, and wherever dog shows are held. Many individual specimens have realised from £100 to £500, which is the largest price ever paid for an Irish Terrier, this sum, I believe, having been given by an American for Mr. Oates' Ch. Straight Tip, although it is said that Mr. Sam Wilson once refused £700 for his famous Ch. Bolton Woods Mixer.

In the evolution of this beautiful Terrier, who has not his superior as an intelligent companion and game, all-round sportsman, controversies have cropped up from time to time on the correctness of his type, the size question, and the colour and texture of his coat. At one time it was alleged that he was getting too big; at another that many of the winners on the show bench were nothing more nor less than red wire-haired Fox-terriers. At another time the colour question would be trotted out, some holding that the deep red was the correct colour, whilst others would contend, and give evidence and data for their contention, that the wheaten colour was quite orthodox.

I might here mention that there is a blue variety, which seems to have been propagated mostly in the South of Ireland, special classes having been provided for them at several of the Cork and other shows many years ago. This variety, under the name of Kerry Blue, has now become very popular, so I have devoted a new chapter to it. It is, no doubt, an offshoot of the original red, created probably by a cross at some distant date with a Blue Bedlington Terrier.

A consensus of expert opinion holds a dog if from 24lb. to 27lb. to be the most desirable weight.

One common defect in the Irish Terrier is indifferent front, legs, and feet. Although greater perfection has been arrived at at the present time than ever existed probably before during his exhibition career, yet the breed does not equal the Fox or Airedale Terrier in these particular points, and this is one of the features which requires the careful attention of breeders and enthusiasts. The Irish Terrier, like all broken-haired breeds, is a victim of the trimming trouble, but, even in the matter of good texture of coat, I am inclined to think that the breed will bear favourable comparison to-day with what it was at any time previously. The wheaten-coloured specimens are inclined to be softer than the deeper red dogs.

The Irish Terrier has a style of physiognomy and expression peculiarly his own. The chiselling of his head should not be like that of the Airedale or the Fox-terrier; perhaps a little stronger than either, without being coarse, and his eyes hazel rather than very dark, as in the case of the breeds named, and so set in as to give the dog a "dare devil" sort of expression distinctly Irish. In describing a good-headed Irish Terrier, it is a common boast of exhibitors that their dog has "the map of Ireland on his face."

In a litter of Irish Terriers, bred from pedigree stock, very often many of the puppies will be darker in colour than the others, and have shorter coats as the coats of the puppies develop. These are most likely to turn out the best coated and coloured puppies in the litter, and if these lines should catch the eye of a novice, pray let me advise him not to drown puppies with a little white on chest (which is no real detriment, even in the show ring) or on their toes, which will most likely disappear with the puppy coat.

The chief points to be aimed at in breeding are long, level, and fairly lean heads, with strength of muzzle to the end, rather long neck, short back, big ribs, sloping shoulders, narrow front, with short, strong feet, nice round bone, with hind limbs well let down in hocks, which should be quite parallel and not incline to "cow hocks."

The chief points to look for in the selection of Irish Terrier puppies at from two to four months old and after are: A long, level head, strong muzzle, comparatively narrow skull, dark eye, small, neat V-shaped, drop ears, short back, deep chest, narrow shoulders, and straight forelegs, showing good bone, with strong, well-knit feet. The coat should not be long, but hard to the touch.

The following is the Irish Terrier Club's standard description referred to:

SCALE OF POINTS FOR JUDGING IRISH TERRIERS.

POSITIVE POINTS.

Head, ears, and expression	20
Legs and feet	15
Neck	5
Shoulders and chest	10
Back and loin	5
Hindquarters and stern	10
Coat	15
Colour	10
Size and symmetry	10
Total	**100**

NEGATIVE POINTS.

White nails, toes, and feet	minus 10
Much white on chest	,, 10
Dark shadings on face	,, 5
Mouth undershot or cankered	,, 10
Coat shaggy, curly, or soft	,, 10
Uneven in colour	,, 5
Total	**50**

DESCRIPTIVE PARTICULARS.

HEAD.—Long; skull flat, and rather narrow between ears, getting slightly narrower towards the eye; free from wrinkles; stop hardly visible except in profile. The jaw must be strong and muscular, but not too full in the cheek, and of a good punishing length. There should be a slight falling away below the eye, so as not to have a Greyhound appearance. Hair on face of same description as on body, but short (about a quarter of an inch long), in appearance almost smooth and straight; a slight beard is the only longish hair (and it is only long in comparison with the rest) that is permissible, and that is characteristic.

TEETH.—Should be strong and level.

LIPS.—Not so tight as a Bull-terrier's, but well-fitting, showing through the hair their black lining.

NOSE.—Must be black.

Eyes.—A dark hazel colour, small, not prominent, and full of life, fire, and intelligence.

Ears.—Small and V-shaped, of moderate thickness, set well on the head, and dropping forward closely to the cheek. The ear must be free of fringe, and the hair thereon shorter and darker in colour than the body.

Neck.—Should be of a fair length, and gradually widening towards the shoulders, well carried, and free of throatiness. There is generally a slight sort of frill visible at each side of the neck, running nearly to the corner of the ear.

Shoulders and Chest.—Shoulders must be fine, long, and sloping well into the back; the chest deep and muscular, but neither full nor wide.

Back and Loin.—Body moderately long; back should be strong and straight, with no appearance of slackness behind the shoulders; the loin broad and powerful, and slightly arched; ribs fairly sprung, rather deep than round, and well-ribbed back.

Hindquarters.—Should be strong and muscular, thighs powerful, hocks near ground, stifles moderately bent.

Stern.—Generally docked; should be free of fringe or feather, but well covered with rough hair, set on pretty high, carried gaily, but not over the back or curled.

Feet and Legs.—Feet should be strong, tolerably round, and moderately small; toes arched, and neither turned out nor in; black toe nails most desirable. Legs moderately long, well set from the shoulders, perfectly straight, with plenty of bone and muscle; the elbows working freely clear of the sides; pasterns short and straight, hardly noticeable. Both fore and hind legs should be moved straight forward when travelling, the stifles not turned outwards, the legs free of feather, and covered, like the head, with as hard a texture of coat as body, but not so long.

Coat.—Hard and wiry, free of softness or silkiness, not so long as to hide the outlines of the body, particularly in the hindquarters, straight and flat, no shagginess, and free of lock or curl.

Colour.—Should be " whole-coloured," the most preferable being bright red, red-wheaten, or yellow-red. White sometimes appears on chest and feet; it is more objectionable on the latter than on the chest, as a speck of white on chest is frequently to be seen in all self-coloured breeds.

Size and Symmetry.—The most desirable weight in show condition is for a dog 27lb., and for a bitch 25lb. The dog must present an active, lively, lithe, and wiry appearance; lots of substance, at the same time free of clumsiness, as speed and endurance as well as power are very essential. They must be neither " cloddy nor cobby," but should be framed on the " lines of speed," showing a graceful " racing outline."

Temperament.—Dogs that are very game are usually surly or snappish. The Irish Terrier as a breed is an exception, being remarkably good-tempered, notably so with mankind, it being admitted, however, that he is perhaps a little too ready to resent interference on the part of other dogs. There is a heedless, reckless pluck about the Irish Terrier which is characteristic, and, coupled with the headlong dash, blind to all consequences, with which he rushes at his adversary, has earned for the breed the proud epithet of " The Dare Devils." When " off duty " they are characterised by a quiet, caress-inviting appearance, and when one sees them endearingly, timidly pushing their heads into their masters' hands, it is difficult to realise that on occasions, at the " set on," they can prove they have the courage of a lion, and will fight unto the last breath in their bodies. They develop an extraordinary devotion to, and have been known to track their masters almost incredible distances.

CHAPTER XXI.

The Kerry Blue Terrier.

The advent of the Kerry Blue Terrier in England as a show specimen only dates back to about 1920, but in Ireland the dog is of considerable antiquity, and it is possible greater than that of his first cousin, the Irish Terrier, certainly in the county of Kerry.

Mr. Cotton, in my old and esteemed friend, the late Rawdon B. Lee's work, " Modern Dogs," published in 1894, writes as follows :—

There is a glen, Imaal, in the Wicklow mountains, that has always been, and still is, justly celebrated for its Terriers. It would be hard to specify their colour in particular—the wheaten in all shades to that of bright red. In Kerry I think the black-blue is most prevalent; quite black very uncommon, and I hardly ever saw a good specimen

KERRY BLUE TERRIER.

that colour. Mr. Charles Galway, of Waterford, the breeder of the celebrated Greyhound, Master McGrath, for years—long before the Irish Terrier came into fashion—always kept and bred the variety, and, I am told, there was no getting one from him. I am also informed the coats of his Terriers were rather inclined to curl, and that the dogs themselves were undeniably game.

The Kerry Blue Terrier has been exhibited at shows in Ireland as far back as towards the close of the last century, but in no great numbers. At the Cork shows there were special classes for them, where they were judged by local enthusiasts on the lines which appealed most to each individual judge, as there was no club for the breed and no standard of points laid down as a guide.

The Kerry Blue Terrier has always been a game, hard-bitten Terrier, specimens having been attached to Fox-hunts and otter hounds and Badger "Digs" in different parts of Ireland, owing to his gameness and hardihood.

It was not until about 1920 that the breed began to come to the front as a show dog, and devotees of the Kerry Blue subsequently banded themselves together and formed themselves into a club for the purpose of the dog's promotion and advancement, which took place almost simultaneously in both England and Ireland—England taking the lead.

In connection with the Irish club I cull the following paragraph from the pen of Mr. J. A. Carbery, a devotee of the breed, in the "Echoes from Erin" columns of "Our Dogs" Christmas number of 1924:—

At a general meeting of the Dublin Blue Irish Terrier Club, recently held, a standard which was passed unanimously may be given as the perfect one—and from which I quote a few points. The most desirable weight for a fully developed dog is 33 to 40lb., bitches proportionately less. Coat, soft. and plentiful. Head, strong and well balanced, showing plenty of hair, with a slight "stop." Foreface of medium length. Jaw strong and muscular. Nose (black nostrils), strong and wide. Teeth, level, large, and white. Gums and roof of mouth, dark. Ears, thin and not large, carried in front or close to the sides of the head. Eyes, dark, or dark to hazel. Back, medium length, not long over loins. Ribs, well sprung. Thighs, muscular, well developed, strong hocks. Hind legs, well set under the dog. Colour, blue of any shade from light blue to dark blue, or blue and tan (*i.e.*, tan on head and legs). In any adult dog, while a little white on the front (chest) may be tentatively permitted, the object of the Club is to obliterate the hereditary blemish ; and, while a judge may not disqualify an otherwise typical dog because of a few white hairs on the chest, yet this blemish should be penalised.

The Kerry Blue Terrier Club of England was founded in 1922, with the Earl of Kenmare, a great Irish devotee of the breed, as first President, Mrs. Fred Appleby chairman, and Mr. J. H. F. Barlow honorary secretary-treasurer. This was at Cruft's great International Show in the Royal Agricultural Hall, London, where classes for the breed were given for the first time in England. From this time on the dog rapidly grew in public favour and esteem, classes for the breed being given at all the leading shows, and the breed being recognised by the Kennel Club and placed upon its register. The rise in public esteem and popularity of the breed was simultaneous in Ireland, where the Irish Kennel Club took the breed specially under its wing. The All-Ireland Kerry Blue Terrier Club was founded, and was a huge success from the start. The entries at the Irish Kennel Club's Show of 1923 were 290, and, in 1924, 351. Those at the All-Ireland Kerry Blue Terrier Club's Specialist Show in 1923 were 246, and, in 1924, 307.

In England the breed progressed similarly or to an even greater extent, the barometer of entries of the breed rising at each leading show, and the breed, as time went on, enlisting fresh recruits in all parts of both England and Ireland.

The following is the standard description of the Kerry Blue Terrier Club of England :—

HEIGHT AT SHOULDER.—Dogs, 18in. ; bitches, slightly less.
WEIGHT.—Dogs, 33 to 35lb. ; bitches, 30 to 33lb.
HEAD.—Long and strong.
SKULL.—Flat, very slight "stop."
JAWS.—Strong and deep, nearly level with cheeks.
MOUTH.—Even, strong, level teeth.
NOSE.—Black.
EARS.—Not too heavy, V-shaped, and carried close to sides of the head or over the eyes.
EYES.—Black or dark brown, showing fire and intelligence.
NECK.—Muscular and moderately long.
SHOULDERS.—Well sloped to back.

CHEST.—Muscular and deep, neither full nor too wide.
BACK.—Strong and straight, medium length, well coupled.
LOINS.—Broad and powerful.
RIBS.—Fairly well sprung; deep, rather than round.
HINDQUARTERS.—Strong and muscular, showing good development.
THIGHS.—Powerful. Hocks strong and near to the ground. Dew claws preferably absent.
FEET.—Strong and fairly round. Toe nails, black; pads, clear of cracks.
FORELEGS.—Straight, plenty of bone and muscle; elbows working clear of sides.
TAIL.—Carried gaily, but not curled over the back.
COLOUR.—Any shade of blue from light to dark; slight tan allowable up to age of 18 months, after which tan markings to constitute a disqualification.
COAT.—Soft to touch; weather-resisting. The head and feet should be clear; body fullcoated, but tidy. The whole of the coat must be soft.
GENERAL APPEARANCE.—Active, hardy, and wiry, with plenty of substance, indicating strength without clumsiness. Must show gameness and intelligence.

SERIOUS DEFECTS.

Weak mouth and jaw, bumpy cheeks, white toe nails, light eyes.

DISQUALIFICATIONS.

Faking or dyeing.

Under the ægis of the standard descriptions and points of the first Irish and English Clubs (although, in the writer's opinion, a little irrational in places), the breed has been greatly improved from its original crude character to a sound, symmetrical, and utility-looking Terrier. The thick skulls, short forefaces, crooked fronts, and long backs, so objectionable in any Terrier, are fast disappearing and giving place to more proportionate skulls, powerful jaws, straight fronts and nicely balanced frames. The description of the head as being "long and strong" would indicate that the longer and stronger the head the better; but a very long head in a dog is rarely strong, and a strong head rarely long. A well-balanced head in proportion to the body, neither too long and narrow, nor too broad, possesses the most ntelligence. The provision for toe nails being black reminds one of the mythical notion that a dog is not pure-bred unless the roof of its mouth is black. There is an old saying that "a good horse cannot be a bad colour," and I would say that in such a small and absolutely unimportant detail as toe nails they could not be a bad colour in a good dog.

The best points to look for in a Kerry Blue puppy are: short back, deep chest, great bone, strong foreface, and small ears. Puppies are usually born black, the blue colour developing later.

CHAPTER XXII.

The Sealyham Terrier.

The following article on the breed is reprinted from " Our Dogs," and was contributed by Mr. Fred W. Lewis, a keen admirer and a successful breeder and exhibitor, who, being on the spot, has studied the subject closely :—

The Sealyham Terrier's rise to fame and popularity has been rapid and permanent. Previous to the Kennel Club Show in October, 1910, the breed was comparatively unknown to the English exhibitor, and it fell to my privilege to be chiefly instrumental in introducing the Pembrokeshire production to the English public.

At the show in question I offered personally to guarantee several classes, provided the Kennel Club consented to their inclusion in the schedule. The

SEALYHAM TERRIER.

ruling authority agreed to this course, and four classes were allocated to Sealyhams, and also, on my suggestion, Mr. H. Ridley was appointed to judge. The result was quite a decent entry, averaging, I think, six exhibits per class. In Open Dogs, Ch. Dandy Bach, which I had just sold to Lord Kensington, was placed 1st ; Ch. Whisky Bach, then my property, came 2nd ; while Ch. St. Bride's Demon, exhibited by Lord Kensington, was placed 3rd. In Open Bitches, Ch. St. Bride's Delight took premier honours, 2nd going to Ch. Bess Bach, then owned by Mr. Charles Wynn-Griffith. It will thus be seen that the winners of that time must have been pretty good specimens, inasmuch as most of them subsequently acquired championship honours, and have continued their successful show-bench career down to the present day. This is more or less an interesting feature, as showing that, notwithstanding the enormous amount of breeding that has since taken place, few individual good specimens have been produced. But there can be no question that the breed, as a whole, has vastly improved during the last four years, and the noticeable uniformity amongst the large numbers of Sealyhams which now appear at all the leading shows is evidence of much care and attention on the part of breeders.

The origin of the Sealyham is more or less wrapped in obscurity, but there are several features of interest which I think I am in a position to lay before my readers, and which will give an approximate idea of how the Sealyham was first evolved and came to be recognised as a distinct breed.

Captain John Edwardes was an eccentric sporting gentleman of noble birth, and resided at Sealyham, an attractive country mansion situate between Haverfordwest and Fishguard, and which is now in the occupation of Mr. and Mrs. Victor Higgon, the latter a well-known breeder and judge, and chairman of the Sealyham Terrier Club since its formation in January, 1908. The Terrier is called after the residence of its founder.

Captain Edwardes, as I have just stated, was a great sportsman, and he conceived the idea that the mongrel dog of sixty or more years ago which he was obliged to use in his numerous sporting excursions was not quite the kind of animal for bolting the fox and otter, or digging out the badger, which he wished for. There seems little doubt that the Terrier of that date was more or less a nondescript kind of creature, with no pretension to beauty or breeding, nor with the least claim to uniformity of type. It will therefore be apparent that to evolve a short-legged, smart, workmanlike Terrier which, above all other considerations, must be dead game, was a problem not easy of solution, and only a man possessed of indomitable courage and tenacity would have persevered in his efforts to realise an ideal which repeated failures must sometimes have indicated was incapable of accomplishment. But Captain Edwardes, in his lonely country mansion, plodded on, and by careful selection and judicious breeding eventually established a short-legged, rough-haired Terrier capable of facing any vermin then prevalent in the county. At this period the polecat was fairly plentiful in the dense woods abounding in the vicinity of the Captain's residence, and the old gent made it a *sine qua non* that no dog should be given lodging at Sealyham which would not dispose of a full-grown specimen of the *Putorius fœtidus;* and anyone who has seen these denizens of the forest will at once realise that the standard of pluck fixed by the gallant Captain was by no means insignificant.

His method of testing the young dogs, which took place when they were about a year old, was as follows : A live polecat was dragged across a field, and then enclosed in a small pit, roughly a couple of feet deep, with an entrance about the size of an ordinary badger's hole. The quarry was secured with sufficient liberty to enable him to put up a fair and square fight. As the polecat is a notoriously odoriferous animal, the dog, which would previously have done plenty of ratting, usually experienced no difficulty in following the trail and arriving at the spot where the length of its stay in the world was to be decided by the character of the combat which then took place. If the dog "went in" and killed, all well and good ; if he funked the encounter and minced about outside, and declined to tackle his quarry, his doom was sealed. But our old friend was not always wise in his estimate of the character of his dog. One day a particularly good ratting dog turned craven, and refused to tackle the polecat. Every facility and encouragement was given, but without effect. The verdict was soon pronounced—the coward must die. The man who had walked the dog had become attached to the Terrier, and begged hard that, as he was such an excellent ratter and so useful to him about the farm, he might be allowed to keep him. A reluctant consent was given, and before the dog was a year older he turned out one of the gamest Terriers ever bred at Sealyham, and the old Captain subsequently purchased him from the farmer. The dog lived to a ripe old age, and when he died was mourned as one of the best tykes that ever went to earth. There is nothing exceptional in this experience, and I have no doubt that many readers, like myself, could relate similar examples of a dog not really developing until he had reached two years of age or so.

To come to the present-day Sealyham it is necessary to jump several decades.

The standard of points drawn up, and subsequently adopted in a slightly amended form by the Sealyham Terrier Club at its first meeting in January, 1908, conveys, I think, a very fair and accurate description of a Sealyham Terrier.

It is often stated that there must be no resemblance to the Fox-terrier. I agree, but I don't agree with those breeders who prefer a Sealyham showing more resemblance to a Clumber Spaniel than to a Fox-terrier. Of two evils, I prefer the Fox-terrier type. But it is certainly not necessary to have either. I think the Sealyham should have a wider skull, shorter and wider jaw, broader chest, longer body, more profuse and harder coat, and, of course, very much shorter legs, than the Fox-terrier. When I add that larger ears are also permissible, I think I have covered the chief characteristics of the dog.

I am surprised to find in the standard of points issued by a new club that "black markings are objectionable, even on head and ears, and a large black spot on the body should almost be a disqualification as showing Fox-terrier blood." Now, such rubbish should not be permitted to pass unchallenged. I agree that none of us care for body markings of any description, but to say that black body markings are evidence of Fox-terrier blood shows an astonishing ignorance of the history of the Sealyham in particular, and of dogs in general.

My object in referring to this matter is to prevent novices from being misled by such nonsense, and they will no doubt be surprised to learn that I have bred scores of puppies by Huntsman and Peer Gynt with any amount of dark body markings, and I do not suppose anyone will dare dispute the statement that the Sealyham Terrier of to-day owes more to these two dogs than to any other specimen, living or dead.

In conclusion, I do hope the novice will not be led away by the glamour of misleading descriptions. Let him be careful to consult a rational standard, and then endeavour to breed specimens as near to it as possible, and consign the fantastic fallacies of the newly fledged theorists to the melting-pot of immaturity.

Standard of Points adopted by the Sealyham Terrier Club.

Head.—The skull slightly domed, and wide between the ears.

Jaw.—Powerful and long, with a punishing and squarer jaw.

Nose.—Black.

Teeth.—Level and square, strong, and canines fitting well into each other, and long for size of dog.

Eyes.—Dark, well set, round, and of medium size.

Ears.—Size, medium; slightly rounded at tip, and carried at side of cheek.

Neck.—Fairly long, thick and muscular, strongly set on sloping shoulders.

Chest.—Broad and deep, well let down between forelegs.

Body.—Medium length and ribs well sprung, hindquarters very strong, body very flexible.

Legs and Feet.—The legs short, strong, and straight as possible; feet round and catlike, with thick pads.

Stern.—Carried gaily.

Coat.—Long, hard, and wiry.

Colour.—Mostly all white, or white with lemon, brown, or badger-pied markings on head and ears.

Weight.—Dogs not to exceed 20lb.; bitches not to exceed 18lb.

Height.—Not exceeding 12in. at the shoulder.

Action.—Free and active.

FAULTS.

EYES.—Light-coloured or small.

NOSE.—White, cherry, or spotted to a considerable extent with either of these colours.

EARS.—Prick, tulip, or rose.

COLOUR.—Much black objectionable.

TEETH.—Defective.

DISQUALIFYING POINTS.

MUZZLE much undershot or overshot.

SCALE OF POINTS.

	Value.
Head	10
Eyes	10
Ears	5
Neck	5
Body	15
Tail	2
Legs and feet	15
Coat	20
Colour	3
Size and weight	15
Total	100

The most desirable points to look for in the selection of a puppy are: Short legs, great bone, a strong, long jaw, level mouth, and a coat as harsh to the touch as possible.

CHAPTER XXIII.

The Scottish Terrier

Occupies a foremost position in the affections of the fancying public, whilst his immediate admirers are very enthusiastic in singing his praises as an intelligent member of the canine race, a sensible and devoted companion, and a hardy, game, and useful vermin dog and watchman.

As the dog's name implies, he is of Scottish origin. Scotland boasts of several distinct varieties of Terriers—the Skye, the Scottish, the Dandie Dinmont, the Paisley, the Clydesdale, the West Highland White, and Cairn Terriers—all indigenous to different districts of Scotland, all rough-haired, all prick-eared (except the Dandie), all more or less of the long and low type, and doubtless all of one common origin.

The original *habitat* of the Scottish Terrier was the North of Scotland, and more particularly the neighbourhood of Aberdeen, this being the name

SCOTTISH TERRIER.

with which he was at first identified, over fifty years ago. As, however, specimens were found in other parts of Scotland, the dog, by common consent, gradually lost his local nomenclature, and received the more general appellation. Being a smaller dog than most of his confrères in Scotland, he was and is still used more generally as an underground dog, and more especially as a Fox-terrier, his wiry coat being a greater protection to him than that of the English Fox-terrier during the rigours of a Highland winter; indeed, in some parts of Scotland he was called Fox-terrier—at least, such of the rough-haired Terriers as were used, who were doubtless somewhat different from the ideal Scottie of to-day.

It is due to the advent of dog shows that the beautiful Scottish Terrier of to-day, with his marked characteristics, differing from any and every other variety of Terrier, has been produced from the material that existed at the time.

" Scotch Terriers," so-called, were exhibited at the earliest dog shows in

England, but they included Skyes and what we would now term nondescripts—Scottish Terriers of various colours, sizes, and shapes. At the Birmingham Show of 1860 there was a class for "Scotch Terriers," the winners in which were all Skyes, while this variety was first classified at the Manchester (Belle Vue) Show in 1861. At Leeds Show in that year the entries in the "Scotch Terrier" classes consisted of a sort of enlarged Yorkshire Terrier, which were doubtless the foundation of the present-day liliputian beauties of this variety. At Birmingham, in 1862, Dandies were classified, and a class was given for "Other Scotch Terriers," which included these shorter-backed and smaller editions of the early Scottish Terrier (the progenitors of the Yorkshire), Skyes, etc. At the Cremorne Show of 1863 " Scotch " Terriers were classified as follows: White, fawn, blue, Skye, and Dandie Dinmont. At the Agricultural Hall Show (London) in 1864 there were two classes for Scotch Terriers, which were divided by weight—viz., over 7lb. and under 7lb.,—and the same at Manchester in the same year, with the qualification added in the over-weight class of "ears uncut." At the Crystal Palace Show (K.C.), in 1875, they were termed "Rough Scotch Terriers," at which show there was a class for "Broken-haired Scotch or Yorkshire Terriers."

Here, then, we see the first introduction of the Scottish Terrier as a show dog, contemporaneously with the Yorkshire Terrier, from whom he sprang, the one in its evolution making in the direction of a diminutive silken-haired Toy, and the other, in his development, taking a course more in the direction of a utility dog, a hardy little sportsman.

In 1882 a club was formed for the breed, with the following office-bearers : President: J. B. Morrison. Vice-presidents: D. J. Thomson Gray, Scotland; Albert Krehl, England. Hon. Secretaries: J. A. Adamson, Scotland; H. Blomfield, England. Hon. Treasurers: W. H. Benoil, Scotland; H. J. Ludlow, England. Committee: J. L. Grainger, Capt. Mackie, A. S. Sutherland, Scotland; John Pirie, W. W. Spelman, England.

This club was in existence for some considerable time, and the formation of the two other clubs was the outcome of its dissolution. From the complexion of its officers, the club was national in its constitution, embracing zealots in both Scotland and England. Mr. J. B. Morrison, President and life member of the Scottish Terrier Club (Scotland), drew up the standard of points, which was approved by the committee, and this standard, with a few minor alterations, is still the one by which the breed is judged.

The Scottish Terrier Club (England) was founded in 1887, being the first club responsible for the dog's change of name. A year later the Scottish Terrier Club (Scotland) was launched. In due course other clubs, offshoots of the parent clubs, in the North of England Scottish Terrier Club, the South of England Scottish Terrier Club, and others, came into being.

There are few breeds in which the type and characteristics are so fixed and undisputed by the cognoscenti. Therefore it is pretty plain sailing for the novice and amateur in his efforts to arrive at the ideal.

The original Scottish Terrier was, like most breeds, bred purely for work and upon no recognised lines. That accounted for the great divergence of type. Some of the early exhibition specimens even differed greatly in size and type, the crudeness of which has now almost entirely disappeared. Many specimens were too big, and most were very long in body and very crooked in their forelegs. In later years breeders seem to have set themselves the task of obliterating the two last-named defects, in which they have not entirely, but eminently, succeeded. Shorter bodies and better fronts having been, as it were, the watchword in the breed for years, to-day a long-backed or crooked-fronted dog very properly will not, for a moment, be tolerated. In this connection I think the Scottish Terrier Club's description, given herewith, requires revision, especially where it provides for the sides of the dog being rather flat. This body formation would, to-day, surely be regarded as a defect. With the short bodies have naturally come *well-sprung ribs*, which all our best dogs possess, and which ought to be rigidly enforced. Flat sides are a sure indication of a faint heart, just as well-sprung ribs give great heart room and denote pluck and perseverance. Another blemish in the earlier specimens was big ears. Nowadays, happily, big ears are the exception, and not the rule. The Club's description makes half-prick ears admissible, but this is a rule honoured more in the breach than the observance, for few judges would, I opine, to-day give a prize to a half-prick-eared Scottie. This clause, with that of flat sides, might well be eliminated from the Club's code, and small prick ears and well-sprung ribs be substituted. In almost all other respects, the standard may be said to describe fairly accurately our very best specimens of to-day, and to be such as any breeder and exhibitor may well hold before him as a guide to the cult of the Diehard as viewed through the most modern optics. His features may be summed up as follows :—A sturdy, shortish-coupled dog, with compact body, well-sprung ribs, big quarters, standing on short legs, perfectly straight front, a long head, powerful punishing jaws, small dark eye, and small sharp-pointed, erect ears, with a weather-resisting wiry coat—a dog of from 16lb. to 20lb. weight, who gives the impression of gameness and hardihood, and whose sound architecture and symmetry together are such as to enable him to go to ground, and to be of some use when he gets there. The defects to avoid are pig jaws (it is very rare that a Scottie is undershot, although it is also a defect), thick heads, full eyes, big ears, long backs, bad fronts, and soft coats, whilst weeds are just as objectionable as dogs of elephantine proportions. Colour is of little consequence, but the darker colours are preferable, giving the appearance of greater hardihood, although, of course, colour cannot affect this most desirable quality in the dog.

The chief points to look for in the selection of Scottish Terrier puppies at from two to four months old and after are :—A long, level head, strong jaw, small, dark eye, small. erect ears, carried close together, short, round body, short sickle tail, great bone, straight forelegs, and a dense, hard coat.

The standard is as follows :—

SKULL.—Proportionately long, slightly domed, and covered with short hard hair, about ¾in. long, or less. It should not be quite flat, as there should be a sort of stop, or drop, between the eyes.

MUZZLE.—Very powerful, and gradually tapering towards the nose, which should always be black, and of a good size. The jaws should be perfectly level, and the teeth square, though the nose projects somewhat over the mouth, which gives the impression of the upper jaw being longer than the under one.

EYES.—A dark brown or hazel colour ; small, piercing, very bright, and rather sunken.

EARS.—Very small, prick or half-prick (the former is preferable), but never drop. They should also be sharp-pointed, and the hair on them should not be long, but velvety, and they should not be cut. The ears should be free from any fringe at the top.

NECK.—Short, thick, and muscular ; strongly set on sloping shoulders.

CHEST.—Broad in comparison to the size of the dog, and proportionately deep.

BODY.—Of moderate length, but not so long as a Skye's, and rather flat-sided ; well ribbed-up, and exceedingly strong in hindquarters.

LEGS AND FEET.—Both fore and hind legs should be short, and very heavy in bone, the former being straight, and well set-on under the body, as the Scottish Terrier should not be out at elbows. The hocks should be bent, and the thighs very muscular ; and the feet strong, small, and thickly covered with short hair, the forefeet being larger than the hind ones.

THE TAIL.—Should be about 7in. long, never docked, carried with a slight bend, and often gaily.

THE COAT.—Should be rather short (about 2in.), intensely hard and wiry in texture, and very dense all over the body.

SIZE.—From 15lb. to 20lb.; the best weight being as near as possible 18lb. for dogs, and 16lb. for bitches, when in condition for work.

COLOUR.—Steel or iron grey, black-brindle, brown-brindle, grey-brindle, black, sandy, and wheaten. White markings are objectionable, and can only be allowed on the chest, and to a small extent.

GENERAL APPEARANCE.—The face should wear a very sharp, bright, and active expression, and the head should be carried up. The dog (owing to the shortness of his coat) should appear to be higher on the leg than he really is; but, at the same time, he should look compact, and possessed of great muscle in his hindquarters. In fact, a Scottish Terrier, though essentially a Terrier, cannot be too powerfully put together, and should be from about 9in. to 12in. in height.

SPECIAL FAULTS.

MUZZLE.—Either under or over hung.

EYES.—Large or light-coloured.

EARS.—Large, round at the points, or drop. It is also a fault if they are too heavily covered with hair.

LEGS.—Bent or slightly bent, and out at elbows.

COAT.—Any silkiness, wave, or tendency to curl is a serious blemish, as is also an open coat.

SIZE.—Specimens of over 20lb. should be discouraged.

SCALE OF POINTS.

Skull	Value 7½
Muzzle	,, 7½
Eyes	,, 5
Ears	,, 5
Neck	,, 5
Chest	,, 5
Body	,, 15
Legs and feet	,, 10
Tail	,, 2½
Coat	,, 15
Size	,, 10
Colour	,, 2½
General appearance	,, 10
	100

CHAPTER XXIV.

The Welsh Terrier,

Which saw the light as a show dog about the year 1886, has not "caught on" with the public as his merit deserves. It was in that year that the Welsh Terrier Club was founded, mainly through the instrumentality of Mr. Weldon Williams, Mr. W. A. Dew, of Bangor, and one or two others who took up cudgels in his behalf against a rival section of Englishmen, who contended that the black-and-tan broken-haired Terrier was of English origin. In this connection, Welshmen forestalled their English friends by forming themselves into a club, and getting the name of the breed registered with the Kennel Club, while the latter were discussing the subject. The breed was first exhibited in that year under its new nomenclature.

WELSH TERRIER.

In spite of the dog's comparatively modern origin as a show dog, Welshmen claim considerable antiquity for the present-day Welsh Terrier, and that he is indigenous to the Principality, in which they are no doubt perfectly correct. The English edition of the dog, if I may so put it, was exhibited anterior to this, under the name of the Old English Broken-haired Black-and-tan Terrier, the two dogs or breeds being very similar, and doubtless have one common origin. For a time much rivalry existed between the two contingents, Old English Broken-haired Black-and-tan Terriers being exhibited in Welsh Terrier classes, and *vice versa*. At one show—Darlington—much comment was created by Mr. H. M. Bryans' dog, Dick Turpin, being entered, competing, and winning under *both* classifications. I mention this to show that at this time the two breeds were very similar, although later developments separated them somewhat, when they began to take up a more distinctive form. Welshmen were content with a shorter and thicker head and fuller eye, whilst for the Old English Broken-haired Terrier Englishmen insisted upon a long, lean, punishing jaw, and did not object to the dog's legs being shorter than that of his Welsh rival, and the general size a shade larger. Upon these details of anatomy the two sections were now content to a peaceful dissolution of partnership, with the result that the Welsh Terrier forged his way to the front, leaving his English duplicate far behind, until, by the apathy of his admirers, he has almost become extinct as a show dog.

That the Welsh Terrier is a smart, gay, game, and useful little dog goes without saying. A dog of about 20lbs. weight, he is beautiful in his proportions, and well balanced throughout, with a wiry, workmanlike coat, an intelligent outlook, and a buoyant disposition. He should have straight forelegs, and short, cat-like feet, and although most of the best dogs on the show bench excel in these points, an indifferent front is one of the prevailing defects in the breed. Worse than this, however, are the short heads, which are an even more common defect in the breed. In the earlier stages of the evolution of the breed, Englishmen sought to " improve " the head by crosses with good-headed Wire-haired Fox-terriers, which I always considered a very judicious cross, and which for a time improved the breed. The Welsh Terrier Club, however, resolutely set its face against such a cross, and refused to recognise any dogs whose pedigree was not pure Welsh. Thus it is that the breed has suffered, and there can be little doubt that this head question has been one of the causes of the breed failing to maintain the progress it was at one time making, coupled probably with the fact of the breed having largely drifted into the hands of a few keen enthusiasts, who have established large kennels, and so exercised a sort of monopoly over the prize lists at shows.

As the " head and front of his offending," it would seem to be wise policy on the part of his present devotees to pay more attention to the improvement of this portion of the dog's anatomy, which I feel sure would go far to assist him in regaining his popularity. In all Terrier varieties, the head is one of the most important properties, for what is a Terrier with a short head and weak foreface worth or fit for? Welsh Terriers generally excel in body, coat, and colour, and if these two prevailing defects could be improved we should have an ideal Terrier as either a workman or a companion.

The chief points to look for in the selection of Welsh Terrier puppies at from two to four months old and after are almost identical with those detailed for Wire-haired Fox-terriers, with the variation of colour.

The following is the standard description formulated by the Welsh Terrier Club, to which little exception can be taken, unless it is to the skull being " rather wide between the ears " :—

Points of the Welsh Terrier

(As Defined and Adopted by the Welsh Terrier Club since the Year 1886).

HEAD.—The skull should be flat, and rather wider between the ears than the Wire-haired Fox-terrier. The jaw should be powerful, clean cut, rather deeper, and more punishing—giving the head a more masculine appearance than that usually seen on a Fox-terrier. Stop not too defined ; fair length from stop to end of nose, the latter being of a black colour.

EARS.—The ear should be V-shaped, small, not too thin, set on airly high, carried forward and close to the cheek.

EYES.—The eye should be small, not being too deeply set in or protruding out of skull, of a dark hazel colour, expressive, and indicating abundant pluck.

NECK.—The neck should be of moderate length and thickness, slightly arched, and sloping gracefully into the shoulders.

BODY.—The back should be short and well ribbed-up, the loin strong, good depth, and moderate width of chest. The shoulders should be long, sloping, and well set back. The hindquarters should be strong, thighs muscular, and of good length, with the hocks moderately straight, well let down, and fair amount of bone. The stern should be set on moderately high, but not too gaily carried.

LEGS AND FEET.—The legs should be straight and muscular, possessing fair amount of bone, with upright and powerful pasterns. The feet should be small, round, and cat-like.

COAT.—The coat should be wiry, hard, very close, and abundant.

COLOUR.—The colour should be black-and-tan, or black grizzle-and-tan, free from black pencilling on toes.

SIZE.—The height at shoulder should be 15in. for dogs, bitches proportionately less. 20lb. shall be considered a fair average weight in working condition, but this may vary a pound or so either way.

STANDARD OF POINTS.

Head and jaws	10
Ears	5
Eyes	5
Neck and shoulders	10
Body	10
Loins and hindquarters	10
Legs and feet	10
Coat	15
Colour	5
Stern	5
General appearance	15
Total	100

DISQUALIFYING POINTS.

1. Nose white or cherry, or spotted to a considerable extent with either of these colours.
2. Ears prick, tulip, or rose.
3. Undershot jaw or Pug-jawed mouth.
4. Black below the hocks to any appreciable extent.

CHAPTER XXV.

The Old English Broken-haired Terrier.

As I have already stated, in the matter of a club this ancient English breed was, as an exhibition specimen with a club to watch over his interests and guide his destiny, forestalled by his Welsh brother, and is one of the few breeds for which a specialist club does not exist, but perhaps *the only* breed which calls for one to save it from utter extinction. Somewhere about a quarter of a century must have elapsed since a specimen of this breed was exhibited, and indeed the dog has never had much acquaintance with the show bench. As a kennel Terrier and companion, however, his name is writ large in the history of country sport, and he is doubtless to a great degree the progenitor of the more popular and plentiful Fox-terrier and Airedale Terrier. The black-and-tan broken-haired Old English Terrier is a dog of very great antiquity. He is shown in some of the oldest sporting prints and paintings, no sportsman's establishment in the olden time being considered complete without him. His ranks seem to have been thinned, even in the hunting field, whilst he is now nearly unknown on the show bench. One feels at a loss to conceive how such a sterling Terrier in make and shape, in hardihood and grit, should have been allowed to lapse into obscurity. No breed, alike from the point of view of antiquity, tradition, appearance, and utility, was or is more deserving of perpetuation. Those who knew only the two dogs, Old Adam and Young Adam, their deeds of valour underground, and their behaviour above ground, would be constrained to admit they possessed traits to be cherished in the heart of anyone who loved a dog for his worth and not for what he would fetch in the market. While the world admires the beautiful Fox-terrier and Airedale Terrier, who abound in the land and who owe most of their Terrier traits, external and internal, to this ancestor, the Old English Broken-haired Terrier, the latter has been lost sight of, and has almost entirely passed into history "unhonoured and unsung."

The chief differences between the O.E.B. Terrier and the Welsh Terrier, as already stated, are in size, the latter being a few pounds heavier, say from 20lb. to 25lb., in body, and head, both of which are longer. The Englishman should have a long, strong, punishing jaw, level mouth, and flat skull, free from cheekiness, and a small, dark, determined eye. His fault was in length of body and front, and in anyone taking up the breed these are the defects to correct. His bone was always good, and coat hard to the touch. His colours are black-and-tan and grizzle-and-tan.

CHAPTER XXVI.

The Dandie Dinmont Terrier

Is a variety of Terrier of considerable antiquity. Originating on the borders of Scotland, and made famous by Sir Walter Scott in his "Guy Mannering," he is doubtless a descendant of the Scottish Terriers—the Scottie or Skye,—since he partakes of both, to some extent, in type and character (being short on leg and long in body), more particularly the former, except that his ears drop instead of being prick. Doubtless the Dandie and Border Terrier, which is a smaller dog with drop ears, and with which the Dandie is often confounded, have a common origin. The Dandie *was* doubtless also a Border Terrier long anterior to the appearance of Sir Walter Scott's novel, to the author of which is due the name given to the type of Terriers kept by such personages of the time as James Davidson, of Hindlee, who died in 1820, or six years after the appearance of "Guy Mannering," and other yeomen of the time, in the Liddesdale district, with whom Sir Walter came

DANDIE DINMONT TERRIER

in contact in his peregrinations in this wild and romantic country, which inspired his famous novel. We read, for instance, of the Allans of Holystone, one of whom was the famous "Piper" Allan, born at Bellingham, Northumberland, in 1704, who kept a breed of rough-haired Terriers, doubtless more or less of the Dandie Dinmont type, and who is credited with originating the Bedlington Terrier, another game, hard-bitten breed, of similar type to some extent, but a leggier dog, which used to abound in the more southern mining district of Bedlington, from which town the dog took its name.

The difference in the type of these three Border Terriers—the recognised Border Terrier (who may or may not be the original), the Bedlington, and the Dandie—is due to breeding by selection and to crossing. The Dandie is the one breed who retains most of his Scottish ancestry in body conformation and in head in some respects, and his fusion with the English Broken-haired Terriers is seen in his drop ears, since, while prick ears are characteristic of almost all the Scottish varieties of Terriers, drop ears are a fixed feature of their English brothers.

Some Dandie Dinmont enthusiasts pride themselves on the purity of their strains, for which they allege they can claim direct descent, through the

Terriers of Mr. E. Bradshaw Smith, of Ecclefechan, a great enthusiast in the breed in the early part and middle of the nineteenth century ; of Hugh Purvis and others, to the " Guy Mannering " dogs. Such descent in no way denotes " purity," because it is alleged, for instance, that Purvis crossed his dogs more than once with a brindled Bull-terrier, in order to maintain their courage.

However, the type of the Dandie has long been so fixed, both in colour and conformation, that occasional crosses have not, according to the records, in any way altered it; and to-day it is more sharply defined than at any other period in its history. The great novelist singularly omitted to give us a definite description of his dogs when he created the " Dandie Dinmont," but subsequently he wrote : " The race of pepper and mustard are in the highest estimation at the present day, not only for vermin killing, but for intelligence and fidelity. Those who, like the author, possess a brace of them, consider them as very desirable companions." This proves that Sir Walter Scott kept Dandie Dinmonts, and that he gave a true definition of the dog's splendid character and disposition ; all those who have ever kept the breed since that time will bear willing testimony to the fact.

The Dandie is one of the gamest of Terriers, the most sensible of dogs, and most devoted of canine companions. He is, besides, a hardy, handy-sized dog, makes a capital house dog, and is just as much at home in the kennel—a rough and tumble sort, to which nothing comes wrong, the tackling of fox or badger underground or one of his own species above ground,—and yet, despite his exceptional power and pluck, he stands unexcelled, and rarely equalled, for common sense and docility.

The impetus given to the breed by Sir Walter Scott's " Guy Mannering " is seen in the zest with which it was subsequently taken up by admirers of every rank in society, from peer to peasant. Passing from James Davidson, Dr. Brown, of Bonjedward, and other of their contemporaries, such names as the Duke of Buccleuch, the Hon. G. H. Baillie, of Mellerstain ; John Stoddard, of Selkirk ; Lord Polwarth, F. Somers (Kelso), D. McDougall, Dr. Grant (Hawick), Nicol Milne (owner of Old Jock and Jenny), and James Scott were names to conjure with in the Dandie world following Davidson, as were Dr. William Brown, James Patterson (owner of Old Miss Fame), Miss Mathers, James Hamilton, and J. B. Richardson, of Dumfries, a well-known judge and writer on the breed.

When the Dandie Dinmont Terrier Club became established, the breed, of course, received an additional fillip, further popularising it and bringing to the cult a fresh crop of enthusiasts. The breed was one of the most patronised at dog shows, the great amount of ink which was being expended upon the dog by such keen admirers as my old friends the late Hugh Dalziel (the original author of " British Dogs "), D. J. Thomson Gray (Author of " The Dogs of Scotland "), and Charles Cook, whose monograph on the breed is both interesting and exhaustive, riveting public attention to its quaintness and merit.

The size of the Dandie is somewhat flexible, but the best weights (by which his size can best be ascertained) are : Dogs, from 18lb. to 24lb. ; bitches, a pound or two lighter. No Dandie should be less than 15lb. nor more than 24lb. in weight. The chief features of the dog are his round skull, full eyes, flatly-carried ears, strong jaw, short, stout legs, long, weasel-shaped body, and soft linty coat and topknot. These features have, in later years, been more and more accentuated by the hand of the fancier, who often manipulates the coat, where its growth permits, in "improving upon nature" in the direction of adding to this necessary character and conformation. The defects to avoid, and which are to be deprecated in any Dandie, are snipy forefaces, flat skulls, small or light-coloured eyes, flat backs, light bone, and unsound limbs. The coat should be neither hard nor soft, but of a crisp, linty texture, peculiar to the Dandie. A soft coat—except the topknot, which is always softer than the other part of the coat, and which should be of a lighter shade, profuse, and pronounced—is objectionable, just as a very harsh or wiry coat denotes coarseness in this breed. The forelegs are never straight, showing a curvature in the forearm, but the elbows should never be out, and the pasterns and feet should always be strong. Unsoundness in the forelegs should be a disqualification, and all the defects enumerated should be heavily penalised in the show ring. Colour is of little consequence, but a sound mustard, or what is called a pepper colour, in its various shades, is the correct thing, and, indeed, the only true colours in the breed. A long tail is objectionable, but not a serious blemish, the short, sickle tail being the sort of caudal appendage desired. A point strongly demanded in the Dandie is the size and carriage of the ears, which should be almond shaped, set on low, and lie very close to the head, being smooth-coated, with the edges fringed with longer hair.

Most of the foregoing details are fancier developments from the crude material they found in the original specimens, and which it is considered give a finish to the dog, without detracting in any way from his fundamental requirements, and give to him a feature and character all his own.

The chief points to look for in the selection of Dandie puppies at from two to four months old and after are: A moderately short head, strong muzzle, large dark eye, rather strong, well-bevelled skull, close-set, drop ears, strong neck, rather long body, distinct arch of loin, great bone, and short legs.

The following are the points and description laid down by the Dandie Dinmont Terrier Club :—

HEAD.—Strongly made and large, not out of proportion to the dog's size, the muscles showing extraordinary development, more especially the maxillary. Skull broad between the ears, getting gradually less towards the eyes, and measuring about the same from the inner corner of the eyes to back of skull as it does from ear to ear. The forehead well domed. The head is covered with very soft silky hair, which should not be confined to a mere topknot, and the lighter in colour and silkier it is the better. The cheeks, starting from the ears proportionately with the skull, have a gradual taper towards the muzzle, which is deep and strongly made, and measures about three inches in length, or in proportion to skull as three is to five. The muzzle is covered with hair of a little darker shade than the topknot, and of the same texture as the feather of the forelegs. The top of the muzzle is generally bare for about an inch from the back part of the nose, the bareness coming to a point towards the eye, and being about one inch broad at the nose. The nose and inside of mouth black or dark coloured. The teeth very strong, especially the canine, which are of extraordinary size for such a small dog. The canines fit well into each other, so as to give the greatest available holding and punishing power, and the teeth are level in front, the upper ones very slightly overlapping the under ones. [Many of the finest specimens have a " swine mouth," which is very objectionable, but it is not so great an objection as the protrusion of the underjaw.]

EYES.—Set wide apart, large, full, round, bright, expressive of great determination, intelligence, and dignity; set low and prominent in front of the head; colour, a rich dark hazel.

EARS.—Pendulous, set well back, wide apart, and low on the skull hanging close to the cheek, with a very slight projection at the base, broad at the junction of the head, and tapering almost to a point, the fore part of the ear tapering very little—the tapering being mostly on the back part, the fore part of the ear coming almost straight down from its junction with the head to the tip. They should harmonise in colour with the body colour. In the case of a Pepper dog they are covered with a soft, straight, brownish hair (in some cases almost black). In the case of a Mustard dog the hair should be mustard in colour, a shade darker than the body, but not black. All should have a thin feather of light hair starting about two inches from the tip, and of nearly the same colour and texture as the topknot, which gives the ear the appearance of a distinct point. The animal is often one or two years old before the feather is shown. The cartilage and skin of the ear should not be thick, but rather thin. Length of ear from three to four inches.

NECK.—Very muscular, well developed, and strong, showing great power of resistance, being well set into the shoulders.

BODY.—Long, strong, and flexible; ribs well sprung and round, chest well developed, and let well down between the forelegs; the back rather low at the shoulder, having a slight downward curve, and a corresponding arch over the loins, with a very slight gradual drop from top of loins to root of tail; both sides of backbone well supplied with muscle.

TAIL.—Rather short, say from eight inches to ten inches, and covered on the upper side with wiry hair of darker colour than that of the body, the hair on the under side being lighter in colour, and not so wiry, with nice feather about two inches long, getting shorter as it nears the tip; rather thick at the root, getting thicker for about four inches, then tapering off to a point. It should not be twisted or curled in any way, but should come up with a curve like a scimitar, the tip, when excited, being in a perpendicular line with the root of the tail. It should not be set on too high nor too low. When not excited it is carried gaily, and a little above the level of the body.

LEGS.—The forelegs short, with immense muscular development and bone, set wide apart, the chest coming well down between them. The feet well formed and not flat, with very strong brown or dark-coloured claws. Bandy legs and flat feet are objectionable. The hair on the forelegs and feet of a Pepper dog should be tan, varying according to the body colour from a rich tan to a pale fawn; of a Mustard dog they are of a darker shade than its head, which is a creamy white. In both colours there is a nice feather, about two inches long, rather lighter in colour than the hair on the forepart of the leg. The hind legs are a little longer than the fore ones, and are set rather wide apart, but not spread out in an unnatural manner, while the feet are much smaller; the thighs are well developed, and the hair of the same colour and texture as the fore ones, but having no feather or dew claws; the whole claws should be dark; but the claws of all vary in shade according to the colour of the dog's body.

COAT.—This is a very important point; the hair should be about two inches long; that from skull to root of tail a mixture of hardish and soft hair, which gives a sort of crisp feel to the hand. The hard should not be wiry; the coat is what is termed pily or pencilled. The hair on the under part of the body is lighter in colour and softer than on the top. The skin on the belly accords with the colour of the dog.

COLOUR.—The colour is Pepper or Mustard. The Pepper ranges from a dark bluish black to a light silvery grey, the intermediate shades being preferred, the body colour coming well down the shoulder and hips, gradually merging into the leg colour. The Mustards vary from a reddish brown to a pale fawn, the head being a creamy white, the legs and feet of a shade darker than the head. The claws are dark as in other colours. [Nearly all Dandie Dinmont Terriers have some white on the chest, and some have also white claws.]

SIZE.—The height should be from eight to eleven inches at the top of shoulder. Length from top of shoulder to root of tail should not be more than twice the dog's height, but, preferably, one or two inches less.

WEIGHT.—From fourteen pounds to twenty-four pounds; the best weight as near eighteen pounds as possible. These weights are for dogs in good working condition.

The relative value of several points in the standard are apportioned as follows :—

Head	10
Eyes	10
Ears	10
Neck	5
Body	20
Tail	5
Legs and feet	10
Coat	15
Colour	5
Size and weight	5
General appearance	5
	100

CHAPTER XXVII.

The Skye Terrier

Is probably one of the oldest breeds in Scotland, having its origin in the islands from which it now takes its name. The breed was originally called Scotch Terrier, just in the same way that the now favourite Diehard, and, indeed, all the Scottish varieties of Terriers were first designated. Dr. Caius, one of the earliest writers on dogs, indicates the existence and type of the Skye Terrier in his work, "Englishe Dogges." He describes them as " Iseland dogges," " brought out of barborous borders from the uttermost countryes northwards," and says that " they, by reason of the length of their heare, make show neither of face nor body, and yet these curres, forsooth, because they are so strange, are greatly set by, esteemed, taken up, and made of, in room of the Spaniell gentle, or comforter." The Bishop of Ross, who wrote a little later—in the sixteenth century—says: " There is also another kind of scenting dog of low height, but of bulkier body, which, creeping into subterraneous burrows, routs out foxes, badgers, martens, and wild cats from their lurking places and dens," which, doubtless, referred to the ancestors

SKYE TERRIER (Drop-eared).

of our modern Skye Terrier. Professor Low describes the dogs of the Island of Skye as follows :—" The Terriers of the western islands of Scotland have long, lank hair almost trailing to the ground."

In the Western Islands of Scotland themselves the Terriers used for work in the cairns in drawing fox and badger were for the most part called Scotch Terriers, but this name was given to most of Scotland's Terriers in different parts of the country. This we learn from the writings of Mr. Hugh Dalziel and Mr. D. J. Thomson Gray. It is the very long and low dog with the long coat, which is indigenous to these Islands, and more particularly to Skye, which have doubtless given rise to the appellation.

Although the prick-eared dogs predominate, there are a number of the drop-eared specimens to be found in their native haunts, and which are preferred for actual work, since this form of ear acts as a protection to the interior of the ear when the dog is burrowing. Indeed, prick-eared and drop-eared specimens will often occur in one and the same litter.

The records show that Skye Terriers were first exhibited in England about 1860, in which year they were shown at Birmingham in the Scotch Terrier class. The first occasion on which Skye Terriers were classified was at the Manchester Show in 1861. From that date onward the breed gradually came in favour as a show dog both in England and Scotland, in each of which countries specialist clubs in due course became established for the purpose of promoting the interests of the breed and formulating a standard description and code of points. It is doubtless due to the efforts and influence of these clubs that the breed has been brought to such perfection as a show dog, but the dog's enormous coat can hardly be considered in his favour as a worker. It is the coat question, and perhaps the enormous size of some of our most successful Skye Terriers, to which utilitarians take exception, and which, with much reason, they contend are distinct disadvantages to the dog in pursuing his natural calling. Few, if any, show dogs are used for actual work, and, therefore, it is needless to decry the bench type, which are calculated to keep intact the distinctive features and characteristics of this game, hard-bitten, and very handsome Terrier. Whilst the Skye Terrier is all this, and a most companionable and faithful dog to those to whom he attaches himself, he is not, speaking generally, as open in disposition as his cousin the Scottie. Whether this surliness in the Skye Terrier is a natural characteristic inherited through long generations, or the result of nervousness created by the dog being so buried in long, thick hair that he can scarcely see, I cannot say, but he is certainly one of the most snappish dogs that goes to a show, and one that is rather dangerous to handle. In this breed, lady owners and exhibitors, I should say, predominate, and it has sometimes occurred to me whether this blemish in the dog's character, if it can be called a blemish, may not be traceable to the great care and kindness—in some cases mistaken kindness probably, amounting to over-indulgence—which their fair owners lavish on their pets. We learn from "British Dogs" that even as long ago as 1837 the Skye Terrier was a popular variety with the fair sex, Lady Fanny Cowper being a great owner and enthusiast in the breed, whilst Lady Macdonald, of Armadale Castle, Skye, had a famous strain.

The great features of the breed are a long, punishing jaw, long, level back free from roach, short, straight, strong forelegs, powerful hindquarters, and a long, straight, thick, harsh coat. The favourite colour is dark steel grey, but colour is not of much consequence, mustards being quite admissible.

The defects to avoid are: Pig-jaws or undershot jaws, light eyes, snipy muzzles, soft coats, and roach backs.

The chief points to look for in the selection of Skye Terrier puppies at from two to four months old and after are: A long head, strong muzzle, dark eye, long body, well-sprung ribs, deep chest, short, heavy-boned legs, and a profuse coat of good texture. In the prick-eared variety the ears should be bolt upright, and in the drop-eared the ears should fall forward in the manner of other drop-eared Terriers.

The following are the standard description and code of points, etc., laid down by the Skye Terrier Club of Scotland:—

HEAD.—Long, with powerful jaws, and incisive teeth closing level, or upper just fitting over under. Skull wide at front of brow, narrowing between ears, and tapering gradually towards muzzle, with little falling in between or behind the eyes. Eyes hazel, medium size, close set. Muzzle always black.

EARS (prick or pendant).—When *prick*, not large, erect at outer edges, and slanting towards each other at inner, from peak to skull, When *pendant*, larger, hanging straight, lying flat, and close at front.

BODY.—Pre-eminently long and low. Shoulders broad, chest deep, ribs well sprung and oval shaped, giving flattish appearance to sides. Hindquarters and flank full and well developed. Back level and slightly declining from top of hip joint to shoulders. Neck long and gently crested.

TAIL.—When *hanging*, upper half perpendicular, under half thrown backwards in a curve. When *raised*, a prolongation of the incline of the back, and not rising higher nor curling up.

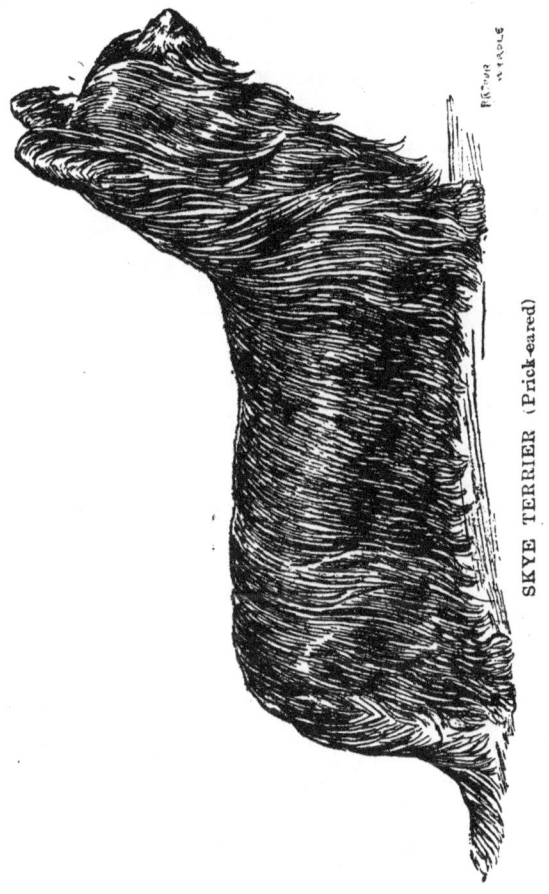

SKYE TERRIER (Prick-eared)

LEGS.—Short, straight, and muscular. No dew claws. Feet large and pointing forwards.

COAT (double).— An *under*, short, close, soft, and woolly. An *over*, long—averaging 5½in.—hard, straight, flat, and free from crisp or curl. Hair on head shorter, softer, and veiling forehead and eyes; on ears, overhanging inside, falling down and mingling with side locks, not heavily, but surrounding the ear like a fringe, and allowing its shape to appear. Tail also gracefully feathered.

COLOUR (any variety).—Dark or light blue or grey, or fawn with black points. Shade of head and legs approximating that of body.

STANDARD.

1—AVERAGE MEASURE.

DOG.—Height at shoulder, 9in.
    Length back of skull to root of tail, 22½in.
        ,, muzzle to back of skull, 8½in.
        ,, root of tail to tip joint, 9in.
        Total length, 40in.

BITCH.—Half an inch lower, and 2½in. shorter than dog, all parts proportional; thus, body 21in., head 8in., and tail 8½in.; total, 37½in.

2.—AVERAGE WEIGHT.

Dog, 18lb.; bitch, 16lb.
No dog should be over 20lb. nor under 16lb.; and no bitch should be over 18lb. nor under 14lb.

3.—POINTS, WITH VALUE.

1.—SIZE	Height, with	10in. high	5	
	Length and	19in. high..	10	15
	Proportions,	8½in. high	15	
2.—HEAD (skull and eyes, 10; jaws and teeth, 5) ..				15
3.—EARS (carriage, with shape, size, and feather) ..				10
4.—BODY (back and neck, 10; chest and ribs, 5) ..				15
5.—TAIL (carriage and feather)				10
6.—LEGS (straightness and shortness, 5; strength, 5)				10
7.—COAT (hardness, 10; lankness, 5; length, 5) ..				20
8.—COLOUR AND CONDITION				5
Total				100

4.—JUDICIAL AWARDS.

1.—Over extreme weight to be handicapped 5 per lb. of excess.
2.—Over- or under-shot mouth to disqualify.
3.—Doctored ears or tail to disqualify.
4.—No *extra* value for greater length of coat than 5½in.
5.—Not to be commended under a total of 60. Not to be highly commended under a total of 65. Not to be very highly commended under a total of 70. No specials to be given under a total of 75.

CHAPTER XXVIII.

The Airedale Terrier

Is one of the later creations of the Terrier family. As his name indicates, he had his origin in this picturesque Yorkshire dale, a little more than half a century ago. All authorities and data point conclusively to the dog having been evolved from a cross with the Otterhound and a Terrier of some sort. My esteemed friend, Mr. Holland Buckley, author of that excellent monograph on the breed, thinks the Welsh Harrier, most of which are broken-haired, has played a part in the manufacture of the Airedale Terrier. As there are no records of either Welsh Harriers or Welsh Terriers having existed in the district at the time the variety was

AIREDALE TERRIER.

produced, I, at any rate, am forced to the position of having to rob " gallant little Wales " of this honour. On the other hand, otter-hunting in the Yorkshire rivers was then, and is still, a great pastime, in which the peasantry and operatives of the district, as well as the squires and landlords, took part. With the hunts were used for unearthing the otter, when, hard-pressed by the Hounds and he took refuge in the cairns and recesses of the rivers, various Terriers, for the most part nondescripts, but some of which were of the Black-and-tan Old English Broken-haired Terrier persuasion, a breed which, alas ! is now nearly extinct as a show dog, but one which, for gameness and good looks, had few equals and no superior. These Terriers would run probably from 18lb. to 30lb. in weight. I can quite understand that on occasions a bigger dog was required to cope with some of the big dog otters that were met with, and naturally a cross between an Otterhound and one of these broken-haired Terriers would at once suggest itself. These dogs were both available; there was no necessity to go farther afield, and both contained the elements in their character required for the specific sport, and I think, in the absence of exact data, this is the most rational explanation of the origin of the Airedale Terrier. The earlier specimens were far from the finished article we possess to-day. Many of them were big, coarse, open-coated dogs, with big lugs, partaking of the Otterhound. Others were on the small side, mostly with Beagle-like ears hanging down by the side of the head. I think the first class made for them was at Bingley Show, somewhere in the 'seventies, which was for " Waterside Terriers." There had, of course, been classes previously, both at this show and others, for " Working Terriers," which included all sorts of Terriers—Waterside, Fox-terriers, Bedlingtons, Dandies, etc. After this they were called " Bingley Terriers," but on the suggestion, I believe, of my old, but, alas! departed friend, Mr. Hugh Dalziel, the more correct appellation of " Airedale " Terrier became generally adopted. The old-established show of the Wharfedale Agricultural Society in due course took up the cause of the local Terrier, and as time went on this old-time fixture gradually developed into a Mecca of the breed, where the finest collections of Airedales in the country have in late years been annually benched.

The formation of the Airedale Terrier Club naturally gave a fillip to the breed, which rapidly came in favour, and since its foundation quite a number of other Airedale Terrier clubs have sprung into being in Scotland, Ireland, the North of England, and Midlands, the last-named club being second only in importance to the parent club.

There can be little wonder at the Airedale Terrier becoming so popular, because he is such a sensible and companionable dog, game to the core, and of a size which enables him to ably defend not only his master against human attack, but himself against attack by the canine tribe. At the same time, he is not a quarrelsome dog, but, as Shakespeare says, " being in " a canine quarrel, he makes his " opposer beware of him."

A standard was formulated from the conception of the founders of the breed, which, with but little modification, prevails to this day. That provides for a dog of, roughly, from 40lbs. to 50lbs., with a well-knit frame, great bone for his size, and with a long, punishing jaw and lean head, keen expression, and a wiry, weather-resisting coat. Those are the chief essentials, but good shoulders, straight forelegs and short cat-like feet, small V-shaped ears, colour, etc., are other details which are nowadays insisted on in aiming at the ideal. The Airedale Terrier architecture may be compared to that of a prize Hackney, on whose lines he should be built throughout. In the matter of colour, black-and-tan or grizzle-and-tan is the correct colour, but, as in a horse, a good Airedale can hardly be a bad colour. Like the Bedlington Terrier, the Dandie, and Wire-haired Fox-terrier, the coat of the Airedale is one of its most troublesome features. Fluffy-coated but otherwise good Airedales will still insist upon being born, and as they are often too good to drown, they get brought up, and find their way on the show bench—not, of course, quite as nature made them, but as the standard says they should be. Some of these dogs become champions, and are bred from, and so the " fluff " is perpetuated. Happily, however, there are a very large number of naturally good-coated Airedales amongst our cracks, and " trimming " to excess is not nearly so much practised as it used to be some years ago, which marks a distinct improvement in the texture of the coats of Airedales generally.

In breeding, or buying, the defects to avoid are either over-sized (which spells coarseness) or under-sized dogs, bad coats, light bone, thin feet, big ears, light eyes, snipy muzzles, or shelly middlepieces. In docking, about half the tail (or a little less) should be removed.

The chief points to look for in the selection of Airedale puppies at from two to four months old and after are : A long, level head, strong muzzle, small dark eye, narrow skull, neat, small, V-shaped drop ears, a long neck, narrow shoulders, short body, deep chest, straight forelegs, and hard dense coat. The standard description and points printed below give readers a clear outline of what a perfect Airedale Terrier ought to be :—

DESCRIPTION AND STANDARD OF THE AIREDALE TERRIER.

HEAD.—Long, with flat skull, but not too broad between the ears, narrowing slightly to the eyes, free from wrinkle ; stop hardly visible, and cheeks free from fulness ; jaw deep and powerful, well filled up before the eyes ; lips tight.

EARS.—V-shaped, with a side carriage ; small, but not out of proportion to the size of the dog.

NOSE.—Black.

EYES.—Small and dark in colour, not prominent, but full of Terrier expression, with teeth strong and level.

NECK.—Should be of moderate length and thickness, gradually widening towards the shoulders, and free from throatiness.

SHOULDERS AND CHEST.—Shoulders long and sloping well into the back ; shoulder blades flat, chest deep, but not broad.

BODY.—Back short, strong, and straight ; ribs well sprung.

HINDQUARTERS.—Strong and muscular, with no droop ; hocks well let down.

TAIL.—Set on high and carried gaily, but not curled over at the back.

LEGS AND FEET.—Legs perfectly straight, with plenty of bone ; feet small and round, with good depth of pad.

COAT.—Hard and wiry, and not so long as to appear ragged ; it should also lie straight and close, covering the dog well all over the body and legs.

COLOUR.—The head and ears, with the exception of dark markings on each side of the skull, should be tan, the ears being of a darker shade than the rest, the legs up to the thighs and elbows being also tan ; the body black or dark grizzle.

SIZE.—Dogs, 40lbs. to 45lbs. weight ; bitches, slightly less.

SCALE OF POINTS.

	Value.
Head	5
Eye	5
Colour	10
Ears	5
Body, loins, and hindquarters	20
Jaw	10
Nose	5
Teeth	5
Legs and feet	10
Neck and shoulders	10
Coat	15
Total	100

CHAPTER XXIX.

The Bedlington Terrier

Is one of the gamest, most sensible, and companionable of all the Terrier varieties. His precise origin and manufacture are, like those of many other breeds, obscured in the mists of the silent past, but there can be no doubt that if he had not his origin on the pit banks of Bedlington, he is, in his present form, largely the product of the Tyneside pitman, who invariably kept, and still keeps, a "Tarrier" for ratting, and if the dog could pick up a rabbit now and then for the Sunday's dinner for his owner, wife, and bairns, he was none the worse thought of in those more primitive days. For this latter purpose a little legginess is required, and that accounts for the rabbiting inference, for legginess is not necessary for ratting; in fact, a short-legged

BEDLINGTON TERRIER.

dog would be better adapted for that purpose purely, being nearer his work. For the same reason, a Bedlington is not well adapted for underground work.

Some canine historians tell us that the Bedlington Terrier originated with that famous Northumbrian "sport," "Piper Allan," in the beginning of the nineteenth century, at which time he was called the Rodberry or Rothbury Terrier, the name of the place at which "Piper Allan" lived. Others associate this local worthy with the origin of the Dandie, but there can be little doubt that the Dandie has had something to do with the manufacture of the Bedlington Terrier (or *vice versa*), with possibly an admixture in the Bedlington of Whippet, then called the "Snap" dog, since the latter was much used later on by the pitmen for rabbit coursing, another of their diversions, then and now.

Mr. Harold Warnes, a reliable authority, in the "Kennel Encyclopædia" states that a Joseph Ainsley, a mason, first gave the name of "Bedlington" to the breed in 1825, and that his dog, Young Piper, was the first true specimen of the more modern and now recognised type. He was bred from "Phœbe, a black bitch with brindle legs and a tuft of light-coloured hair on her head . . . . who was brought to Bedlington in 1820." Put to James Anderson's Piper, a slenderly built, liver-coloured dog, weighing 15lb. and standing 15in. high (the latter surely a mis-print for 13in.) produced the Young Piper referred to. The nomenclature of these two dogs, however, does suggest a connection with "Piper Allan," who died in 1774, or half a century earlier, which particular name has been more or less associated with the breed continuously from that time up to the present.

Whatever may be the dog's actual origin, the foregoing facts and data are sufficient for the purposes of this article, and show him to have been a purely British-bred animal. Despite his lowly surroundings, he has always been noted for his pluck and sporting instincts. The prize dogs of to-day are a little heavier and taller than the weight and height quoted in the case of the first recorded "Piper," but the *type* otherwise seems to have been much the same.

The Bedlington Terrier, briefly summed up, is a long, snaky-headed, racily-built, and lathy Terrier, of about 22lb. to 24lb. weight, with a linty coat, topknot, and closely hanging pendulous ears, which, with his coat, he doubtless inherits from the Dandie, or the Dandie from him. These are the salient points of the breed, about which all Bedlington experts are agreed, which they assiduously strive to preserve, and which give to the breed a distinctiveness, and, where the coat is trimmed *a la mode*, a quaintness all its own. With the bigger dogs, naturally, comes greater length of head, and it is wonderful the length and strength of jaw which some Bedlingtons possess, and which is a great desideratum. The difficulty is in getting a long head on a short, compact body, for, despite the fact that a Bedlington is a lathy, flat-sided dog, he should have a comparatively short back. His lung power is found in the *depth*, not *width*, of his chest, for his chest must be deep. Then again, his head must be lean, and showing a distinct development of the occipital bone. A short, snipy face is all wrong, and should be avoided in both breeding and buying. A slight arch in the loin is as desirable as a flat back is objectionable. A Bedlington should have a nice length of neck, set into obliquely placed shoulders, which, with a *deep* as against a *wide* chest, are a guarantee of a narrow front, from Nature's ordinary laws of reproduction, which is what is required. A feature of the Bedlington's ears is that they should be rather long, almost smooth-coated, fringed with long hair at the edges, and lie close to the head. Any deviation in either carriage or character of the ears is a departure from the true type as laid down by experts. The Bedlington should have a closely knit, strong, hare foot, but many prize dogs are defective in this point, being either open or flat in feet. The original colours of Bedlingtons are blue, blue-and-tan, liver, liver-and-tan, and sandy, to which another shade or two have since been added. The coat is a very important feature of the dog, and its artistic manipulation, in these later times, has been the bane, if not the ban, of the breed which alone has retarded its progress and prevented it from achieving that popularity to which the dog's many virtues justly entitle it. Fashion has ordained that the topknot shall be more profuse and more clearly defined than Nature prescribes, and that the coat generally shall be of a certain length and texture. Where these arbitrary requirements are not present naturally, the skill of the tonsorial artist steps in and furnishes the deficiency. Trimming, of course, always was, and always will be, necessary in many cases in connection with the rough or wire-haired varieties, and there will always be a difficulty in clearly defining where legitimate trimming finishes and "faking" begins. This difficulty will always offer a temptation to the unscrupulous to "o'erstep the modesty of Nature," as Shakespeare says, in order to present a picture which from the standpoint of skill, and even art, is pleasing but not natural. The undue trimming of this breed has prevented many admirers from taking it up, and has caused many to desert it, who have declared that it is the best-barbered dog, not the best dog, which wins. Instances of this sort, no doubt, have occurred, but, speaking generally, with a full knowledge of the facts and no prejudice one way or the other, I am of the opinion that in ninety-nine cases out of every hundred it is the best dog who wins, and that is as near as we can ever hope to get in any variety.

The chief points to look for in the selection of Bedlington puppies at from two to four months old and after are : A long, snaky head, narrow skull, small dark eye, drop ears lying close to the side of the head, short body, short sickle tail, straight forelegs, and dense linty coat.

The original Bedlington Terrier Club formulated the first standard description and points, and there are also the National Bedlington Terrier Club and the British Bedlington Terrier Club.

Below is the standard description of the first-named Club :—

	Value.
SKULL.—Narrow, but deep and rounded ; high at occiput, and covered with a nice silky tuft or topknot	15
JAW.—Long, tapering, sharp, and muscular ; as little stop as possible between the eyes, so as to form nearly a line from the nose-end along the jaw of the skull to the occiput ; the lips close-fitting, and no flew	5
EYES.—Should be small and well sunk in head ; the blues should have a dark eye ; the blue-and-tan ditto, with amber shade ; livers, sandies, etc., a light brown eye	5
NOSE.—Large, well angled ; blues and blue-and-tans should have black noses ; livers and sandies flesh-coloured noses	5
TEETH.—Level, or pincer-jawed	5
EARS.—Moderately large, well formed, flat to the cheek, thinly covered and tipped with fine silky hair ; they should be filbert-shaped	5
LEGS.—Of moderate length, not wide apart, straight and square set, and with good-sized feet, which are rather long	10
TAIL.—Thick at root, tapering to a point, slightly feathered on lower side, 9in. to 11in. long, and scimitar-shaped	5
NECK AND SHOULDERS.—Neck long, deep at base, rising well from shoulders, which should be flat	5
BODY.—Moderately long and well proportioned, flat-ribbed, and deep ; not wide in chest ; back slightly arched, well ribbed up, with light quarters	15
COAT.—Hard, with soft undercoat, and not lying flat to the sides ; twisty outercoat	10
COLOUR.—Dark blue, blue-and-tan, liver, liver-and-tan, sandy, sandy-and-tan	5
HEIGHT.—About 15in. or 16in.	5
WEIGHT.—Dogs, about 24lb. ; bitches, about 22lb.	5
Total points	100
GENERAL APPEARANCE.—A lightly made-up, lathy dog, but not shelly	

CHAPTER XXX.

The Border Terrier.

The Border Terrier's name indicates his nativity. These dogs have existed in the Border districts of England and Scotland for centuries, but have only comparatively recently been given the appellation of "Border" Terrier. They are attached to many of the hunts in those districts for use as a Fox Terrier, viz., in bolting the fox when Reynard goes to ground. The Border Terrier is a sturdy, rather low-set, rough-haired, but shortish-coated dog of from 12lbs. to 16lbs., with a strong jaw, drop ears, and "as game as a pebble," as the saying goes.

The Border Terrier is a dog of considerable antiquity, but, like that of many other breeds, his precise origin is unrecorded. Judged by his form and features the Dandie Dinmont and some local small working Terrier would seem to have had something to do with his make-up. He is a workman every inch—a *multum in parvo*—having been kept small, so that he could the better engage his quarry, the fox or badger, in his natural earth. A game, hardy little fellow, he possesses utility traits from stem to stern and from top to toe.

BORDER TERRIER.

It is only in late years that the Border Terrier has come to the front as a show dog outside his immediate locality. He was rarely exhibited before the war; but, since, his many admirers have been determined that his great merit should be more publicly recognised and that the dog and his many virtues should not be longer kept in the local shade at the expense of the importation of other alien canines.

To attain this desirable position one of his great admirers and enthusiasts—to wit, Mr. T. Hamilton-Adams—set to work to found a club to promote the dog's best interests, and got around him quite a galaxy of prominent ducal and noble sportsmen, including about a dozen M.F.H. and an executive of Border and other zealots, who, together, have done much to popularise the breed, which was promptly recognised by the Kennel Club and placed upon its register.

The Northumberland Border Terrier Club was really the pioneer in the emancipation of this game Terrier, and eventually this club and the Border Terrier Club became amalgamated under the latter title.

The following excerpt from an article written by another Border Terrier enthusiast, Mr. F. W. Morris, gives a somewhat graphic account of the unearthing of this little Terrier from his haunts in the pursuit of his calling along the borders of England and Scotland, and bringing him out into the limelight of public exhibition :—

The year 1920 will ever be a red-letter year in the history of the Border Terrier, for in 1920 this game British Terrier has been "recognised" by the Kennel Club, a special club has been formed to further the interests of the breed, and a standard of points has been drawn up and accepted. So far so good. It is in the recollection of many how for years I have fought for this "recognition," and advocated a club being formed. With all the above results—and do not forget that *Our Dogs* was the first and only paper which took up the question years before any other doggie paper gave even one line to advocate the claims of the Border Terrier—we Border Terrier fanciers are pleased, and realise that this little dog is now making headway in the fancy.

We have had classes at several of the best shows in the London district and large provincial cities, and at all these shows much interest has been aroused. At Richmond, where I judged, a very large number of ladies and gentlemen asked me many questions on the breed, and I felt that my propaganda visit to the royal borough had not been in vain. We have had challenge certificates allotted to the breed at Carlisle, Edinburgh, and the K.C. Shows, and every week proves that the Border Terrier has come to stay; but he must be protected from some of his friends. I was at Bellingham Show when the standard was read out, and it was Mr. J. Dodds, a gentleman I have always held to be the greatest authority on the Border Terrier, who objected, I think, to the size. The standard says : "Dogs should be between 14lb. and 17lb. in weight, and 13in. and 16in. in height at shoulder. Bitches should not exceed 15lb. in weight and 15in. in height at shoulder," for, as Mr. Dodds said, "the Border Terrier is essentially a working Terrier, and, being of necessity able to follow a horse, must combine great activity with gameness." I think, and I feel confident, that all who can speak with authority will endorse Mr. Dodds' views. We do not desire to breed Whippets. Do fanciers realise what a dog 16in. at shoulder and 17lb. in weight is ? The Border Terrier is to bolt foxes, otters, and badgers, and at such a weight and size he would be perfectly useless.

Then my old and esteemed friend, Mr. F. E. Schofield, voiced a matter which brought forth great laughter. Was it the laugh of the ignorant?—for Mr. Schofield was right in his question. He asked what about the "moustache," for the Border Terrier should have what cannot be better termed than "moustache," for "moustache" it is. Are we to lose sight of this characteristic? I was amazed to hear such laughter, but Mr. Schofield has certainly the laugh on his side, and I again say that this characteristic of the Border Terrier must not be overlooked or lost. Border Terriers require no trimming, and this "tuft of hair," or "moustache" must not be "trimmed out" like some other varieties of Terriers. Do not forget this fact, that quite fifty years ago Mr. Schofield was breeding Border Terriers, and to my certain knowledge—and few know him better than I do—Mr. Schofield has kept himself in touch with the Border Terrier ever since.

He is making great progress. We have had some remarkable entries at Wooler, Hexham, Bellingham, etc., shows, and with a club of over 100 members the day is not far distant when the Border Terrier will have a show of his own—a club show—where there should be a great " gathering of the clans."

The following is the description of the Border Terrier, as formulated by the Border Terrier Club:—

The Border Terrier is essentially a working Terrier, and, being of necessity able to follow a horse, must combine great activity with gameness.

N.B.—The points following are placed in their order of importance.

SIZE.—Dogs should be between 14 and 17lb. in weight and 13 and 16in. in height at shoulder. Bitches should not exceed 15lb. in weight and 15in. in height at shoulder.

HEAD.—Like that of an otter, moderately broad in skull, with short, strong muzzle, level teeth, black nose preferred, but liver and flesh-coloured not to disqualify.

EYES.—Dark, with keen expression.

EARS.—Small V-drop.

BODY.—Deep, narrow, and fairly long, ribs carried well back, but not oversprung, as a Terrier should be capable of being spanned by both hands behind the shoulder.

FORELEGS.—Straight, not too heavy in bone.

FEET.—Small and catlike.

STERN.—Short, undocked, thick at base, then tapering, set high, carried gaily, but not curled over back.

HINDQUARTERS.—Racing.

COAT.—Harsh and dense, with close undercoat.

SKIN.—Thick.

COLOUR.—Red-wheaten, grizzle, or blue-and-tan.

DISQUALIFICATION.—Mouth undershot, or much overshot.

The chief points to look for in the selection of a puppy are:—

A strong muzzle, small ears, great bone, deep chest, big quarters, and hard coat, leaving the rest to the natural development of the dog.

Since the above was written the Border Terrier Club has altered the standard weight to:—Dogs, 13 to $15\frac{1}{2}$ lbs.; and Bitches, $11\frac{1}{2}$ to 14 lbs.]

CHAPTER XXXI.

The West Highland White Terrier.

Like the Clydesdale, this comparatively new variety as a show dog is an offshoot of the Scottish Terrier and Cairn Terrier, who is undoubtedly his very near, and probably only, prototype, and whom he should resemble in every feature almost, except that his followers have ordained that he shall be a little smaller than the average exhibition Scottie, and shorter in foreface.

White Terriers have been carefully bred at Poltalloch for a hundred years, to destroy foxes and other vermin; and probably very much longer. Colonel Malcolm's father and grandfather kept them, and it is probable that their lineage goes back to the days of James I., who asked for " some earth-dogges out of Argyleshire." In Skye, too, there was a well-known strain of them long before dog shows were thought of.

WEST HIGHLAND WHITE TERRIER.

Doubtless the origin of this variety can be traced to the breeding from " Sports," to which albinos the northern latitudes—which, without any process of selection, produces in its white hares, white wild rabbits, white grouse, and white heather—readily lends itself.

The same " sports " have occurred in the Skye Terrier ranks, to which one of the Dukes of Argyll paid close attention, and produced a race of white or creamy coloured small Skye Terriers, some prick- and some semi-drop eared, to which are given the name of Roseneath Terriers, taken from the Duke's place in Dumbartonshire. Some few years ago the late Mr. J. C. Macdona, an ardent admirer of these little West Highlanders, induced the Committee of Cruft's Show to provide a class for them. Dr. Flaxman, of Pittenweem, Fife, made a speciality of the albinos, as did the late Capt. Keene and

Donald Ferguson, the Lochgilphead fox-hunter. The late Queen Victoria was given a brace by the Duke of Argyll. Col. Malcolm, C.B., of Poltalloch, devoted much time and care in the propagation of these attractive Highlanders, and bred them for many years. The Colonel's strain were at first described as "Poltalloch" Terriers. They were much on the same lines as Dr. Flaxman's dogs, and more on the lines of the exhibition Scottie than the Duke of Argyll's strain. It has been suggested that a Spanish vessel once brought a collection of Maltese Terriers with its cargo, which were distributed in the Highlands, but there is nothing authentic about this story, which most likely is legendary.

It has been left to the West Highland White Terrier Club of Scotland to collect the albino forces of the canine inhabitants of the Western Highlands of Scotland into one recognised clan. The West Highland White Terrier Club of England, founded in 1905, formulated a standard description and code of points in keeping with the most generally approved type.

In all white varieties, which are produced from coloured originals, there is a tendency for the noses and eyelids to come flesh colour. So it is in these West Highlanders, but it is interesting to see that the club, in its very lucid and comprehensive description, lays down that the nose at least must be black, but why the roof of the mouth should be black is difficult to understand. This provision must surely be a relic of a superstitious age, when it was held that a dog could not be pure bred unless the roof of its mouth was black, a theory long since exploded, and every day refuted by facts, since hosts of our best and purest bred dogs do not possess black roofs to their mouths. There is some semblance of logic in the foot of the pad being black, on the ground, possibly, of a black pad being harder than a white or flesh-coloured one, although I do not know that this is actually the case. I think the description would have been better with both these " black list " items left out, and also the sentimental one of " self-esteem," which is an attribute of most quadrupeds, and bipeds, too.

There is but an infinitesimal difference between the points required in a White West Highlander and a Scottish Terrier puppy—therefore in their selection in early puppyhood one may well stand for the other.

The following is the description in question :—

THE GENERAL APPEARANCE of the West Highland White Terrier is that of a small, game, hardy-looking Terrier, possessed with no small amount of self-esteem, with a varminty appearance, strongly built, deep in chest and back ribs, straight back and powerful quarters on muscular legs, and exhibiting in a marked degree a great combination of strength and activity. The coat should be about 2½in. long, white in colour, hard, with plenty of soft undercoat, with no tendency to wave or curl. The tail should be as straight as possible, and carried not too gaily, and covered with hard hair, but not bushy. The skull should not be too broad, being in proportion to the terribly powerful jaws. The ears should be as small and sharp-pointed as possible, and carried tightly up, and must be absolutely erect. The eyes of moderate size, dark hazel in colour, widely placed, with a sharp, bright, intelligent expression. The muzzle should not be too long ; powerful, and gradually tapering towards the nose. The nose, roof of mouth, and pads of feet distinctly black in colour.

COLOUR.—Pure white ; any other colour objectionable.

COAT.—Very important, and seldom seen to perfection ; must be double-coated. The outer coat consists of hard hair, about 2in. long, and free from any curl. The under coat, which resembles fur ,is short, soft, and close. Open coats are objectionable.

SIZE.—Dogs to weigh from 14lb. to 18lb., and bitches from 12lb. to 16lb., and measure from 8in. to 12in. at the shoulder.

SKULL.—Should not be too narrow, being in proportion to his powerful jaw, not too long, slightly domed, and gradually tapering to the eyes, between which there should be a slight indentation or stop, eyebrows heavy. Head and neck thickly coated with hair.

EYES.—Widely set apart, medium in size, dark hazel in colour, slightly sunk in the head, sharp and intelligent, which, looking from under the heavy eyebrows, give a piercing look. Full eyes and also light-coloured eyes are very objectionable.

MUZZLE.—Should be nearly equal in length to the rest of the skull, powerful, and gradually tapering towards the nose, which should be fairly wide. The jaws level and powerful, the teeth square or evenly met, well set, and large for the size of the dog. The nose and roof of mouth should be distinctly black in colour.

EARS.—Small, erect, carried tightly up, and terminating in a sharp point. The hair of them should be short, smooth (velvety), and they should not be cut. The ears should be free from any fringe at the top. Round-pointed, broad, and large ears are very objectionable, also ears too heavily covered with hair.

NECK.—Muscular and nicely set on sloping shoulders.

CHEST.—Very deep, with breadth in proportion to the size of the dog.

BODY.—Compact, straight back, ribs deep and well arched in the upper half of rib, presenting a flattish side appearance, loins broad and strong, hindquarters strong, muscular, and wide across the top.

LEGS AND FEET.—Both fore and hind legs should be short and muscular. The shoulder blades should be comparatively broad, and well sloped backwards. The points of the shoulder blades should be closely knitted into the backbone, so that very little movement of them should be noticeable when the dog is walking. The elbow should be close in to the body, both when moving and standing, thus causing the foreleg to be well placed in under the shoulder. The forelegs should be straight and thickly covered with short, hard hair. The hind legs should be short and sinewy. The thighs very muscular and not too wide apart. The hocks bent and well set in under the body so as to be fairly close to each other when standing, walking, or trotting. The forefeet are larger than the hind ones, are round, proportionate in size, strong, thickly padded, and covered with short, hard hair. The hind feet are smaller and thickly padded. The under surface of the pads of feet and all the nails should be distinctly black in colour. Cow hocks detract from the general appearance. Straight or weak hocks, both kinds, are undesirable, and should be guarded against.

TAIL.—Five or six inches long, covered with hard hairs, no feather, as straight as possible, carried gaily, but not curled over back. A long tail is objectionable. On no account should tails be docked, *vide* K.C. Rule V., Appendix II.

MOVEMENT.—Should be free, straight, and easy all round. In front the leg should be freely extended forward by the shoulder. The hind movement should be free, strong, and close. The hocks should be freely flexed and drawn close in under the body, so that when moving off the foot the body is thrown or pushed forward with some force. Stiff, stilty movement behind is ever objectionable.

FAULTS.

COAT.—Any silkiness, wave, or tendency to curl is a serious blemish, as is also an open coat, and any black, grey, or wheaten hairs.

SIZE.—Any specimens under the minimum weight, or above the maximum weight, are objectionable.

EYES.—Full or light-coloured.

EARS.—Round-pointed, drop, semi-erect, also ears too heavily covered with hair.

MUZZLE.—Either under- or over-shot, and defective teeth.

Scale of Points.

	Value
General appearance	5
Colour	10
Coat	10
Size	7½
Skull	7½
Eyes	5
Muzzle	5
Ears	5
Neck	7½
Chest	7½
Body	10
Legs and feet	7½
Tail	5
Movement	7½
	100

CHAPTER XXXII.

The Cairn Terrier

Is one of the latest distinct breeds to claim recognition in the classic curriculum of the show ring. An ancient Scottish variety, like his clansmen the Skye, the Scottie, and the West Highlander, he represents in his coat and character the same rugged nature which characterises his native haunts, and, like his canine kinsmen, he is the embodiment of gameness and hardihood, and as sensible as a Christian. The specific avocation of the Cairn is, as his name implies, to follow his quarry—the fox, the otter, the wild-cat, and other burrowing animals—underground and into the cairns which abound in "Bonny Scotland."

I cannot do better than reprint a little article of mine on the origin and progress of this handsome and quaint little Highlander, which appeared in the Christmas Number of *Our Dogs*. It is as follows:—

"It may perhaps appear somewhat presumptuous on my part as an Anglo-Saxon to essay to discuss the above subject in the face of so many Scottish experts, who, I am sure, know a great deal more than I

CAIRN TERRIER.

do about Cairn Terriers. As one whose professional duty it is to observe the advent of new breeds, and to watch their rise or fall, their progress or deterioration, I venture, without desiring in any way to usurp the delicate domain of specialism, to offer a few observations upon the Cairn as I found him, and give my 'impressions' as to his progress, for whatever they may be worth.

"It so happens that I am in the unique position of being the first person to ever judge Cairn Terriers at a show in public competition. This was at the Inverness Show in 1909, at which a class was given for 'short-haired Skye Terriers.' The exhibits, about ten or a dozen in number, were all Cairns, many of them somewhat unkempt in coat, and in various colours—sandy, black, grizzle, and one of a bluish shade, if I remember correctly,—but they were all Cairns. Mrs. Macdonald won first with Fassie, and Mrs. J. Alastair Campbell the other two prizes and reserve with her dogs, Macleod of Macleod, Doran Bhan, and Roy Mohr respectively,

"The 'points' and features of the breed at that time existed only in the imagination of most people, as they had not then been categorically ascertained and reduced to writing. With a limited knowledge of the breed (which I do not mind confessing), I was left to form my own conception of their specific functions and appraise the merits and demerits of the dogs accordingly. To begin with, the description of the class was, to me at least, a misnomer. I looked upon these rugged, game-looking, compact little tykes as underground dogs, and to my mind they appeared to be more closely allied in type and character to the West Highland White Terrier, which was at that time just coming to the front.

"We may probably take it that the dogs exhibited at this show would be a fair sample of the breed as it then existed in its native haunts—for they had never before been exhibited, I understand,—from which the present more uniform exhibition Cairn Terrier has sprung.

"It was not until the Scottish breeders and enthusiasts of the Cairn had decided upon launching a new club to promote its interests, and if possible to popularise it, that its 'points' and a description of the breed were evolved. This club, the Cairn Terrier Club, is now one of the most flourishing of specialist clubs, and has done wonders for the breed. Its followers include the nobility, and ladies and gentlemen high in the social scale, including the hon. secretary, Mrs. Alastair Campbell, who may be said to be the great pioneer of the breed, and to whom the credit is due for digging the little dog out of his obscurity and bringing him bang to the front and placing the Cairn among the most popular of the Terrier varieties.

"The Cairn is a rare little fellow for which I have a great admiration—a *multum in parvo*,—containing the finest combination of good traits in the smallest compass. I predict a great future for the dog under the auspices of the Cairn Terrier Club.

"The standard says that the 'head should be small,' but yet 'in proportion to the body.' A 'small' head is rather a vague term, but the expression is also paradoxical, for if it is 'in proportion to the body' it cannot be *small*—but the correct size. I scarcely think the Club really desires the ribs of the Cairn to be 'deep.' This description of ribs is always applied to Greyhounds, Deerhounds, Borzois, Bloodhounds, and most hunting dogs, but never to Terriers, whose ribs should be well sprung—not particularly deep, especially in a short-legged dog. I must apologise for pointing out these little commissions in the code, which may form food for Club discussion, if not digestion!

"There is one thing I notice the Club is doing—endeavouring to prevent the infusion into the Cairn of the type of the modern Scottie. This appears to be one of the Club's watchwords, and a laudable one."

The chief points to look for in the selection of a Cairn Terrier puppy are: Compactness of body, great bone, a long head with strong jaw, small ears, and a hard coat.

The standard description and points adopted by the Cairn Terrier Club are as follows :—

GENERAL APPEARANCE.—Active, game, hardy, and " shaggy " in appearance ; strong, though compactly built. Should stand well forward on forepaws. Strong quarters, deep in ribs. Very free in movement. Coat hard enough to resist rain. Head small, but in proportion to body. A general foxy appearance is the chief characteristic of this working Terrier.

SKULL.—Broad in proportion; strong, but not too long or heavy jaw. A decided indentation between eyes; hair should be full on forehead.

MUZZLE.—Powerful, but not heavy. Very strong jaw, with large teeth, which should be neither undershot nor overshot.

EYES.—Set wide apart; medium in size; dark hazel, rather sunk, with shaggy eyebrows.

EARS.—Small, pointed, well carried and erect, but not too closely set.

TAIL.—Short, well furnished with hair, but not feathery; carried gaily, but should not turn down towards back.

BODY.—Compact, straight back; well-sprung deep ribs; strong sinews; hindquarters very strong. Back medium in length and well coupled.

SHOULDERS, LEGS, AND FEET.—A sloping shoulder and a medium length of leg; good, but not too large, bone. Forelegs should not be out at elbow, but forefeet may be slightly turned out. Forefeet larger than hind. Legs must be covered with hard hair. Pads should be thick and strong. Thin and ferrety feet are objectionable.

COAT.—Very important. Must be double-coated, with profuse, hard, but not coarse, outer coat, and undercoat which resembles fur, and is short, soft, and close. Open coats are objectionable. Head should be well furnished. Colour, red, sandy, grey, brindled, or nearly black. Dark points, such as ears and muzzle, very typical.

In order to keep this breed to the best old working type, any cross with a modern Scottish Terrier will be considered objectionable.

FAULTS.

MUZZLE.—Undershot or overshot.

EYES.—Too prominent or too light.

EARS.—Too large or round at points. They must not be too heavily coated with hair.

COAT.—Silkiness or curliness objectionable; a slight wave permissible.

NOSE.—Flesh or light-coloured most objectionable.

SCALE OF POINTS.

Skull	5
Muzzle	10
Eyes	5
Ears	5
Body	20
Shoulders, legs, and feet	20
Tail	5
General appearance (size and coat)	30
	100

IDEAL WEIGHT.—14lb.

CHAPTER XXXIII.

The Alsatian Wolfdog.

There is not, in the history of the dog in England, any canine parallel to the great post-war invasion of this country by the Alsatian Wolfdog (*alias* German Sheepdog, under which nomenclature the breed is still recognised in Germany and in the United States of America, where it also abounds), nor to the rapidity with which the breed came into public favour, and maintained and increased its popularity to limits never reached by any other breed in so short a time.

All this speaks well for the intrinsic merit of the Alsatian Wolfdog, which Britishers were not slow to discover, and which may be said to comprise, in the more cultivated specimens, first a rational form of canine architecture, consisting of due proportion strength and symmetry of body and limb, providing for great power, pace and activity ; long. punishing jaws, enabling the dog to attack his quarry, or foes, on the one hand, and defend his master to the best advantage on the other ; a keen, intelligent eye and expression, and highly developed aural appendages to enable the dog to hear the sounds of his master's call, or the bleating of the sheep at an enormous distance ; and a close, weather-resisting coat to protect the dog under all meteorological conditions.

With such a form and faculties it is not to be wondered that the Alsatian Wolfdog should have become such a great favourite with Britishers, nor that it should have attracted to its ranks of owners such a great array of well-to-do and intelligent fanciers, who have taken up the breeding and cultivation, training, and exhibition of the Alsatian with an almost bewildering zest and success in this country, far exceeding that of any other foreign breed of dog.

To demonstrate this, one has only to look at its brief history in this country. There were a few Alsatians in England before the war, one or two appearing at shows from time to time in variety classes, which were shown as German Sheepdogs, but not until after the war, when the British officers saw the clever scout, sentinel, and signal work, and other valuable war activities, which the German and French Sheepdog put in as adjuncts to the army in the field in the Great War, that they became enamoured of his great intelligence, aptitude, fidelity, and endurance, and determined to firmly transplant the breed in England when the war was over.

The Alsatian Wolfdog was undoubtedly originally a German and French Sheepdog and used only in pastoral pursuits, having much in common with all European Sheepdogs, including the English smooth-haired, Dutch, Belgian, Scandinavian, and Slavonic Sheepdogs. And that he has been crossed with the wolf at some time or other there can be little doubt, although there does not appear to be any exact records of this having taken place, for the simple reason that such a cross would be looked upon as somewhat illicit, carrying with it the possibility of a deterioration of the dog if indulged in to any great extent. We have, therefore, to first ask ourselves is such a cross between wolf and dog physically possible, and, having ascertained that it is (but not between dog and fox), then the question arises as to what it was that induced owners of Sheepdogs to resort to such a cross. The answer is not far to seek. There can be no doubt that it was to give the Sheepdog greater fierceness and ability to defend his charges, the sheep, from marauding wild animals in the wastes and the pastoral countries of Europe. This added faculty, with that of the greater cunning of the wolf, has been an acquisition to the Alsatian in the later

ALSATIAN WOLFDOG.

vocation to which he was applied in the Continental countries, viz., as a watch, police dog, and guard. Apart from historical records of the wolf cross, which may not be very reliable, there are several physical features of the Alsatian Wolfdog, such as a certain formation of the skull, feet, and tail, and the fact that the œstrum of some bitches of the alleged first crosses were like that of the she-wolf—annual, instead of bi-annual as in a canine bitch.

It was these facts, no doubt, which led the combined Alsatian zealots in this country, when they formed themselves into a club—the first club in England devoted to the breed, viz., " The Alsatian Wolfdog Club "—to alter the nomenclature of the breed from German Sheepdog (Deutsches Schaeferlund) to Alsatian Wolfdog.

That well-informed continental correspondent to *Our Dogs*, our esteemed friend and confrere, Mr. George Horowitz, has written a very interesting and authoritative monogram on the Alsatian Wolfdog. In that standard work on the breed occurs the following :—

We find the first trace of the Alsatian Wolfdog in the seventh century, when a paragraph in the old Germanic Law says : " Si quis canem pastoralem, qui lupum mordit et pecus exore ejus tollit, et clamor ad aliam vel ad tertiam villam currit occiderit, cum tribus solidis componat," which in translation means : " The one who kills a Sheepdog capable of killing a wolf and of depriving it of its quarry, if capable of barking loud enough so that his voice can be heard at the second or third neighbouring farm, will be punished by a fine of three solidis (about 38s. in English money)."

From then until 1606 we have absolutely no documentary evidence of the breed, but in the latter year P. C. Gessner describes the Alsatian in the following manner : "Many of these large dogs are trained to guard the house and the cattle, and they are generally called ' dogs for the sheep.' The Schaffhunde (Sheepdogster) must be large, strong, courageous, and enterprising, and must possess a very strong voice. They must be white as the sheep, so that the latter should not be afraid of them, and that they should be easily distinguished from the wolf, so that they be not shot at in the night by mistake. There is a collar with sharp points put round their neck, which does not allow the wolf to catch them by the throat."

* * * *

In spite of the dominating position which she has so long held in its fancy, Germany was comparatively late in taking up the breeding of the Alsatian of distinct type, but when she did so she made very rapid strides in this respect. If we examine the German Stud Books for Dogs, we find that there are no Alsatians mentioned in the first half of 1880, not even amongst the entries, and in the second half of that year only Collies figure, so that it appears that even then the Germans preferred to their own dogs those that came from England. " Always the old story !" complains Strebel. It was only in 1882 that two Alsatians made their appearance at the Hanover Show, exhibited by the Master of Hounds, Baron von Knigge, of Beyenrode. One of them was called Kirass, was born in 1878, and was grey and white in colour. The other's name, Greif ; was born in 1879, and was white in colour. Three years later, at the Neubrandenburg Show, Herr Gr. Duderstadt, of Dernburg, exhibited the yellow-brown Alsatian, Moreau, born in 1878. In 1887 there were shown at Hanover, besides the already mentioned Greif, the Alsatians, Foss, born in 1884, a brown-yellow, the property of the Captain Deinhard, of Kiel ; and Russin, a daughter of Greif, born in 1876, and belonging to the shepherd, Froemling, of Bey. In 1888, at the Hamburg Show, we find Foss and Russin and also Greifa, the property of Baron von Knigge ; Greifa was a white. In the same year there were benched at the Berlin Show the white-and-yellow Greif, belonging to Herr Hewald, of Vogelsdorf the black-and-yellow Franz Fleck, the property of Herr Fleck, of Berlin ; and the red-and-black

Peter, owned by Herr Schnetze, of Heinsdorf. It was at Cassell Show, in 1899, that Herr Riechelmann first exhibited an Alsatian; it was named Stummel, and was yellow in colour; and side by side with it was Grief II., a white belonging to Baron von Knigge. After this Herr Riechelmann proceeded very energetically with the popularising of the Alsatian, and it was thanks to him that the breed continued to be exhibited and ultimately received its place "in the sun."

* * * * *

It would not be out of place here to give credit to one who, in pre-war days, during the war, and for some time afterwards, probably did more to further the cause of the Alsatian in England than anyone else. I refer to Mr. Will Hally, my predecessor as scribe for the breed in the columns of *Our Dogs*, whose versatile and fluent pen was always at the service of the breed and its followers, and whose profound knowledge of the Alsatian was at all times willingly placed at their disposal.

* * * * *

As a matter of fact, the Alsatian has long been an excellent dog for guarding and driving sheep, and his elongated gait, which is so typical of the breed, thanks to his anatomical formation, enables him, better than any other variety of Sheepdog, to bring back the sheep that goes astray from the flock, without approaching it at a gallop—in other words, without frightening it. I will go further, and say that it would be desirable if all varieties of Sheepdogs possessed the gait of the Alsatian.

* * * * *

As showing further the widespread influence which the advent of the Alsatian Wolfdog has exercised upon the fancier instincts of Britishers, following the establishment of the Alsatian Wolfdog Club in 1919, was the formation in October, 1923, of a working club for the breed, to wit, the Alsatian, Sheep, Police, and Army Dog Society, whose chief aim is "to promote and encourage the breeding and training of high-class working Alsatian Wolfdogs." This new club decided to adopt the Continental standard of points and methods of judging as far as possible. The first president was Col. Lawrie, D.S.O., Assistant Commissioner of Police; and the first chairman, Major Robert Long; the first committee including such household names in the breed as Mesdames Rex Walker, Veitch, and Richardson, and Messrs Pickett, Barnes, and Horowitz, Major Beddoes, etc.

This Society holds field trials periodically in different parts of the country, which are very successful, and which, no doubt, aid in the development and maintenance of the innate qualities and capabilities of the Alsatian Wolfdog.

Scarcely had the Alsatian, Sheep, Police, and Army Dog Society got itself in working harness than an even greater combination was suddenly launched on the Alsatian horizon in "The Alsatian League of Great Britain," which was founded in April, 1924, mainly at the instance of that devoted Alsatianist, Mr. Rex Walker, who was the prime mover, and whose memorable tribute to the dog uttered by him at the dinner of the Canton and Ely Canine Society's Show at Cardiff in May of the same year, is fit to rank with those of Lord Byron, Senator West, and other great poets and philosophers, who have proclaimed and made memorable for all time the virtues of "the friend of man."

The Alsatian League of Great Britain, as showing the ripe condition of the community for any and every scheme which had for its object the promotion and benefit of the Alsatian Wolfdog, within the brief period of six months from the foundation gathered round its banner no fewer than 500 enthusiasts as members, and further extended its ramifications by the establishment of eight geographical branches of the main body to further consolidate the League and promote its cherished objects.

These branches are as follows:—the Northern, North-western, Midland, Southern, South-western and Welsh, Eastern, North London, and Scottish, each of which are doing yeoman service in both propaganda and practical development of the breed to further the objects of the League, which are officially summarised as follows :—

(1) Immediately starting and publishing a stud book.

(2) Establishing an office from which unbiassed advice on mating and correct information with regard to the general subject of breeding may be obtained. The characteristics of leading sires and dams and those which they are known to transmit to their progeny, etc., etc.

(3) To immediately form local branches all over Great Britain, and, working through them, to as soon as possible obtain classes for Alsatians at every recognised show.

(4) To hold annual shows under the world's most famous judges, and to hold these in different centres of the country for the purpose of allowing people all over the country to see the best specimens of the breed.

(5) To do the same with intelligence trials and police-work exhibitions.

(6) To make arrangements whereby members can obtain the best possible foods at much under shop prices.

(7) To give advice and facilities for training.

(8) To place certain special veterinary facilities at the disposal of members.

(9) To obtain, where possible, reduced rates of stud fees to members of the League.

(10) To establish a training kennel at which members' dogs will receive instruction at cost price. The subscription is one guinea per annum.

The first exhibition promoted by the League was that held at Birmingham on August 22 and 23, 1924, at which 368 entries were returned and that great German authority, Capt. von Stephanitz, specially imported to judge.

The second show of the League was held in London on February 3, 1925, when there were returned an entry of 490. At this show Continental judicial talent was discarded, and a triumvirate of native experts empanelled in the persons of the Hon. Miss E. Lindley Wood, Mr. H. Robbins, and Mr. A. Cornish Bowden, M.R.C.V.S., and later the British Alsatian Association was launched.

Thus the wave of enthusiasm in this country for this popular alien specimen of the canine race has been given a setting not exceeded (if approached) in magnitude and popularity by any other native or foreign breed, which surely portends greater lustre and achievement in the future.

The chief points to look for in an Alsatian puppy of three of four months are : good length of face, small ears, great bone, sound limbs, body rather long than short, and a dense coat.

The following is a copy of the standard description and points of the Alsatian Wolfdog Club, which are recognised by all the Alsatian Clubs and combinations :—

STANDARD OF POINTS.

GENERAL APPEARANCE.—The general appearance of the Alsatian Wolfdog is a well-proportioned dog, showing great suppleness of limb, neither massive nor heavy, but at the same time free from any suggestion of weediness. It must not approach the greyhound type. The ideal height (measured to the shoulder) not less than 22in. in bitches and 24in. in dogs, and not more than 26in. in either sex. The body, rather long, is strong boned, with plenty of muscle, obviously capable of endurance and speed, and of quick and sudden movement. Its method of locomotion is a tireless, long striding gait, and all its movements should be entirely free from stiltiness. The whole dog and its expression give the impression of perpetual vigilance, strong fidelity ; lively, and ever watchful, alert to every sight and sound, nothing escaping its attention, showing no fear, but with a decided suspiciousness towards strangers—in striking contra-distinction to the immediate friendliness of some breeds ; possessing highly developed senses, a vivid mentality, and plenty of temperament, strongly individualistic, and showing unique powers of intelligence. Three of its most outstanding traits are its incorruptibility, its discernment, and its ability to think for itself.

THE HEAD.—The head is proportionate to the size of the body, long, lean, and clean cut, broad at the back of the skull, but without coarseness, tapering to the nose with only a slight stop between the eyes. The skull is slightly domed, and the top of the nose should be parallel to the forehead. The cheeks must not be full or in any way prominent, and the whole head, when viewed from the top, should be much in the form of a V, well filled in under the eyes. There should be plenty of substance in foreface, with a good depth from top to bottom. A long, narrow, show Collie or Borzoi head is a serious fault.

THE MUZZLE.—The muzzle is strong and long, and, while tapering to the nose, it must not be carried to such an extreme as to give the appearance of being overshot. It must not show any weakness, or be snipey or lippy. The lips must be tight fitting and clean. The nose should be black whatever colour the dog may be. A pink or liver-coloured nose is a disqualification.

THE TEETH.—The teeth should be sound and strong, gripping with a scissor-like action, the lower incisors just behind, but touching the upper. To be undershot or overshot is a bad fault.

THE EYES.—The eyes are almond-shaped, of average size, as nearly as possible matching the surrounding coat, but darker rather than lighter in shade, and placed to look straight forward. They must not be in any way bulging or prominent, and must show a lively, alert, and highly intelligent expression.

THE EARS.—The ears should be of moderate size, but rather large than small, broad at the base, and pointed at the tips, placed rather high on the skull, and carried erect—all adding to the alert expression of the dog as a whole. It should be noted, in case novice breeders may be misled, that in Alsatian Wolfdog puppies the ears often hang until the age of six months, and sometimes longer, becoming erect with the replacement of the milk teeth.

THE NECK.—The neck should be strong, fairly long, with plenty of muscle, fitting gracefully into the body, joining the head without sharp angles, and free from throatiness.

THE FOREQUARTERS.—In the forequarters the shoulders should slope well back; the ideal being that a line drawn through the centre of the shoulder blade should form a right angle with the humerus when the leg is perpendicular to the ground. Upright shoulders are a bad fault. They should show plenty of muscle, which is quite distinct from, and must not be confused with, coarse or loaded bone, which is a fault. The shoulder-bone should be clean. The forelegs should be perfectly straight, viewed from the front, but the pastern should show a slight angle with the forearm when regarded from the side; too great an angle denotes weakness, and, while carrying plenty of bone, it should be of good quality. Anything approaching the massive bone of the Newfoundland, for example, being a decided fault.

THE HINDQUARTERS.—The hindquarters should show breadth and strength, the loins being broad and strong, the rump rather long and sloping, and the legs, when viewed from behind, must be quite straight, without any tendency to cowhocks, or bowhocks, which are an extremely serious fault. The stifles are well turned, and the hocks strong and well let down. The ability to turn quickly is a necessary asset in the Alsatian Wolfdog, and this can only be got by a good length of thigh-bone and leg, and by the bending of the hock.

BODY PROPERTIES.—The body is muscular, the back is broadish and straight, rather long, but strong boned and well developed. The belly shows a waist without being tucked up. There should be a good depth of brisket or chest, and that should not be too broad. The sides are flat compared to some breeds, and while the dog must not be barrel-ribbed it must not be so flat as to be actually slabsided. While quick in movement, and speedy, the Alsatian Wolfdog is not a greyhound in any way. As giving an idea of the body proportions, it may be added that the length of body from the front point of the breast-bone in a straight line to the buttocks should be greater than the height to the shoulder as is 10 to 9. Short-backed dogs with high legs should be discarded. A weak back is a decided fault.

THE GAIT.—The gait should be supple, smooth, and long-reaching, carrying the body along with a minimum of up-and-down movement.

THE TAIL.—The tail, during rest, should hang in a slight curve. During movement and excitement it will be raised, but under no circumstances should the tail be carried past a vertical line drawn through the root. The tails with curls and pronounced hooks are faulty.

THE FEET.—The feet should be round and short, the toes strong, slightly arched, and held close together. The pads should be hard, the nails short and strong. Dew claws are neither a fault nor a virtue, but are better removed, as they are liable to spoil the gait.

THE COAT.—The coat is smooth, but it is at the same time a double coat. The undercoat is woolly in texture, thick, and close, and to it the animal owes its characteristic resistance to cold. The outer coat is also close, each hair straight, hard, and lying flat, so that it is rain-resisting. Under the body, to behind the legs, the coat is longer, and forms near the thigh a mild form of breeching. On the head (including the inside of the ears), to the front of the legs and the feet, the hair is short. Along the neck it is longer and thicker, and in winter approaches a form of ruff. A coat either too long or too short is a fault. As an average, the hairs on the back should be from $1\frac{1}{2}$in. to $2\frac{1}{2}$in. in length. The lack of heavy undercoat is a grave fault.

THE COLOUR.—The colour of the Alsatian Wolfdog has no effect on its character or on its fitness for work, and so colour is, in reason, a secondary consideration. It may be brown, iron-grey, cinder-grey, fawn, black, or black-and-tan, etc. Colour in itself must not influence judicial decisions. The definite colour of puppies cannot be determined until arrival of the upper coat. White should be debarred in Alsatian Wolfdogs, as it makes the animal much too conspicuous for its legitimate work.

SCALE OF POINTS.

Nature and expression	20
General appearance	15
Gait	15
Bone	7
Back	7
Coat	5
Hindquarters	7
Forequarters	7
Chest	7
Seat	5
Head	5
	100

CHAPTER XXXIV.

The British Bulldog.

The British Bulldog must occupy, and deservedly, the pride of place in the Non-Sporting breeds, since it is one of the oldest of them, in the first place, and, in the second, because this breed has been selected, probably by the British themselves, to typify the national character, as a result of which the English Bulldog is often termed the "national" breed. In this latter connection it is indisputable that the English race (in which we, of course, include the Scotch, Irish, and Welsh people) are dogged, determined, courageous, and tenacious, which are the chief characteristics of the Bulldog in respect of his innate virtues, for he knows no fear, will fight to the death, and attack anything with hair on it. At the same time, the Bulldog is one of the

BULLDOG.

most docile of the canine species, and absolutely free from treachery, which together make him a most desirable companion and in this way accounts for his great popularity. The breed for years has been eagerly sought after by admirers in every part of the world, £200, £300, and £500 being prices which have frequently been paid for winning specimens, whilst in one case £1,000 was paid by an American, Mr. Richard Croker, junr., to Mr. Walter Jefferies for the dog Ch. Rodney Stone. A higher price than this, even—£1,200—was, I believe, refused by Mr. Atkinson Jowett for Ch. Pressgang, a similar price or a little less being rejected by Mrs. Edgar Waterlow for her Ch. Nuthurst Doctor, whilst Mr. Luke Crabtree's refusal of American dollars to the amount of £800 for Ch. Prince Albert and £700 for Ch. Moston Michael is a matter of history, as is a similar offer for Ch. Broadlea Squire and Menestrel (an unshown dog), which the late Mr. John W. Proctor was offered and which he declined.

Although similar big prices have been paid for St. Bernards in years gone by, and for Collies still later, no such prices are nowadays realised for the saintly breed, and the sales in Collies can hardly be said to equal those of the British Bulldog, who is thus given the proud position of pre-eminence in public esteem and marketable value at the present moment.

As to the origin of the Bulldog, it seems to be clearly set forth by the historian that he is descended from the Old English Mastiff, which appears to be the dog first used for bull and bear baiting. Jesse says the first mention of a Bulldog was in 1631 or 1632, in a letter written by Prestwich Eaton from St. Sebastian to George Wellingham, London, for a good Mastiff and two good " Bulldogs." The former sport was initiated with the disappearance of the wild oxen from the woods, in the reign of King John, towards the close of the twelfth or beginning of the thirteenth century. We read that " William, Earl Warren, Lord of Stamford, standing upon the castle walls of this town, saw two bulls fighting for a cow in the meadow. The butcher's dog pursued one of the bulls, which, maddened with the noise and the multitude, galloped through the town. This sight so pleased the Earl that he gave those meadows (called the Castle Meadows), where first the bull duel began, for a common to the butchers of the town, on condition that they find a mad bull six weeks before Christmas Day for the continuance of the sport, every year." Bull-baiting became a very fashionable British sport, and was at one time patronised by persons of the highest rank, from the King and Queen of England down, just as bull-baiting in Spain is to-day the leading and most fashionable sport, in which matadors take the place of Bulldogs. As the sport developed, and became popular, naturally the breeding of dogs best adapted for bringing down the bull followed, and in this way originals of our present-day Bulldogs were produced, but, of course, not so pronounced in type nor so perfectly fitted structurally and anatomically for their specific avocation as they are to-day. It was, no doubt, found that a less and more agile dog than a Mastiff would be better for the purpose of this sport, and either smaller specimens would be used or the Mastiff become dwarfed by crossing, probably with a Terrier. As the bull always attacks his canine foes head down, so as to catch them up with his horns, the dogs would be taught to seize him by the nose, which indeed would be the natural mode of attack of the dog in such circumstances. The type of dog that would be suggested to careful students of the sport, even in the old days, would be a low-set, powerful fronted and jawed dog, with light quarters, and whose nose receded from his lower jaw, to enable him to breathe while hanging on to his quarry, his light hindquarters further assisting him in hanging on to the bull, whose habit in such circumstances invariably is to whirl the dog in the air in his frantic endeavour to shake him off.

The engraving dated 1734, from a picture by Morland, of three Bulldogs of the same time and very similar to indifferent specimens of present-day type, is of dogs of 40lbs. or 50lbs. weight. Then, again, in the Crib and Rosa picture, dated 1817, we have the same type as I have outlined. It was about this time, early in the nineteenth century, that bull-baiting was prohibited by Act of Parliament, and the Bulldog's specific occupation, like that of Othello, was gone. Still, the dog, as a breed, was firmly established, and was preserved by his admirers. With the disappearance of bull-baiting, a substitute sport appears to have been found for the Bulldog—viz., dog-fighting, for which he was largely used by the lower classes, and to which (as in cock-fighting, a sport that flourished in those days) many of the aristocracy gave tacit countenance if not openly took part.

In the matter of type, the true Bulldog, from the abolition of bull-baiting in the beginning of the nineteenth century to about the middle of it, somewhat degenerated, not in courage, but in type and outward characteristics. He was in this degenerate state when the earliest showmen found him, which included the late Mr. William George, Mr. James Hinks, Mr. Jacob Lamphier,

Mr. Stockdale, and one or two others, who were great Bulldog breeders and enthusiasts, to whom we largely owe the restoration of the pure breed.

The Bulldog has now been completely lifted out of his "Bill Sikes" surroundings, and it has been made possible for the most cultured lady of the highest social position to be closely associated with his breeding and exhibition.

The Bulldog Club (Incorporated) is no doubt largely responsible not only for framing, after very careful investigation of his antecedents, a well thought-out description of a perfect Bulldog and a code of points, which it published in 1875, but for purifying the Bulldog atmosphere, and assisting to popularise the breed with the general public as well as with fanciers. How far it succeeded is shown in the fact of some twenty other Bulldog clubs having subsequently sprung into being in the British Isles, all devoted to the breed and working for its propagation and advancement. These include the following :—

> The Bulldog Club (Incorporated), The British, The London, Manchester and Counties, Leeds and County, Leodensian, Northumberland and Durham, Bristol and West of England, Scottish, Sheffield, Hull and District, Liverpool and District, Yorkshire, Birmingham and Midland Counties, The Irish, and others.

The Allied Clubs of Great Britain is a comparatively new federation of the Bulldog clubs, which gave great promise of usefulness and the combining of the Bulldog forces into one concrete body for the purpose of the better promotion of its interests and the bringing into harmony of the various tenets of the different clubs, and more particularly the divergence in the standard descriptions and points. The Bulldog Club (Incorporated), however, fought shy of this scheme, and refused to sacrifice its individuality and antiquity. The federation formulated a 500-point standard, but it does not seem to have "taken on," nor the federation to have made much progress.

In looking for a perfect specimen of a Bulldog, his ancient but obsolete avocation should be carefully borne in mind, because the standard description and points have been framed on such lines as to enable the dog to bait the bull in the most successful manner.

In general appearance the dog should therefore be a low-set, heavy-boned and wide-fronted animal, with a broad, turned-up underjaw and large receding nostrils, a big skull and small ears, and light hindquarters, the purpose of which has already been described. Although his quarters should be light, his hind limbs should be perfectly sound, his hocks well let down, and his stifles nicely bent. His chest should be both wide and deep—making provision for any amount of lung power—and let down somewhat between his forelegs, which should be well set on outside, slightly curved at the armpits, to allow of the dog getting down to his work, but they should be perfectly sound, and in no way deformed. The neck is required to be very short and thick, which gives to it additional strength. The jaws should be wide and strong for the same purpose, additional strength and leverage being given by the turn-up of the jaw. The object of the layback is, as I have already stated, to allow the dog to breathe freely when pinning the bull and hanging on to him. The arched loin gives the dog a little additional spring, whilst spring of rib is always an indication of a big heart. The dog should move with a roll, occasioned by his heavy front and light quarters, but he should move freely, and show great activity for his size.

Such details as great width of skull from eye to ear, small ears, large eyes, short low-set tail, quality of coat, are what I may term little finishing touches to the animal.

The most flagrant defects are legginess and light bone, flat sides, down face, straight, narrow underjaw, long back, and big ears or drop ears, any one of which seriously discounts an otherwise good specimen.

Colour is of little consequence, except the disqualifying colour prohibited by rule, together with a " Dudley " nose—that is, a liver or flesh-coloured nose, which is due to great inbreeding.

Weight, again, is of no consequence, now that the dog is not required for his legitimate sport, all weights being permissible from the miniatures of 15lbs. weight or less to a dog 6olbs. or even 7olbs. in weight.

The chief points to look for in the selection of Bulldog puppies at from two to four months old and after are : A massive head, with long, sweeping underjaw, well turned up, not necessarily short nose, but it must be *retrousse* —laid well back, massive, broad foreface, big skull, little ears, short back and tail, short legs, with enormous bone.

The following are the description and standard of points referred to :—

THE GENERAL APPEARANCE of the Bulldog is that of a smooth-coated, thick-set dog, rather low in stature, but broad, powerful, and compact. Its head strikingly massive, and large in proportion to the dog's size ; its face extremely short ; its muzzle very broad, blunt, and inclined upwards ; its body short and well-knit, the limbs stout and muscular ; its hindquarters high and strong, but rather lightly made in comparison with its heavily made foreparts. The dog should convey an impression of determination, strength, and activity, similar to that suggested by the appearance of a thick-set Ayrshire bull.

THE SKULL should be very large—the larger the better,—and in circumference should measure (round in front of the ears) at least the height of the dog at the shoulders. Viewed from the front, it should appear very high from the corner of the lower jaw to the apex of the skull, and also very broad and square. The cheeks should be well rounded and extended sideways beyond the eyes. Viewed at the side, the head should appear very high, and very short from its back to the point of nose.

THE FOREHEAD should be flat, neither prominent nor overhanging the face ; and the skin upon it and about the head very loose, and well wrinkled.

The projections of the FRONTAL BONES should be very prominent, broad, square, and high, causing a deep and wide indentation between the eyes, termed the " stop." From the " stop " a furrow both broad and deep should extend up the middle of the skull, being traceable to the apex.

THE EYES, seen from the front, should be situated low down in the skull, as far from the ears as possible. The eyes and " stop " should be in the same straight line, which should be at right angles to the furrow. They should be as wide apart as possible, provided their outer corners are within the outline of the cheeks. They should be quite round in shape, of moderate size, neither sunken nor prominent, and in colour should be very dark—almost, if not quite, black, showing no white when looking directly forward.

THE EARS should be set high on the head—*i.e.*, the front inner edge of each ear should (as viewed from the front) join the outline of the skull at the top corner of such outline, so as to place them as wide apart and as high and as far from the eyes as possible. In size they should be small and thin. The shape termed " rose ear " is correct and folds inward at its back, the upper or front edge curving over outwards and backwards, showing part of the inside of the burr.

THE FACE, measured from the front of the cheekbone to the nose, should be as short as possible, and its skin should be deeply and closely wrinkled.

THE MUZZLE should be short, broad, turned upwards, and very deep from the corner of the eye to the corner of the mouth.

THE NOSE should be large, broad, and black; its top should be deeply set back, almost between the eyes. The distance from the inner corner of the eye (or from the centre of the stop between the eyes) to the extreme tip of the nose should not exceed the length from the tip of the nose to the edge of the under lip. *The Nostrils* should be large, wide, and black, with a well-defined vertical straight line between them.

THE FLEWS, called the " chop," should be thick, broad, pendant, and very deep, hanging completely over the lower jaw at the sides (not in front). They should join the under lip in front, and quite cover the teeth, which should not be seen when the mouth is closed.

THE JAW should be broad, massive, and square, the canine teeth, or tusks, wide apart. The lower jaw should project considerably in front of the upper, and turn up. It should be broad and square, and have the six small front teeth between the canines in an even row. The teeth should be large and strong.

THE NECK should be moderate in length (rather short than long) very thick, deep, and strong. It should be well arched at the back, with much loose, thick, and wrinkled skin about the throat, forming a dewlap on each side, from the lower jaw to the chest. *The Chest* should be very wide laterally, round, prominent, and deep, making the dog appear very broad and short-legged in front.

THE SHOULDERS should be broad, sloping, and deep, very powerful and muscular, giving the appearance of having been " tacked " on to the body.

THE BRISKET should be capacious, round, and very deep from the top of the shoulders to its lowest part where it joins the chest, and be well let down between the forelegs. It should be large in diameter, and round behind the forelegs (not flat-sided, the ribs being well rounded). The body should be well ribbed up behind, with the belly tucked up, and not pendulous.

THE BACK should be short and strong, very broad at the shoulders, and comparatively narrow at the loins. There should be a slight fall to the back close behind the shoulders (its lowest part), whence the spine should rise to the loins (the top of which should be higher than the top of the shoulders), thence curving again more suddenly to the tail, forming an arch—a distinctive characteristic of the breed, termed " roach-back."

THE FORELEGS should be very stout and strong, set wide apart, thick, muscular, and straight, with well-developed forearms, presenting a rather bowed outline, but the bones of the legs should be large and straight, not bandy or curved. They should be rather short in proportion to the hind legs, but not so short as to make the back appear long and detract from the dog's activity, and so cripple him. The elbows should be low, and stand well away from the ribs. The pasterns should be short, straight, and strong. The forefeet should be straight, and turn very slightly outwards, of medium size, and moderately round. The toes compact and thick, being well split up, making the knuckles prominent and high.

THE HIND LEGS should be large and muscular, and longer in proportion than the forelegs, so as to elevate the loins. The hocks should be slightly bent and well let down, so as to be long and muscular from the loins to the point of the hock. The lower part of the leg should be short, straight, and strong. The stifles should be round, and turned slightly outwards away from the body. The hocks are thereby made to approach each other, and the hind feet to turn outwards. The latter, like the forefeet, should be round and compact, with the toes well split up and the knuckles prominent. From its formation the dog has a peculiar, heavy, and constrained gait, appearing to walk with short, quick steps on the tip of its toes, its hind feet not being lifted high, but appearing to skim the ground, and running with the right shoulder rather advanced, similar to the manner of a horse in cantering.

SIZE.—The most desirable size for the Bulldog is about 50lb.

THE TAIL, termed the "stern," should be set on low, jut out rather straight, and then turn downwards. It should be round, smooth, and devoid of fringe or coarse hair. It should be moderate in length—rather short than long—thick at the root, and tapering quickly to a fine point. It should have a downward carriage (not having a decided upward curve at the end), and the dog should not be able to raise it over its back.

THE COLOUR should be whole or smut (that is, a whole colour with a black mask or muzzle). The only colours (which should be brilliant and pure of their sort) are whole colours—viz., brindles, reds, with their varieties; fawns, fallows, etc.; whites, and also pied (*i.e.*, a combination of white with any other of the foregoing colours).

THE COAT should be fine in texture, short, close, and smooth (hard only from the shortness and closeness, not wiry).

The following 100 points show the relative value of the properties mentioned in the foregoing standard description.

SKULL AND HEAD.—Size, 3; height, 1; breadth and squareness, 3; shape, 2; wrinkles, 4	13
STOP.—Depth, 2; breadth, 1; extent of furrow, 1 ..	4
EYES.—Position, 2; size, 1; shape, 1; colour, 1 ..	5
EARS.—Position, 1; shape, 1; size, 1; thinness, 1 ..	4
FACE.—Shortness, 1; breadth, 1; depth, 1; shape and upward turn of muzzle, 1; wrinkles, 1; nose and nostrils, 5	10
CHOP.—Breadth, 1; depth, 1; complete covering of front teeth, 1	3
MOUTH.—Width and squareness of jaw, 2; projection and upward turn of lower jaw, 2; size and condition of teeth, 2	6
CHEST AND NECK.—Length, 1; thickness, 1; arch, 1; dewlap, 1; width, depth, and roundness of chest, 1	5
SHOULDERS.—Size, 2; breadth, 2; muscle, 1 ..	5
BODY.—Depth and thickness of brisket, 2; capacity and roundness of ribs, 3	5
BACK (ROACH).—Shortness, 2; width of shoulders, 1; shape, strength, and arch at loin, 2	5
FORELEGS. — Stoutness, 1½; shortness, 1; development, 1; feet, 1½	5
HIND LEGS.—Stoutness, 1; length, 1; shape and development, 2; feet, 1	5
SIZE..	5
TAIL	5
COAT AND COLOUR	5
GENERAL APPEARANCE	10
	100

The following are disqualified: "Dudleys," Blacks, and Black-and-tans.

The size of Bulldogs is usually divided as follows:—

Dogs: Exceeding 55lbs., exceeding 45lbs. but not exceeding 55lbs., not exceeding 45lbs. Bitches: Exceeding 45lbs., exceeding 35lbs. but not exceeding 45lbs., not exceeding 35lbs.

BULLDOG (MINIATURE).

The weight of the Bulldog (Miniature), according to the rules of the Miniature Bulldog Club, should not exceed 25lbs. for dogs nor 22lbs. for bitches, but classes are often given and encouraged for dogs and bitches not exceeding 20lbs.

The points and characteristics of this sub-division of the British Bulldog may be summed up in the simple statement that he should be an exact replica, in miniature, of the larger specimens in every point and detail; in fact, just like looking at a large Bulldog through the reverse end of the telescope. Their origin is not very clear, but is doubtless of a later date than that of their bigger brothers. In the breeding of any variety odd miniature specimens will crop up in litters, and these have, no doubt, suggested to some fanciers the idea of propagating a race of pigmy Bulldogs, probably as ladies' pets. It is on record that many Toy specimens, as they were first called, have been produced in the Bulldog breeding centres of London, Sheffield, Birmingham, Nottingham, etc., and it is doubtless from these that the present-day and more perfected race of Miniatures or Bantam Bulldogs have sprung. It is also on record that in the distant past many of these Toy specimens were exported to France. They were, for the most part, prick-eared or tulip-eared in the old days, and in later years re-imported French Bulldogs have been used to cross with English-bred Toys for the purpose of fixing the size. This cross, happily not largely resorted to, had the disadvantage of perpetuating the hideous bat and tulip ears, and of rather spoiling the correct British type.

BULLDOG (MINIATURE).

The institution of the Miniature Bulldog Club in 1898 marked an epoch in the history and manufacture of the Toy or Miniature Bulldog. The Club was composed for the most part of ladies of title and position who have taken up the cult of the Miniature Bulldog, and to whose efforts the improved position and features of the dog are due. The first aim of this club was to breed out the defects—fortunately not deep-rooted—implanted in the variety by the French cross, in which its devotees have been eminently successful. Breeders have been largely assisted in their efforts in this direction by the advent of very typical Toys, which, singularly, have been bred by accident and without design from notable specimens of the larger variety; perfect in ear carriage, and with no foreign taint whatever in their blood. These include Ch. No Trumps, Baby Bullet, Minnie Surewyn, Mersham Planet, Ch. Little Truefit, and others.

The type of the Bulldog (Miniature) was never more fixed, probably, than it is to-day, nor were there so many real Miniatures coming under the regulation weight in normal condition without starving them down to it, than exist at the present moment, which is a hopeful sign, and if breeders will only make good use of the position they have gained in bantamising the larger Bulldog, by careful selection and great patience, the future of the variety is undoubtedly a bright one. Although the French Bulldog has got a good hold on the British public's fancy, the bat ears are a great drawback to the dog in the estimation of many, in addition to the general type being somewhat removed from what have come to be regarded as salient features in a Bulldog—a dog intended for bull-baiting,—viz., great width and turnup of underjaw, very short nose and good layback, wide chest, let well down between the forelegs, features that are still required in the Miniature, but that are absent in the Frenchman, whose straight foreface and Terrier-like limbs some consider disentitle him to the appellation of " Bulldog " altogether.

The chief points to look for in Miniature puppies are identical with those in the larger variety, except that the smaller the puppy the better, if good in points.

Points of the Bulldog (Miniature).

THE GENERAL APPEARANCE of the Miniature Bulldog must as nearly as possible resemble that of the big Bulldog.

THE SKULL should be large, forehead flat, the skin about it well wrinkled, the " stop " broad and deep, extending up the middle of the forehead.

EYES of moderate size, situated low down on the skull, and as wide apart as possible.

EARS to be " rose." " Bat " ears are a disqualification.

FACE as short as possible.

NOSE jet black, deeply set back, almost between the eyes.

MUZZLE to be short, broad, and turned upwards.

THE LOWER JAW should project considerably in front of the upper, and turn up.

NECK to be short with much loose skin about it. " Frogginess " is objectionable.

CHEST to be very wide, round, and deep.

BACK short and strong, narrow towards the loins and broad at the shoulder. A roach back is desirable.

TAIL to be short and not carried above the back.

FORELEGS to be short in proportion to the hind legs.

HINDQUARTERS much lighter in proportion than forequarters.

THE WEIGHT must be 22lb. and under for bitches ; 25lb. and under for dogs.

Scale of Points.

General appearance and character	20
Head	10
Underjaw	10
Ears	5
Body	15
Size	5
Roach back	5
Chest and set-on of shoulders	10
Tail	$2\frac{1}{2}$
Legs and feet	$7\frac{1}{2}$
Soundness	10
	100

Since the above chapter was written the Kennel Club has abolished any weight limit in Bulldogs, so that the Miniature Bulldog does not now exist as a separate variety.

It is claimed for

THE FRENCH BULLDOG (OR BOULEDOGUE FRANCAIS) (to give the popular alien his correct nomenclature) that he is a pure French breed. Mr. F. W. Cousens, M.R.C.V.S., who has made the variety a study, in " The New Book of the Dog," says :—

Authorities across the Channel are of the opinion that the French Bulldog is strictly a breed of French origin, yet they are willing to admit that of comparatively recent years there have been from time to time importations from England which have been used as a cross with the native dog, and that this cross has, perhaps, led to a nearer approximation to the British type than was the case prior to the admixture of British blood. M. J. Boutroue, the Secretary of the French Bulldog Club of Paris, and Secretary of the French Kennel Club, holds this opinion very strongly, as do Mr. Gordon Bennet, President of the Paris Club, and Prince de Wagram, its President d'Honneur. Mr. Max Hartenstein, of Berlin, who was first interested in the French Bulldog in 1870, and has owned and bred great numbers of them, declares that " there can be no two opinions as to the fact of the French Bulldog being a distinct French breed, with a longer history and more remote origin than is generally understood." He is aware of the introduction of small British specimens into France; not, however, necessarily for the purpose of interbreeding, but principally because French fanciers desired to have

FRENCH BULLDOG.

a bright, vivacious, bantam specimen. He is of opinion that in Paris in 1870, the breed, as a whole, was smaller than it is to-day.

The late Mr. George R. Krehl, of London, one of the greatest authorities, with whom the subject of the French Bulldog was very thoroughly discussed by the present writer, went still further back into the past (nearly three hundred years), and from his researches built up a plausible and very probable theory as to the origin of this breed in France. In a letter written by him to the *Stock-Keeper* Christmas Supplement, 1900, he showed grounds for believing that the variety came originally from Spain. There was published with Mr. Krehl's letter a copy of an antique bronze placque dated 1625, bearing in *bas-relief* the head of a Bulldog with either cropped, or bat, ears, and the inscription, " *Dogue de Burgos, Espana, anno MDCXXV.*," the artist's name being Cazalla. This placque has been examined by a connoisseur and pronounced authentic. The historic value of this bronze will be at once appreciated when it is remembered that Burgos is the principal town of old Castile, in Spain, noted for the breeding of dogs used in the arena for bull-baiting.

On the other hand, it is contended here in England that the breed has been founded in France by importations of Toy Dogs from England, which undoubtedly took place as far back as the middle of last century, or perhaps, earlier, and subsequently. Our French cousins admit these importations, but contend they were only for the purpose of outcrossing, and, if the information and data furnished by such authorities as our friend the late M. Boutroue, Secretary of the French Bulldog Club and Paris Dog Show; by Mr. Gordon Bennet, proprietor of the great *New York Herald*, and president of the former club; by Prince de Wagram, and by the late Mr. Geo. R. Krehl, who made considerable research into the history of the breed, be reliable, the contention must be correct.

The differences of opinion in the ranks of the Bulldog Club Miniature led, in 1902, to a split, those who favoured the French type, headed by Lady Lewis, forming themselves into a separate club, called the French Bulldog Club, which deserted its English favourite and embraced the French type, which was ultimately placed on the Kennel Club's register under the native title of Bouledogue Français; a standard description was formulated on purely recognised French lines, and thus the two breeds received a sharp and wholesome distinction.

The chief difference between the English Miniature and the French is in foreface and front; in most other points the two breeds are very nearly identical. The body of the Frenchman should be short and rotund, with a distinct roach, and light but sound quarters. His shoulders should be strong, and he should stand on short, fairly stout limbs for his size, not exceeding 22lb., being extremely agile, and, indeed, almost Terrier-like in action and movement. The fundamental difference is seen in the foreface, which in the French should show some slight protrusion of the underjaw and some turnup, but no layback, which, through English Bulldog optics, gives the dog the appearance of being frog-faced. The eyes should be set wide apart, and a good distance shown between the eye and ears, and the skull flat. The ears, of course, should be on the lines of the ears of a bat, but it is satisfactory to note that large ears are deprecated. The tail, again, like that of the English variety, should be short, low set, and tapering to a point, but nothing is said in the standard about a " screw " tail.

The chief points to look for in the selection of Bouledogue Français puppies at from two to four months old and after are: Squareness and shortness of foreface, massiveness of skull, large eye, deep stop, small neat ears, shortness of body, good spring of rib, and straight legs, showing great bone.

The following is the description of the French Bulldog Club of England :—

GENERAL APPEARANCE.—A French Bulldog should be sound, active, and intelligent, of compact build, medium or small sized, with good bone, a short smooth coat, and the various points so evenly balanced that the dog does not look ill-proportioned.

COLOUR.—Colours allowed are all the brindles, also pied dogs (white and brindle).

HEAD AND MUZZLE.—Head massive, square, and broad. Skull nearly flat between the ears, with a domed forehead, the loose skin forming symmetrical wrinkles. Muzzle laid back; nose and lips back. Stop well defined. Lower jaw powerful and turned up square. Nose extremely short, black, and wide, with opened nostrils, and the line well defined. Lips thick, the lower meeting the upper in the middle, completely hiding the teeth. The upper lip should cover the lower on each side with plenty of cushion, but not so exaggerated as to hang too much below the level of the lower jaw. Teeth sound and regular, but not visible when mouth is closed. Tongue must not protrude.

EARS.—" Bat ears " of medium size, wide at the base, rounded at the top, set high, carried upright and parallel, a sufficient width of skull preventing them being too close together, the skin soft and fine, and the orifice, as seen from the front, showing entirely.

EYES.—Eyes dark, of moderate size, round, neither sunken nor prominent, showing no white when looking straight, set wide apart.

BODY.—Tail very short, set low, thick at the root, and tapering quickly towards the tip, and either straight or kinked but never curling over the back. A good tail is placed so that it cannot be carried gaily. Body short, cobby, muscular, with deep and wide brisket, roach back, good "cut up" and well sprung ribs. Neck powerful, with loose skin at the throat, but not exaggerated. Coat texture fine, smooth, lustrous, short, and close.

LEGS.—Fore-legs set wide apart, straight boned, strong, muscular, and short. Hind-legs strong, muscular, and well-proportioned. Hocks well let down and with very fine movement.

FEET.—Feet small, compact, and placed in continuation of the line of the leg, with absolutely sound pasterns. The hind rather longer than the fore. Toes compact, knuckles high, nails short and thick.

HINTS TO BREEDERS ON POINTS TO AVOID.

Too prominent an underjaw, allowing teeth to show. Tongue protruding when mouth shut. Light-coloured or prominent eyes. Long and coarse coat. Tail carried above the level of the back. Dewlap. Bad movement. Too long in the back. Too high on the leg.

DISQUALIFICATION.—Faults which disqualify are :—Any but erect ears. The colours, pure black, black and white, black and tan, mouse grey (blue). Eyes of different colours. Nose other than black. Hare lip. Docked tail.

SCALE OF POINTS.

	Value.
GENERAL APPEARANCE.—Soundness, 15; action, build and bone, 10; colour, 5	30
HEAD.—Skull and forehead, 10; ears, 10; eyes, 5	25
MUZZLE.—Jaws and Teeth, 5; nose, 5	10
BODY.—Tail, 10; neck, chest, and shoulders, 5; back and cut-up, 5; coat, 5	25
LEGS.—Fore legs, feet, and toes, 5; hind legs, feet, and toes, 5	10
Total	100

CHAPTER XXXV.

The Mastiff.

The Old English Mastiff, as it is now termed, is one of the very oldest breeds known to the British Isles. Respecting its origin, I cannot do better than reprint the account given by my old friend, Mr. W. K. Taunton, hon. secretary of the Old English Mastiff Club, one of our very oldest breeders, exhibitors, and judges, and a great authority on the breed, which appears in that most comprehensive work, " The Book of the Dog." He says :

It is possible that the Mastiff owes his origin to some remote ancestor of alien strain. The Assyrian kings possessed a large dog of decided Mastiff type, and used it in the hunting of lions, and credible authorities perceived a similarity in size and form between the British Mastiff and the fierce Molossian dog of the ancient Greeks. It is supposed by many students that the breed was introduced into early Britain by the adventurous Phœnician traders who in the sixth century B.C. voyaged to the Scilly Islands and Cornwall to barter their own commodities in exchange for the useful metals. Knowing the requirements of their barbarian customers, these early merchants from Tyre and Sidon are believed to have brought some of the larger *Pugnaces*, which would be readily accepted by the Britons to supplement, or improve, their courageous but undersized fighting dogs.

Before the invasion by Julius Cæsar, 55 B.C., the name of Britain was little known to the Romans, and it is not to be wondered at that Virgil makes no reference to British dogs ; but Gratius Faliscus, writing in the eighth year of the Christian era, recorded that the *Pugnaces* of Epirus—the true Molossian dogs—were pitted against the *Pugnaces* of Britain, which overpowered them. Gratius further indicates that there were two kinds of the British *Pugnaces*, a larger and a smaller, suggesting the existence of both the Bulldog and the Mastiff, the latter being employed to protect flocks and herds. Strabo, writing some thirty years later, refers to British dogs used in hunting and in warfare, and mentioning the *Pugnaces*, he especially remarks that they had flabby lips and drooping ears.

The courage of the " broad-mouthed dogs of Britain " was recognised and highly prized by the Romans, who employed them for combat in the amphitheatre. Many writers have alleged that in order to secure the best specimens the Roman Emperors appointed a special officer, Procurator Cynegii, who was stationed at Winchester, and entrusted with the duty of selecting and exporting Mastiffs from England to Rome.

By degrees the Mastiff was substituted as a hunting dog in England, and became an all-round guard of person and property—including cattle, of course. Mr. Taunton goes on to say, in his most interesting history of the breed, that—

The names Tie-dog and Bandog intimate that the Mastiff was commonly kept for guard, but many were especially trained for baiting bears, imported lions, and bulls. The sport of bear-baiting reached its glory in the sixteenth century. Queen Elizabeth was fond of witnessing these displays of animal conflict, and during her progresses through her realm bear-baiting was a customary entertainment at the places, such as Kenilworth and Hatfield, at which she rested. Three trained Mastiffs were accounted a fair match against a bear, four against a lion ; but Lord Buckhurst, Elizabeth's ambassador to France in 1572, owned a great Mastiff which, unassisted, successfully baited a bear, a leopard, and a lion, and pulled them all down.

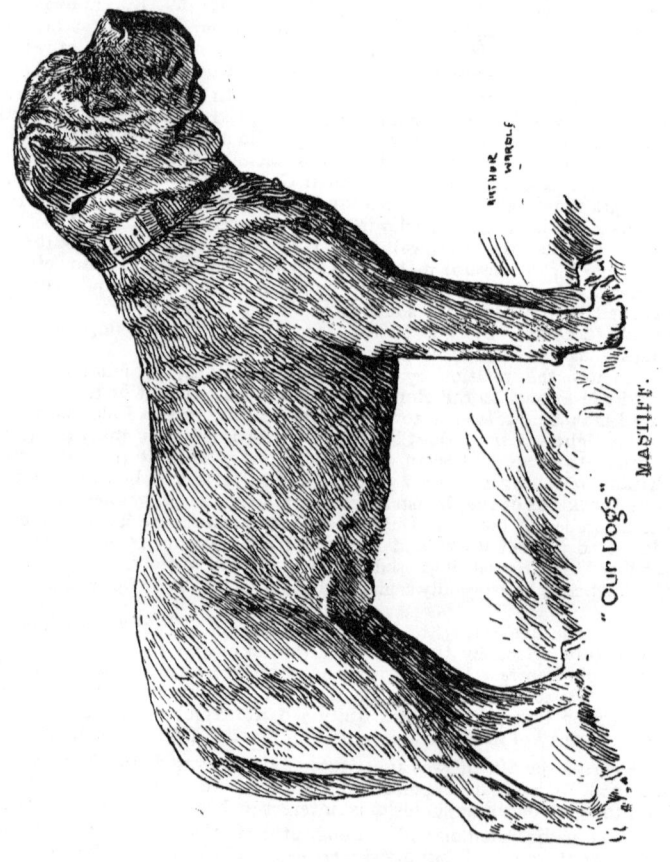

Barnaby Googe, in the early part of the seventeenth century, gives a splendid description of the features and uses of the Mastiff in those days as follows :—

First the Maistie that keepeth the house. For this purpose you must provide you such a one as hath a large and mightie body, a great and shrill voyce, that both with his barking he may discover, and with his sight dismaye, the theefe, yea being not seene, with the horror of his voyce put him to flight. His stature must be neither long nor short, but well set; his head great; his eyes sharp and fiery, either browne or grey; his lippes, blackish, neither turning up nor hanging too much down; his mouth, black and wide; his neather jaw, fat and coming out of it on either side, a fang appearing more outward than his other teeth; his upper teeth, even with his neather, not hanging too much over, sharpe and sudden with his lippes; his countenance, like a lion; his breast, great and shaghayred; his shoulders, broad; his legges, bigge; his tayle, short; his feet, very great. His disposition must be neither too gentle nor too curst, that he neither faune upon a theefe, nor flee upon his friends; very waking; no gadder abroad, nor lavish of his mouth, barking without cause; neither maketh it any matter though he be not swifte, for he is but to fight at home, and to give warning of the enemie.

The Rev. M. B. Wynn says the word Mastiff is of Norman introduction, and he derives it from the Latin *massivus*, massive; *massa*, a massy form of animal.

So much, then, for the origin and early history of this noble breed, which, it is sad to reflect, has in these " pursy times " been allowed to degenerate and become supplanted by several alien breeds. I often think that if some enterprising fancier of wealth and influence would set to work in grim earnest to restore the Old English Mastiff, which is so rich in antiquity and historical lore, to his once proud position of pre-eminence, he would be a national benefactor, and be handed down to posterity as such. The Mastiff, being a large breed, to thrive well requires almost unlimited space and great attention in the breeding and rearing, and is not therefore " anybody's dog." It must be someone who possesses a pretty long purse and spacious premises ; but I feel sure that, even on commercial lines, the investment of capital in the foundation of a kennel started on a good basis—that is to say, stocked by dogs descended from our best strains, and bred true to the type laid down by the Old English Mastiff Club—would result in a remunerative undertaking financially. There probably never was such an opportunity for a fancier to distinguish himself and confer upon the cause of British dogdom the everlasting benefit that the resuscitation of the Old English Mastiff at this moment offers.

Fashion in all breeds of dogs somewhat fluctuates. It is a process of evolution and development—we cannot remain stationary. Sometimes little changes and innovations in type, which come about as the result of either the fads of fanciers or the freaks of nature, are not for the general good of the breed—abnormalities in one point obtained at the expense and sacrifice of others, equally undesirable. These idiosyncrasies, however, generally find their own level, and the changes are often ephemeral. For instance, at one time our type of Mastiffs drifted in the direction of too Bulldoggy heads—that is to say, very short forefaces, with slightly protruding underjaws, and even a suspicion of turnup. This shows an unmistakable Bulldog cross, and the light quarters and weak hind legs, the antithesis of what is required in a Mastiff, were additional evidence of that cross. Massiveness is, of course, required in the head, but also in the body and quarters, and in breeding this should be kept steadily in view. A perfect Mastiff is a massive dog of great size, but who excels in symmetry and proportion, with straight forelegs, great bone, a deep chest, well-sprung ribs, broad loins and hindquarters. His head should be in proportion to his body, and comprise a broad, square skull, decided stop, muzzle not too long nor too short, but deep, broad, and powerful, teeth perfectly level and large. His eyes should be medium in size, not houndy nor too small, but keenly intelligent without being cruel or vicious. A thick coat is an indication of coarseness, just as a thin one denotes delicacy—both of which are objectionable. A short, close coat on a thick skin is what is required. Colour is of little consequence, the recognised colours being fawn and brindle, but a black mask is indispensable. A little white on chest is in no way detrimental, and I hope it will never be regarded as such.

The chief points to look for in the selection of Mastiff puppies at from two to four months old and after are : Great size, massive short head, deep square muzzle, big well-chiselled skull, short deep round body, straight forelegs, and enormous bone.

The Lyme Hall (Cheshire) is generally regarded as the most ancient strain which survives in England, and which the Leghs, the owners, have kept up for many centuries. The Dukes of Devonshire also kept a very noted strain.

The standard description of the Old English Mastiff Club is as follows :—

GENERAL CHARACTER AND SYMMETRY (value 10).—Large, massive, powerful, symmetrical, and well-knit frame. A combination of grandeur and good nature, courage, and docility.

GENERAL DESCRIPTION OF HEAD. — In general outline giving a square appearance when viewed from any point. Breadth greatly to be desired, and should be in ratio to length of the whole head and face as 2 to 3.

GENERAL DESCRIPTION OF BODY (HEIGHT AND SUBSTANCE) (value 10).—Massive, broad, deep, long, powerfully built, on legs wide apart and squarely set. Muscles sharply defined. Size a great desideratum, if combined with quality. Height and substance important, if both points are proportionately combined.

SKULL (value 12).—Broad between the ears, forehead flat, but wrinkled when attention is excited. Brows (superciliary ridges) slightly raised. Muscles of the temples and cheeks (temporal and masseter) well developed. Arch across the skull of a rounded, flattened curve, with a depression up the centre of the forehead from the medium line between the eyes to half-way up the sagittal suture.

FACE OR MUZZLE (value 18).—Short, broad under the eyes, and keeping nearly parallel in width to the end of the nose ; truncated, *i.e.*, blunt and cut off square, thus forming a right angle with the upper line of the face, of great depth from the point of the nose to underjaw. Underjaw broad to the end ; canine teeth healthy, powerful, and wide apart ; incisors level, or the lower projecting beyond the upper, but never sufficiently so as to become visible when the mouth is closed. Nose broad, with widely spreading nostrils when viewed from the front ; flat (not pointed or turned up) in profile. Lips diverging at obtuse angles with the septum, and slightly pendulous, so as to show a square profile. Length of muzzle to whole head and face as 1 to 3. Circumference of muzzle (measured midway between the eyes and nose) to that of the head (measured before the ears) as 3 to 5.

EARS (value 4).—Small, thin to the touch, wide apart, set on at the highest points of the sides of the skull, so as to continue the outline across the summit, and lying flat and close to the cheeks when in repose.

EYES (value 6).—Small, wide apart, divided by at least the space of two eyes. The stops between the eyes well marked, but not too abrupt. Colour hazel-brown, the darker the better, showing no haw.

CHEST AND RIBS (value 8).—Neck slightly arched, moderately long, very muscular, and measuring in circumference about 1in. or 2in. less than the skull before the ears. Chest wide, deep, and well let down between the forelegs. Ribs arched and well rounded. False ribs deep and well set back to the hips. Girth should be one-third more than the height at the shoulder. Shoulder and arm slightly sloping, heavy, and muscular.

FORELEGS AND FEET (value 6).—Legs straight, strong, and set wide apart; bones very large. Elbows square. Pasterns upright. Feet large and round. Toes well arched up. Nails black.

BACK, LOINS, AND FLANKS (value 8).—Back and loins wide and muscular; flat and very wide in a bitch, slightly arched in a dog. Great depth of flanks.

HIND LEGS AND FEET (value 10).—Hindquarters broad, wide, and muscular, with well-developed second thighs. Hocks bent, wide apart, and quite squarely set when standing or walking. Feet round.

TAIL (value 3).—Put on high up, and reaching to the hocks, or a little below them, wide at its root and tapering to the end, hanging straight in repose, but forming a curve, with the end pointing upwards, but not over the back, when the dog is excited.

COAT COLOUR (value 5).—Coat short and close lying, but not too fine over the shoulders, neck, and back. Colour, apricot or silver fawn, or dark fawn-brindle. In any case, muzzle, ears, and nose should be black, with black round the orbits, and extending upwards between them.

CHAPTER XXXVI.

The Great Dane.

The Great Dane is one of the most imposing of the canine species—an alien who has "caught on" with the British doggy public. A German breed, it has now becomes so acclimatised in this country and engrafted in the affections of Englishmen as to be classified by the Kennel Club in its calendar of breeds under the head of home as against foreign varieties. The peculiar part of this classification, however, is that our kennel authority has placed the breed in the Non-Sporting division; but a Boarhound is surely a sporting dog. True, the Great Dane is not used for hunting the boar in the British Isles, for the simple reason that there are no wild boars to hunt; neither is the Borzoi, for the same reason, used for hunting the wolf, and yet the Kennel Club places this latter breed under the head of Sporting Dogs. The two breeds are exactly on all fours with each other in their sporting use and English relationship, which makes it difficult to understand by what line of logic the Kennel Club has thus differentiated between them on its register.

The Great Dane, or Boarhound, as it was formerly called, is of very ancient origin. In its native country, where its ears are still cropped, doubtless for the purpose of preventing the boar from seizing the dog by the ears, and in order to give it a more alert and striking appearance, old coins and prints carry the breed back to some hundreds of years before the Christian era—at least, a very similar dog,—that is to say, a large, long-headed, powerful dog of the proportions and type of the present Great Dane. In earlier times the breed was used in Germany as a protector of property and person, as well as a hunter, a stronger type of dog obtaining in some parts of the Fatherland, which was designated the Ulmer Mastiff. No German palace or castle is considered complete without one or more of these powerful and imposing canines, the breed being an especial favourite with the Iron Chancellor, the late Prince Bismarck, who made them his bodyguard and constant companions. With the introduction of dog shows the breed received greater attention in its native country, where a club has been established for the purpose of promoting and encouraging the propagation of the breed upon lines which the club has laid down as being the most correct according to its conception of what the type and features should be.

The Great Dane was introduced into England long before it was known to the English show bench. Sydenham Edwards, says "British Dogs," writing in the early part of last century, said that the Harlequin Dane was occasionally used in England as an ornamental appendage to run with the coaches of the wealthy, instead of the smaller Dalmatians. Again, Richardson was well acquainted with the dog, which he describes as rarely standing less than 30in. at the shoulder. He refers to the Great Dane, Hector, the property of the Duke of Buccleuch, which measured 32in. at the shoulder at eighteen years of age, when it was no doubt much shrunken. Others of our nobility have been known to possess imported specimens.

The advent of dog shows in England gave the breed an impetus, although the attainment of its present popularity was a somewhat slow process. This is accounted for by the fact that only the wealthier classes at first could afford to take it up, by reason of the expense involved in importing dogs and keeping up a kennel of them, which necessitated great kennel accommodation and a kennelman. By degrees, however, the smaller fanciers embraced the breed, and now devotees of the species may be numbered by the hundred, with

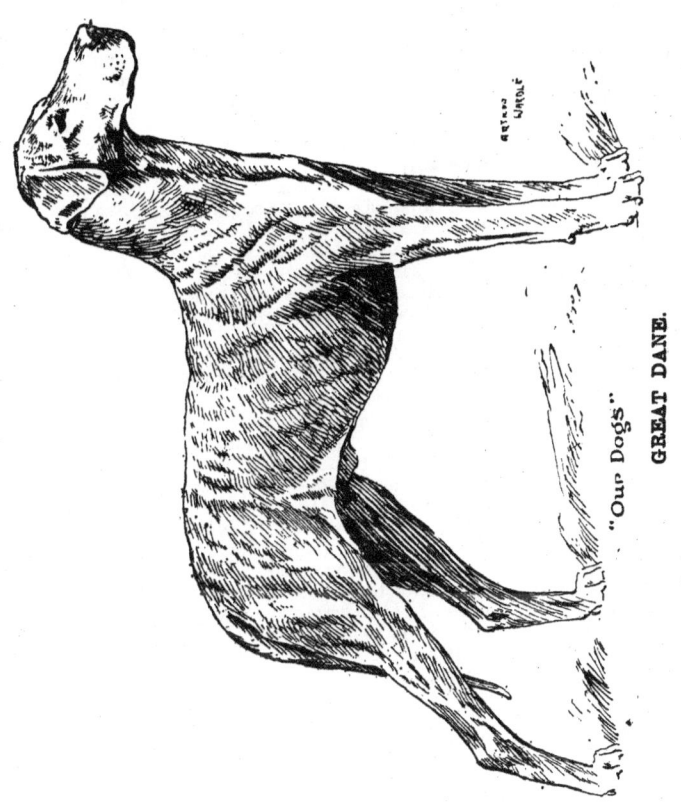

"Our Dogs" GREAT DANE.

several clubs—the Great Dane Club and the Northern Great Dane Club—in existence to look after its interests.

All the earlier specimens were, of course, cropped. The abolition of cropping in England in 1898 dealt a blow to the Great Dane, just as it affected other cropped English breeds, all of which have, however, happily survived the edict. For a time the ears of Great Danes were very unsightly, being large and, for the most part, carried irregularly. The paramount duty of the Great Dane Club at this particular epoch was to concentrate its attention upon the improvement of the ears. This meant a total reversal of the old policy, which had been to produce a strong, big ear, which would ensure a stout, erect, aural appendage, or what remained of it, when cropped. What was now considered the most pleasing form of ear was a small, thin ear, to fall over the head, much in the same way as that of a Fox, Irish, or Airedale Terrier, and it is marvellous how, in the course of a few years, the ugly ears of the Dane have been almost obliterated, and small, neat, nicely carried ears, which are now the rule and not the exception, substituted. With the improvement in ears gradually came an influx of Dane admirers and enthusiasts, although there are among the older school of fanciers some who look back with pride to the cropped champions of the past, and declare that an uncropped Great Dane of otherwise equal merit has not nearly the same character in head. But even if there is a little difference, it is, of course, more than compensated for by the great cruelty which is saved the breed. Breeding for ears to a great extent seems to have involved a little sacrifice in the matter of soundness of limb, which is probably the weakest spot in the Great Dane armour of to-day, and upon this point it will be to the everlasting good of the breed if breeders will concentrate their attention and energies, instead of making colour a *sine qua non*—an innovation with which a large portion of the fraternity has recently been seized, and which has gone so far as to have become one of the tenets of the Great Dane Club, and incorporated in its code of points. It is a German introduction, since colour is a cardinal point in connection with the breed in the Fatherland; but then, the dog is found in greater perfection there than in England, speaking generally. The breed, however, is making rapid strides now, if this colour fad does not retard its legitimate progress. I always think a good Great Dane cannot be a bad colour, and I know many prominent Great Dane enthusiasts in England who hold the same opinion. In all British breeds, except a few purely fancy breeds, such as Black-and-tan Terriers, Pomeranians, and one or two Toy Dog breeds, colour is of quite secondary importance. It is not so on the Continent. A good red, or black-and-tan, or liver-and-tan Dachshund with a white foot or white on chest would not be handicapped even at an English show, whereas it would involve disqualification in Germany.

What should be the first and paramount considerations in a Great Dane, which is essentially a sporting dog, and one of the finest in existence for big game, are size, soundness of limb, and symmetry, power, and elegance. After these desiderata have been obtained, then, and then only, should colour step in. To sacrifice any one of those cardinal points for mere colour is, in my opinion, pure sacrilege.

The most popular colours are brindles, harlequins, and fawns of several shades, although blacks and blues are frequently met with.

The head, as the index of all breeds, is a part of the anatomy which must be emphasised in a Great Dane. The long telescopic head, narrow, deep, square muzzle, with a majestically poised neck, are great features in the Great Dane. Other desiderata are great height, a well-balanced frame, obliquely placed shoulders, and a pair of forelegs as straight as gun barrels, with short, stout feet and strong pads. The hindquarters should be thick through, which means wide, powerful loins, nicely rounded at the extremity, and thighs wide, with hocks perfectly parallel and well let down, and stifles well bent. A dog so formed will be comparatively short in the back, but covering a lot of ground below, which formation and anatomy mean that the dog cannot move badly if it wanted to, and that it must have pace, and be a stayer if it has a big heart. An indication of the latter property is well-sprung ribs, which are an essential and which invariably accompany a dog formed as described. **Flat, slab sides** usually are to be found in long, flat-backed dogs, and, with light bone, thick skulls, snipy muzzles, and cow-hocks, should be scrupulously avoided in the Great Dane. Light eyes are another blemish, of less importance, but still one to be eradicated where it exists if perfection is to be attained.

The disposition of the Great Dane—like that of all dogs, naturally—is docile, although dogs vary in their temperament somewhat. This docility should be fostered when young, at which time character in the dog, as in the youth, is, to a great extent, moulded. If a Great Dane is spoiled in his upbringing, he is, on account of his great size and power, more than ordinarily dangerous, which fact emphasises the necessity for great care being exercised in his rearing, and absolute control being obtained over the animal.

The chief points to look for in the selection of Great Dane puppies at from two to four months old and after are: Great size, a long telescopic head, almost free from stop, deep square muzzle, small deep-set eye, narrow skull, small ears, short body, deep chest, well-sprung ribs, straight forelegs, and great bone.

One of the earliest exhibitors was Mr. Frank Adcock, solicitor, of Wigan, who used to show his imported dog, Satan, a huge, savage beast of the Ulmer type; also the bitch, Proserpina. This was in the 'seventies, before the breed was classified by the Kennel Club, and the dog, of course, was relegated to the Variety classes. The breed was first classified as Boarhounds in 1883 and as Great Danes in 1885.

The following are the standard description and points of the Great Dane, as promulgated by the Great Dane Club :—

STANDARD OF POINTS.

1.—GENERAL APPEARANCE.—The Great Dane should be remarkable in size and very muscular, strongly though elegantly built; the head and neck should be carried high, and the tail in line with the back, or slightly upwards, but not curled over the hindquarters. Elegance of outline and grace of form are most essential to a Dane; size is absolutely necessary; but there must be that alertness of expression and briskness of movement without which the Dane character is lost. He should have a look of dash and daring, of being ready to go anywhere and do anything.

2.—HEIGHT.—The minimum height of an adult dog over 18 months must be 30in.; that of a bitch, 28in.

3.—WEIGHT.—The minimum weight of an adult dog over 18 months should be 120lb.; that of a bitch, 100lb.

4.—HEAD.—Taken altogether the head should give the idea of great length and strength of jaw. The muzzle, or foreface, is broad, and the skull proportionately narrow, so that the whole head when viewed from above and in front has the appearance of equal breadth throughout. The entire length of head varies with the height of the dog; 13in. from the tip of the nose to the back of the occiput is a good measurement for a dog of 32in. at the shoulder. The length from the end of the nose to the point between the eyes should be about equal or preferably of greater length than from this point to the back of the occiput. The skull should be flat and have a slight indentation running up the centre, the occipital peak not prominent. There should be a decided rise or brow over the eyes, but no abrupt stop between them—the face should be well chiselled, well filled in below the eyes, with no appearance of being pinched—the foreface long, of equal depth throughout. The cheeks should show as little lumpiness as possible compatible with strength.

5.—LIPS.—The lips should hang quite square in front, forming a right angle with the upper line of foreface.

6.—UNDERLINE.—The underline of the head, viewed in profile, should run almost in a straight line from the corner of the lip to the corner of the jawbone, allowing for the fold of the lip, but with no loose skin to hang down.

7.—JAW.—The teeth should be level, and not project one way or the other.

8.—NOSE AND NOSTRILS.—The bridge of the nose should be very wide, with a slight ridge where the cartilage joins the bone. (This is quite a characteristic of the breed.) The nostrils should be large, wide and open, giving a blunt look to the nose. A butterfly- or flesh-coloured nose is not objected to in harlequins.

9.—EARS.—The ears should be small, set high on the skull, and carried slightly erect with the tips falling forward.

10.—NECK.—The neck should be long, well arched, and quite clean and free from loose skin, held well up, snakelike in carriage, well set in the shoulders, and the junction of head and neck well defined.

11.—SHOULDERS.—The shoulders should be muscular, but not loaded, and well sloped back, with the elbows well under the body.

12.—FORELEGS AND FEET.—The forelegs should be perfectly straight, with big bone. The feet should be catlike, the toes well arched and close, the nails strong and curved.

13.—BODY.—The body should be very deep, with ribs well sprung and belly well drawn up.

14.—BACK AND LOINS.—The back and loins should be strong, the latter slightly arched.

15.—TAIL.—The tail should be thick at the root, and taper towards the end, reaching to or just below the hocks. It should be carried, when the dog is in action, in a straight line level with the back, slightly curved towards the end, but in no case should it curl or be carried over the back.

16.—HINDQUARTERS.—The hindquarters and thighs should be extremely muscular, giving the idea of great strength and galloping power. The second thigh is long and well developed, the stifle and hock are well bent, the hocks set low, turning neither out nor in.

17.—COAT.—The hair is short and dense and sleek-looking, and in no case should it incline to roughness.

18.—MOVEMENT.—The action should be lithe, springy, and free. The hocks move freely, and the head be carried high, except when galloping.

19.—COLOUR.—(*a*) Brindles. Brindles must be striped. Ground colour from the lightest yellow to deep orange, and the stripes must always be black. (*b*) Fawns. The colour varies from lightest buff to deepest orange; darker shadings on the muzzle and ears and around the eyes are by no means objectionable. (*c*) Blues. The colour varies from light grey to deepest slate. (*d*) Blacks. In all the above colours white is only admissible on the chest and feet, but it is not desirable even there. The nose is always black (except in blues). Eyes and nails preferably dark. (*e*) Harlequins. Colour pure white underground, with preferably black patches (blue patches permitted), having the appearance of being torn. In this variety, wall eyes, pink noses, or butterfly noses are not a fault.

CHAPTER XXXVII.

The Newfoundland.

The Newfoundland forms one of the only two really life-saving breeds among the canine species, all others having the natural propensity, more or less, to kill. Its name denotes its origin, where the breed is still used, and always has been, as far as history can trace, as a beast of burden and a working dog—that is to say, it is used for the purpose of assisting in the hauling in of nets of fish and for other purposes connected with the great fishing industry of that interesting country. Whether the dog is indigenous to Newfoundland there are no records to show, not even the Frenchman, Cabot, the discoverer of the island, having left behind any information on the point. It is more than probable that European settlers took over dogs of large and powerful size, which were likely to be useful in the specific pursuit and calling they intended to follow, and which Newfoundland offered, and that from these originals the Newfoundland dog has descended. His drop ears are against the theory of the Newfoundland dog being a native, but suggest that he is also an aboriginal settler, since all Arctic dogs and those of extreme northern latitudes have prick ears. The breed in Newfoundland is very similar to that seen in England, but is not, of course, bred to any arbitrary standard, dogs being mated not for their fancy points, but for their working capabilities, intelligence, and tractability. The colour, black-and-white, fur-like coat, and big pads are developments of the Arctic or northern latitudes. Whatever the colours of imported dogs, or whatever their type, in the course of years and inbreeding, from the same originals, they would from a big race be sure to develop, in such northern latitudes, into a dog similar to the Newfoundland as we know him.

It is not very clear when the Newfoundland first set foot on English shores, but certainly before the advent of dog shows, and it is from the material then existing, with a few importations from time to time, that the present show dog, one of the most beautiful and rational specimens of the canine species, has been evolved. With regard to size, it is very clear that it varied, and varies very considerably, in Newfoundland, but a medium-sized dog is always the most useful for general purposes, and especially for drawing, if he is compact and thick-set, which the Newfoundland is and should be. The best of the Continental cart dogs are all medium-sized dogs, and the Arctic sledge dogs are even less in size. Since, however, the dogs are not used for work in England, but merely as companions and guards, a little additional size gives the animal a somewhat more imposing appearance and avails him more in self-defence against his own species, or in defending his master or mistress. The size laid down by the Newfoundland Club, therefore, seems to be a sensible one—viz., of an average height at shoulder of 27in. for a dog and 25in. for a bitch, weighing from 140lb. to 150lb. and 110lb. to 120lb. respectively. This, if anything, rather *under*-estimates the size which prevails to-day, but is a very rational guide of what the size of the Newfoundland dog should be.

The two colours recognised are white-and-black and black, but black-and-tan dogs and very bronzy black dogs have been known to take prizes on the show bench. These two latter colours are, however, not looked upon with favour, and will probably never become popular. The white-and-black dogs—which means a preponderance of white—are sometimes called Landseer Newfoundland, this variety having been immortalised by the well-known painting by this famous artist of a white-and-black Newfoundland on a raft. The coat of the dog should be perfectly straight, dense, close, and fur-like,

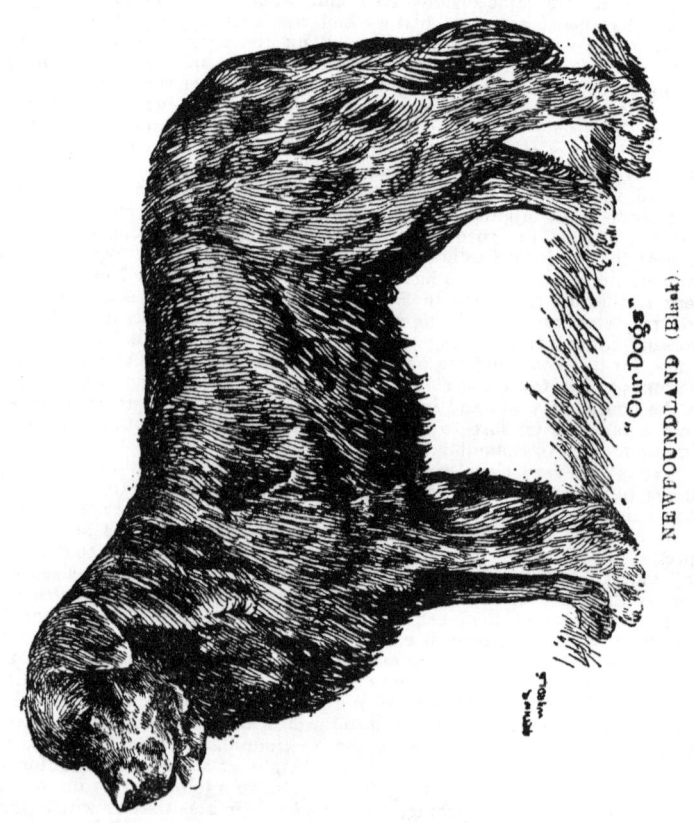

NEWFOUNDLAND (Black).
"Our Dogs"

in order to resist the water. In Newfoundland, where the dog spends most of his time in the water, his coat naturally is somewhat wavy, which is due to the action of the water, but in England, where the dog is not so engaged, there is no difficulty in producing and perpetuating the desirable straight, dense, close, fur-like coat.

The Newfoundland is essentially an aquatic, whether natural or acquired, being by instinct a water dog and without his equal. It is with this necessary quality in view that the standard description and points have been laid down, and which should enable him to perform any and every necessary evolution in the water. The dog's power and prowess in the water have often been turned to good account in the saving of human life, both in Newfoundland and in England, where his record and deeds form an imperishable monument to his worth. More than one Newfoundland dog has been awarded the medal of the Royal Humane Society for life saving, and if only for his noble character in this direction the breed is one which must excite the admiration and affection of all civilised and humane communities.

At Maidstone Dog Show, somewhere in the 'seventies, I think, water trials for Newfoundlands were instituted as an experiment, but, from whatever cause, they were not regarded at the time as a great success. The following are the regulations which were formulated for the trials:—

TESTS FOR WATER DOGS.

FIRST.—Courage displayed in jumping into the water from a height to recover an object. The effigy of a man is the most suitable thing.

SECOND.—The quickness displayed in bringing the object ashore.

THIRD.—Intelligence and speed in bringing a boat to shore—the boat must, of course, be adrift, and the painter have a piece of white wood attached to keep it afloat, mark its position, and facilitate the dog's work.

FOURTH.—To carry a rope from shore to a boat with a stranger, not the master, in it.

FIFTH.—Swimming races, to show speed and power against stream or tide.

SIXTH.—Diving. A common flag basket, with a stone in the bottom of it, to sink it, answers well, as it is white enough to be seen, and soft enough to the dog's mouth.

If the Newfoundland Club would take up the subject of competitive water trials for Newfoundlands, I feel sure they would do the breed itself incalculable good, and add greatly to its popularity. Working trials for show dogs are now the fashion, and are increasing in popularity and interest. The Newfoundland Club, therefore, would only be consulting its own interest and that of the noble and handsome breed whose welfare it espouses if it brought itself in line with the times. It would be a calamity for the water propensity in the Newfoundland to become degenerate. It is there, varying in degree in individual dogs, and only requires developing, which competitive trials, conducted on proper and well-thought-out lines, would be calculated to accomplish.

Coming to the type of the dog, the Club's standard description gives at a glance lucid details and a correct idea of the dog. The main features of the dog are a short body, compact frame, great bone and strength, and a broad, powerful pad. The head should be moderate in length, level, and not lippy in muzzle, which is a distinct disadvantage in a dog that has to grasp objects, sometimes hard objects, with its mouth. The ears are required to lie flat to the head in order to keep the water out. A prevailing defect in Newfoundlands is light eyes. A light eye in any dog is an indication of an uncertain temper to a smaller or greater degree, which in a Newfoundland is, of course, a heinous fault. Very light-eyed Newfoundlands should not, therefore, be bred from, if this blemish is to be eradicated, and the reputation for docility and sweetness of temper in the breed are to be maintained. Coat has already been referred to. A dog possessing such a coat as described is very quickly dry when he shakes himself after coming out of the water, whereas a soft, woolly, or wavy coat lets in and retains the water.

The chief points to look for in the selection of Newfoundland puppies at from two to four months old and after are : Great size if typical, moderately long head, muzzle free from lippiness, but not snipy, dark eye, not much stop, medium ears set close to side of head, big short body, set on rather short legs, showing enormous bone, coat dense, almost like fur. In the white-and-blacks the colour should be equally distributed.

The following are the Newfoundland Club's standard description and scale of points :—

SYMMETRY AND GENERAL APPEARANCE.—The dog should impress the eye with strength and great activity. He should move freely on his legs, with the body swung loosely between them, so that a slight roll in gait should not be objectionable; but at the same time a weak or hollow back, slackness of the loins, or cow-hocks should be a decided fault.

NEWFOUNDLAND (White-and-black).

HEAD.—Should be broad and massive, the occipital bone well developed; there should be no decided stop, and the muzzle should be short, clean cut, rather square in shape, and covered with short fine hair.

COAT.—Should be flat and dense, of a coarsish texture and oily nature, and capable of resisting the water. If brushed the wrong way, it should fall back into its place naturally.

BODY.—Should be well ribbed-up, with a broad back. A neck strong, well set-on to the shoulders and back, and strong muscular loins.

FORELEGS.—Should be perfectly straight, well covered with muscle, elbows in but well let down, and feathered all down.

HINDQUARTERS AND LEGS.—Should be very strong; the legs should have great freedom of action, and a little feather. Slackness of loins and cow-hocks are a great defect; dew-claws are objectionable, and should be removed.

CHEST.—Should be deep and fairly broad, and well covered with hair, but not to such an extent as to form a frill.

BONE.—Massive throughout, but not to give a heavy, inactive appearance.

FEET.—Should be large and well shaped. Splayed or turned-out feet are objectionable.

TAIL.—Should be of moderate length, reaching down a little below the hocks; it should be of fair thickness and well covered with long hair, but not to form a flag. When the dog is standing still and not excited it should hang downwards, with a slight curve at the end; but when the dog is in motion, it should be carried a trifle up, and when he is excited, straight out, with a slight curve at the end. Tails with a kink in them, or curled over the back, are very objectionable.

EARS.—Should be small, set well back, square with the skull, lie close to the head, and covered with short hair, and no fringe.

EYES.—Should be small, of a dark brown colour, rather deeply set, but not showing any haw, and they should be rather widely apart.

COLOUR.—Dull jet black. A slight tinge of bronze or a splash of white on chest and toes is not objectionable.

HEIGHT AND WEIGHT.—Size and weight are very desirable so long as symmetry is maintained. A fair average height at the shoulders is 28in. for a dog and 26in. for a bitch, and a fair average weight is respectively: Dogs, 140lb. to 150lb.; bitches, 110lb. to 120lb.

OTHER THAN BLACK.—Should in all respects follow the black except in colour, which may be almost any, so long as it disqualifies for the Black class, but the colours most to be encouraged are white-and-black or bronze. Beauty in markings to be taken greatly into consideration.

Black dogs that have only white toes and white breasts and white tip to tail should be exhibited in the classes provided for Black.

SCALE OF POINTS.

	Value.
HEAD	34
Shape of skull	8
Ears	10
Eyes	8
Muzzle	8
BODY	66
Neck	4
Chest	6
Shoulders	4
Loin and back	12
Hindquarters and tail	10
Legs and feet	10
Coat	12
Size, height, and general appearance	8
Total points in all	100

MARKINGS OF WHITE-AND-BLACK DOGS.

Head	3 points	
Saddle	5 points	Total 10 points.
Rump	2 points	

DEFINITION FOR PREFERENCE.

Black head marking, with narrow blaze. Even-marked saddle. Black rump, extending on to tail.

CHAPTER XXXVIII.

The St. Bernard.

The St. Bernard, or "Saintly" breed, as this splendid Swiss specimen of the canine race is sometimes designated, may, by its great size, magnificent appearance, beautiful temper, docility, and "holy" mission in its native country combined, be justly regarded as the finest example and most noble member of the canine species. The St. Bernard shares with the Newfoundland the honour of being the only two breeds of dogs whose special mission and characteristics are the saving of life, in contradistinction to those of all

ST. BERNARD (Rough-coated).

other breeds, which, more or less, lie in the direction of its destruction. No wonder, therefore, that the breed should at once appeal to the feelings and sentiment of humane England, where it has taken thorough hold of the affections of dog lovers and the public, and, by careful and persistent breeding for half a century or more, now surpasses in size and type anything to be found in its Alpine home. Indeed, the St. Bernard, unlike some breeds, which have become more or less degenerate as the result of alien invasions of this country, has maintained and improved its position, character, and popularity.

The breed has been kept at the Hospice and propagated by the monks of St. Bernard for hundreds of years, where it was, and is still, employed for the purpose of discovering and rescuing lost travellers in the Alps. The dogs are trained for the purpose and sent over the snow-capped mountains, with a barrel fastened round their necks, containing restoratives, should they happen to discover any wayward travellers. A pathetic story is told of the fate which befell the famous dog, Barry, who rescued no fewer than forty wanderers on the Alps, and whose body is preserved in the Museum at Berne. Barry was sent out one day on his usual mission, and, being mistaken for a wolf, he was shot dead by a benighted traveller, to whom he was taking succour. This was in 1815, when the dog was fifteen years old.

About this period the Holy Fathers of the Hospice, who had kept the breed pure for a long series of years, found that, unless some outcross was resorted to, the breed, with all its fine record of life-saving on the pages of history, was becoming somewhat degenerate and was indeed threatened with extinction. An outcross was, therefore, decided upon, and, of course, the nearest available dogs suitable were the Great Dane, or Ulmer Mastiff, and Pyrenean Sheepdog, which breeds were in turn employed for its resuscitation, the one imparting size and courage and the other hardihood. It is said that later the Newfoundland and Bloodhound were used as outcrosses.

Be that as it may, the intermixture, whatever it was, restored the breed and kept up both its stamina and, to a great extent, its type. The monks, in their inbreeding process, inclined to the smooth-coats, as they found that a very rough coat impeded the progress and handicapped the dog by its coat and feathering becoming clogged with snow. On the matter of type, they paid more attention to markings than to architecture, so long as the dogs were big and strong. They aimed at producing an orange-and-white patched dog, with a white blaze running right up the face from the nose to the neck, and with a white collar encircling the neck and traversing the shoulders and chest. The orange colour on the head deepened towards the white until it became black at the fringe. In the centre of the white on the forehead they divined that there should be a spot. These markings were said to represent the stole, chasuble, and scapular which form part of the vestments worn by the monks.

Among the earliest importers of the St. Bernard in England the name of the late Mr. J. C. Macdona will for ever be associated. His Tell, a famous dog, was one of the first, others following later. Indeed, he founded one of the first English kennels of the breed at West Kirby, in Cheshire, of which parish he was then the rector. The Rev. A. N. Bate was another clergyman who espoused the cause of the " saintly " breed, and who, with Mr. Macdona, was among the first exhibitors. Bernard was another successful dog imported by Mr. Macdona, and who really laid the foundation of the kennel of the late Mr. F. Gresham. Moltke, Alp, Hedwig, Hospice, and others followed in the West Kirby kennel. The late Mr. J. H. Murchison, of Fox Terrier renown, was first a St. Bernard fancier, obtaining his dogs from M. Schumacher, a great Swiss breeder and authority. Sir Charles Isham's Leo was a famous dog in the earliest days of the breed in England. Abbess and Thor were names to conjure with, from whom came Ch. Hector and Shah.

The most famous dog probably of the " middle ages " in St. Bernard lore was Mr. T. D. Green's Ch. Sir Bedivere, whom he bred, who stood 33in. at the shoulder and weighed 200lb., and who, after winning hundreds of prizes and cups, including the Halsey 200 guineas cup, given in the dog's honour, was sold to America for £1,300. About this period scores of English champions were exported to America, from which the breed was established in the United States.

When Dr. George Inman and Mr. B. Walmsley came upon the scene, establishing separate kennels, but later going into partnership at Bowdon, Cheshire, this incident marked an epoch in the breed. The St. Bernard Club, which had been formed some years earlier, and which had promoted several successful shows for St. Bernards only at Alexandra Palace, Knightsbridge, and Southport, was the victim of a split, mostly on the question of type, the success of the Bowdon Kennel arousing a little jealousy in the ranks. This feud culminated in the formation of the Northern St. Bernard Club, of which Dr. Inman and Mr. Walmsley were leading lights.

From the notions of the doughty doctor, who with Mr. Walmsley established the finest kennel of St. Bernards the world has ever seen, whose dogs held absolute sway in the show ring for a decade or more, and whose breed and type are still paramount in England, the St. Bernards in the country had degenerated, becoming too small and snipy, like the earlier importations. It is said, with what truth I do not know, that the success of the breeding of Messrs. Inman and Walmsley was due partly to a Mastiff outcross. Even if this were so, I see no reason to quote it either as a reproach upon the breeder or a stain on the escutcheon of the breed, any more than were the undoubted alien outcrosses of the monks of St. Bernard.

ST. BERNARD (Smooth-coated)

The great success of the Bowdon Kennel was no doubt due first to very careful selection in breeding, after a great study of pedigree, and to faultless rearing. The Bowdon dogs, rough and smooth, were noted for their great size, soundness, massiveness in body and head, and uniformity of type—a combination of virtues no other kennel in the country that ever existed could show. Many of the bench winners of the day, although good dogs, were defective in limbs, and the few which were sound in limbs lacked type in head. The grandeur of the heads of the Bowdon dogs was simply a marvel to the canine world—the deep square forefaces, massive yet well chiselled skulls, beautiful expression, nice placement of ears, and intense character, which, together with great bone, soundness of limb fore and aft, marked not some, but almost all, of the Bowdon dogs. This kennel at one time contained no fewer than a dozen home-bred champions. On the death of Dr. Inman, abroad, the kennel was dispersed, and the famous champions found new homes in different parts of the country. In one sense this dispersal was a boon to the breed, for it terminated the monopoly the kennel had long held, which was distinctly disheartening to the smaller fanciers and to novices in particular, to whom the distribution of the dogs now gave a wholesome and healthy stimulus. Although the stud services of the dogs were always available under the Bowdon régime, the real secret of the great success of the owners in their breeding operations was locked in the breasts of Messrs. Inman and Walmsley, who kept the key.

Their breeding arithmetic was followed by the various new owners, as far as registrations would furnish, but the sequence of champion after champion being turned out of the Bowdon mint was by no means maintained. True, a few stars later made their appearance in the scattered constellation, but somehow or other there appeared to be a general falling off. The dogs themselves, or at least, most of them, with the change of kennel lost much of the Bowdon bloom with which they always went into the show ring. Of course, to but few fanciers is given the opportunity which Dr. Inman and Mr. B. Walmsley had, two bachelors in the prime of life, with unlimited time and means at their disposal to devote to their hobby. However, one great fact remains, that, although the type of this kennel was at first somewhat tabooed by some of the leaders of the St. Bernard Club, by the sheer force of circumstances it became recognised as *the* type, and even its detractors, who ultimately even kept and bred from the very dogs they had despised, gradually came to recognise it.

As a matter of fact, there is nothing in this " Bowdon " type to which any legitimate or honest exception could be taken. With the wholesale exportations to America from time to time, the breed in England was becoming degenerate, and snipy, plain-headed dogs, undersized and crippled in limbs, were more the rule than the exception. This firm established a race of dogs as sound as Terriers, big and massive in size, with heads the chiselling and grandeur of which even their greatest enemies were ultimately constrained to admit. With the exception of one dog, probably, there was no trace of Mastiff or any other alien cross. Their enormously deep, square forefaces, nice " stop," beautifully chiselled skulls, pellucid eyes, and benevolent expression denoting beautiful dispositions, which all the dogs possessed, were at once the admiration and marvel of the fancy.

Happily, the Bowdon type is the type now universally recognised, and the Bowdon dogs and their descendants are still invulnerable on the show bench, which is the finest monument that could be erected to the skill of the firm as breeders of this most noble and imposing animal. It is to be hoped it will continue to be perpetuated by succeeding generations, for there can be no disputing the fact that it is the acme of perfection in the breed.

The points to be avoided by breeders are weak heads, light bone, shelliness, and crooked limbs. Stud dogs possessing any of these defects should be given a wide berth. Any of the defects detailed are more pardonable in a bitch, especially if she is a big-framed, roomy sort, which are always the best to breed from. Size is a most desirable feature, but it should not be sacrificed at the expense of " type," which must always come first in the St. Bernard. A sound, good, typical little dog, with the correct type of head, must always supersede a big, tall, plain-headed dog.

Englishmen, not all being of the same religious persuasion as the monks of St. Bernard, or so keenly imbued with their ritual, do not attach the same supreme importance to markings in the " saintly " breed. Still, the broad white blaze and collarette and the dark shadings of its fringe on the face are considered very desirable points, since these markings, with the patched body, give a picturesqueness to the colour of the dog.

The chief points to look for in the selection of St. Bernard puppies at from two to four months old and after are : Great size and massiveness all through, head medium in length, with very deep square muzzle, decided stop, massive skull, but the substance well distributed, not broad like a Mastiff. The puppy should show signs of growing tall, and have enormous bone and short deep body. A rich orange is the favourite colour, with white collar, blaze, and dark shadings. The roughs show more coat as puppies than the smooths.

The following are the standard description and points of the breed, as laid down by the St. Bernard Club, the only difference in the two varieties being a little more coat in the case of the roughs :—

Standard of Points.

HEAD.—Large and massive, circumference of skull being rather more than double the length of the head from nose to occiput. Muzzle short, full in front of the eye, and square at nose end. Cheeks flat, and great depth from eye to lower jaw. Lips deep, but not too pendulous. From nose to stop perfectly straight and broad. Stop somewhat abrupt and well defined. Skull broad, slightly rounded at the top, with somewhat prominent brow.

EARS.—Of medium size, lying close to the cheeks, and not heavily feathered.

EYES.—Rather small and deep set, dark in colour, not too close together, the lower eyelid drooping so as to show a fair amount of haw at the inner corner, the upper eyelid falling well over the eye.

NOSE.—Large and black, with well-developed nostrils.

MOUTH.—Level.

EXPRESSION.—Should betoken benevolence, dignity, and intelligence.

NECK.—Lengthy, thick, muscular, and slightly arched, with dewlap well developed.

SHOULDERS.—Broad and sloping, well up at the withers.

CHEST.—Wide and deep. The lower part should not project below the elbows.

BODY.—Back broad and straight, ribs well rounded. Loin wide and very muscular.

TAIL.—Set on rather high, long, and in long-coated variety well feathered. Carried low when in repose, and when excited or in motion should not be curled over the back.

LEGS AND FEET.—Forelegs perfectly straight, strong in bone, and of good length. Hind legs heavy in bone, hocks well bent, and thighs very muscular. Feet large and compact, with well-arched toes.

SIZE.—The taller the better, provided the symmetry is maintained; thoroughly well proportioned, and of great substance. The general outline should suggest great power and capability of endurance.

COAT.—In the long-coated variety should be dense and flat, rather fuller round the neck; thighs well feathered. In the short-coated variety it should be close and hound-like, slightly feathered on thighs and tail.

COLOUR AND MARKINGS.—Orange, mahogany-brindle, red-brindle, or white with patches on body of either of the above-named colours. The markings should be as follows :—white muzzle, white blaze up face white collar round neck, white chest, white forelegs, feet, and end of tail ; black shadings on face and ears.

DEW CLAWS.—Of no value.

MOVEMENT.—Is most important, and St. Bernards have often failed in this direction, the hind legs being especially faulty.

OBJECTIONABLE POINTS.—Dudley, liver, flesh-coloured, or split nose ; over or undershot mouth ; snipy muzzle ; light or staring eyes ; cheek bumps ; wedge head ; flat skull ; badly set or carried, or heavily feathered ears ; too much peak ; short neck ; curly coat ; flat sides ; hollow back ; roach back ; flat thighs ; ring tail ; open or hare feet ; cow hocks ; straight hocks ; fawn or self-coloured.

SCALE OF POINTS.

Head—Skull	3	
Ears	4	
Eyes	5	
Stop	3	
Depth	5	
Muzzle	10	
Expression	10	
		40
Neck and shoulders		5
Chest, body, and loin		10
Hindquarters		10
Legs, feet and movement		10
Size		15
Coat		5
Colour and markings		5
		100

CHAPTER XXXIX.

The Rough-coated Collie.

The Rough-coated Collie is a purely Scottish dog, and, like all varieties of sheep and cattle dogs used in pastoral life and agricultural pursuits, is of great antiquity. Indeed, it is sometimes contended that, of all the varieties of the domesticated dog, the Collie or Sheepdog is the oldest, and probably the one variety from which all breeds have been evolved. This idea has doubtless arisen from the fact that the Collie most resembles the wild dog, and that there is a great similarity in form and character between the sheep and cattle dogs of all countries, which incident certainly does point to a common origin. The little differences in the dogs may easily be accounted for by the exigencies of the variations in the character of the different countries, which call for dogs somewhat different in build, but all are more or less of the same type and character—the Dutch, German, Belgian, French, Spanish, etc.

Mr. Drury, author of " British Dogs," whilst agreeing as to the similarity of the Collie of all countries, and as to his close alliance with the wild dog, does not think he is the origin of all the varieties of the domestic dog. He says :

" The Collie is one among many Sheepdogs that writers have credited with being the origin of all our varieties of domestic dog ; but this seems an untenable position to take on the question. Far more feasible is it to suppose that the Collie, like other breeds, is the result of crosses and selection to adapt him to the special requirements of his country and the work he is called upon to perform.

"There is one point upon which most people will agree—namely, that the Collie is in physical properties more nearly allied to several races of wild dogs than any other of our domestic breeds. The Aguara dogs, and especially the Hoary Aguara, as depicted by Lieut.-Col. Charles Hamilton Smith in Jardine's ' Naturalist's Library,' bear a strong resemblance to a smooth or half-rough Collie with prick ears, which feature is not uncommon in the Collie. The likeness between the Collie and the Indian Haredog, as given by Youatt, is very striking."

Upon the question of the origin of the name " Collie," the same author has the following :—

" If we endeavour to learn anything of the Collie's origin from his name, we are again met with a host of difficulties. Some writers have assumed that the name is of Gaelic origin ; but they advance no satisfactory reason, and before that can be accepted, we must have proofs that the dog is Celtic.

" In Chaucer, ' Coll our dog ' occurs, and it may be the name was used in reference to the colour—black prevailing in this variety of dog. It has been suggested that Coll and Collie may be from the same root as Collar, and the name given to the dog because of the white collar round the neck, which is very common in this, and indeed in all breeds where we get a mixture of a dark colour and white.

" Dr. Ogilvie, in his ' Imperial Dictionary,' and Jamieson, in his ' Scottish Dictionary,' both give Collie ; and it is not improbable that Collie is merely the diminutive and familiar form of Coll, for in all Scotch words the ' i e ' is thus used :—Will becomes Willie, and lass, lassie. Bewick, in his ' British Quadrupeds,' indeed, had his own peculiar and original spelling of the word, which was Coaly—pardonable in a book published in a town the subject of the proverb, ' Carry coals to Newcastle.' "

COLLIE (Rough-coated).

In the absence of any definite data, both the origin of the Collie and its name will, to a great extent, as in most breeds, remain somewhat obscure and ever be a matter of mere conjecture.

Coming to the dog as we find him, the modern example, while in the main identical with the animal bred (for use only) for centuries in the highlands and lowlands of Scotland, is, of course, a more refined creature, which is the result of the hand of the showman. The question of a correct carriage of ear, a certain formation of skull and muzzle, size and colour of eye, and even formation of body, never entered into the philosophy of the Gaelic shepherds and herdsmen. They bred from their dogs because of their prowess in connection with sheep on the Grampian or other hills, and the best worker, whatever his anatomy, was in their rustic opinion the best dog.

With the institution of dog shows both Scottish and English fanciers took the breeding of the Collie in hand upon scientific lines, the result of which has been that as a show dog his marketable value has been raised from a few pounds to hundreds, reaching even to four figures, which price more than one Collie has fetched during the last thirty or so years. Indeed, it is a very moderate dog that is not now worth in the market £100, whilst it is on record that Mr. Stretch's Ch. Christopher was sold for £1,000, the same gentleman's Ch. Ormskirk Emerald to Mr. Megson for £1,300, Ch. Southport Perfection for four figures, and later Mr. Mason's Ch. Squire of Tytton and Mr. Tait's Ch. Wishaw Leader for, it is said, well on to £1,000 each.

Such sales at once prove the popularity of the Collie, which Scottish fanciers, with the proverbial cuteness of their race, foresaw, and although the same high prices do not rule to-day, because of the market having been largely supplied, the dog's popularity is still well maintained, and good specimens always command very good prices.

Comparing the modern Collie with his early ancestor at the time of the advent of dog shows, I can see nothing but improvement everywhere. In place of the thick, coarse head we have a long, refined physiognomy, and a sharp, intelligent eye. Pessimists of the old school declare that the show Collie has no brains, because of his narrow skull; but this is not a fact, and a theory that has often been exploded. Ch. Ormskirk Charlie (Mr. R. S. Piggin's), which was both a pedigree dog and a show dog (as his prefix indicates), was also one of the most celebrated field triallers that ever lived, in which line he gained his championship spurs. Others could be mentioned. Again, in place of the big, ugly ears irregularly carried, we have now a neat ear carried erect, with the tips only falling forward, so that the Collie can the better catch the sound of the bleating sheep or his master's voice or whistle, as the case may be. Indeed, the whole points and standard description of the Collie as formulated by the Scottish Collie Club, the British Collie Club, which with other local Collie Clubs have been established to promote his welfare and protect his interests, have been framed on such lines as should enable the dog to perform his vocation in the field to the best possible advantage. The question of his ability to do so must, of course, always depend upon his tuition, training, and employment as a worker. Dogs vary in their intelligence and aptitude, and whilst fools in the ante-dog show days found a watery grave, they have since gone to ornament the show bench where such dogs have shown sufficient merit, and have doubtless been bred from. It is in this connection that some anti-showmen contend that the breed has degenerated in intelligence, and doubtless there may be some truth in it in the case of all breeds, but just as intelligent and sagacious dogs will breed fools, so may intelligent dogs be bred from fools. This is one of the subtleties of Nature in breeding, which scientists cannot solve, and which applies to mankind as well as to dogkind. It may be an exception which proves the rule, but still it is there.

The modern rough-coated Scotch Collie is, without doubt, one of the handsomest examples of the canine species, his long, intelligent head, enormous coat and frill, proportionate frame and symmetry, and great buoyancy of disposition appealing to all dog lovers, and which account for his at once coming into popularity. It took years to evolve the dog from the rough original, and not even the most pessimistic would have the temerity to say that such specimens as those just mentioned were not infinitely more beautiful in every way than the earliest nondescripts of the show bench, or of such later champions as Old Cockie, Rutland, or others of the 'seventies and 'eighties.

In the show Collie we have size and substance with symmetry and without coarseness, quality without effeminateness, and all the essential traits, including a weather-resisting coat for warmth and protection, which should enable the dog to fulfil his function as a workman to the best advantage.

A good Collie can hardly be a bad colour, but sable-and-white and black-tan-and-white are the prevailing and most favoured and predominating colours, although the picturesque blue-merle, which has been years in incubating, is now in great favour, and specimens of this colour are more typical generally than they used to be.

In breeding, the points to aim at are long, lean, level heads, small dark eyes, small highly carried ears, short bodies, straight forelegs, and big coats. And the bad points to avoid are big, badly carried ears, coarse skulls, and thin coats. It is just as foolish to breed from small, weedy specimens as from big, coarse dogs. Big, roomy (but not coarse) bitches make the best brood bitches, and dogs of fair size, with the greatest length of head, free from coarseness, the best stud dogs. The great length of head of some of our show dogs has given rise to the theory of the Borzoi having been employed as a cross with the Collie, but we have no record of such cross, nor actual evidence upon which to base such a theory.

The question of pig-jaw—that is, an overshot mouth,—which some of our winning Collies possess to a smaller or greater degree, is one which has greatly exercised the mind of experts. Many a most classical specimen has been marred by this common blemish. I say common, because where great length of head is sought, overshot mouths are sure to result when they reach the abnormal. I should not discourage breeding from such a specimen, however, and for two reasons. First, because although some of the progeny might and would be overshot, yet the probability is that the desired length of head would be obtained in others whose mouths were sufficiently level to be passable. I say " sufficiently " level, because it is not necessary, and few dogs are so formed, for a Collie's mouth to be absolutely level as is required in a working Terrier. It is not necessary, since a Collie is not expected to " bite " his charges, but only to " nip " them, and a slightly overshot mouth is quite equal to that requirement. Of course, if the mouth is overshot to the extent of half an inch or more, then it amounts to a malformation, and should incur disqualification in the show ring.

The chief points to look for in the selection of Collie puppies at from two to four months old and after are : Great length of head, which should be level and wedge-shaped, but should not run into coarseness or width at the base of skull, which should be narrow. Ears small, body short and round, tail short, forelegs straight. The biggest puppies are likely to be the best, if they are not coarse, but possess the desired points. The foregoing applies to both roughs and smooths, the latter requiring to be very smooth in coat, short but dense ; the more coat the roughs have the better.

The following are the standard description and points as laid down by the Collie Club for the two varieties :

DESCRIPTIVE TYPE OF COLLIE.

THE SKULL should be flat, moderately wide between the ears, and gradually tapering towards the eyes. There should only be a slight depression at the stop. The width of skull necessarily depends upon the combined length of skull and muzzle, and the whole must be considered in connection with the size of the dog. The cheek should not be full or prominent.

THE MUZZLE should be of fair length, tapering to the nose, and must not show weakness or be snipy or lippy. Whatever the colour of the dog may be, the nose must be black.

THE TEETH should be of good size, sound, and level; very slight unevenness is permissible.

THE JAWS should be clean cut and powerful.

THE EYES are a very important feature, and give expression to the dog. They should be of medium size, set somewhat obliquely, of almond shape, and of brown colour except in the case of merles, when the eyes are frequently (one or both) blue-and-white or china; expression full of intelligence, with a quick alert look when listening.

THE EARS should be small and moderately wide at the base, and placed not too close together on top of the skull nor too much to the side of the head. When in repose they should be usually carried thrown back, but when on the alert brought forward and carried semi-erect, with tips slightly drooping in attitude of listening.

FAULTS.—Length of head apparently out of proportion to the body and of the Borzoi type are to be strongly condemned. Weak, snipy muzzle, overshot mouth, heavy or gooseberry-coloured, also glassy or staring, eyes are very objectionable. Domed skull, high peaked occiput, prominent cheek, dish-faced, or Roman-nosed.

THE NECK should be muscular, powerful, and of fair length, and somewhat arched.

THE BODY should be rather long, with well-sprung ribs, chest deep, fairly broad behind the shoulders, which should be sloped, loins slightly arched and powerful. The legs should be straight in front. Faults: Flat-sided, short, or cobby.

THE FORELEGS should be straight and muscular, neither in nor out at elbows, with a fair amount of bone; the forearm somewhat fleshy, with pasterns showing flexibility without weakness. Faults: Weak long pasterns, out at elbows, crooked forearms.

THE HIND LEGS should be muscular at the thighs, clean and sinewy below the hocks, with well-bent stifles. Faults: Cow-hocks, straight hocks.

THE FEET should be oval in shape, soles well padded, and the toes arched and close together. The hind feet less arched, the hocks well let down and powerful. Faults: Large, open, flat, or hare feet; feet turned outwards or inwards.

THE BRUSH should be moderately long, carried low when the dog is quiet, with a slight upward "swirl" at the end, and may be gaily carried when the dog is excited, and not over the back. Faults: Short tail, or tail carried over the back, or twisted to one side.

THE COAT should be very dense, the outer coat harsh to the touch, the inner or under coat soft, furry, and very close, so close as to almost hide the skin. The mane and frill should be very abundant, the mask or face smooth, as also the ears at the tips, but they should carry more hair towards the base; the forelegs well feathered, the hind legs above the hocks profusely so; but below the hocks fairly smooth, although all heavily coated Collies are liable to grow a slight feathering. Hair on the brush very profuse. Faults: A soft, silky, or wavy coat, or insufficient undercoat.

COLOUR AND MARKING are immaterial, but other points being equal, a nice showily marked dog is preferred. All white or red Setter colour is most objectionable.

GENERAL CHARACTER.—To enable the Collie to fulfil his natural bent for sheepdog work, he should be built on lines of strength, activity, and grace, with a shapely body and sound legs and feet. He should be lithe and active in his movements, and entirely free from cloddiness and coarseness in any part of his conformation; and, lastly, he must be gifted with true expression. Expression is obtained by the perfect combination of head and muzzle, size, shape, and colour, and placement of eye, and correct position and carriage of ears, which give the dog that sweet, dreamy, semi-cunning, yet alert outlook that makes the perfect Collie the most beautiful of the canine race.

SIZE AND WEIGHT.—Dogs, 22in. to 24in. at the shoulders; **bitches,** 20in. to 22in. Dogs, 45lb. to 65lb.; bitches, 40lb. to 55lb.

THE SMOOTH COLLIE only differs from the rough in its coat, **which** should be hard, dense, and quite smooth.

SCALE OF POINTS.

Head and expression	15
Ears	10
Neck and shoulders	10
Legs and feet	15
Hindquarters	10
Back and loins	10
Brush	5
Coat and frill	20
Size	5
Total	100

THE SMOOTH-COATED COLLIE.

The smooth-coated Collie is, or should be, an exact replica of his rough-coated brother in every detail and particular, but with a short, dense, double coat, which looks smooth to the eye, but which is harsh and weather-resisting. The smooth-coated Collie is an English edition of his Scotch cousin, and is doubtless a manufactured variety to a great extent, as seen to-day on the show bench, although a form of smooth Collie or Sheepdog has been indigenous to the agricultural districts of England from time immemorial almost.

He doubtless has been "improved" by alternate crosses with the Scotch Collie, and the Greyhound and Lurcher maybe, but the dog to be a good specimen should not show any trace of the two latter crosses. I am speaking now of the earlier days of the smooth show Collie, which is somewhat later than when the rough made his appearance on the show bench, since when he has been greatly improved, and has now been firmly established as a full-blooded pedigree variety, with heaps of admirers, the ranks of whom embrace all classes of fanciers from the nobility down, and which are ever being swelled by recruits.

COLLIE (Smooth-coated).

The smooth Collie, as an all-round utility dog, probably cannot be excelled. His short, sleek, dense, weather-resisting coat is undoubtedly an advantage to him over his rough brother in snowy weather, and is less cumbersome to carry. He is more difficult to breed true to type because of his smooth coat, which lays bare an anatomy which a rough coat covers, and with it defects of body that cannot be hidden in the smooth variety. The orthodox colour of the smooth is much the same as in the rough-coated variety.

THE BEARDED COLLIE.

The Bearded Collie is a very old Scottish variety, and indigenous to Scotland, but undoubtedly is a member of the same family as the Old English Sheepdog, both of which no doubt have had one common origin. The breed is kept largely in the mountainous districts of Scotland, and is a dog that is valued for his all-round utility. The breed is quite distinct from either the Collie or Old English Sheepdog, and although recognised as such and frequently exhibited in Scotland, it has not yet come under the direct ken of the fancier and showman. In this way no standard description and points have been evolved for the breed, the type and merit of the dogs exhibited being left entirely to the individual judgment and opinion of the gentlemen who have adjudicated upon them.

SCOTTISH BEARDED COLLIE.

The Scottish Bearded Collie or Sheepdog resembles the Old English Sheepdog in the shagginess of his coat, in ears and head, but he is a somewhat smaller dog, more snipy in muzzle, and has the suggestion of a "Billygoat" beard under his jaw, with, of course, the difference that his caudal appendage is not removed as in the case of his English cousin.

Their colours are mostly grizzle, sandy, black, and blue, with the varying complement of white markings.

The chief points to look for in the selection of Bearded Collie puppies are much the same as for the Old English Sheepdog.

CHAPTER XL.

The Old English Sheepdog.

This ancient and quaint variety of the canine species was never more popular than at the present time. Indeed, in this connection he is a close rival to his Scottish kinsman, the rough-coated Collie, the "fever" having caught on in the United States, to which country scores of show cracks have in late years been expatriated and at prices ranging from £20 to £200 each. America, in fact, can at the present time probably present as good a show of the breed as the Old Country.

The precise origin of the Old English Sheepdog is again shrouded in obscurity. He is doubtless a relic of those early pastoral days when the wolf and other wild animals inhabited these isles, and from which the flocks and herds had to be protected, necessitating the employment of a powerful and hardy sheepdog which could hold his own against marauding beasts of prey. A similar sheepdog exists in Russia, Northern India, the Pyrenees, and coming nearer home, in France, where the wolf and other wild animals still infest the pastoral plains of these countries, and to which the Old English Sheepdog doubtless is closely allied. These dogs are mostly somewhat larger, but in the matter of type there is a great deal in common.

The incident of docking the Old English Sheepdog may have arisen in the first place from notions of cleanliness, which practice doubtless prompted the docking of sheep. It could not have been from considerations of utility, because the tail of the dog greatly assists him in his vocation of collecting and folding sheep, being to him, in fact, just what the rudder is to a boat. It is in making sudden turns and other movements and evolutions that the tail of a dog is of such great advantage. Be that as it may, however, custom has ordained that the variety for exhibition purposes at least shall be tailless, and this is embodied in the standard description and code of points promulgated by the Old English Sheepdog Club, which was established in 1888 for the purpose of promoting the pure breeding and welfare of the breed. Some time previous to this the breed was perpetuated promiscuously and aimlessly so far as preserving the dog's unique type and character goes, the main object being the propagation of the rare working qualities and hardihood in the dog.

Beneath the shaggy, unkempt coat of this canine rustic there lay virtues of intelligence and sagacity equal to any in the most cultivated and domesticated breed, and this appealed to the fancier, who saw in the dog a sensible and devoted companion, coupled with a quaintness which was at once fascinating. He therefore took the dog in hand, weaned him, as it were, from his agricultural pursuits, and brought him into that condition of civilisation and culture best adapted for city life and the family circle. In this process very little alteration has been made to the dog's outward conformation and character from that in which he was found, except, of course, that greater symmetry and a more gracefully formed animal, more uniform in size, with a sensible head, and frame covered by a weather-resisting coat, have been obtained. Some attention has, of course, been paid to colour, the favourite colour being pigeon-blue, with white blaze, collar, and points, which is both pretty and picturesque. Colour, however, is not a cardinal virtue, but only the finishing touch of the artist, since grizzle and black-and-white are admissible.

OLD ENGLISH SHEEPDOG.

The defects to be avoided in Old English Sheepdogs are undersize, snipy foreface, cow-hocks, and soft coat, one or other of which often mars otherwise good specimens.

The chief points to look for in the selection of Old English Sheepdog puppies at from two to four months old and after are: Great size, big massive heads and heavy muzzles, short round bodies, deep chest, and great bone, with as much coat as possible.

The following are the Old English Sheepdog Club's standard description and scale of points:—

DESCRIPTION.

SKULL.—Capacious, and rather squarely formed, giving plenty of room for brain power. The parts over the eyes should be well arched, and the whole well covered with hair.

JAW.—Fairly long, strong, square, and truncated; the stop should be defined, to avoid a Deerhound face.

[*The attention of judges is particularly called to the above properties, as a long narrow head is a deformity.*]

EYES.—Dark or wall eyes are to be preferred.

NOSE.—Always black, large and capacious.

TEETH.—Strong and large, evenly placed, and level in opposition.

EARS.—Small, and carried flat to side of head, coated moderately.

LEGS.—The forelegs should be dead straight, with plenty of bone, removing the body a medium height from the ground, without approaching legginess; well-coated all round.

FEET.—Small round; toes well arched, and pads thick and round.

TAIL.—Puppies requiring docking should have the operation performed within a week from birth, preferably within four days.

NECK AND SHOULDERS.—The neck should be fairly long, arched gracefully, and well coated with hair; the shoulders sloping and narrow at the points, the dog standing lower at the shoulder than at the loin.

BODY.—Rather short and very compact, ribs well sprung, and brisket deep and capacious. The loin should be very stout and gently arched, while the hindquarters should be round and muscular, and with well let down hocks, and the hams densely coated with a thick, long jacket in excess of any other part.

COAT.—Profuse, and of good hard texture; not straight, but shaggy and free from curl. The undercoat should be a waterproof pile, when not removed by grooming or season.

COLOUR.—Any shade of grey, grizzle, blue, or blue-merle, with or without white markings, or in reverse; any shade of brown or sable to be considered distinctly objectionable, and not to be encouraged.

HEIGHT.—Twenty-two inches and upwards for dogs, slightly less for bitches. Type, symmetry, and character are of the greatest importance, and on no account to be sacrificed to size alone.

GENERAL APPEARANCE.—A strong, compact looking dog of great symmetry, absolutely free of legginess or weazleness, profusely coated all over, very elastic in its gallop, but in walking or trotting he has a characteristic ambling or pacing movement, and his bark should be loud, with a peculiar *pot easse* ring in it. Taking him all round, he is a thick-set, muscular, able-bodied dog, with a most intelligent expression, free of all *Poodle* or *Deerhound* character.

SCALE OF POINTS.

	Value
Head	5
Eyes	5
Colour	10
Ears	5
Body, loins, and hindquarters	20
Jaw	10
Nose	5
Teeth	5
Legs	10
Neck and shoulders	10
Coat	15
Total	100

N.B.—The Northern Old English Sheepdog Club gives the height as 24 in. and upwards.

CHAPTER XLI.

The Dalmatian.

The Dalmatian is a very popular variety in England at the present time, being a very pretty and picturesque animal. Two clubs are in existence for the purpose of promoting his welfare—viz., The Dalmatian Club and The North of England Dalmatian Club.

Although individual specimens have been kept by the nobility and aristocracy as a carriage dog for very many years back, as an exhibition dog the Dalmatian seems to be, for the most part, in the hands of the middle and lower classes, some of whom are exceedingly enthusiastic over his virtues.

As to the dog's origin there seems to be no precise data or information, but there is little or no doubt that he comes from Dalmatia, on the eastern

DALMATIAN.

shores of the Gulf of Venice. In Italy and some other countries the dog is used as a Pointer, and that he possesses sporting proclivities is beyond dispute. Indeed, the Pointer make and shape seem to have formed the foundation upon which the Dalmatian Club built its standard description and code of points for the breed, with the addition of well-distributed distinct spots instead of patches. In England the conception of his vocation is purely as a carriage dog—that is, a dog to run under or follow a carriage or other conveyance, and protect the occupants and property therein, to do which he has a natural instinct—and he is a devoted companion of the horse. In this way usage has become second nature with him, and any Dalmatian almost will fall into his duty practically without tuition and as if to the manner born. No handsomer dog could be used for the purpose. His clear white colour evenly spotted all over with black spots, and proportionate and symmetrically-made body and intelligent head, are features which appeal to anyone as lines of canine beauty. He is, moreover, a dog that is better seen at night in the dark than many varieties, which, in the case of driving in the country, is a distinct advantage. Besides, a Dalmatian loves the association of a horse and trap.

There are no records of the date of his introduction into England, which was early in the last century, if not before. That he was in existence in England during the advent of dog shows is a fact, for good specimens were exhibited at our earliest dog shows, before any club had been established or any standard description formulated. He must have been bred in those days haphazard, or by mere finger and thumb rule, and yet no better Dalmatian exists to-day than some of those early specimens, who were merely an adjunct to the stable, and bred, for the most part, by ostlers or stablemen.

There are few breeds which breed truer to type than the Dalmatian. Dogs may be bred with thick heads, ring tails, and many of the spots running in, but they are Dalmatians in type and character. These are among the chief defects to avoid in breeding. The spots should be perfectly distinct all over the dog, and the size of a circle that a threepenny-piece or a sixpence would make. They should be either black or liver, soundness as well as distinctness being a great desideratum. Patch on the cheek or ears is permissible, but one on the body very objectionable, both handicapping the dog, as against one entirely free from patches. Some Dalmatians have a wall eye, about which controversies have taken place among the cognoscenti; the clubs have now decided that it is permissible, but handicaps a dog in the show ring. Ch. Palette, a beautiful bitch which did an immense amount of winning, had a wall eye. In harlequin Great Danes and merle Sheepdogs a wall eye is quite permissible, and, indeed, quite in keeping with the colour of the dog, to which varieties the Dalmatian has some affinity in colour, and as the dog can see just as well out of a wall eye as one of any other colour, there seems to be no logical or valid objection to it.

The head of the Dalmatian should be much on the lines of a good Pointer, and his tail much like that of a Bull-terrier, carried straight. Bad extremities, heads, and tails are prevailing defects in the Dalmatians of to-day, and few possess the beautifully clear and sound spots of the late Mr. Fawdry's Captain, exhibited so far back as 1875. Snipiness of muzzle and the black spots merging into tan markings on the legs are defects which often mar otherwise good specimens. A Dalmatian should have good straight forelegs and short well-knit feet, and his hocks should be well let down. He should be short in back, but cover a lot of ground, all points required in a dog which is required to travel. A perfect Dalmatian is a most proportionately formed, graceful, and picturesque animal. It should be stated, for the information of novices, that all pure-bred Dalmatian puppies are pure white when born, the puppies beginning to develop their spots at from two to three months old.

The chief points to look for in the selection of Dalmatian puppies at from two to four months old and after are: Size and symmetry, smallness, soundness, and distinctness of spot, free from patches, head long and Pointer-like, tail short and carried straight as possible, although all puppies curl their tails when young, which often afterwards become straight.

The following are the standard description and code of points of the Dalmatian Club:—

THE DALMATIAN in many particulars much resembles the Pointer, more especially in size, build, and outline, though the markings peculiar to this breed are a very important feature, and very highly valued.

IN GENERAL APPEARANCE the Dalmatian should represent a strong, muscular, and active dog, symmetrical in outline, and free from coarseness and lumber, capable of great endurance, combined with a fair amount of speed.

THE HEAD should be of fair length, the skull flat, rather broad between the ears, and moderately well defined at the temples—*i.e.*, exhibiting a moderate amount of "stop,"—and not in one straight line, from the nose to the occiput bone, as required in a Bull-terrier. It should be entirely free from wrinkle.

The Muzzle should be long and powerful, the lips clean, fitting the jaws moderately close.

The Eyes should be set moderately well apart, and of medium size, round, bright, and sparkling, with an intelligent expression, their colour greatly depending on the markings of the dog : in the black-spotted variety the eyes should be dark (black or dark brown) ; in the liver-spotted variety they should be light (yellow or light brown). The rim round the eyes in the black-spotted variety should be black, in the liver-spotted variety brown,—never flesh-coloured in either.

The Ears should be set on rather high, of moderate size, rather wide at the base, and gradually tapering to a rounded point. They should be carried close to the head, be thin and fine in texture, and always spotted, the more profusely the better.

The Nose in the black-spotted variety should always be black ; in the liver-spotted variety always brown.

Neck and Shoulders.—The neck should be fairly long, nicely arched, light and tapering, and entirely free from throatiness. The shoulders should be moderately oblique, clean, and muscular, denoting speed.

Body, Back, Chest, and Loins.—The chest should not be too wide, but very deep and capacious ; ribs moderately well sprung ; never rounded like barrel hoops (which would indicate want of speed) ; the back powerful ; loin strong, muscular, and slightly arched.

Legs and Feet of great importance. The forelegs should be perfectly straight, strong, and heavy in bone ; elbows close to the body ; forefeet round, compact, with well-arched toes (cat-foot), and round, tough, elastic pads. In the hind legs the muscles should be clean, though well defined, hocks well let down.

Nails.—In the black-spotted variety, black-and-white ; in the liver-spotted variety, brown-and-white.

The Tail should not be too long, strong at the insertion and gradually tapering towards the end, free from coarseness. It should not be inserted too low down, but carried with a slight curve upwards, and never curled. It should be spotted, the more profusely the better.

The Coat should be short, hard, dense, and fine, sleek and glossy in appearance, but neither woolly nor silky.

Colour and Markings.—These are most important points. The ground-colour in both varieties should be pure white, very decided, and not intermixed. The colour of the spots in the black-spotted variety should be black, the deeper and richer the black the better ; in the liver-spotted variety they should be brown. The spots should not intermingle, but be as round and well defined as possible, the more distinct the better ; in size they should be from that of a sixpence to a florin. The spots on head, face, ears, legs, tail, and extremities to be smaller than those on the body.

Size.—Dogs, 55lb. ; bitches, 50lb.

Standard of Excellence.

	Value.
Head and eyes ..	10
Legs and feet ..	15
Ears ..	5
Coat ..	5
Neck and shoulders ..	10
Body, back, chest, and loins ..	10
Colour and markings ..	30
Tail ..	5
Size, symmetry, etc. ..	10
Total ..	100

CHAPTER XLII.

The Poodle.

The Poodle is, of course, a Frenchman pure and simple. He is considered by some enthusiasts to be the most intelligent member of the canine species, and does, without doubt, stand high in the scale of canine sagacity, intelligence, and tractability. For this reason the French Poodle is often selected by itinerant showmen and music-hall artists as a trick and performing dog, and with the greatest success. The Punch and Judy shows of country fairs very often include a French Poodle as a " handy man," whilst he is equally familiar to the circus as to the stage, and is always a most reliable performer.

The show bench is, of course, altogether a different matter, and it is in this connection that I have to consider the dog. Whilst the Poodle is undoubtedly of French origin, and, indeed, has been regarded for ages as the national

POODLE (Corded).

breed, a larger variety of corded specimens is to be found in Russia and Germany, which doubtless have emanated from France. The Russian specimens, a few of which at one time found their way to the English show bench, were sometimes called Russian Retrievers, their characteristics, however, being wholly those of the Poodle. The breed is of very ancient origin, into which it is not necessary for us to dig, and seems to have preserved its type and features through long ages. In this connection no breed probably has been less varying or more uniform than it is to-day. The aquatic instincts of the Poodle, and his natural propensity to retrieve game off the water, denotes that he is by nature a sporting dog, in which capacity he was formerly and is still used in France. The breed is divided into two varieties—viz., the corded and curly, several clubs being in existence in England to look after its interests and advancement, the chief being the Poodle Club and the Curly Poodle Club. The only difference in the two varieties is in coat, the coat of the corded being allowed to grow sometimes to an abnormal length, being carefully cultivated to that end, whilst the coat of the curlies is kept short and is combed out, giving it a fluffy appearance. In shape of head, body properties, limbs, and character, the two varieties are identical. The breed is now sub-divided by both size and colour. Some of the corded and curly dogs will scale as much as 70lb., whilst we now have both Toy cordeds and curlies (Poodles Miniature), some of the latter being as small as 4lb. or 5lb. in weight. In the matter of colour, the foundations of both varieties are, of course, the blacks and the whites, from which blues, browns, fawns, oranges, etc., have been produced, for the most part in the curly variety. Some of the Miniatures (the height of which is limited to 15in.) are as pretty as the larger varieties are imposing and picturesque. Soundness of colour is a great desideratum in either variety, and in the corded, tightness, distinctiveness, quality, and length of curl are always aimed at. In most breeds, when the type and features have been fixed, by individual authorities, custom, or a club, a craze often sets in for exaggerations and abnormalities. Take, for instance, the Field Spaniel. Directly it was ordained that this dog should be long and low, which were his chief characteristics, breeders laid emphasis upon these points, and by degrees, until a reaction set in, bred Field Spaniels almost as long and low as alligators. So it has been with corded Poodles, the great feature of which variety is length of coat. As a result the cords of some dogs have been cultivated to such an abnormal extent as to render locomotion by the dog almost impossible. In this connection at a Kennel Club show two very noted and indisputably good dogs were put back, purely on the ground of their coats, which the judge contended had been cultivated to an unreasonable excess in length—in fact, so as to impede their locomotion. How far the judge was justified in his extraordinary action I am not going to discuss here. It must be conceded, however, that a Poodle, whatever else, should be an active dog. It was for this reason that the curly-coated variety was evolved and a club instituted in its behalf. But the Poodle is, after all, a purely "fancy" breed, not being used in England for any purpose other than as a companion, leaving out the trick dogs, and, therefore, there is no reason why he should not be made ornamental, so long as the form and features of the breed, as laid down by the club, are not infringed. The owner of the dogs banned contended that they were as active and agile as any corded Poodle could be, and in this connection it cannot, of course, be expected that a corded Poodle, with his wealth of ringlets to carry, can possibly be as agile as the curly variety.

Before leaving coat, I may mention that fashion has ordained that the Poodle shall be "shaven and shorn" to pattern, this varying in detail in accordance with the particular taste of the owner, but in the main providing for a lion-like mane and body-covering of hair, the loins, face, and legs being shaved, except for tufts of hair left here and there. These sometimes take the form of the owner's crest or coat of arms and other designs.

The great features of the Poodle are his long clean-cut head, dark intelligent eye, short body, well-balanced frame, and beautiful straight forelegs and catlike feet. Indeed, he is the embodiment of symmetry in his architecture, which should in every detail be such as to ensure the handiwork of a dog capable of unlimited activity and the agility of a cat. Full eyes, a thick head, flat sides, a long back, straight stifles, and thin or open feet are faults to be avoided in any Poodle, whether corded or curly, large, medium, or Toy.

The chief points to look for in the selection of Poodle puppies at from two to four months old, whether large or Toy, are: Great length of head, dark eyes, narrow skull, short back, well-sprung ribs, clean neck and shoulders, and straight forelegs.

The following are the description and points as laid down by the Poodle Club.

Points of the Perfect Poodle.

GENERAL APPEARANCE.—That of a very active, intelligent, and elegant-looking dog, well built, and carrying himself proudly.

HEAD.—Long, straight, and fine, the skull not broad, with a slight peak at the back.

MUZZLE.—Long (but not snipy) and strong—not full in cheek, teeth white, strong, and level, gums black, lips black and not showing lippiness.

EYES.—Almond shaped, very dark, full of fire and intelligence.

NOSE.—Black and sharp.

EARS.—The leather long and wide, low set and hanging close to the face.

NECK.—Well proportioned and strong, to admit of the head being carried high and with dignity.

SHOULDERS.—Strong and muscular, sloping well to the back.

POODLE (Curly-coated).

CHEST.—Deep and moderately wide.

BACK.—Short, strong, and slightly hollowed, the loins broad and muscular, the ribs well sprung and braced up.

FEET.—Rather small, and of good shape, the toes well arched, pads thick and hard.

LEGS.—The forelegs set straight from shoulder, with plenty of bone and muscle. Hind legs very muscular and well bent, with the hocks well let down.

TAIL.—Set on rather high, well carried, never curled or carried over back.

COAT.—The coat should be very profuse, and of good hard texture; if corded, hanging in tight even cords; if non-corded, very thick and strong, of even length, the curls close and thick, without knots or cords.

COLOUR.—All black, all white, all red, all blue.

The White Poodle should have dark eyes, black or very dark liver nose, lips, and toe nails.

The Red Poodle should have dark amber eyes, dark liver nose, lips, and toe nails.

The Blue Poodle should be of even colour, and have dark eyes, lips, and toe nails.

All other points of White, Red, and Blue Poodles should be the same as the perfect Black Poodle.

N.B.—It is strongly recommended that only one-third of the body be clipped or shaved, and that the hair on the forehead be left on.

Value of Points.

General appearance and movement	15
Head and ears	15
Eyes and expression	10
Neck and shoulders	10
Shape of body, loin, back, and carriage of stern	15
Legs and feet	10
Coat, colour, and texture of coat	15
Bone, muscle, and condition	10
Total	100

Points of the Perfect Poodle (Miniature).

The definition of Miniature Poodles as agreed to by the Miniature Poodle Club:—

Size.—Must be under 15in. at shoulder, but the smaller the better, as long as the Poodle type is kept to.

General Appearance.—That of a very active, intelligent, smart, and elegant-looking little dog, well built, and carrying himself proudly.

Head.—To be as long, straight, and fine as possible; very slight stop; fine skull.

Muzzle.—Long and fine, not full in the cheek, teeth white and level, black lips not showing lippiness.

Eyes.—Oval shaped, very dark, full of fire and intelligence.

Nose.—Black and pointed.

Ears.—The leather long and wide, low set, and hanging close to the face.

Neck.—Well proportioned, the head being carried high and with dignity.

Shoulders.—To slope well to the back.

Chest.—Deep and moderately wide.

Back.—Very short, very slightly hollowed, loins not too broad, ribs well sprung and braced up.

Feet.—Very small and dainty, of oval shape, the toes not to open when set on ground.

Legs.—The forelegs set very straight from shoulder with fine bone and muscle. Hind legs muscular and well bent; hocks well let down.

Tail.—Set on high, gaily carried, never curled or carried over back.

Coat.—For curly: Very profuse, of hard texture, of even length; very frizzy, not at all open. For corded: Very thick, hanging in tight, even cords.

Colours.—Any even colour.

White Miniature to have black eyes, black rims to eyes, black nose and lips.

The Red and Brown Miniature to have brown eyes, brown nose and lips.

The Blue Miniature to have dark eyes, black nose and lips.

The Cream or Apricot Miniature to have black eyes, nose, and lips.

FAULTS IN THE MINIATURE POODLE.—Heavy build, clumsiness, long back, light and prominent eyes, bad stern carriage, heavy gait, coarse head, over- or under-shot mouth, flesh-coloured nose, coarse legs and feet, open and rusty coats; white markings on black and coloured poodles, lemon markings on white poodles.

VALUE OF POINTS.

General appearance and movement	20
Head and ears	15
Eyes and expression	10
Shape of body, loin, back, and carriage of stern	15
Legs and feet	10
Coat, colour and texture of coat	10
Condition	10
Size	10
Total	100

CHAPTER XLIII.

The White English Terrier.

The White English Terrier has declined so much in public favour in late years as to become threatened with extinction. Indeed, I very much doubt if there are twenty pure-bred specimens of the breed at this moment in the whole of the British Isles. This grim fact is much to be deplored, for it is a very nice variety, makes a desirable companion, and is a rare vermin dog. The origin of the White English Terrier is difficult to fix, but there can be little doubt that it is a very near relative of the Bull-terrier. Whether the latter was largely used in its manufacture or *vice versa* is not clear. If the former, the Fox-terrier and Whippet will doubtless have been employed to reduce the size, for many White English Terriers show traces in their architecture of either one or other of these breeds. There is little doubt that the breed is a Lancashire production, where it has for the most part abounded, particularly in its palmier days of nearly half a century ago. One of the earliest enthusiasts of the breed was Mr. Robert Lee, of Bolton, and this Lancashire cotton borough once boasted of other fanciers famous in the breed in the late Mr. James Roocroft and Mr. Walker. Other centres had their zealots—viz., Birmingham, in the Hinks and Mr. Yardley; London, Mr. Alf. George; whilst the breed has had a few devotees in Scotland, the most prominent being Mr. William Ballantyne, manager of the show of the Scottish Kennel Club, whose famous bitch, Ch. Queen, had a most brilliant career on the show bench. The breed in its early days was, like Bull-terriers, cropped, and in this the cropping trouble has also been successfully surmounted. The breed was not classified by the Kennel Club separately until early in the 'nineties.

The White English Terrier has much in common with the Bull-terrier, being on very similar lines throughout, in miniature, except that its head should be finer and muzzle a little squarer. In body, legs, feet, and stern one is a counterpart of the other. The eye of the White English Terrier should be dark, but not so small, in proportion, and cruel-looking as that of the Bull-terrier. The ears should be small, V-shaped, and drop like those of the Fox-terrier. Before the abolition of cropping in 1895 the ears of White English Terriers were cropped, and doubtless the cropping edict of the Kennel Club has had much to do with the decline of the breed, which was none too strong when it came into force. The records do not reveal the fact of there ever having been any other colour than white, although it is on record that a good Black-and-tan Terrier once existed which was by a dog of this breed, out of a White English Terrier bitch, and it was so good that it won at one of the Manchester Dog Shows. This is very much akin to the white blackbird, except that the dog is reversed.

The best weight for a White English Terrier is from 12lb. to 14lb., the lighter weight for bitches and the heavier for dogs.

The chief points to look for in the selection of White English Terrier puppies at from two to four months old are much the same as those given for Bull-terriers, except that a leaner head is required and a little stronger muzzle in proportion.

There used to be a White English Terrier Club, but, alack, that has become extinct. The following are the standard description and code of points it formulated for the breed :—

HEAD.—Long and narrow, flat from the back of the skull to the nose, and with no bumps at sides or cheeks.

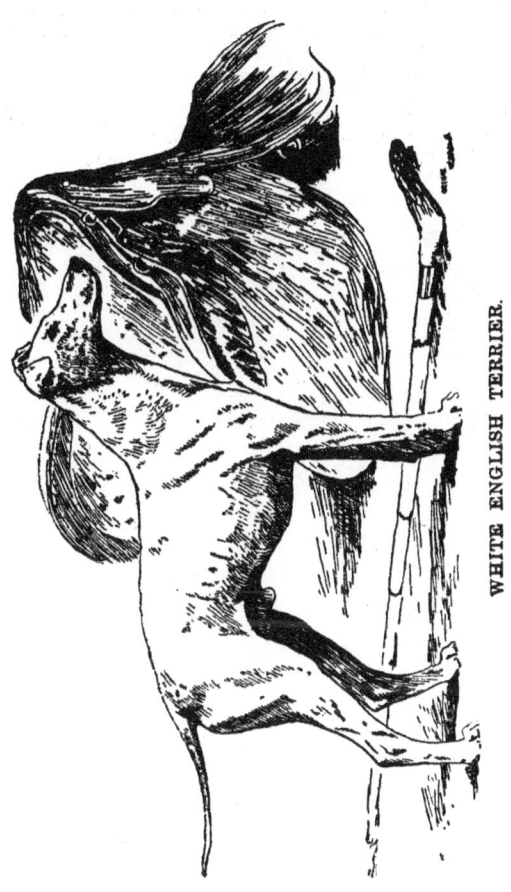

WHITE ENGLISH TERRIER.

MUZZLE.—Long and tapering, but not weak.
JAWS.—Strong, teeth close-fitting and even, with no lippiness.
EYES.—Small, oval-shaped, bright in expression, and dark, nearly black in colour.
NOSE.—Well defined, quite black, and of moderate size.
EARS.—Small, fine in texture, V-shaped, and hanging close to the head.
NECK.—Light and graceful, rather long, slightly arched.
SHOULDERS.—Sloping; chest rather narrow but deep.
BODY.—A little arched, with good back ribs.
FORELEGS.—Quite straight, with well-arched toes and black nails.
HINDQUARTERS.—Strong and powerful, with hocks well let down.
TAIL.—Very fine, and carried almost straight or with a slight curve, but never curled over the back.
COAT.—Short, fine, and glossy.
COLOUR.—Pure white.
WEIGHT.—Should not exceed 20lb.; even less is desirable.
GENERAL APPEARANCE.—That of a well-bred and high-class, smart and neat-looking dog, well suited for a companion or a house guard.

STANDARD OF EXCELLENCE.

Head, including jaws	20
Ears	10
Eyes	5
Legs and feet	10
Body and quarters	10
Colour	20
Tail	5
General appearance (including size) and action	20
Total	100

CHAPTER XLIV.

The Manchester Terrier.

The Manchester or Black-and-tan Terrier is another breed that came under the ban of the Kennel Club in the matter of the cropping edict, which gave the popularity of the breed a shake from which it has nearly recovered. Although the ear question, as in the case of Great Danes, Irish, Bull, and White English Terriers, has, by dint of perseverance on the part of breeders, been effectually solved by the establishment of a neat drop-ear in this breed, there are a number of fanciers who still cling to the theory that a cropped Manchester is ever so much smarter and possesses more "character" than one possessing its aural appendages in their entirety, no matter how neat or orthodox they may be carried, and many of them have deserted the breed entirely on that account. Cropping is a custom, like many others, which dies hard, and it will probably pass entirely away only with the generation which saw it in vogue.

MANCHESTER TERRIER.

The Manchester Terrier in his present form is comparatively a new breed, and yet no reliable data exist as to his original manufacture, which may, however, be fixed to almost synchronise with the advent of dog shows, and to be the work of the Mancunian fancier, from whence the breed first emerged, and where it has been and is to-day more largely propagated than in any other part of the kingdom. Hence its nomenclature, by which name it was solely identified originally, even by the Kennel Club; but as time advanced and the breed became disseminated and bred largely in other parts of the kingdom (notably in Scotland, where it has firmly "caught on," and where many specimens of the first water have been bred), and abroad, especially in the United States, where it was at one time very popular, the word "Manchester" was gradually dropped, and it became known everywhere as the Black-and-tan Terrier. Recently, however, the Kennel Club has again reverted to the old name of the Manchester Terrier.

Smooth-haired Manchester Terriers have existed in England for centuries, being formerly used, with Terriers of other colours and rough in coat, for underground work; but they were, of course, very different dogs from the modern show article. At the same time, it is from these dogs that the present-day Manchester Terrier, with his fine, long head, glossy coat, whip-tail, and general brilliancy of appearance, has been evolved by the Manchester dog fancier, who, with his quick commercial eye, saw money in such a breed, which made a most desirable pet and companion for both lady and gentleman. And there can be no question that the Manchester Terrier as a companion has few, if any, compeers. He is a splendid house-dog, very sagacious, intelligent, and discriminative, whilst his smooth, sleek, lustrous coat not only appeals to the eye, but has the additional advantage of greater cleanliness in a dog kept entirely in the house than can be said of a rough-haired Terrier, whose coat means in wet and snowy weather the introduction of dirt and wet into the house, which is particularly objectionable to the frugal housewife, and involves the " poor dog " in many a thrashing he really does not deserve, and which the Manchester Terrier, of course, escapes.

Although the imported refinement in the Manchester Terrier has deprived the dog of a great deal of his original hardihood, he has retained all his innate Terrier virtues of gameness, for assuredly the show Manchester Terrier can hold his own in combat with his own species, and cannot be excelled by any other breed as a vermin dog where he has been properly reared and trained. Indeed, in his earlier career, he was used almost entirely as a vermin dog, and the invention of cropping was originally prompted by considerations of humanity, in saving his ears from mutilation. In this way usage or habit became " second nature," and a Manchester Terrier un-cropped came to be regarded by the fancier and the public, very paradoxically, as an incomplete article!

By what process the metamorphosis was effected from the crude original to the beautiful modern show specimen is not very clear. The system of breeding by selection, which in itself has revolutionised many breeds of dogs and other livestock, has, doubtless, played the most prominent part in the dog's evolution. Possibly the Whippet, Bull-terrier, or White English Terrier, may have been employed as outcrosses occasionally, to add refinement to the head, limbs, and outline in the one case, and coat and tail in the other; but such crosses would naturally be kept a secret, and could more easily be practised in those days, before pedigrees were recorded or as much importance was attached to lineage as is the case nowadays. Whatever the process, the breed has long been well established and pedigrees have been sufficiently authenticated as to avoid the risk of alien blood being introduced into the breed.

Coming to the chief features of the breed, what are necessary to constitute an ideal specimen are an exceptionally long, level head and lean, flat skull, free from even a suspicion of cheekiness or lippiness, with small, almond-shaped, dark eyes, set in pretty close together in a slightly oblique position. The great length of head is given by an abnormal length of muzzle (which must still be strong, and the mouth neither overshot nor undershot) in proportion to the length of skull, which should be short. Any great amount of " stop," suspicion of cheekiness, full or light eyes, or snipiness, are serious blemishes. The body should be short, ribs well sprung, and back level, with a short whip-tail carried straight out from the root. In proportion the dog should be well balanced—viz., neither too long nor too low on leg, but showing the symmetry and proportion of a perfect hackney. The forelegs should be straight and feet closely knit, but not cat-like—more hare-footed. It is in the forelegs where so many Manchester Terriers fail, out at elbows being a common defect, even among prize-winners. The hind legs should be well bent; the stifles and the hocks well let down. The quality of coat and colour are, of course, very important features. The hair should be short and lustrous, but not soft. To the touch it should be crisp, but to the eye have the appearance of fineness and quality. The body, top of the head, tail, and front of legs are, of course, jet black, the tan beginning in an almost straight line across the cheeks, running to the nose. The tan on the legs begins just above the pasterns, running into black pencillings down the toes. These should be distinct. A streak of tan, beginning under the root of the tail, runs down the rectum to the under part of the body; it is called the "vent," and should be so narrow that when the tail is put down flat to the dog the tan is covered. The hind feet should be similarly "pencilled," markings being of the greatest importance. The tan should be of a rich mahogany colour, pale or too dark tan or indistinct markings being very objectionable. The ears should be small, V-shaped, and carried flat on the head.

It is probably the necessity for tan of a particular hue, and certain markings (in addition to make and shape), that has had much to do with the want of progress in the breed—points that are not required in any other breed.

The chief points to look for in the selection of Manchester Terrier puppies at from two to four months old are :—Great length of head, which should be flat and free from stop, eyes small and dark, skull lean, lengthy neck, short back and short whip-tail, clean shoulders, and straight forelegs, medium as to bone. The colour and markings are, of course, important, and should be taken into account, those laid down in the standard being the guide.

The following are the standard and scale of points promulgated by the Black-and-tan Terrier Club :—

HEAD.—Long, flat, and narrow, level and wedge-shaped, without showing cheek muscles; well filled up under the eyes, with tapering, tightly lipped jaws and level teeth.

EYES.—Very small, sparkling, and dark, set fairly close together, and oblong in shape.

NOSE.—Black.

EARS.—The correct carriage of the ears is a debatable point since cropping has been abolished. Probably in the larger breed the drop ear is correct, but for Toys either erect or semi-erect carriage of the ear is most desirable.

NECK AND SHOULDERS.—The neck should be fairly long, and tapering from the shoulders to the head, with sloping shoulders, the neck being free from throatiness, and slightly arched at the occiput.

CHEST.—Narrow but deep.

BODY.—Moderately short and curving upwards at the loin; ribs well sprung, back slightly arched at the loin and falling again at the joining of the tail to the same height as the shoulders.

LEGS.—Must be quite straight, set on well under the dog, and of fair length.

FEET.—More inclined to be cat- than hare-footed.

TAIL.—Moderate length, and set on where the arch of the back ends; thick where it joins the body, tapering to a point, and not carried higher than the back.

COAT.—Close, smooth, short, and glossy.

COLOUR.—Jet black and rich mahogany tan, distributed over the body as follows: On the head the muzzle is tanned to the nose, which, with the nasal bone, is jet black; there is also a bright spot on each cheek, and above each eye, the underjaw and throat are tanned, and the hair *inside* the ear is of the same colour; the forelegs tanned up to the knees, with black lines (pencil marks) up each toe, and a black mark (thumb mark) above the foot; *inside* the hind legs tanned, but divided with black at the hock joint; and under the tail also tanned; and so is the vent, but only sufficiently to be easily covered by the tail; also slightly tanned on each side of chest. Tan *outside* of hind legs—commonly called breeching—is a serious defect. In all cases the black should not run into the tan, or *vice versa*, but the division between the two colours should be well defined.

GENERAL APPEARANCE.—A Terrier calculated to take his own part in the rat pit, and not of the Whippet type.

WEIGHT.—10lb. to 20lb. is most desirable.

SCALE OF POINTS.

	Value.
Head and eyes	25
Neck	5
Ears	5
Legs and feet	15
Body	10
Tail	10
Colour and markings	15
General appearance	15
Total	100

CHAPTER XLV.

Black and Tan Terrier (Miniature)

The Toy Black-and-tan Terrier is a sub-variety of the Manchester Terrier, from which he has been bantamised by careful selection, and to-day is probably as numerous and popular as his larger prototype. His points are identical with the latter in every particular and detail; indeed, he should be an exact replica of him in miniature, and that is why the Kennel Club adopted the distinguishing word " miniature." The smaller he is the more valuable, so long as length and leanness of head and symmetry are preserved—the two most difficult points to obtain in the miniature variety. Apple heads and

BLACK-AND-TAN TERRIER (MINIATURE).

long bodies are more the rule than the exception, and big bat ears are a big disfigurement often found on some of our best specimens. Where a good long lean head, nice short body, and straight forelegs are found in a small specimen he is sure to go " nap " on the show bench, and these are the points, with small ears, which should be emphasised and aimed at by breeders. The regulation weight limit is 7lb., but many of our best specimens are much under that weight.

The chief points to look for in the selection of Black-and-tan Terrier (Miniature) puppies at from two to four months old are :—Length of head, which should be flat and free from stop, eyes small and dark, skull lean, lengthy neck, short back and short whip-tail, clean shoulders, and straight forelegs. The colour and markings are, of course, important, and should be taken into account, those laid down in the standard being the guide.

The description and standard of points is the same as that for the Manchester Terrier, except that the most desirable weight for a miniature is not exceeding 7lb.

CHAPTER XLVI.

The King Charles Spaniel.

There are four recognised varieties of the King Charles Spaniel—viz., the Black-and-tan, Tricolour or Prince Charles, Ruby, and Blenheim—all of which have, doubtless, one common origin, since all are, and may be, interbred without losing their individuality. What that origin is is not clearly authenticated beyond the fact that the breed has been given to us by Spain, from which the name is derived. History tells us that King Charles Spaniels were associated with British monarchs as far back as Henry VIII. and Queen Elizabeth, with both of whom they were great favourites. This was during the sixteenth century. The Black-and-tan King Charles Spaniel was the especial favourite of King Charles II., who doubtless obtained

KING CHARLES SPANIEL (Black-and-tan).

specimens from Spain and propagated the variety which ultimately became associated with the name of this monarch. This was in the early part of the seventeenth century. The first Duke of Marlborough about this time cultivated a red-and-white King Charles Spaniel at his famous seat, Blenheim Palace, which gave the name Blenheim to the red-and-white variety. The Blenheim Spaniel has been preserved by the Marlborough family from that time to the present, but they are very different from the Blenheims exhibited at our shows of to-day, doubtless resembling more the original, being larger and longer in face. The short-faced and almost noseless diminutive modern Blenheim, is, of course, the work of the showman and fancier of the nineteenth century, who from these two varieties has evolved the Prince Charles and Ruby, which are comparatively modern creations, first appearing in the K.C.S.B. for 1892. The difference between the old Blenheim of the Duke of Marlborough and the modern article has become so marked that the name Blenheim, as applied to the former, is gradually being dropped, and that of " Marlborough " substituted, so as to distinguish it from its modern descendant.

The King Charles Spaniel, according to ancient records, has ever been a favourite of the English court and nobility in the olden time, its long associations with Royalty and the aristocracy having doubtless had an effect upon its character, general bearing, and demeanour, which is most markedly that of the little canine aristocrat. W. D. Drury, in his revised edition of Dalziel's " British Dogs," has the following interesting references to the early history and latter-day associations of the King Charles Spaniel :—

History records that the hapless Queen of Scots was accompanied to the scaffold by her little Spaniel, and that while a fugitive or prisoner at Carisbrooke Castle, King Charles was attended by his favourite Spaniels, with whom he often amused himself ; it is certainly a fact that he was rarely unattended by his four-footed pets. They were so numerous

KING CHARLES SPANIEL (Blenheim).

in his time that they bred in his bedroom and over-ran Hampton Court and York Palace,—now Whitehall,—to which, according to Pepys' Diary, they had free access, even upon State occasions. Although harsh censors may declare these facts fitting to a frivolous age, the popularity of these little animals has ebbed and flowed ever since, and the Toy Spaniel still maintains his exalted associations.

The aristocrat seems born in each variety—they cannot be otherwise. Psychologically, they are sensitive and observant, as quickly noticing the difference between poorly-clad and well-to-do people as between people kind and unkind. They are more at home on the pillow or the counterpane and in the drawing-room than in the kitchen or the kennel. Their lives have correspondingly " fallen in pleasant places." It is interesting to note what vicissitudes of fortune have attended this little dog—from being the chosen company of ye daintie dames and monarchs, they were found as late as thirty years ago bred in the slums of London, and some of the best specimens now on the show bench are related to grand-dames and sires bred and reared in Whitechapel. Many are the experiences old fanciers can tell of visits to underground kitchens and dark apartments, and discoveries of rare specimens huddled in corners or extracted from boxes and cupboards. How these delicate animals survived under such conditions, or retained their charming characteristics, is a matter of conjecture.

Those are practically the associations of the King Charles Spaniel life of to-day, with the difference that the middle-class element of society is now probably the most numerous among his enthusiasts.

The chief features required in the four varieties are practically identical. The leading characteristic is, of course, the head. In each extreme shortness of foreface with great depth and width and finish is a great desideratum, together with a lofty globular type of skull, large lustrous eyes, and low-set ears, which, of course, naturally follow a phenomenally occipitally developed head. In each shortness and roundness of body and soundness of limb are points to be aimed at, as well as flatness of coat and abundance of feathering, which latter is a characteristic of all Spaniels, whether Sporting or Toy. All the points enumerated in the foregoing are what may be termed cardinal points, except flatness of coat, which is strongly desirable, although a wavy

KING CHARLES SPANIEL (Ruby or Red).

coat is not objectionable and a curly coat not fatal where a dog excels in the other leading features. In the matter of size, present-day fashion has drifted and is still drifting, as in the case of most, if not all, "fancy" breeds of dogs, in the direction of diminutiveness, the result being that the smallest specimens which excel in the breed's leading points are the most prized and most valuable, on account probably of their being the most difficult to produce and the most rare. Greater massiveness in head, with most of the desirable head points accentuated, is generally to be found in the larger specimens, which should by no means be discarded, but, on the other hand, retained, and even cultivated, as a foundation for the propagation of the medium and small sized specimens. Practice has discovered that breeding from medium-sized specimens good in themselves is not always successful in producing facsimile reproductions, whilst greater mediocrity still is produced by the alliance of very diminutive specimens. The best results are usually obtained by the mating of a good medium-sized bitch to a big massive-headed dog, and a biggish roomy sound-limbed bitch to a small but massive-headed dog.

The sire in every case should be a very short, good-headed dog if great bench merit in the progeny is looked for, since the bitch, as a rule, puts on the bodies and limbs and the dog the heads. In this way great care should be taken that the bitch is exceptionally sound in limb, well sprung in ribs, and an active, agile specimen, for one of the great defects of the King Charles Spaniels of to-day is weak, and even crippled, hindquarters, which often mar an otherwise beautiful bench specimen. Fashion has ordained that the tails of all King Charles Spaniels shall be docked, about one-half the tail being removed.

The chief points to look for in the selection of all English King Charles Spaniel puppies at from two to four months old are the same, except, of course, colour, to which some weight should be given according to the standard laid down. They are :—Diminutiveness compatible with soundness and robustness, extreme shortness of face, large eyes, lofty skull, short body, nicely proportioned all round, low set and rather long ears.

KING CHARLES SPANIEL (Tricolour or Prince Charles).

The following are the description and standard of points of the four varieties as laid down by the King Charles Spaniel Club :—

SKULL.—Massive in comparison to size, well domed, and full over the eyes.

EYES.—Very large and dark, set wide apart, with eyelids block square to face line, and with pleasing expression.

NOSE.—Black with large wide open nostrils, very short, and turned up to meet skull. The stop between skull and nose should be well defined.

JAW.—Muzzle square, wide, and deep, and well turned up, lower jaw wide, lips exactly meeting, giving a nice finish. The cheeks should not fall away under the eyes, but be well cushioned up. A protruding tongue is objectionable, but does not disqualify.

EARS.—Set on low, and to hang quite flat to cheeks, very long and well feathered.

SIZE.—The most desirable size is from 6lb. to 12lb.

SHAPE.—Compact and cobby, on refined lines, chest wide and deep, legs short and straight, back short, and level. Tail well flagged, and not carried over the level of back.

MOVEMENT.—Free, active, and elegant.

COAT.—Long, silky, and straight, a slight wave allowed, not curly. The legs, ears, and tail should be profusely feathered.

COLOUR.—King Charles: A rich glossy black, with bright mahogany tan markings on muzzle, legs, chest, lining of ears, under tail, and spots over eyes. Tricolour: A ground of pearly white with well distributed black patches, brilliant tan markings on cheeks, lining of ears, under tail, and spots over the eyes. A wide white blaze between the eyes, and up the forehead. Blenheim: A ground of pearly white with well distributed chestnut red patches. A wide clear blaze with the "spot" in centre of skull. The Spot: A clear chestnut red mark about the size of a sixpence in the centre of skull. Ruby: Whole coloured; a rich chestnut red.

DISQUALIFICATION.—The presence of a few white hairs on the chest of a Black-and-tan or Ruby is undesirable, but a white patch shall disqualify.

The popularity of the King Charles Spaniel, which was for a time dimmed somewhat by the introduction of the Japanese and Pekingese, has been considerably recovered, and a new boom set in.

CHAPTER XLVII.

The Japanese.

The Japanese is of the King Charles Spaniel species, but in no way a kinsman so far as historical records reveal. Still, he has much in common with his English counterpart, being a short-faced Toy dog, similar in shape, coat, and not unlike the Blenheim in colour, except that, although red-and-whites and yellow-and-whites are numerous, black-and-white is the prevailing colour. The chief points of divergence are in the shape of head and placement of the eye, the former being less domed and the latter set in more at the side of the head, but still large. The ears are placed higher on the head than those of the King Charles Spaniel, and the nostrils are smaller, the nose being equally as short or shorter, and the foreface somewhat wider and not quite so deep. Shortness of body is a great desideratum in the Japanese, whose tail is left intact and not docked as in the case of the King Charles Spaniel, and curls over the back, in the fashion of the

JAPANESE.

Pomeranian, being well feathered. The coat of the "Jap" should be flat, entirely free from waviness, and the legs well feathered, with a large frill or mane. The size of the Japanese is a feature which has undergone considerable modification since the breed was first imported and exhibited in England about fifty years ago. A dog I myself owned about that time in Ming Seng, who was imported with a cargo of tea, was about 12lb. weight. He was one of if not the first Japanese exhibited, and so little known was the breed in the North of England that some judges at that time hesitated to give the dog a prize, although he really was a very good Jap for his size. The late Rev. F. Hodgson, an authority on the breed, once gave this dog the gold medal at the Crystal Palace Show as the best foreign dog. An article on the breed appears from my pen in the first edition of Dalziel's "British Dogs," published about that time, at which period the name of the breed was in some doubt, some holding that they were a Japanese rough Pug, and others inclining to the idea that they more closely resembled the King Charles Spaniel. The latter view was the more rational, and Japanese Spaniel ultimately became the name with which the breed was associated.

As people became more and more informed on the breed, it was found that the most valuable specimens in the Mikado's dominion were the very diminutive dogs, those so small indeed that they could be and which were carried in the sleeves of the ladies of rank and fashion. Such dogs in Japan were almost priceless, besides an increased risk involved in importing them. In this way for a long time the medium-sized dogs were those which found their way into England—dogs of from 7lb. to 11lb. weight—but the fashion was set, the "sleeve dog" was the ideal, and English breeders at once entered upon the native enterprise of dwarfing the breed, and with much success. Since then the closer relations which happily have been brought about between this country and Japan, and the consequent greater intercourse of the two peoples, have resulted in an impetus being given to the breed, and a natural demand among the English aristocracy and fancying element for the diminutive Japs, dogs of from 2½lb. to 4½lb. weight, which have since been largely imported. The result has been that what with the original stock, the efforts of breeders in bantamising them and the diminutive importations together, England can now offer a grand show of Japs. Their ranks, however, have often been decimated by distemper, since the Japanese is one of the most delicate of all the Asiatic breeds, and this has been its greatest drawback. So susceptible is the breed to this fell disease that it has been humorously remarked that to talk of distemper only in a kennel of Japs is enough for the whole kennel to be stricken down with the disease! Another cause of the breed's later somewhat modified popularity is the craze for a kindred alien in the Pekingese, which has supplanted the Jap to some extent.

The latter possesses many of the notable characteristics of his Chinese cousin in the direction of consummate dignity and aristocratic bearing altogether disproportionate to his diminutive size and capability. The Jap is a dog who at once impresses you with his supreme importance and innate contempt for Western associations, either human or canine, and that doubtless is one of the causes of his having "caught on" with the "hupper suckle," as the Cockney would say, and for the large prices which many winning specimens have realised. And his diminutiveness, his elegance, and his aristocratic mien will be likely to cause him to retain the affection of the wealthy classes, who do not count kennel losses in the same way as those who have to earn their livelihood. A separate classification was allotted to the breed by the Kennel Club in 1894.

The chief points to look for in the selection of Japanese puppies at from two to four months old are almost identical with those given for King Charles Spaniels, except that the ears should be shorter and set higher on the head, the foreface broader, and the eyes set wider apart, more in the direction of the side of the head. The colour is not very material, but is better well distributed, profuse coat and feathering and tail showing an indication to curl well over back.

The following are the standard description and code of points laid down by the Japanese Chin Club :—

GENERAL APPEARANCE.—That of a lively, highly-bred little dog, with dainty appearance, smart, compact carriage, and profuse coat. These dogs should be essentially stylish in movement, lifting the feet high when in motion, carrying the tail (which is heavily feathered) proudly curved or plumed over the back. In size they vary considerably, but the smaller they are the better, provided type and quality are not sacrificed. When divided by weight, classes should be for under and over 7lb.

COAT.—The coat should be long, profuse, and straight, free from curl or wave, and not too flat. It should have a tendency to stand out, more particularly at the frill, with profuse feathering on the tail and thighs.

COLOUR.—The dogs should be either black-and-white or red-and-white—*i.e.*, parti-coloured. The term red includes all shades of sable, brindle, lemon, and orange, but the brighter and clearer the red the better. The white should be clear white, and the colour, whether black or red, should be evenly distributed patches over the body, cheek, and ears.

HEAD.—Should be large for size of dog, with broad skull, rounded in front; eyes large, dark, set far apart; muzzle very short and wide and well cushioned—*i.e.*, the upper lips rounded on each side of nostrils, which should be large and black, except in the case of red-and-white dogs, when a brown-coloured nose is as common as a black one.

EARS.—Should be small, set wide apart, and high on the dog's head, and carried slightly forward, V-shaped.

BODY.—Should be squarely and compactly built, wide in chest, "cobby" in shape. The length of the dog's body should be about its height.

LEGS AND FEET.—The legs should be straight and the bone fine; the feet should be long and hare-shaped. The legs should be well feathered to the feet on the front legs and to the thighs behind. The feet should also be feathered.

NUMERICAL SCALE OF POINTS.

	Value.
Head.—Size of head	5
Shape of skull	5
Shortness of nose	5
Width of muzzle	5
Eyes	10
Ears	5
Coat and feathering	15
Colour and markings	10
Legs and feet	10
Action, shape, style, and carriage of tail	20
Size	10
Total	100

CHAPTER XLVIII.

The Pekingese.

The Pekingese is probably the most fashionable ladies' dog in England at the present moment. Introduced into this country as a show dog about forty to forty-five years ago, the breed has "caught on" immensely with the nobility and aristocracy, especially so since the advent of the present century, since which Pekingese have been propagated to an enormous extent, many shows having been promoted specially for Pekingese by the Pekingese Club, the Pekin Palace Dog Association, and the British Pekingese Club, at each of which over 200 entries were made. Quarantine has compelled breeders to resort to inbreeding to a very great extent, although there have been a few importations from China, which must have been most beneficial to a breed in which the artificial and luxurious conditions under which they live, and consanguinity together, were beginning to have a most deleterious

PEKINGESE.

effect, as shown in the many weedy or coarse and typeless specimens seen in the show ring from time to time.

The breed was a great favourite with the late Queen Alexandra, but the earliest importations were made by Lord John Hay and Lord Algernon Gordon Lennox, who, having access to the very exclusive Court of Pekin, were privileged to procure reliable specimens. Others of the earlier importers and zealots are Lady Gooch, Mrs. Douglas Murray, Mrs. Loftus Allen, who I believe was the first exhibitor of these dogs, and one or two others.

Although the Pekingese has doubtless been largely propagated, and become a great favourite with the Emperors and Court of China, now abolished, it was by no means confined to the Court and capital of Pekin, but is to be found in other parts of the Celestial Empire, being with the Chow Chow a distinctive national breed. The incident of this Royal favour and the fact that almost all the importations to England have been brought from Pekin together determined the dog's nomenclature in England, just in the same way that the Bedlington and Manchester Terrier and Sussex Spaniels came to be called after the place of their origin. Whether the breed should come under the Spaniel category, or be classed with the Pug species, is a problem which the English cynologists with all their expert knowledge of the races of dogs have hitherto not attempted to solve. Doubtless there is a difficulty, as in the first place the Pekingese possesses few Spaniel instincts, nor is he used as a sporting or water dog in his native country. Drury, however, designates him as a Chinese Spaniel, although the earlier specimens were called Pekingese Pugs, and there can be little doubt that the Pekingese is the prototype and progenitor of the English Pug—in all probability the latter came from the smooth specimens, called " Happa " dogs, of which there are but few in England, although they abound in Pekin. In character and disposition the Pekingese has all the pugnacity of the English Pug, and the same dignity and aristocratic bearing, but intensified, which he has doubtless imbibed through his long association with Royalty and the Court. The great care and attention which his Royal and noble masters and mistresses have bestowed upon him, and the manner in which they have jealously guarded him and provided him with every luxury and comfort, have moulded in the dog a character full of dignity and sublime pride, and disgust for anything menial or common. This feature of the breed is most marked, whether at home or at the shows, where his airs and graces are often most embarrassing to the dogs' fair owners in their sometimes frantic efforts to induce particular celebrities to observe the necessary show-ring etiquette and fall in with its requirements.

The earlier specimens were the larger dogs of from 12lb. to 16lb., but, as in most " fancy " breeds, a craze soon set in for Toys, which was accentuated by the information that the very diminutive Pekingese, dogs of 3lb. or 4lb., such as could be carried in the sleeves of ladies, were valued the most by the ladies of the court, and this led to the formation of the Pekin Palace Dog Association, whose mission is in the main the cultivation of the Toy Dog, and whose creed does not even provide for dogs exceeding 10lb. in weight. This craze has become infectious, and most breeders are now directing their efforts to the production of the most diminutive specimens, which shall possess all the character and features of their larger brethren. These are extreme shortness of muzzle, which, unlike the King Charles Spaniel, but like the Pug, should be as square as possible, and the mouth neither overshot nor undershot. The head should be massive, skull lofty, and ears rather small and set high on the head, the antithesis of what is required in the King Charles Spaniel. A large eye, set widely apart, which gives the dog an expression all his own, and quite Asiatic, and with a profusion of wrinkle, furnishes the finishing touches to the physiognomy of this quaint breed. The bodies of earlier specimens which came to England were much longer and more Skye Terrier-like than those possessed by the best dogs of the present day. In fact, compactness of body, with a slight "waist " (formerly termed loin), is now an acknowledged desideratum among the cognoscenti. The dog should be low set, have great bone for his size, his forelegs being bowed, somewhat in the manner of the Dachshund or Dandie Dinmont. This curvature of the foreleg, together with the four white feet and white collar, are said to be symbolical of some native legendary theory of dogmatic belief, which can hardly enter into the philosophy of Christian England, where it is gradually losing its original emphasis, and the native white markings and their significance are now likely to become a feature honoured more in the breach than the observance by breeders and experts. Whole self colours are most favoured and likely to be, rich red or biscuit colour having preference, although blacks have many adherents. It is generally considered that a good Peke. can hardly be a bad colour. As the breed progressed, however, colour became one of its features, and the clubs provide separate classes for reds, fawns, blacks, brindles, particolours, etc. The coat is a very important point. In the smooths it should, of course, be quite smooth, like a Pug's, and in the rough variety it should be profuse but straight, a lion-like mane, which is much prized, well-feathered legs and culotte, and profusely feathered tail, which should be curled up on the back, being absolute requisites. The black masks in reds and fawns are much coveted, and black noses in all colours are insisted upon. The features to avoid are snipy forefaces, long backs, legginess, shelly bodies, and small eyes, all more or less unpardonable blemishes.

No Toy Dog, or what I may term " fancy " breed, has ever reached such a high monetary value in England. Fifty to one hundred pounds is not at all an uncommon price to pay for brood bitches, and I believe as much as £1,000 has been offered and refused for one particular show and brood bitch, who bred big winners of the most approved type in every litter, whilst on two occasions double that amount is said to have been offered for two celebrated dogs. The country at present is flooded with a large number of mediocre specimens, some of which may be bought cheap, and others can hardly be given away, but really good specimens will always readily command a good price, and are likely to do so for some time to come.

The chief points to look for in the selection of Pekingese puppies at from two to four months old are : Diminutiveness compatible with soundness and robustness, shortness and width of foreface, large eyes, deep stop, well-wrinkled forehead, moderately short and compact body, shortness of leg and great bone, with an abundant and dense fur-like coat, tail well feathered, and showing an indication to curl well over body.

The following are the standard description and standard of points of the Pekingese Club :—

HEAD.—Massive, broad skull, wide and flat between the ears (not dome-shaped) ; wide between the eyes..	10
NOSE.—Black, broad, very short and flat	5
EYES.—Large, dark, prominent, round, lustrous	5
STOP.—Deep	5
EARS.—Heart shaped, not set too high, leather never long enough to come below the muzzle, not carried erect, but rather drooping, long feather..	5
MUZZLE.—Very short and broad, not underhung nor pointed, wrinkled ..	5
SHAPE OF BODY.—Heavy in front, broad chest, falling away lighter behind, lion-like, not too long in the body	10
LEGS.—Short, forelegs heavy, bowed out at elbows, hind legs lighter but firm and well shaped	5
FEET.—Flat, not round, should stand well up on toes, not on ankles ..	5
COAT AND FEATHER AND CONDITION.—Long, with thick undercoat, straight and flat, not curly nor wavy, rather coarse but soft, feather on thighs, legs, tail, and toes, long and profuse ..	10
MANE.—Profuse, extending beyond shoulder blades, forming ruff or frill round front of neck..	5
TAIL.—Curled and carried well up on loins, long, profuse, straight feather..	10
SIZE.—Being a Toy dog, the smaller the better, provided type and points are not sacrificed. When divided by weight, classes should be over 10lb. and under 10lb.	5
COLOUR.—All colours are allowable, red, fawn, black, black-and-tan, sable, brindle, white, and particoloured; black masks, and spectacles round eyes, with lines to ears are desirable ..	5

ACTION.—Free, strong, and high, crossing the feet or throwing them out in running should not take off marks. Weakness of joints should be penalised 10

Total 100

The Pekin Palace Dog Association's description and standard of points are as follows :—

HEAD.—Massive, broad skull, wide and flat between the ears, wide between the eyes .. ..
NOSE.—Black essential, broad, very short and flat..
EYES.—Large, dark, round, and lustrous .. ..
EARS.—Long and drooping, leather not to reach below the muzzle, long feather.. .. .. } 25
MUZZLE.—Wrinkled, very short and broad, with level mouth ; muzzle preferably black, except in black-and-tans and parti-colours .. ..

SHAPE OF BODY.—Broad deep chest ; body light in loins ; lion-like ; not long in body. Due allowance should be made for the natural difference in shape between dog and bitch in regard to lightness of loin 20

LEGS.—Short ; forelegs heavy, bowed out at elbows ; hind legs lighter, but firm and well shaped .. .. } 15
FEET.—Flat, toes turned outwards. Toes should be feathered .. ..

MANE.—Profuse, and coarser than the rest of coat..
COAT AND FEATHER.—Long with thick undercoat, straight and soft, not curly nor wavy : feather on thighs and legs long and profuse .. .. } 15

TAIL.—Carried high on loins in a loose curl ; long profuse straight feather 5
SIZE.—Maximum weight, 10lb.
COLOUR.—All colours are allowable. In particolours the colour must be evenly broken.
ACTION.—Free, strong, and high 10
GENERAL APPEARANCE.—A sturdy compact little dog of dignified and fearless carriage and sound and healthy condition 10

Total 100

DISQUALIFICATIONS.—Blindness, if total ; docked tail ; cropped ears.
PENALISATIONS.—Nose any other colour than black, straight legs, lightness of bone, smallness of eye, paralysed tongue, mouth other than level.

CHAPTER XLIX.

The Miniature Trawler Toy Spaniel.

Lady Wentworth kindly furnished us with some interesting particulars and a photograph of the Trawler Toy Spaniel, which she alleges is a distinct breed, and to be found in Holland and Italy, and in which the lady interested herself. She does not tell us who formulated the description and points. They are as follows :—

Head small and light, with very pointed rather short nose, fine and tapery, with a very slight curve upwards of tip of nose. A curve downwards (as in the Borzoi) should be an absolute disqualification. The " stop " well marked and the skull rather raised but flat on the top, not dome-shaped. Muzzle just finished, not overshot. Long ears set high, and carried pricked forwards framing the face. Large dark eyes set wide apart, and showing the white when turned. They must be set perfectly straight, not obliquely, in the head. Whatever colour the dog may be, the nose and lips must be black. Neck arched. Back broad and short. Tail set on a level with the back and carried gaily, though not straight up in the air, or curled over the back like a Pomeranian. It should be docked to about 4in. or 5in., and well furnished with long feathering. General carriage very smart and gay. Legs reasonably short, and perfectly straight, bone light though strong. Build square, sturdy, and compact, but never heavy. The action should be smart and prancing; coat very curly, but not woolly. It should be rather silky in texture and very glossy. Liberal feathering, waistcoat, and breechings. Shape is all important; colour a secondary matter. Best colour a brilliant black, with white waistcoat. Next red, with white waistcoat, black-and-white, and red-and-white. Best size from 11in. to 13in. at shoulder. Any tendency to weediness should be carefully avoided, and the height at shoulders should just about equal the length from top of shoulders to root of tail. The size should not be judged by weight, but by height, as they should weigh heavily for their size. A dog about 13in. high should weigh about 15lb. Very small specimens—*i.e.*, under 9in. high —are only desirable if the type, soundness, compactness, and sturdiness are unimpaired. Feet close, firm, and hard. They and the lower part of the legs should not be too heavily feathered.

The expression of face should be very alert, and very sweet. The dogs should be very bold and courageous. Timidity is a great fault, and should tell against them in the ring. They are excellent ratters and rabbiters.

As to proportion of head, if the total length of head be about 6in. the ears should be set about 4in. apart. The whole head, seen from a bird's-eye point of view, should be a triangle, with the tip of nose as apex. General appearance should be that of an exquisitely pretty little sporting dog, very strong, and exceedingly smart and compact.

These dogs must not be confounded with Cockers, the type being absolutely different.

The origin of the breed is unknown, but it is *supposed*, without any certainty, to be descended from the original curly King Charles Spaniel (see Mr. Watson's " Book of the Dog ") and the old-fashioned curly Sussex Spaniel, now extinct. A quantity of these Spaniels exist in Holland and Italy.

Scale of Points.

	Value.
General appearance, including condition and smartness	12
Coat	10
Head and expression	15
Eyes	6
Curve and proportion of muzzle	6
Set-on of ears	5
Legs and feet	5
Colour	5
Action and soundness of limb	10
Size	5
Compactness, levelness of back, and set of tail	10
Boldness and alertness	8
Soundness of teeth	3
Total	100

Points that should Disqualify.

1. A flesh-coloured nose.
2. A downward curve of muzzle.
3. No "stop."
4. Hanging lips.
5. Crooked forelegs.
6. Light-coloured eyes.
7. Slanting eyes.
8. A very long body.
9. Bad action.

Points that are very Undesirable.

1. Timidity.
2. A straight coat.
3. Low-set ears.
4. Exaggeratedly short or long legs.
5. Exaggeration of any kind.
6. Sluggishness.
7. Drooping tail.
8. Showing teeth or tongue.
9. An "apple" head.

Measurements of a Perfect Specimen.

	Inches.
Breadth of skull at eyes from each outside corner of eyes across head	5
Length of skull	4
Length of nose	2¼
Circumference of skull	10½
Circumference of muzzle under eyes	6¾
Space between eyes	1⅜
Length of ears (leather)	4
Space between ears when not pricked	4¼
Height at shoulders	13
Length from top of shoulders to root of tail	13
Length of forelegs to elbow	7½
Breadth at shoulders	6
Breadth at quarters	6
Girth	19
Feathering on tail flag	6
Waistcoat feathering	4

CHAPTER L.

The Yorkshire Terrier.

Despite our many foreign Toy Dog importations, which have in great measure supplanted him in the affections of the fair, the Yorkshire Terrier is still the prettiest and most elegant morsel of Toy Dog flesh on the British show bench.

As his name implies, he is a production of the "county of broad acres," and his origin dates from the advent of dog shows—shortly after the middle of last century. He is the product of the Leeds and Halifax working-men fanciers, but was not designated Yorkshire Terrier at first. He came under the category at shows of "Scotch Terrier," "Rough or Broken-haired Terrier," "Broken-haired Scotch and Yorkshire Terrier," and "Toy Terrier, Rough." At the Leeds Show in 1861 there was a class for "Scotch Terriers," the entries in which were all Yorkshires of a crude pattern, while at the Birmingham Show of the year previous, in the same class, all the winners were Skye Terriers. It was not until 1886 that the Kennel Club classed the then more perfected breed as Yorkshire Terriers.

YORKSHIRE TERRIER.

Although his origin is comparatively modern, it is a most singular fact that no precise data exist as to the dog's exact component parts. In the very earliest days of dog shows, Skye Terriers, Dandie Dinmonts, and almost every conceivable specimen of long broken-haired Terriers came under the category of "Scotch Terrier." In particular, a short-backed, broken-haired, rather blue-and-tan dog, and it is doubtless from this dog, crossed with the Maltese, that the Yorkshire Terrier has been evolved, and which may be taken to represent a Yorkshire fancier's conception of what a Toy house-dog should be like. The earlier specimens, or many of them, were somewhat pale or silvery in colour, taking more after the Maltese, and there can be little doubt that the old broken-haired black-and-tan English Terrier, which would be available and on the spot, has been employed to enrich the tan.

The earlier exhibition specimens were much larger than the best dogs of to-day, weighing from 7lb. to 10lb. probably. Having firmly established the breed, which would faithfully reproduce facsimiles of itself by intercrossing, breeders next laid themselves out to bantamise it, which they have succeeded in doing with the greatest success, the weights of our best show specimens now ranging from about 2¼lb. to 5¼lb., sound and perfect in symmetry and shape, and with good Terrier heads and enormous coats of great quality. In my opinion the evolution of the Yorkshire Terrier reflects more lustre on the British breeder than does that of any other breed of dog. He is, with the exception of coat—which, of course, can be regulated according to taste—a dog free from abnormalities and full of Terrier characteristics and intelligence, which he, of course, inherits from his ancestors on all sides. Beautiful to look at, active as a kitten, vivacious as the most " perky Pom.," the perfect Yorkshire Terrier is the acme of Toy Dog virtue and perfection, looked at from every standpoint.

The length, colour, and quantity of coat are nowadays his leading features, and as the greatest care and experience are required, first, in the production of such a coat and afterwards in its preservation, general fanciers, and more especially ladies, who are wont to become rapturous in their admiration of these charming lilliputian luminaries, find difficulty in keeping pace with the dogged working-man fancier, who lives with, and almost for, his dog, which receives the attentions of himself and his wife and family in their little cottage almost hourly.

The incident of some of our most beautiful specimens having been sold, at the zenith of their fame on the show bench, for large prices to inexperienced admirers, in whose hands they have "fallen off" and degenerated into mediocrity, has, no doubt, been one of the causes of the lack of progressive popularity in connection with the breed, and the admission to the heart and affections of the British fancying public of alien Toy Dogs which, however, cannot compare with the beauty and charm of the native Yorkshire Terrier.

The chief points to aim at in breeding and to look for in buying a good mature Yorkshire Terrier are diminutiveness, shortness and straightness of back, length, straightness, and quality of coat, soundness of colour. That is to say, the body coat should be a sound blue, and the fall, which should be long, should be of a rich golden tan, deepening as the hair reaches the head, which, with the ears and legs, should be deeper in colour—almost mahogany. The head should be Terrier-like—that is to say, the skull somewhat lean, and the muzzle free from snipiness—eyes small, and mouth quite level, although the exact chiselling of the head and head points generally are secondary to the others detailed.

All Yorkshire Terrier puppies are black when they are born. The coat begins to "break" in puppies—that is to say, a blue shade begins to develop at the roots of the coat at from three to six months. The development of the black puppy or chrysalis into the beautiful, fully-matured Yorkshire Terrier butterfly is a process which varies in the period it occupies—from 12 to 18 months—but usually the coat has, or ought to have, entirely "cleared" by the time the dog reaches the age of 18 months at latest. If it has not cleared by this, its due transition in colour is hopeless.

A roomy pedigree brood bitch of 5lb. to 7lb. weight, of very dark tan, is the best to breed from, and mated to a quality little dog with plenty of coat and fall, and free from any waviness. Waviness and mixed colouring on back are two of the most troublesome defects Yorkshire Terrier breeders have to contend with, and which handicap a dog heavily in the show ring.

Yorkshire Terriers must be kept and bred from in the house. One of the secrets of the success of Yorkshire Terrier breeders of the working-man section, who are by far the most numerous, is the fact that the dogs are kept in the kitchen, where the housewife or children can give them constantly those little attentions which spell success. They usually convert the kitchen dresser into a kennel by taking out the drawers and making the interior into three distinct little houses, with little brass-railed gates. They are given a woollen cloth to lie on, which is kept quite clean by washing and changing as required. The feet of the dogs, as soon as they leave the dam almost, are " stockinged " to prevent them scratching the hair off any part of them, and the regular attention to their " toilette " now begins. They are combed and brushed almost daily, and the skin kept in a soft and perfectly healthy condition. If there is the slightest suspicion of mange or eczema, it is promptly attended to by an application of some well-tried specific, which is always kept in the house. As the coat grows it is kept constantly in oil, the finest olive oil, with the least drop of paraffin in it, being generally used, but there are other preparations, such as cocoa-nut oil, and a very excellent pomade is recommended in Jessop's work on this breed, which is sold by " Our Dogs " Publishing Co., Ltd. These applications not only keep the hair from getting matted, but act as a good hair stimulant. The dogs should be washed periodically with either a good dog soap or soft soap sparingly used.

Valuable Yorkshire Terriers are not given their absolute liberty. They are, or should be, frequently exercised during the day, out in the open when fine and in the house when wet, but it should always be done under the supervision of one of the household, as, being such diminutive, active little creatures, accidents may easily happen, or the dog pick up something it should not have, and the flower of the breeder's efforts become extinguished almost as quickly as the light of a candle.

In this way Yorkshire Terriers do lead a life of imprisonment, but not solitary confinement. They see all that is going on in the house, are given frequent runs (where they are well cared for), and their life made happy in many ways, by the attentions of the family, in a dietary being rigidly observed, which is conducive to good health, and accidents and death avoided, which would, and do more or less, befall all Toy Dogs that are given their full and unrestricted liberty. Thus, although at times a cry has been raised by the humane against the system of rearing Yorkshire Terriers, where they are well cared for, as in the case of all good specimens which are too valuable to be neglected, the method and treatment together are a " blessing in disguise."

The chief points to look for in the selection of Yorkshire Terrier puppies at from two to four months old are : Diminutiveness, shortness of back, lightness of bone, and giving indications of a long straight class of coat, and dark tan on head and legs.

Amongst the very earliest and most famous exhibition specimens, which, however, were much behind present-day specimens in point of diminutiveness and general merit, may be mentioned :—

Mrs. M. A. Foster's immortal Huddersfield Ben, bred by W. Eastwood, of Huddersfield ; was born in 1865, and died in 1871. He is the progenitor of all our best Yorkshire Terriers, and will ever remain the greatest pillar of the breed ; Mr. Midgley Marsden's Bright, Mr. Abe Boulton's Bright II., Mr. W. J. Lucas' Empress, Mr. J. Henshall's Punch, Mr. Crossley's Wasp, etc.

The following are the description and standard of points as laid down by the Yorkshire Terrier Club :—

GENERAL APPEARANCE.—Should be that of a long-coated Toy Terrier, the coat hanging quite straight and evenly down each side, a parting extending from the nose to the end of the tail.

The animal should be very compact and neat, the carriage being very upright, and having an important air. The general outline should convey the existence of a vigorous and well-proportioned body.

HEAD.—Should be rather small and flat, not too prominent or round in the skull, nor too long in the muzzle, with a perfectly black nose. The fall on the head to be long, of a rich golden tan, deeper in colour at the sides of the head about the ear roots, and on the muzzle, where it should be very long. The hair on the chest a rich bright tan. On no account must the tan on the head extend on to the neck, nor must there be any sooty or dark hair intermingled with any of the tan.

EYES.—Medium, dark, and sparkling, having a sharp intelligent expression, and placed so as to look directly forward. They should not be prominent, and the edge of the eyelids should be of a dark colour.

EARS.—Small V-shaped, and carried semi-erect, or erect, and not far apart, covered with short hair, colour to be of a very deep rich tan.

MOUTH.—Perfectly even, with teeth as sound as possible. An animal having lost any teeth through accident not a fault, providing the jaws are even.

BODY.—Very compact, and a good loin. Level on the top of the back.

COAT.—The hair on body moderately long and perfectly straight (not wavy), glossy like silk, and of a fine silky texture. Colour, a dark steel blue (not silver blue) extending from the occiput (or back of skull) to the root of tail, and on no account mingled with fawn, bronze, or dark hairs.

LEGS.—Quite straight, well covered with hair of a rich golden tan, a few shades lighter at the ends than at the roots, not extending higher on the forelegs than the elbow, nor on the hind legs than the stifle.

FEET.—As round as possible, and the toe-nails black.

TAIL.—Cut to medium length; with plenty of hair, darker blue in colour than the rest of the body, especially at the end of the tail, and carried a little higher than the level of the back.

TAN.—All tan hair should be darker at the roots than in the middle, shading to a still lighter tan at the tips.

VALUE OF POINTS.

Formation and Terrier appearance	15
Colour of hair on body	15
Richness of tan on head and legs	15
Quality and texture of coat	10
Quantity and length of coat	10
Head	10
Mouth	5
Legs and feet	5
Ears	5
Eyes	5
Tail (carriage of)	5
Total	100

CHAPTER LI.

The Clydesdale Terrier

Is, without doubt, a misfit Skye Terrier, with which he has a common origin. In the early exhibition days he was exhibited as a Skye Terrier—that is to say, the more silky-haired specimens of this variety—but he did not curry favour with the general body of Skye Terrier enthusiasts, who simply regarded the dog as a bad-coated Skye, and more fit for the drawing-room than the Cairns, just as Fox-terrier experts would regard a soft-coated Wire-haired specimen as a bad Fox-terrier. The dog, however, had his devotees, and the upshot of the strife which at one time raged over his head culminated in a dissolution of partnership and the division of the variety, the hard-coated, long and low variety by the weight of public opinion being accorded the title of Skye Terrier, to which their character, working fitness, and tradition gave them an irresistible claim, whilst the leggier and more silky-coated specimens, under the banner of the Clydesdale and Paisley fanciers, parted company, and gradually assumed the former appellation. This was somewhere in the 'eighties. Since then the Clydesdale fanciers have developed the difference in the two dogs—namely, have cultivated by

CLYDESDALE TERRIER.

selection the silkiness and lighter colour of the coat, which they have made a *sine qua non* of the variety. In all other essentials the character and conformation of the two varieties are practically one and the same. The coat should be long, straight, and silky in texture, colour and quality being very similar to that of the very best Yorkshire Terriers, of which the Clydesdale, or, as it was then called, the Scottish Terrier, has been largely used in its manufacture.

The formation of a Club for the Clydesdale Terrier naturally gave the variety an impetus in Scotland, but, singular to say, it has never " caught on " in England, where very few specimens indeed are to be found. Why, it is difficult to imagine, unless it is that the Anglo-Saxon does not look for or appreciate anything effeminate coming from the land of the hardy Celts, and, whatever his admirers may think to the contrary, the Clydesdale Terrier is essentially a lady's dog, a companion and a pet. Singular to say, however, even ladies have not fastened on to the breed, for very few kennels of Clydesdales are owned by the fair sex, whilst the majority of the exhibition kennels of Skye Terriers are in the hands of women enthusiasts.

The chief points to look for in the selection of Clydesdale Terrier puppies are almost identical with those in Skye Terriers.

The following are the standard description and code of points formulated by the Skye and Clydesdale Terrier Club, which was purely a Scottish combination, from which it will be seen that colour and coat absorb only one-half of the complement of 100 points:—

GENERAL APPEARANCE.—A long, low, level dog with heavily fringed, erect ears, and a long coat like the finest silk or spun glass, which hangs quite straight and evenly down each side, a parting extending from the nose to the root of the tail.

HEAD.—Fairly long, skull flat, and very narrow between the ears, gradually widening towards the eyes and tapering very slightly to the nose, which must be black. The jaws strong and the teeth level.

EYES.—Medium in size, dark in colour, not prominent, but having a sharp, Terrier-like expression. Eyelids black.

EARS.—Small, set very high on the top of the head, carried perfectly erect, and covered with long, silky hair, hanging in a heavy fringe down the sides of the head.

BODY.—Long, deep in chest, well ribbed up, the back being perfectly level.

TAIL.—Perfectly straight, carried almost level with the back, and heavily feathered.

LEGS.—As short and straight as possible, well set under the body, and entirely covered with silky hair. Feet round and cat-like.

COAT.—As long and straight as possible, free from all trace of curl or waviness; very glossy and silky in texture, with an entire absence of undercoat.

COLOUR.—A level, bright steel-blue, extending from the back of the head to the root of the tail, and on no account intermingled with any fawn, light, or dark hairs. The head, legs, and feet should be a clear, bright, golden tan, free from grey, sooty, or dark hairs. The tail should be very dark blue or black.

SCALE OF POINTS.

	Value.
Texture of coat	25
Colour	25
Head	10
Ears	10
Tail	10
Body	10
Legs and feet	10
Total	100

CHAPTER LII.

The Maltese.

The Maltese, as its name implies, is undoubtedly a native of the island of Malta, the well-known British possession in the Mediterranean. Dr. Johannes Caius, a very ancient writer, describes them as a Toy Spaniel. He says : " They are called Meliti, of the Island of Malta." Strabo, one of the earliest writers, ascribes their origin not to Malta, but to a town in Sicily called Melita, and states that they were the particular favourites of women.

The Maltese is a very ancient breed, and has been kept in purity for centuries. In Malta, Greece, and Italy the breed abounds, many of the specimens being coloured. Fawn-coloured specimens, which are shaved like a Poodle, and described as the " Lion " dogs of Malta, are often exhibited at Continental shows and occasionally in England. We in England, however, nowadays really recognise only the pure-white specimens. In character the breed partakes of both the Terrier and the King Charles Spaniel, and that is probably why some writers ally them to the one and some to the other. The Kennel Club recognised neither, but simply placed the breed on its list as " Maltese," whilst by their size they also come under the category of a " Toy " Dog.

MALTESE.

Maltese have been exhibited in England at the very earliest exhibitions, and whilst most other breeds have undergone a metamorphosis at the hands of the enterprising fancier, the Maltese has remained the same, being to-day, in type, size, coat, and general characteristics, exactly what it was when first exhibited on the English show bench.

The breed is a very handsome one, and one that breeds to type without any difficulty. Of course, coloured spots and pink noses keep cropping up, but all such marked puppies ought to be drowned. The chief features to be aimed at are : Diminutiveness, purity, and straightness and quantity of coat. Black noses and black-rimmed eyelashes are essential. The head should resemble that of a Skye Terrier in miniature, the ears should drop at the side of the head and be covered with a profusion of hair, extending all over the head (forming a "fall") and body. Indeed, the dog should be literally buried in pure-white spotless hair of great quality. Legginess is another fault ; the dog should be on short legs, quite straight in front, and the body should be moderately short. Many Maltese are somewhat long in body, which is not desirable. The tail should curl on the back, and be covered with long hair. The coat of the Maltese, like that of the Yorkshire Terrier, is parted down the centre of the back, extending to the forehead and fall. The Maltese requires, like all long-haired dogs, considerable attention to its toilette—washing and grooming frequently, and particularly the day before going to a show. They should be dried quickly, being combed the while.

In selecting Maltese puppies at from two to four months old, those are likely to make the best dogs which are the smallest (not weaklings), possess most coat, shortest bodies, and shortest legs.

The following are the standard description and points of the Maltese Club :—

1. HEAD.—Should not be too narrow, but should be of a Terrier shape, not too long, but not apple-headed.

2. EARS.—Should be long and well feathered, and hang close to the side of the head, the hair to be mingled with the coat at the shoulders.

3. EYES.—Should be a dark brown, with black eyerims and not too far apart.

4. NOSE.—Should be pure black.

5. LEGS AND FEET.—Legs should be short and straight, feet round, and the pads of the feet should be black.

6. BODY AND SHAPE.—Should be short and cobby, low to the ground, and the back should be straight from the top of the shoulders to the tail.

7. TAIL.—Should be well arched over the back and well feathered.

8. COAT, LENGTH AND TEXTURE.—Should be a good length, the longer the better, of a silky texture, not in any way woolly, and should be straight.

9. COLOUR.—Any self-colour is admitted, but it is desirable that they should be pure white ; slight lemon marks should not disqualify.

10. CONDITION AND APPEARANCE.—Should be of a sharp Terrier appearance, with a lively action, the coat should not be stained, but should be well groomed.

11. SIZE.—The most approved weights should be from 4lb. to 9lb., the smaller the better, but it is desirable that they should not exceed 10lb.

VALUE OF THE POINTS OF THE MALTESE.

Head	5
Ears	5
Eyes	5
Nose	5
Legs and feet	5
Body and shape	10
Tail	10
Coat (texture and length)	20
Colour	15
Condition and appearance	10
Size	10
Total	100

CHAPTER LIII.

The Italian Greyhound.

The Italian Greyhound is given to us by Italy, where it is the domestic favourite of Royalty and the nobility, and has been for centuries. The pure Italian Greyhound is the *beau idéal* of canine delicacy and refinement, and as an adjunct to "my lady's chamber," or boudoir, has no superior. As the Whippet is a Greyhound in miniature, so the Italian Greyhound is a Whippet in miniature, with an added elegance of figure and more aristocratic bearing and mien.

The breed has been brought to great perfection in England, many of the original importations being large and coarse by comparison. The smaller the specimen the more valuable, providing it is not Terrier-like in its anatomy,

ITALIAN GREYHOUND.

but has the goat neck, the narrow shoulders, deep chest, flat sides, an extremely arched loin, with the slightest of limbs. These are the chief features of the breed, coupled with a high-stepping gait, in the fashion of a circus horse stepping over the serried circle of poles in the arena of the ring.

With regard to size, the Italian Greyhound Club give two weights, over and under 8lb., but the smaller are, of course, preferable and most valuable, providing they possess the necessary characteristics—dogs of from 5lb. to 7lb. The most prized colour is golden fawn, but the various shades of fawn are quite admissible, and even blue, brindle, and black-and-white, which, however, are not favoured.

The chief points to select in puppies at from two to four months old are diminutiveness, slightness, and apparent fragility, with a distinct arch of loin.

The following are the points and standard description of the Italian Greyhound Club:—

Points of the Italian Greyhound.

GENERAL APPEARANCE.—A miniature English Greyhound, more slender in all proportions, and of ideal elegance and grace in shape, symmetry, and action.

	Value of Points.
HEAD.	
SKULL.—Long, flat, and narrow	6
MUZZLE.—Very fine. Nose dark in colour. Teeth level	8
EARS.—Rose-shaped, placed well back, soft and delicate	8
EYES.—Rather large, bright, and full of expression..	5
BODY.	**27**
NECK.—Long and gracefully arched..	8
SHOULDERS.—Long and sloping	5
CHEST.—Deep and narrow	5
BACK.—Curved, drooping at hindquarters	8
LEGS AND FEET.	**26**
FORELEGS.—Straight, well set under the shoulder; fine pasterns, small and delicate bones	8
HIND LEGS.—Hocks well let down. Thighs muscular.	8
FEET.—The long "hare's foot"	8
TAIL, COAT, AND COLOUR.	**24**
TAIL.—Rather long, fine, with low carriage..	8
COAT.—Skin fine and supple. Hair thin and glossy like satin	4
COLOUR.—Preferably self-coloured. The colour most prized is golden fawn, but all shades of fawn—red, mouse, blue, cream, and silver—are recognised; and blacks, brindles, and pied are considered less desirable. Black-and-tan Terrier markings not allowed	3
ACTION.—High stepping and free	8
	23

WEIGHT.—Two classes. One of 8lb. and under, and one over 8lb. A good small dog is preferable to an equally good large one, but a good large dog is preferable to a poor small one.

Total value of points	100

CHAPTER LIV.

The Chow Chow.

The Chow Chow, as his name indicates, is a " Heathen Chinee " pure and **simple**. He is sometimes described as the " edible dog of China," since the dog has long been and still is used as an article of food by the poorer classes of the Celestial Empire, the Chow Chow being bred specially for human consumption in various parts of China, where they are killed when quite young puppies of from 5 to 10 months old.

There are no records showing the origin of the Chow Chow, but there can be little doubt that he is closely allied to the arctic dog, with whom he has a great deal in common, in head, his prick ears, fur-like coat, and curled tail. This is to some extent proved by the fact that in Northern China the breed abounds, where it is not only used for hunting, but in winter time is employed to draw sledges across the snow, like the Esquimaux.

CHOW CHOW (Rough-coated).

Odd specimens of the Chow Chow have been imported into England from time to time during the last century, but not until from 30 to 40 years ago has the breed become at all popular, when the public seem to have " gone in " for it and made it one of the fashionable breeds of the day. A club was formed, a standard description formulated from the best and most authentic material at hand, and a list of qualified judges appointed, which gave the breed a great fillip, and to-day the Chow Chow classes are amongst the best filled at our leading shows, and the breed one of the most interesting sections at the shows.

The Chow Chow is a breed that, unlike many, breeds very true to type, although, of course, every puppy is not a champion. Looking over the Chow

Chow section at the Kennel Club or other important show, greater uniformity of type will be noticed than in any other breed.

There are two varieties, the rough-coated and the smooth. The only difference is in coat, the coat of the roughs being perhaps about two inches long on the back, but very dense and more like fur than hair. The coat of the smooths is much like that of the smooth Sheepdog.

The great features of the breed may be said to be concentrated in the head and coat. The head should be short, the muzzle thick and blunt, the eyes small and sunken, temples prominent, and with the loose skin overhanging and wrinkles on the forehead forming a scowl quite distinct from the expression of any other breed of dog, the nearest approach being that of the Pekingese. The ears should be very small, prick, and pointed. Shortness of body is a great desideratum in the breed, and straight forelegs and cat-like feet are equally desirable, and a black roof of the mouth and black tongue, which are said to indicate purity of race, indispensable points in the breed. The

CHOW CHOW (Smooth-coated).

tail should curl on the back, and the dog when moving present the appearance of a compact, strong, sturdy, yet agile animal of a sullen disposition, which most but not all Chow Chows are. In disposition they are, speaking generally, what may be termed an unsocial dog, shrinking from the society of their own species, or even humans, except their own master or mistress, to whom they become much devoted. They are a very game dog, and usually can hold their own in combat with any dog their own size. Another quality they have is their wonderful topographical knowledge. Many stories are told of Chow Chows who have accidentally lost their owners in a crowd, threading their way through the labyrinth of the throng until they have found them, and of their wonderful homing instinct, dogs having been known to find their way home a score or more miles through country they had never before traversed.

There are four or five colours of Chow Chows, the reds being most in favour, blacks next, then red with white shadings, fawn, white, and blue.

The Toy Dog craze has not yet reached the Chow Chow, the best size for which is a dog of from 40lb. to 50lb. The standard description issued by the Chow Chow Club is as follows :—

HEAD.—Skull flat and broad, with little stop, well filled out under the eyes.

MUZZLE.—Moderate in length and broad from the eyes to the point (not pointed at the end like a fox's).

NOSE.—Black, large, and wide. (In cream or light coloured specimens a pink nose is allowable.)

TONGUE.—Black.

EYES.—Dark and small. (In a blue dog light colour is permissible.)

EARS.—Small, pointed, and carried stiffly erect. They should be placed well forward over the eyes, which gives the dog the peculiar characteristic expression of the breed—viz., a sort of scowl.

TEETH.—Strong and level.

NECK.—Strong, full, set well on the shoulders, and slightly arched.

SHOULDERS.—Muscular and sloping.

CHEST.—Broad and deep.

BACK.—Short, straight, and strong.

LOINS.—Powerful.

TAIL.—Curled, well carried over back.

FORELEGS.—Perfectly straight, of moderate length, and with great bone.

HINDLEGS.—Same as forelegs, muscular, and hocks should be perfectly straight.

FEET.—Small, round, and cat-like, standing well on the toes.

COAT.—Abundant, dense, straight, and rather coarse in texture, with a soft woolly undercoat.

COLOUR.—Whole-coloured black, red, yellow, blue, white, not in patches (the under part of tail and of thighs frequently of a lighter colour).

GENERAL APPEARANCE.—A lively, compact, short-coupled dog, well knit in frame, with tail well curled over the back.

DISQUALIFYING POINTS.—Drop ears, red tongue, tail not curled over back, white spots on coat, and red nose, except in yellow or white specimens.

N.B.—Smooth Chows are governed by the same scale of points, except that the coat is smooth.

The points to avoid are :—Other than black tongues, long faces, drop ears, open coats, bad fronts, long backs, and very straight stifles, which latter is a rather common defect in the breed.

The chief points to look for in the selection of puppies of from two to four months old are short faces, short backs, dense coats, great bone, short feet, and well-twisted tails.

CHAPTER LV.

The Samoyed.

The Samoyed, with the Esquimau, is a breed indigenous to the most northern latitudes, extending to the Arctic regions. He is the guard, draught animal, huntsman, general assistant, and companion—in fact, the "all"— of the inhabitants of these snowy regions. He assists them in the fishing industry, in their hunting expeditions, and takes the place of the horse as a beast of burden, being at home in all these avocations; whilst as a guard to the people against marauding animals at night, he is indispensable.

SAMOYED.

The introduction of the Samoyed into England is comparatively recent and the formation of a Club specially to look after his interests more recent still. He is now recognised by the Kennel Club as a distinct breed, and is becoming very popular as a show dog. There are two Samoyed Clubs—the Samoyed Association and the Samoyed Siberian Club. The name used to be spelled Samoyede, but it was recently decided to drop the final "e" at the end of the name of the breed.

Like all dogs of these northern latitudes, he is of the foxy-headed, prick-eared, curled-tail, sturdy-built pattern, with a close, short, fur-like weather-resisting coat, and for the most part white in colour, although white-and-fawn and white-and-black are admissible.

The following are the standard description and points of the Samoyed Association :—

GENERAL APPEARANCE.—The Samoyed being essentially a working dog, should be strong and active and graceful, and as his work lies in cold climates his coat should be heavy and weather-resisting. He should not be long in back, as a weak back would make him practically useless for his legitimate work; but at the same time a cobby body, such as the Chow's, would also place him at a great disadvantage as a draught dog. Breeders should aim for the happy medium—viz., a body not long, but muscular, allowing liberty, with a deep chest and well-sprung ribs, and exceptionally strong loin. A full-grown dog should stand about 21in. at shoulder. On account of the depth of chest required, the legs should be moderately long; a very short-legged dog is to be deprecated. Hindquarters should be particularly well developed, stifles well bent, and any suggestion of unsound stifles or cow-hocks severely penalised.

COAT.—The body should be well covered with a thick, close, soft and short undercoat, with harsh hair growing through it, forming the outer coat, which should stand straight away from the body and be quite free from curl.

HEAD.—Powerful and wedge-shaped, with a broad flat skull, muzzle of medium length, a tapering foreface, not too sharply defined, ears not too long and slightly rounded at tips, set well apart, and well covered inside with hair; eyes dark, set well apart and deep, with alert intelligent expression; lips black; hair short and smooth before the ears; nose and eyerims black for preference, but may be brown or flesh-coloured; strong jaws, with level teeth.

BACK.—Medium in length, broad, and very muscular.

CHEST AND RIBS.—Chest broad and deep; ribs well sprung, giving plenty of heart and lung room.

HINDQUARTERS.—Very muscular, stifles well let down, cow hocks or straight stifles very objectionable.

LEGS.—Straight and muscular; good bone.

FEET.—Long, flattish, and slightly spread out; soles well padded with hair.

TAIL.—Long and profuse, carried over back when alert, sometime dropped down when at rest.

SIZE AND WEIGHT.—Dogs, 20 to 22in. at shoulder, 45 to 55lb.; bitches, 18 to 20in., 36 to 45lb.

COLOUR.—Pure white, white-and-biscuit, cream.

SCALE OF POINTS.

General appearance	20
Coat	15
Head	10
Size	10
Chest and ribs	10
Hindquarters	10
Back	10
Feet	5
Legs	5
Tail	5
Total	100

The chief points to look for in the selection of a puppy are: Short, compact body, very dense coat, foxy head, and very small ears, with good bone.

CHAPTER LVI.

The Pomeranian.

The Pomeranian, as his name implies, is presumed, and rightly, to originate from Pomerania, a northern province of Germany. Less than fifty years ago the few specimens one saw in England were of the very large white variety, dogs weighing from 18lb. to 24lb. It is a fact that dogs of his description, and even larger, mostly white, with some few coloured specimens, more particularly the wolf-sable, called in Germany wolf-spitz, wolf-sable dog, ranging from 20lb. to 40lb., abound in Pomerania and the whole of Northern Germany, where they may be seen in the streets everywhere. He is the common house-dog, carrier's dog, and, indeed, general canine factotum. The Wolf-spitz is the dog of Spitzbergen, in the Arctic

POMERANIAN.

regions, and the white Pomeranian is doubtless closely allied to the Samoyed and Esquimau. They all have a great deal in common—the foxy head, prick ears, curled tail, and dense fur-like coat, which are the characteristics of all the dogs of the extreme northern latitudes.

With such material at hand it was quite an easy matter for the Germans to cultivate the breed, and bantamise it somewhat for the purpose of producing a smaller lady's pet. This they have done, and so popular has the breed become, owing to its vivacity, quick intelligence, and fidelity, that a demand for it sprang up in various European countries. Holland seems to have taken to the Wolf-spitz, which they call Keeshond; the breed has travelled to France and to Italy, where he is known as the Lulu and Volpino; and to England, where it has been the most largely cultivated, and brought to the greatest perfection under the nomenclature of its native country, Pomerania; and through England to the United States, where it has "caught on" immensely, and become *the* Toy dog of that great country.

The breed was first classified by the Kennel Club in 1871, but then only the big white dogs were exhibited. A Pomeranian of any other colour at that time was a *rara avis*, and then it would be a black of probably 10lb. or 12lb. weight at the least. From this time up to the formation of the Pomeranian Club in 1891, in which I took part and was the first hon. secretary, the progress of the breed in England was slow. The founding of the Pomeranian Club, however, gave the breed a great impetus, and fanciers now journeyed to Germany to procure the best specimens of the breed that could be obtained, and soon a number of kennels were firmly established. The perky Pomeranian seemed now to come into popularity at one bound, the craze, of course, being for the smaller specimens, and for coloured Poms. The first coloured Poms. to be exhibited were Mrs. Lynn's Prince of Orange and Ch. Ruffle, and it is from these and Mrs. Thomas's famous dogs, Black Boy and King Pippin, that most of our charming coloured Toy Dogs of to-day can be traced. Miss Hamilton is the pioneer of the white variety, but there were white Poms. exhibited even before this lady's time, notably Mr. Fawdry's Charley, Mr. Boddington's Charlie, Mr. Megson's Shirley, Mr. Swinburne's Scoff, and others. The earliest blacks exhibited were Mr. Goas's Black Peter, and one or two others.

It is some evidence of the genius of the British fancier that during a period of about 25 years he, from a few specimens of blacks, whites, one or two sables, and an orange, none less in weight than 7lb. or 8lb., evolved a race of almost perfect Toy Pomeranians, with all the marked features of the breed—foxy heads, small ears, short backs, enormous coats and plumes, and with all the vivacity, beauty, and activity of the breed.— weighing as little as 1½lb. full grown, and averaging probably 4lb. weight, in the following sound colours :—

Black, blue, beaver, white, sable (various shades), black-and-tan, chocolate, racoon (various shades), black-and-white, brown (several shades), orange, tricolour, etc.

And from a collection of some 25 entries of Pomeranians in 1892, which was the most that could be got together in England, no fewer than 500 entries were obtained at the Northern Pomeranian Club's Show at Belle Vue Gardens, Manchester, in 1907, which comprised all the colours mentioned, and were distributed over upwards of 40 classes, divided by colour, sex, and weight. The foregoing, to some, would almost appear incredible, but it shows the great strides the breed has made in England, leaving Germany, its native country, far and away behind.

The breed is one which appeals to ladies more particularly, and as a pet and lady's companion the Pomeranian doubtless has no superior. His diminutiveness, his charm of manner, his enormous coat and rich colourings, combined, will always keep him in the forefront as a favourite Toy Dog and popular companion for the fair sex generally, and even for the sterner sex.

The aim of all breeders is to produce Toy Pomeranians—that is, dogs weighing from 2½lb. (although there are many winners on the bench less than that) to 5lb., perfect in points, and of various recognised colours. The favourite colours are the various shades of sables and dark chocolates, but orange is rapidly coming into favour, and Toy whites are in demand. In the first instance, breeders wisely confined their efforts to bantamising the Pomeranian, leaving, in most cases, the colour question out of their calculation. But in breeding for diminutiveness and selecting sires, almost irrespective of colour, beautiful coloured puppies made their appearance in litters. For instance, two blacks bred together produced some brown puppies. This is, of course, a fixed feature of nature, for do not two black horses produce a chestnut, and two black Field Spaniels a liver? In turn, a chocolate or brown bitch mated to a black dog produced shaded sables. This was how the immortal king of the sables, Ch. Sable Mite, came, quite haphazard : he electrified the fancy, and may be said to have initiated the rage for shaded sables, as he was such a lovely specimen, weighing 4½lb., with an enormous coat, short body, grand plume, and neat head and ears. He was by The Little Nipper, a black dog, who had a faculty for siring sables and chocolates. Ch. The Sable Mite must have won 250 first prizes and specials, and his owner, Mrs. Wetwan (Mrs. Vale Nicolas then), I believe, refused as many sovereigns for her favourite. It is said that she once refused £500 for Ch. Sable Mite and Ch. Shelton Sable Atom (also by The Little Nipper out of a black bitch), the most perfectly matched brace of shaded sables that ever lived.

Although breeding coloured Pomeranians was, in the first instance, more haphazard than anything, the incident of lovely coloured Pomeranians making their unexpected appearance in litters has encouraged breeders to turn their attention to colour breeding, with the result that, although the Mendelian principle has not yet been applied, by studying the crossing of certain colours, and watching results, a basis has been discovered by which some colours can be produced at will. For instance, it has been discovered that an orange sire and a black or chocolate bitch will produce a preponderance of sound chocolate puppies, without light shadings, whilst a chocolate sire and orange or sable bitch will produce pure orange puppies. Orange sable and blue parents seldom produce blue puppies unless there is more blue behind, but wolf sable and blue parents will produce orange puppies. Blues originally came from blacks, the pioneer of this colour being Miss Ives, whose beautiful Sable dog, Ch. Dragon Fly, has earned immortal fame, not only as one of the greatest show dogs of his day, but as the greatest sire.

Many coloured puppies undergo a process of metamorphosis after birth, blues often developing into beautiful shaded sables, and blacks, or what appear to be black puppies, developing into blues, etc.

The Pomeranian, by reason of his great popularity, is one of the most profitable breeds that can be kept and cultivated. The chief points to breed for in Pomeranians are diminutiveness, lightness of bone, shortness of body, foxy head, flat skull, and small ears, with heavy coat and a good twist of tail. Big ears, long backs, heavy bone, and flat coats should be scrupulously avoided. The best stamp of brood bitch is a well-bred bitch of 6lb. or 7lb. mated to a quality dog of 3½lb. to 4½lb. weight, as perfect as can be procured. Even with a good dog, grooming and attention have a great deal to do with success on the show bench. Poms. should have their coats combed out and brushed " the wrong way of the wool "—that is, from back to front—every day, so that it is impossible for it to become in the least matted. A little hair stimulant such as is recommended in the case of the Yorkshire Terrier should be applied once or twice a week, as it encourages the growth of the coat. Pomeranians should never be thrashed : this " cows " them and renders them unfit for the show ring, where they should show fearlessness, life, and buoyancy, to be successful.

The chief points to look for in the selection of Pomeranian puppies at from two to four months old and after are diminutiveness, short backs, light bone, small ears, and full dense coat.

The following are the standard description and points of the breed as adopted by the Pomeranian Club, the North of England Pomeranian Club, and the Midland Counties Pomeranian Club :—

    APPEARANCE.—The Pomeranian in build and appearance should be a compact, short-coupled dog, well knit in frame. He should exhibit great intelligence in his expression, activity and buoyancy in his deportment 10

    HEAD AND NOSE.—The head and nose should be foxy in outline, or wedge-shaped ; the skull being slightly flat, large in proportion to the muzzle, which should finish rather fine and be free from lippiness .. .. ..
        The teeth should be level, and should on no account be undershot. The hair on the head and face should be smooth and short-coated. The nose should be black in white, orange, and shaded-sable dogs ; but in other colours may be " self-coloured," but never parti-coloured or white 10

EARS.—The ears should be small, not set too far apart nor too low down, but carried perfectly erect like those of a fox 5

EYES.—The eyes should be medium in size, not full nor set too wide apart, bright and dark in colour, and showing great intelligence .. ..
In white, orange, shaded-sable, and cream dogs, the rims round the eyes should be black 5

NECK AND BODY.—The neck should be rather short and well set in.
The back must be short and the body compact, being well ribbed up and the barrel well rounded.
The chest must be fairly deep and not too wide, but in proportion to the size of the dog 15

LEGS.—The forelegs must be well feathered and perfectly straight, of medium length, and not such as would be termed "leggy" or "low on leg," but in length and strength in due proportion to a well-balanced frame.
The shoulders should be clean and well laid back. The hind legs and thighs must be well feathered down to the hocks, and must be neither "cow-hocked" nor wide behind. They must be fine in bone and free in action. The feet should be small and compact in shape 10

TAIL.—The tail is one of the characteristics of the breed, and should be turned over the back and carried flat and straight, being profusely covered with long, harsh, spreading hair 5

COAT.—There should be two coats, an undercoat and an overcoat; the one, a soft, fluffy undercoat, the other, a long perfectly straight coat, harsh in texture and covering the whole of the body, being very abundant round the neck and forepart of the shoulders and chest, where it shall form a frill of profuse, standing-off straight hair, extending over the shoulders. The hindquarters should be clad with long hair or feathering, from the top of the rump to the hocks 25

COLOUR.—All whole colours are admissible, but they should be free from black or white shadings. At present the whole-coloured dogs are: White; black; brown, light or dark; blue, as pale as possible; orange, which should be as self-coloured and bright as possible; beaver; cream, which should have black noses and black rims round the eyes.
Whites must be quite free from lemon or any other colour. A few white hairs in any of the self-coloured dogs shall not necessarily disqualify.
Dogs other than white with white or tan markings are decidedly objectionable, and should be discouraged. They cannot compete as whole-coloured specimens.
In parti-coloured dogs the colours should be evenly distributed on the body in patches;

a dog with white or tan feet or chest would not be a parti-coloured dog.

Shaded sables should be shaded throughout with three or more colours, the hair to be as uniformly shaded as possible, and with no patches of self-colour.

In mixed classes, where whole-coloured and parti-coloured Pomeranians compete together, the preference should, if in other points they are equal, be given to the whole-coloured specimens 15

100

CHAPTER LVII.

The Pug.

We are indebted to China for the Pug, and he is no doubt closely allied to the smooth-haired Pekingese. He is, however, a much earlier immigrant in this country than the Imperial Peke., King William III. being one of the first, if not the first, to import the breed to this country. The dog was always a favourite with the nobility and aristocracy, his dignified bearing and action, and great fidelity and intelligence (although the Pug is not among the most intelligent, since all short-faced varieties of the dog are possessed with more or less stupidity), appealing to the leisured classes.

It was not until about the middle of the last century, however, that his breeding on a larger scale was taken up, and although there can be little doubt

PUG (Fawn).

that black blood was in his veins, all the earlier Pugs were fawns, with black traces down their backs. One of the earliest zealots in the propagation of the Pug upon anything like a systematic scale was the late Lady Willoughby d'Eresby, who established a strain of Pug which ultimately was known as the Willoughby Pug. They were of the silver fawn, remarkable for the distinct trace and very black mask.

Mr. Morrison was another of our earliest breeders, his dogs being more of the golden fawn in colour.

At one time a number of cream-coloured Pugs were exhibited, but they did not find favour, and frequently rough-coated puppies have cropped up in litters, pointing unmistakably to the Pekingese.

The blacks are a more modern creation, dating no further back than about 1886, and it is to the efforts of Lady Brassey that we owe the initiation of these Nubians. Her Ladyship was a great traveller, and, it is said, imported a black Pug (or maybe Pekingese) from China, when she visited that country in her yacht Sunbeam, which she crossed with her darkest coloured fawn Pugs, and so established the colour. The inbreeding of the few blacks that were available with the fawns produced a lot of half-and-half colours, or bronzy blacks, but by judicious selection not only has the colour been deepened, but a race of black Pugs has been founded which in type and character beat the fawns. Indeed, black Pugs now preponderate at our shows.

Some of the earlier Pugs were large dogs of 18lb. or 22lb., but the tendency in late years has been to reduce the size, although the Toy craze has not yet taken thorough hold of the Pug fancy.

PUG (Black).

The chief features of the breed, which all breeders and exhibitors aim at, are compactness and roundness of body, very short, square muzzle, big skull, large eyes, and great wrinkle, small drop ears, and double twist of tail, with straight forelegs. Snipiness or long muzzles, long backs, and straight tails are unpardonable blemishes. Quality of coat is another important feature in both varieties, soundness of colour in the blacks and distinctness of trace in the fawns being most desirable points. A *little* white on chest is not a material blemish in either variety, nor are black toe-nails, which used to be insisted on in the early days, now considered a material point. The medium sizes are the best, and in dogs of this size it is easier to obtain an accentuation of the desired points—dogs of from 10lb. to 14lb.

The chief points to look for in the selection of puppies at from two to four months old are : Short square faces, great wrinkle, short backs, great bone.

The following are the standard description and scale of points issued by the Pug Club:—

	SCALE.					Fawn.	Black.
Symmetry	..	..	..	..	..	10	10
Size	..	..	..	..	..	5	10
Condition	..	..	..	..	..	5	5
Body	..	..	..	..	..	10	10
Legs ⎱ Feet ⎰	..	..	..	..	..	5	5
Head	..	..	..	..	..	5	5
Muzzle	..	..	..	..	..	10	10
Ears	..	..	..	..	..	5	5
Eyes	..	..	..	..	..	10	10
Mask	..	..	..	..	..	5	
Wrinkles	..	..	..	..	..	5	5
Tail	..	..	..	..	..	10	10
Trace	..	..	..	..	..	5	
Coat	..	..	..	..	..	5	5
Colour	..	..	..	..	..	5	10
						100	100

SYMMETRY.—Symmetry and general appearance, decidedly square and cobby. A lean, leggy Pug, and a dog with short legs and a long body, are equally objectionable.

SIZE AND CONDITION.—The Pug should be *multum in parvo*, but this condensation (if the word may be used) should be shown by compactness of form, well-knit proportions, and hardness of developed muscle. Weight from 13lb. to 17lb. (dog or bitch).

BODY.—Short and cobby, wide in chest, and well ribbed up.

LEGS.—Very strong, straight, of moderate length, and well under.

FEET.—Neither so long as the foot of the hare, nor so round as that of the cat, well-split-up toes, and the nails black.

MUZZLE.—Short, blunt, square, but not upfaced.

HEAD.—Large, massive, round, not apple-headed, with no indentation of the skull.

EYES.—Dark in colour, very large, bold and prominent, globular in shape, soft and solicitous in expression, very lustrous, and when excited full of fire.

EAR.—Thin, small, soft, like black velvet. There are two kinds: The "Rose" and "Button." Preference is given to the latter.

MARKINGS.—Clearly defined. The muzzle or mask, ears, moles on cheeks, thumb-mark or diamond on forehead, back trace should be as black as possible.

MASK.—The mask should be black. The more intense and well defined it is the better.

WRINKLES—Large and deep.

TRACE.—A black line extending from the occiput to the tail.

TAIL.—Curled tightly as possible over the hip. The double curl is perfection.

COAT.—Fine, smooth, soft, short, and glossy, neither hard nor woolly.

COLOUR.—Silver or apricot-fawn. Each should be decided to make the contrast complete between the colour and the trace and the mask.

CHAPTER LVIII.

The Papillon.

The Papillon (pronounced pah-peé-yong) or Butterfly dog is among the latest post-war canine importations into England, and a charming Lilliputian beauty of the diminutive rough-coated Toy Dog order, which sprang into popularity at one bound almost, and is now a great and growing favourite, especially with the fair sex.

As to the history of this petite alien, I cannot do better than reprint what Mr. George Horowitz, its well-informed foreign correspondent, wrote about it in *Our Dogs* of January 12, 1923, which is as follows :—

Great French authors, such as the late Monsieur Pierre Mégnin, father of our confrere, Monsieur Paul Mégnin, have it that the Papillon is essentially of French origin, that this breed had been in favour centuries ago, and—and this is very important—that the specimens of to-day are like those of by-gone days. We can say, therefore, that the Papillon has remained true to its original type, and absolutely foreign to any infusion of strange blood.

PAPILLON.

It was in the middle of the sixteenth century that Papillons made their first appearance—namely, at the court of the King of France. We know that up to the reign of Henri III. no trace of them can be found, either on objects of art or in books. The first we hear of them is in the " Popular History of France," vol. II., page 307, as follows :—

Henri III. possessed all the vulgar and low tastes. Once he made a journey to Lyons to buy little dogs, for which that town was known then, and Sully tells us that, having obtained an audience from the King, he found him, " his little cap on the head and with a basket hanging round his neck, in which there were three little dogs, not larger than the fist." He spent more than 100,000 crowns a year on his dogs . . . and he paid high salaries to a crowd of men and women who had no other occupation than to look after them and feed them.

257

The above does not tell us anything of the character and, consequently, of the breed of those little dogs of Henri III., which were then called " chiens lions " (perhaps owing to the town they originated from), and which found favour with the ladies of the court, and of the neighbouring courts, until the French Revolution.

Eleven years after the death of Henri III., who was succeeded by Henri IV., in 1589, the marriage took place of the latter with Marie de Médicis, and the beautiful paintings of Rubens, in the possession of the Louvre, in Paris, consecrated this event. Thus, on the painting representing the marriage itself, we see below, on the left, one of these fashionable little dogs, with long hair on the ears and on the tail, as well as on the back of the legs and feet, and on the neck. Another painting of Rubens, representing Marie de Médicis as Regent of France, again shows us a similar little dog nestling against the Queen. Last, but not least, on the painting of the coronation, by Rubens, we see two more similar dogs.

During the reign of Louis XIV., Louis XV., and Louis XVI., these little dogs remained in favour. There is a painting at the Paris Louvre representing the Duchess of Orleans, sister-in-law of Louis XVI., in which she is seen holding in her arms a charming little Papillon, with long and silky hair, and the same great French museum possesses paintings of two favourite dogs of Madame de Pompadour, Mimi and Ines. These paintings tell us clearly what Papillons were in favour in those times.

I must repeat that the Papillon of to-day is just the same as it was about a hundred years ago—*i.e.*, that it has preserved a skull (separated by a mesial furrow) of an average size, and a pointed muzzle, like that of Madame de Pompadour's Mimi and Ines. The name " Papillon " (butterfly) no doubt arose owing to their ears having not too much hair, and being pricked when at attention, and so spread out, resembling more or less the wings of the butterfly. The Papillon is not only met with in France, but more especially in Belgium. It is called " Chien Ecureuil " (squirrel dog), on account of the shape of its tail. It is a charming companion, very intelligent, and it does not require much care as to its " toilette."

From the foregoing it will be seen that the little Franco-Belgian production is a dog of great antiquity. In his very interesting article, however, Mr. Horowitz does not give us any glimpse into the mists of its origin, which must, to a great extent, like that of many other old breeds, remain a matter of conjecture.

My old and esteemed friend, Count Henri de Bylandt, in his wonderful illustrated work, " Dogs of All Nations," describes the Papillon as of the Spaniel (Spagneuls) family, and there is little doubt that the English King Charles Spaniel and the Papillon have somewhat of a common origin. Some authorities, however, hold that either a cross with the little Mexican dog, the Chihuahua, or *vice versa*, has at some time been effected between the two breeds, which have a great deal in common in size, ears, colouring, and character, the chief variation being in coat, the Chihuahua being mostly smooth-coated.

We are confirmed in this view by the " Foreword," written for the first booklet of rules and standard description of the " Papillon (Butterfly) Dog Club, by my old friend, Robt. Leighton.

This brings us to the formation of the " Papillon (Butterfly) Dog Club, founded in 1924, the chief promoters of which, and pioneers of the breed, were :—Mrs. Gordon Gratrix (the eminent Pekingese expert and enthusiast), Mrs. Cooper (who joined forces in importing some of the most classic specimens of the breed from France and Belgium, and founded a famous kennel in England), Mrs. C. M. Hunter, Mrs. Partridge (mater of Mr. W. R. Partridge, the well-known Alsatian Wolfdog enthusiast), and one or two others.

Application was made to the Kennel Club, and, after due consideration by that august body in kennel matters in this country, the breed was duly placed upon its register.

The new club appears to have adopted the standard description given by Count Bylandt, in his work, "The Dogs of All Nations," which is printed in French, and which Mr. Horowitz translated and published in his original article quoted above. It is described in the Club's booklet as "Points," but the various features of the dog, or "Points," are not appraised and apportioned in a total of 100, in the usual way. The description is as follows:—

POINTS.

GENERAL APPEARANCE.—Smart, very lively, and intelligent.
HEAD.—Small, slightly rounded skull; fine pointed muzzle.
EYES.—Round, and placed rather low in head; dark in colour.
NOSE.—Always dark, preferably black.
EARS.—Carried pricked or falling, but always very fringed.
LIPS.—Thin and tight.
NECK.—Not too short.
SHOULDERS.—Well developed.
CHEST.—Rather deep.
BACK.—Straight, and not too short.
BELLY.—Slightly raised.
LOINS.—Rather arched.
BODY.—Rather long and well formed; not cobby.
PAWS.—Straight, fine, rather short; front paws fringed.
FEET.—Long, comparatively
TAIL.—Long, and very fringed, carried like that of a squirrel—falling over back.
COAT.—Long and silky. On the muzzle and front feet the coat is short.
COLOUR.—Brown, ruby, light brown, dark yellow, black-and-white, tricolour, white with coloured patches.
HEIGHT.—Not over 12in. at shoulder; smaller the better.
WEIGHT.—Not over 12lb.

DISQUALIFICATIONS.—Black colour (unicolour).
FAULTS.—Rose or spotted nose; cobby body.

As in Skye Terriers, there are two varieties, prick (or butterfly) ears and drop ears (retomber), but the former are the most characteristic.

Until the breed had been recognised by the Kennel Club, Papillons had perforce to be entered in the variety classes at shows, where, even so early, they distinguished themselves in competition with better-known English or longer-acclimatised foreign breeds, by judges who had some experience of the breed. One of these was the author of this work, who made himself intimate with it in his judicial peregrinations on the continent years ago, where he occasionally was called upon to judge the breed. Later, however, upon the new devotees of the breed guaranteeing classes for it, many of our leading shows, including that of the Kennel Club, made special classes for Papillons, and thus it became established in the ranks of British Toy Dogs as a new recruit to be reckoned with.

The Papillon is a most intelligent, affectionate, and faithful little creature, and, for its size, active and hardy, since it is free from any physical abnormalities, except diminutiveness.

With the numerous importations that have taken place of the very best products of France and Belgium, there is now in this country ample material to carry on breeding operations for some years and at the same time improve and perfect the breed.

In choosing a puppy the chief points to look for are diminutiveness, soundness fore and aft, light bone, fine head, and dense coat.

CHAPTER LIX.

The Schipperke.

The Schipperke may be said to have been " made in Belgium," where he is used as a watch dog on the various canals which intercept King Albert's dominion. Round the top edge of these canal boats there runs a ledge, probably a foot wide, with a back to it. It is the custom of the boatmen to keep one or two Schipperkes, which are trained to run round this ledge and to keep a sort of sentinel watch. It occurred to one of their class, at what exact

SCHIPPERKE.

date is not on record, that the Schipperke (pronounced skip-per-keé) would the better fulfil his duty if his tail were off, as it appeared to be somewhat in the way, and often precipitated the dog into the water. It was, therefore, ordained that the tails of Schipperkes used as bargees (also in Holland) should be docked, and in due course the docking of the breed became a general custom. The dog was also used to keep down the rats in the boats, and to-day is a splendid ratter.

As in the case of the Old English Sheepdog, the systematic docking of the tail for many long years exercised such an influence upon the breed that bitches often gave birth to some puppies that were already tailless, and to others that had merely a stump. The Schipperke is not, however, as some people have supposed, a naturally tailless variety, like the Manx cat. He was originally always born with his full caudal appendage, and many are so born still, both in Belgium and England, where the dog has become such a favourite. When so born, his tail invariably curls over his back, *a la* Pomeranian, and this fact, taken in conjunction with his general type, his head, prick ears, often profuse coat, more particularly the mane and culotte (breeching), and general character and disposition, strongly points to the dog being very closely allied to the Pomeranian, if not an immediate descendant. Belgium is close to Germany, and doubtless Pomeranians migrated to that country and Holland before they came to England, Italy, or more distant countries. It is very natural to suppose that in the Pomeranian the Belgian boatmen saw a useful little dog for the purpose already defined, but his heavy coat and tail were somewhat against him, the former by retaining the water, and the latter for reasons already described. They therefore set to work to reduce the coat and harden it in texture, and abolish the tail altogether, in which they succeeded, transforming the dog into an article of Belgian manufacture, and giving it also a Belgian name. What process was adopted in the coat transformation is, like the origin of the Schipperke, a mere matter of conjecture, but the most probable that is presented to us, in the absence of any really authentic data, is either that a broken or even smooth-haired Terrier was employed to reduce and harden the coat, or that the metamorphosis has been accomplished by selection.

When the Schipperke was first introduced into England is probably not known, but very few, if any, specimens were known to exist, say, fifteen years before the Schipperke Club was founded in 1890. The institution of this Club naturally gave a fillip to the breed, which was now recognised by the Kennel Club, and quickly became popular. The dog's great intelligence, vivacity, docility, fidelity, and general smartness quickly appealed to the English fancier and public. The Schipperke Club formulated a standard description and code of points, based principally upon those of the Belgian Schipperke Club, and the breed, with this standard laid down, and under the fostering influence of the Club, made rapid progress. Classes were everywhere provided at shows, and breeders sprang up in every direction. Some few years later, however, there was a split in the ranks of the Schipperke Club, and a new club was started as a result, one alleged reason of this defection being that the parent club did not give sufficient weight to mane and culotte, and so these were emphasised in the standard of the new club, which called itself the St. Hubert Schipperke Club. Some years later a club for the breed was started in Scotland, and later still a North of England Club was launched, supported by the leading zealots of the North of England, and even by many in the South. With the dawn of the present century, therefore, the Belgian bargee may be said to have been extremely well catered for in this country—far better than in his native country, where only one club exists to promote his interests and welfare. The breed is, moreover, more perfected in England than in Belgium, at least according to English ideas, just as the Pomeranian surpasses his kinsmen in Germany, the result of the keen fancier instincts and tenacity of the British breeder, whose goal is " perfection " in whatever he takes up.

Although the Schipperke came to us a Nubian, coloured specimens crop up in many litters, and sables, chocolates, and whites even, are not unknown in Belgium, although blacks only are recognised by the Belgian Schipperke Club. This is, to my mind, further proof of the "Schip.'s" Pomeranian descent. Latterly, these "sports," as they have been erroneously termed, have been cultivated by many breeders, with the result that we have in England many really good sable, chocolate, and white Schipperkes, correct in type, many of which have been exhibited with success, and some of the coloured dogs have even been advertised at public stud. It is only right to state, however, that the leading clubs have, so far, taken an official stand against coloured Schipperkes, believing that their breeding and propagation will injure the blacks. They contend that the process of breeding coloured "Schips." will be sure to involve crossing with the Pomeranian, which, it is alleged, will not only seriously affect the colour, but the type, of the black Schipperkes. Personally

I disagree with the attitude of the clubs in this matter, and see no logic in keeping the "Schip." always in mourning. Colour breeding in Pomeranians has not seriously affected the blacks in colour, but it has given the breed a largely increased popularity and raised its status and the value of the breed in the market. This I prophesy would be the result if the Schipperke Clubs embraced the colour question, and instead of attempting to stem its flowing tide devoted themselves to keeping it within the prescribed lines of the Schipperke cult pure and simple.

The breed in Belgium is divided by weight, the one maximum being 12lb., and the other 20lb. This, of course, admits of Toy Dogs, but in England, although the size of the dog has fluctuated somewhat, both Toy Dogs and dogs above 15lb. have been tabooed.

The main features that by a concensus of expert opinion are required in the breed are a foxy head, small erect ears, the inside line of which should be almost straight, short compact body, tapering towards the quarters, but with well-sprung ribs, clean shoulders, and straight forelegs, showing quality of bone, and indeed quality all through. The coat should be crisp to the touch, yet lustrous, and profuse round the neck and at the breeching, and dense but close in other parts of the body, the legs being otherwise free from feathering. Thick heads, big ears, light eyes, long backs, and soft coats are defects to be scrupulously avoided.

The chief points to look for in the selection of puppies at from two to four months old and after are: A foxy head, small ears, short back, dense coat, light bone.

The best age at which to dock puppies is when they leave their dam; the sooner after the better. As the docking of Schipperkes is a more delicate and difficult operation than the docking of Terriers, involving the removal of the whole of the tail, the operation should always be entrusted to a fully qualified veterinary surgeon.

My old and esteemed friend, the late Mr. G. R. Krehl, was one of the great pioneers of the Schipperke in this country, if not actually the first to introduce the breed to the British show bench.

The standard description and code of points adopted by the Schipperke Club (England) are as follows:—

HEAD.—Foxy in type, skull should not be round, but broad, and with little stop. The muzzle should be moderate in length, fine but not weak, should be well filled out under the eyes.

NOSE.—Black and small.

EYES.—Dark brown, small, more oval than round, and not full, bright and full of expression.

EARS.—Shape: Of moderate length, not too broad at the base, tapering to a point. Carriage: Stiffly erect, and when in that position the inside edge to form as near as possible a right angle with the skull and strong enough not to be bent otherwise than lengthways.

TEETH.—Strong and level.

NECK.—Strong and full, rather short, set broad on the shoulders, and slightly arched.

SHOULDERS.—Muscular and sloping.

CHEST.—Broad and deep in brisket.

BACK.—Short, straight, and strong.

LOINS.—Powerful, well drawn up from the brisket.

FORELEGS.—Perfectly straight, well under the body, with bone in proportion to the body.

HIND LEGS.—Strong, muscular, hocks well let down.

FEET.—Small, catlike, and standing well on its toes.

NAILS.—Black.

HINDQUARTERS.—Fine compared to the foreparts, muscular and well-developed thighs, tailless, rump well rounded.

COAT.—Black, abundant, dense and harsh, smooth on the head, ears, and legs, lying close on the back and sides, but erect and thick round the neck, forming a mane and frill, and well feathered on back of thighs.

WEIGHT.—About 12lb.

GENERAL APPEARANCE.—A small cobby animal, with sharp expression, intensely lively, presenting the appearance of being always on the alert.

DISQUALIFYING POINTS.—Drop or semi-erect ears.

FAULTS.—White hairs are objected to, but are not disqualifying.

STANDARD OF POINTS FOR JUDGING.

	Value.
Head, nose, eyes, teeth	20
Ears	10
Neck, shoulders, chest	10
Back, loins	5
Forelegs	5
Hind legs	5
Feet	5
Hindquarters	10
Coat and colour	20
General appearance	10
Total	100

CHAPTER LX.

The Shetland Sheepdog.

The name of the Shetland Sheepdog clearly indicates his origin and habitat. The Shetland Isles are noted for their horses, cattle, sheep, and dogs, all being in miniature. Whether these dwarfed animals on the Island are a provision of Nature, as adapting them the better for their Island home and haunts, or their bantamising has been the work of the Islanders, is a subject which I need not discuss here. Suffice it to say that the Shetland Sheepdog is in perfect keeping with his other island companions. This is in the fitness of things, for it would indeed look strange if the orthodox Scotch Collie were to roam about the Islands amongst the miniature cattle, some specimens of which would exceed in size many of the latter!

It is only a few years since the Shetland Sheepdog found his way on the show bench and fell into the hands of the fancier, who, of course, immediately began to exploit him; and later still the Kennel Club admitted the dog on its register as a distinct breed. On the Islands the dog, like other sheepdogs, is employed for herding the sheep and cattle, and therefore requires the same points as his enlarged brother, who is built for and used for the same purpose. The points of the Scotch Collie have been formulated by experts, and on such well-attested lines as should enable him to prosecute his calling with the greatest facility, and it must be admitted that by years of careful selection and breeding the larger edition has been brought to very great perfection, and is one of the finest examples of canine culture extant.

Bred on the Islands, indiscriminately no doubt—not even by rule of thumb,—the original specimens of Shetland Sheepdog were, and are, naturally of a somewhat nondescript pattern. The only consideration which the Shetland farmers had originally in mating their sheepdog bitches would be proved *working* qualities in the dog to which they were to be mated. Such features as narrow shoulders, straight forelegs, well-sprung ribs, strong loin and quarters, dense weather-proof coats, intelligent eyes, and suitable carriage of ear, were in ninety-nine cases out of every hundred probably points in the anatomy of a Sheepdog which never entered into their philosophy, although all very necessary qualifications and very advantageous to the dog in his specific calling.

That is why I can never understand the force of those who argue that the Shetland Sheepdog should be kept to his original type, which is really no type at all. In the earliest exhibition days of the Shetland Sheepdogs there were all sorts and sizes of dogs shown as Shetland Sheepdogs, many of them hailing from the dog's native heath. Some were more on Pomeranian than Sheepdog lines, and many showed traces of the Spaniel in their physiognomy and anatomy.

If in the various breeds of dogs—or, indeed, any domestic animal—we were to stick to originals, we should not have the beautiful dogs that are on the show bench to-day. If this conservative theory is to be carried to its legitimate end—that is, to the original dog—we should have now only one breed!

The various beautiful breeds we have to-day in England, and which are the wonder of the world, have not been produced by sticking to originals, but by judicious and rational selection, with the one object of improvement in view. The Scotch Collie, as seen at his best on the show bench, is the finest example in the world of a Sheepdog possessing all the attributes, anatomically, to fit him to fulfil his work to the best advantage. Why cannot our Shetland friends take advantage of the half-century's work of their friends

SHETLAND SHEEPDOG.

and copy the larger model and make the Shetlander a replica in miniature of his big brother? And the best way to do this is to breed the Shetland bitches to undersized Scotch Collies. Out-crossing in these days of consanguinity is an absolute necessity, and could there possibly be a better outcross for the Shetlander than the Scotch Collie, who possesses *every attribute required* except size?

The colours of the Shetland are the same—sable-and-white and tricolour. The points to choose for in a puppy are identical with those given in the case of the Scotch Collie, except with regard to size—the smallest puppies in the litter, given other good points, being those to select.

The following is the standard description and points of the Scottish Shetland Sheepdog Club:—

SKULL.—Should be as near as possible flat, moderately wide between the ears, and gradually tapering towards the eyes. There should only be a slight depression at stop. The cheeks should not be full or prominent.

MUZZLE.—Should be of fair length, tapering to the nose, and should not show weakness, or be snipy or lippy. The nose must be black, whatever the colour of the dog may be.

TEETH.—Should be sound, and near as possible level. Very slight unevenness is permissible.

JAWS.—Clean cut and powerful.

EYES.—Should be of medium size, set somewhat obliquely, and close together, of almond shape, and of brown colour; full of intelligence and expression.

EARS.—Should be small, and moderately wide at the base, and placed fairly close together on top of skull. When in repose they should be carried thrown back, but when on the alert brought forward and carried semi-erect, with the tips drooping forward.

NECK.—Should be of fair length, muscular, and somewhat arched.

BODY.—Should be moderately long and level, with well-sprung ribs and strong loins; chest deep.

FORELEGS.—Should be straight and muscular, with a fair amount of bone.

HIND LEGS.—Should be muscular at the thighs, with well-bent hocks.

FEET.—Should be oval in shape, soles well padded, and the toes arched and close together.

TAIL.—Should be moderately long, with abundant hair, carried low when the dog is quiet, with a slight upward swirl at the end; but carried gaily when the dog is excited, but not over the back.

COAT.—Must be double—the outer coat consists of hard hair; the under coat, which resembles fur, is short, soft, and close. The mane and frill should be very abundant, the mask or face smooth, as also the tips of the ears. The forelegs well feathered, the hind legs above the hocks profusely covered with hair, but below the hocks fairly smooth. What is commonly known as smooth-coated specimens are barred.

COLOUR.—Any colour except brindle is permissible.

GENERAL APPEARANCE.—The general appearance of the Shetland Sheepdog is that of the modern show Collie *in miniature* (Collie character and type must be adhered to). Ideal height, $13\frac{1}{2}$in. at maturity, which is fixed at ten months old.

FAULTS.

Domed skull; large dropping ears; weak jaws; snipy muzzle; full or light eyes; crooked forelegs; cow hocks; tail carried over the back; under or over-shot mouth.

SCALE OF POINTS.

Head and expression	15
Ears	15
Neck and shoulders	5
Legs and feet	10
Hindquarters	10
Back and loins	5
Tail	10
Coat and frill	15
Size	15
Total	100

The standard of type contained in the Constitution of the Shetland Sheepdog Club is as follows :—

"The type and points of the Shetland Sheepdog shall be similar to those of the Rough Collie in miniature. The height of the Shetland Sheepdog shall not exceed 15in."

CHAPTER LXI.

The Griffon Bruxellois.

The Griffon Bruxellois, which interpreted into English means Brussels Griffon, is, as its name implies, the product of the Belgian capital. There are no definite data as to the dog's precise origin or evolution, but I have it on good authority that the breeds employed in his manufacture were English, viz., the Yorkshire Terrier, King Charles (Ruby) Spaniel, and Irish Terrier. There are really two varieties in Belgium—viz., the rough-coated Griffon (which word means rough) and the smooth-coated, to which the word Griffon is, of course, a misnomer, and which are called Brabancon—a smooth red Griffon with black points. The rough-coats are the more popular in both Belgium and England, in which latter country the breed has become a great favourite, to such an extent that English fanciers have in late years drained

GRIFFON BRUXELLOIS.

Brussels of most of its choicest specimens. The Griffon Bruxellois is a much later arrival than the Schipperke, and neither so numerous yet nor so generally popular, although a great favourite with many people. There is a quaintness about the little Belgian and a dignity altogether disproportionate to his diminutiveness, for the dog is a Toy Dog—a Toy Terrier really—although for exhibition specimens as large as 10lb. weight is permissible, but a dog of that weight will always be beaten by a good sound specimen half its size.

In Belgium the breed is cropped as well as docked, but the cropping of really good puppies is often considerably delayed by breeders, in the hope of their being wanted for the English market. They are still docked in England. His short and retroussé nose denotes his King Charles Spaniel blood, his coat and colour that of the Irish Terrier, and his lighter-coloured topknot his Yorkshire Terrier cross. No matter what his original ancestry, the type of the breed is now fairly fixed, and he breeds as true as most other breeds. There will be in litters indifferent specimens, some too big, others fluffy in coat, and some too long in face, but this happens in connection with most breeds.

Clubs have been founded in England to cultivate the breed and look after his welfare, the Griffon Bruxellois Club being the first to be launched.

The chief features of the breed are extreme shortness of foreface—the more noseless the dog is the more valuable is he,—good turnup of underjaw, large dark eyes, neat ears, wiry coat, short back, general cobbiness and symmetry. Colour is important, the colour and texture of coat of the Irish Terrier being the most approved. A feature of the face, too, is the profuseness of the moustache and beard. Soft top-knots are a common defect, but a uniform texture and colour of coat throughout is aimed at.

The chief points to look for in the selection of puppies at from two to four months old and after are: Extreme shortness of face, short compact bodies, crisp coats, good sound colour, and diminutiveness.

The following are the standard description and code of points laid down by the Griffon Bruxellois Club, as revised at the general meeting in Brussels, February 5th, 1901 :—

GENERAL APPEARANCE.—A lady's pet dog, intelligent, sprightly, robust, of compact appearance, reminding one of a cob, and captivating the attention by a quasi-human expression.

HEAD.—*Large* and rounded, covered with rather coarse hair, rough, somewhat longer round the eyes, nose, and cheeks.

EARS.—Semi-erect when not clipped, erect when clipped.

EYES.—Very large, black or nearly black, eyelashes long and black, eyelids often edged with black, eyebrows furnished with hair, leaving the eye perfectly uncovered.

NOSE.—Always black, short, surrounded with hair, converging upwards and going to meet those that surround the eyes; the break or stop in the nose well pronounced.

LIPS.—Edged with black, furnished with a moustache; a little black in the moustache is not a fault.

CHIN.—Prominent without showing the teeth, and furnished with a small beard.

CHEST.—Rather wide and *deep*.

LEGS.—As straight as possible, of medium length.

TAIL.—Upwards, and cut to the two-thirds.

COLOUR.—*Red*.

TEXTURE OF COAT.—Harsh and wiry, rather long and *thick*.

WEIGHT.—Small dogs, male and female, $5\frac{1}{2}$lb. maximum. Big dogs, 9lb. maximum. *Large bitches*, 10lb.

FAULTS.—Pale eyes; silky tuft on head; *brown toe nails*; *showing teeth*.

DISQUALIFICATION.—*Brown nose; white marks; tongue protruding*.

The Griffon Belge Club's description of the Griffon Belge :—

GENERAL APPEARANCE.—A lady's little dog, intelligent, sprightly, robust, of compact appearance, reminding one of a cob, and captivating the attention by a quasi-human expression.

HEAD.—Rounded, furnished with somewhat hard, irregular hairs, longer round the eyes, on the nose and cheeks.

EARS.—Semi-erect.

NOSE.—Always black, short, surrounded with hair converging upwards to meet that which surrounds the eyes, very pronounced stop or break.

LIPS.—Edged with black, furnished with a moustache.

CHIN.—Prominent, without showing the teeth, and edged with a small beard.

CHEST.—Rather wide and deep.

LEGS.—As straight as possible, of medium length.

TAIL.—Erect and cut short.

COLOUR.—Must be black, or black with tan markings.

TEXTURE OF COAT.—Irregular, broken, harsh, wiry, and thick (smooth coats not admissible).

WEIGHT.—Not to exceed 9lb.

FAULTS.—Light eyes; silky hair on head; brown nails; teeth showing.

DISQUALIFICATIONS.—Brown nose; white patches; and tongue showing.

The type is the same in the three varieties, the difference being chiefly in coat, colour, and size.

CHAPTER LXII.

Unclassified British Breeds.

Besides the Bearded Collie and Trawler Toy Spaniel, referred to in their respective sections, there are several other British breeds which have come to be regarded as distinct, but which have not as yet been so recognised by the Kennel Club.

THE TURNSPIT

Is a dog of antiquity in both this country and abroad. His occupation was originally fixed—viz., in the kitchen to turn the joint which was roasting before the fire before modern cooking appliances came in vogue; and in the farm to turn a primitive appliance for grinding corn and churning milk—but not the breed of the dog. For these purposes the smaller puppies coming from the farm sheepdogs were often selected for training as Turnspits, or nondescripts which had any appearance of suitability or adaptability to the particular vocation, the dog usually being a short-legged animal, and for the roaster a short-coated dog was generally employed. With the advance of civilisation and invention, the occupation—like that of Othello—has gone and the breed, if it may be termed a breed, has become practically extinct

THE TRUFFLE HUNTER.

Truffle hunting is an ancient sport in both England and France and other wooded countries. The truffle is a subterranean fungi of great delicacy, and much prized by the aristocracy. It is found mostly in beech-grown districts, the succulent vegetable growing just beneath the surface of the ground, and is about the size of the egg of a turkey. The dogs, which are of the Terrier persuasion, mostly crossbred—probably a cross between a white Poodle and Fox-terrier,—are trained to find the truffle by scent, and are able by practice to locate the fungi, distinguishing it from other roots and fungi by its smell. Truffle-hunting was at one time a considerable industry among the peasantry of the pastoral counties of England, mostly in the South, owing to the great demand for the delicacy in London. The importation of truffles from France, however, has in late years done the English trade considerable injury, although English truffles are still sent to the market. Truffle-hunting is a very interesting outdoor sport—interesting to witness with what accuracy good canine hunters can locate the prized vegetable, as if by instinct almost.

THE CORGI.

The Corgi (Cwygi) is a Welsh cur or cattle dog of great antiquity, being used mostly by the small farmers of the Principality in the herding of their cattle and sheep, and found very handy and useful for the purpose, especially in the more mountainous districts of Wales. He is somewhat of the old Collie type, and is a short-legged, rough-coated, rugged-looking little fellow, varying from 20lb. to 30lb. in weight, although some are less and some larger, and is commonly called a "heeler," since "heeling" his charges forms a great part of his vocation, and is a very necessary adjunct to the farmers and cattle-drovers of Welsh Wales.

The Corgi until now had remained outside the domain of the professional dog fancier, but recently he has arrested fanciers' attention, and a " Corgi " Club has been formed for the purpose of formulating a uniform standard of points out of the rough material available, and bringing the little fellow to the front in the same way that the Sealyham Terrier has been popularised. Indeed, many of the earlier devotees of the Sealyham Terrier hold the view that the Corgi has played a great part in the founding of that now very popular South Walian Terrier, who has far outstripped the earlier Welsh Terrier in general favour with the fancier, and certainly in their architecture the two breeds have not a little in common, especially in the earlier editions of the Sealyham.

This little Cambrian cattle dog has at length been lifted from his pastoral obscurity into the limelight of public notoriety, and been added to the long and growing list of classic canines whose original, more or less nondescript, breeding has been obliterated and an ordered genealogy instituted, which will, in the effluxion of time, place the Corgi among the classics of his species.

THE BULL-MASTIFF.

For some years enthusiasts in the crossing of the Bulldog with the English Mastiff have been endeavouring to get the cross, like that of the Bull-terrier, established as a distinct breed. They have importuned the Kennel Club, which has at length evolved a scheme by which Bull-Mastiffs can be registered as a pure breed. The regulation, published in *The Kennel Gazette* of December 1924 issue, is as follows :—

With reference to Bull-Mastiffs, the Committee, at their meeting of December 2nd, decided that it is prepared to open a section among the " Any Other Variety " registrations of Bull-Mastiffs, if *pure-bred* as such, and where sufficient be registered under this heading according to the Rule mentioned above, the breed would be eligible for a place in the Register of Breeds. It is, of course, most important to observe the distinction between a Bull-Mastiff (pure breed) and a Bull-Mastiff (cross breed), the former being a dog bred with both parents and the preceding three generations all Bull-Mastiffs, without the introduction of a Mastiff or Bulldog. The term Bull-Mastiff (cross-bred) implies the existence of a definite cross which has not yet been bred out according to Regulation 12 of the Regulations for Registration.

For the development of the scheme of standardising the Bull-Mastiff, two Clubs have been formed, and give promise of carrying it out successfully under the regulations laid down by the Kennel Club. A standard description and points have been drawn up by the Clubs.

CHAPTER LXIII.

Eastern Greyhounds.

The Greyhounds of Arabia, Persia, and Afghanistan, are very ancient, and, to European eyes, quaint sporting breeds of dogs. The records, some of them somewhat misty, still point to these Greyhounds being the prototype, of first, the Egyptian, Circassian, Caucasian, and Russian, and finally European and English Greyhounds and Deerhounds.

If that is so, while the latter have developed deviations, not in actual type, but in little details only, the former have retained through the ages their quaint distribution of coat and fleet-like conformation and type which they possessed centuries ago, as is proved by ancient sculpture and fossils.

THE SALUKI.

The Saluki, or Gazelle Hound, is the first of the several breeds of Eastern Greyhounds to become specifically recognised by the Kennel Club and to be placed upon its register of breeds. This was in July, 1923.

Mr. Harding Cox, in reviewing the famous kennels of Brigadier-General and Mrs. Fred Lance in the Christmas number of *Our Dogs* of 1924, says :—

The term " Saluki " is a generic one, and is applied to many varieties of Eastern " sight dogs." The type with which we have been familiarised by General Lance and others is the Gazelle Hound, of Bedouin, which is used, as its name implies, for coursing the fleet gazelle, sometimes unaided and sometimes with the co-operation of falcons.

Count Henri de Bylandt, in his great illustrated work on dogs, gives a description and points of the Slongled, under the heading " Levrier drabe " (Arabian), which differs very little from the Saluki, and which, we believe, is included in the Club's repertory.

Count Bylandt's standard is as follows :—

The Arabian Greyhound (Saluki)—
GENERAL APPEARANCE.—A dog with the appearance of an English Greyhound.
USES.—A dog used in hunting the gazelle.
HEAD.—Long.
SKULL.—Rather flat.
FOREHEAD.—Broad.
STOP.—The bridge of the nose is barely visible.
MUZZLE.—Long and slender.
EYES.—Small, soft, dark amber in colour, eyelids bordered with black.
NOSE.—Black and pointed.
LIPS.—Close and black.

Quite a number of Saluki zealots in England, in 1923, banded themselves together for the purpose of the formation of a club under the title of " The Saluki, or Gazelle Hound, Club," which boasted of from 50 to 60 members right off the reel, and the object of which was to formulate a standard description and points for the breed to be bred to, and for its general promotion and advancement in this country.

This standard is as follows :—
HEAD.—Long and narrow, skull moderately wide between ears, not domed, stop not pronounced, the whole showing great quality. Nose black or liver.

SALUKI, OR PERSIAN GAZELLE HOUND.

EARS.—Long and covered with long silky hair hanging close to the skull, and mobile.
EYES.—Dark to hazel and bright, large and oval, but not prominent.
TEETH.—Strong and level.
NECK.—Long, supple, and well muscled.
CHEST.—Deep and moderately narrow.
FOREQUARTERS.—Shoulders sloping and set well back, well muscled without being coarse.
FORELEGS.—Straight and long from the elbow to the knee.
HINDQUARTERS.—Strong, hip bones set wide apart, and stifle moderately bent, hocks low to the ground, showing galloping and jumping power.
LOIN AND BACK.—Back fairly broad, muscles slightly arched over the loin.
FEET.—Of moderate length, toes long, and well arched, not splayed out, but at the same time not cat-footed ; the whole being strong and supple, and well feathered between the toes.
TAIL.—Long, set on low, and carried naturally in a curve, well feathered on the underside with long silky hair, not bushy.
COAT.—Smooth and of a soft silky texture, slight feather on the legs, feather at the back of the thighs, and sometimes with slight woolly feather on thigh and shoulders.
COLOURS.—White, cream, fawn, golden, red, grizzle-and-tan, tricolour (white, black, and tan), and black-and-tan.
GENERAL APPEARANCE.—The whole appearance of this breed should give an impression of grace and symmetry and of great speed and endurance coupled with strength and activity to enable it to kill gazelle or other quarry over deep sand or rocky mountain. The expression should be dignified and gentle, with deep, faithful, far-seeing eyes. Dogs should average in height from 23 to 28in., and the bitches may be considerably smaller, this being very typical of the breed.
THE SMOOTH VARIETY.—In this variety the points should be the same with the exception of the coat, which has no feathering.

From this description it will be seen that there are two varieties of Saluki, the rough-coated and the perfectly smooth-coated dogs. The former develop a rough coat on the pendulous ears and tail only, the remainder of the dog being comparatively smooth, whilst the smooth-coated differ little from the English Greyhound in coat and architecture. These dogs are used more in the deserts and lower-lying and warmer parts of Persia and Arabia, and the rough-coats more in the mountainous parts.

Youatt says of their sporting proclivities that :—

In his native country he is not only used for hunting the hare, but the antelope, the wild ass, and even boar. The antelope is speedier than the Greyhound, therefore the hawk is given to him as an ally. . . . The chase however in which the Persians chiefly delight, and for which these Greyhounds are mostly valued, is that of the ghookham or wild ass, which inhabits the mountainous districts of Persia.

THE AFGHAN HOUND

Differs from the Saluki and Sloughi mostly in coat, this variety possessing a heavy coat on the head, which assumes the form of a hood, almost like the Irish Water Spaniel, and a mass of coat on the body, which hangs down much in the form of the coat of the llama, whilst the face and legs are smooth coated, together with a streak of short hair down the centre of the back.

The Afghan Hound is a great favourite with the sirdars of the Royal Barukhzy family, so much so that they are often called " Barukhzy " Hounds. They are mostly indigenous to Balkh, the north-eastern provinces around, and the Afghan Hound is locally believed to be one of the dogs that Noah collected in his ark.

AFGHAN HOUND.

Count Henri de Bylandt, in his book, "Les Races de Chiens," gives the points of the Afghan Hound, with an illustration by Wardle. His description is as follows:—

GENERAL APPEARANCE.—A dog with a great resemblance to the Persian Greyhound, but of a more powerful build.

HEAD.—Long and fine, with an intelligent expression.

EYES.—Soft and intelligent.

NOSE.—Black, large, and pointed.

EARS.—Large, long, and falling; well trimmed with long hair.

BODY.—Arched neck, sloping shoulders, deep chest, tucked-up belly, and well-developed hindquarters.

FEET.—Straight and fine.

LEGS.—Long.

TAIL.—Carried high, and slightly fringed.

HAIR.—Fine, dense, and soft.

COLOUR.—Black, specked with clear fawn.

HEIGHT AT WITHERS.—About 27½in.

WEIGHT.—About 66lb.

ORIGINATED.—In Afghanistan.

One of the earliest and most typical hounds was Zardin, owned and imported by Mr. Banff. A few others were imported mostly by officers after the war in Afghanistan, since which odd specimens have made their appearance, but the existence of quarantine regulations have prevented importations on any large scale. Still the breed has now a goodish following in this country, and a club is formed, but I have always thought a better plan than the establishment of another club for this other example of the Eastern Greyhound would have been for the existing Saluki or Gazelle Hound Club to take in the kindred Afghan Hound and call it "The Eastern Greyhound Club." The three breeds come from contiguous countries, and have much in common, and if there is any virtue in union, which there is, this incorporation of the Afghan Hound by the Saluki Club would largely strengthen it and bring more "grist to the mill," for its field of operations must be, to a great extent, limited at the present time.

CHAPTER LXIV.

Foreign Dogs.

The Kennel Club group under this heading several breeds of Foreign Dogs other than those which, by long sojourn in England and the extensive breeding and propagation to which they have been subject in this country, have become nationalised, as it were, and recognised as British. The breeds relegated to the Foreign Dog group, however, by no means exhaust the number of Foreign Dogs, whose names are legion, nor even those familiar to the English show bench.

ESKIMO.

It is the latter only that I shall endeavour in this chapter to touch upon and give an outline of, for to treat upon the whole of the well-known Foreign Dogs would occupy a volume in itself, and a very interesting one, too.

The Elkhound and the Esquimaux are breeds which we have often seen exhibited in England, almost since the advent of shows. They come from the most northern parts of Europe and Asia, and have much in common, the Elkhound, which is used in Norway for herding and hunting deer, being the larger, and the Esquimaux (Eskimo) the smaller of the two. They both possess the long-pointed nose, prick ears, curled tail, and dense fur-like coat peculiar to all the dogs of the Arctic regions and extreme northern latitudes, where they are used for all purposes—hunting, drawing sledges, and every other requirement, simply because there are no other breeds available in these snowy regions. They vary in colour; the Elkhound is mostly grey sable, white being the preponderating colour of the Esquimaux.

By whatever means they have been procured, it is a fact that periodically specimens of the dogs of Tibet have been imported to this country, some of which have found their way on to the show bench. Following the expeditionary British Force which some years ago went out to Lhassa, owing to the trouble caused by the Lama of Tibet, there appeared a very fine specimen of Tibetan Mastiff at the Kennel Club's Show at the Crystal Palace. But, despite the fact that no white is supposed to have previously set foot within the sacred precincts of the Tibetan capital, many Lhassa Terriers have been imported to England. The Tibet Mastiff is a most imposing specimen of the canine species, and a dog full of character. He is much on the lines of a black Newfoundland in size, build, colour, and coat, but with a heavier head, which in chiselling and expression is more like that of an enlarged Chow Chow. It is said that these dogs are very savage, and they look it, but why they are called Mastiff is difficult to understand, as they have absolutely no resemblance

LHASSA TERRIER.

to the English Mastiff at any rate. From the Tibet Mastiff to the Lhassa Terrier and Tibet Spaniel is a big descent, the two latter being as lacking in character as the first-named is full of it. The Lhassa Terrier is a shortish-faced, short-legged, rather long-bodied, shaggy-coated dog of some 14lb. to 18lb. weight, much resembling the Maltese in type. The Tibet Spaniel is somewhat larger, and very similar in type, but has more of the Skye Terrier about him than Spaniel. Their colours are black-and white, grey-and-white, black, etc. What the correct type of these dogs should be it is difficult to say.

Several varieties of Asiatic Greyhounds have from time to time made their appearance on the English show bench. They are built much on the lines of the English Greyhound.

China, besides the Pekingese, the Chow Chow, and Pug, gives us the hairless crested dog, an animal of from 15lb. to 20lb. weight, devoid of hair all over his body, with a tuft of bristly hairs on his forehead. They are mostly blue in colour. He, of course, emanates from Southern China, and from other tropical countries, Mexico and Africa, we get a similar type of dog. Mexico

TIBET MASTIFF.

MISS ROSINA CASSELLI AND HER TEAM OF PERFORMING CHIHUAHUAS.

Photo by W. P. Dando, F.Z.S., Regent's Park.

THE AUSTRALIAN DINGO.

also gives us an interesting Toy Terrier in the Chihuahua (pronounced " Shee-wah-wah "), called after a northern province of Mexico, where the breed abounds, and where it is said that at one time it ran wild in the woods, and is almost as clever as the squirrel in running up trees. It is a very game and intelligent dog, much on the lines of our Toy Bull-terrier, but smaller, good Chihuahuas weighing from 3½lb. to 6½lb. only.

Occasional specimens of the Dingo or Australian wild dog have been exhibited in England from time to time, and these dogs seem to carry us back to very primitive times, being in all likelihood a replica of the original of the canine species. They are much on the lines of a smooth-haired English Sheepdog, except that they are a little more wolf-like and have prick ears.

On rare occasions a Kortals Griffon has been exhibited in England it is a German sporting dog, much on the lines of an English Pointer, but broken-haired and docked. The colour of these dogs is mostly liver-flecked. They look a very rational sort of dog, cut out for both speed and endurance. From Belgium, besides the Schipperke and Griffon Bruxellois, there is the Papillon, a long-coated Toy Dog, after the style of a Pomeranian, but flatter in coat and mostly tricolour, although there are blues, greys, and other colours. They are sometimes called the Butterfly dog, because their bat-like ears and markings are said to resemble a butterfly in full flight. They vary in size from 3lb. or 4lb. to 6lb. or 7lb. They are now becoming very popular, so a special chapter has been written for them. And, of course, there is the Belgian Sheepdog, a semi-smooth-haired cur, much on the lines of the English Smooth Sheepdog.

France has a host of hunting Hounds, but few have ever found their way into England besides the Bassethound. Some of the Vendee Hounds are very fine, but the Griffon Courant Francais, a rough-haired Hound, almost a facsimile of our Otterhound, would appeal most to English sportsmen probably. I once saw one exhibited in England, and it is more than probable that our Otterhound originated from France.

On very rare occasions has a Boston Terrier made its appearance on the English show bench, although this dog is as popular and plentiful at American Shows as are our Fox-terriers. He is of American manufacture, and said to have been originally bred from an English Bull-terrier and Bulldog cross. They are bred wonderfully true to type, a dog somewhat on the lines of the French Bulldog, varying from 12lb. to 27lb. in weight, short and compact in body, with straight fronts, well balanced in frame, and a shortish flat head, square muzzle, broad white blaze up face, and screw tail. Their ears are cropped. Some of the cracks of this breed fetch enormous prices in America.

The Pyrenean Sheepdog is now and then exhibited in England, and is a rather imposing breed, about the size and substance of a small, snipy St. Bernard, of which breed they show unmistakable descent in their character. Indeed, one might easily suppose them to be the result of a cross between the St. Bernard and the Old English Sheepdog, many of them resembling the latter in colour, and a great deal in character also. With this exception all the Continental sheepdogs—the French, Belgian, Dutch, and German (the last-named being claimed by France as their Alsatian sheepdog, where it originated)—are very much on the lines of the English smooth-haired Collie, but with prick ears, and they are mostly red-fawn and black in colour. The Dobermann Pinscher is a police dog in Germany. It is a smooth-coated, black-and-tan dog on smooth sheepdog lines, but both cropped and docked. They are very intelligent and of tireless activity, now very popular in America. The Affenpinscher is a vivacious German Toy dog, black-and-tan in colour, and also cropped and docked. A breed of which there have been some importations to England is the Wolfspitz or Keeshonden, known here as the Dutch Barge Dog. They are very like large Pomeranians. There are many other foreign breeds.

PYRENEAN SHEEPDOG.

The Kennel Club Rules.

Copyright. [Entered at Stationers' Hall.]

(*Published by permission of the Kennel Club.*)

---

1. DEFINITIONS.—In these Rules and in any Regulations for the time being in force, unless the contrary intention appears—
   - (a) Words importing the male sex shall include the female.
   - (b) Words in the singular shall include the plural, and words in the plural shall include the singular.
   - (c) The word month shall mean a calendar month.
   - (d) The Committee means a duly constituted meeting of the Committee of the Kennel Club, and if and so far as any powers of the Committee have been delegated includes the delegated authority
   - (e) "Delegated authority" means a duly constituted meeting of a Sub-Committee of the Committee of the Kennel Club or other body to whom powers have been delegated by the Committee of the Kennel Club.
   - (f) A Show or a Dog Show means a Show at which Dogs are exhibited for competition or awards to which the public are admitted
   - (g) A Show Committee means the Committee or other authority duly authorised to manage a Show.
   - (h) Recognised Shows are those held—
     - (1) Under Kennel Club Rules, or other Regulations of the Committee.
     - (2) Under sanction of an authority abroad recognised by the Kennel Club.
     - (3) As Hound Shows under an authority recognised by the Kennel Club.
     - (4) In conjunction with Agricultural or Horticultural Shows, Fetes, or other entertainments for which exemption has been granted by the Committee.
   - (i) Unrecognised Shows are all other Shows.
   - (j) A Hound Show is a Show consisting exclusively of all or any of the following breeds:—Foxhounds, Staghounds, Otterhounds, Bloodhounds, Harriers, Basset Hounds and Beagles.
   - (k) A Puppy.—A Puppy for the purposes of exhibition (except at Sanction Shows) is a Dog of six and not exceeding twelve months of age dating from and inclusive of the day of its birth.
   - (l) A Litter.—A Litter consists of one or more puppies born at the same parturition.
   - (m) The Breeder of any dog is—
     - (1) The owner of the dam at the time of whelping; or
     - (2) The person to whom the dam was lent for breeding purposes, if a declaration of the loan has been registered with the Kennel Club prior to the birth of the litter.
   - (n) A Prize includes a money prize or prize of any description won in a Class, other than a Special Prize.
   - (o) A Challenge Certificate is a Certificate granted by the Kennel Club for offer of award at a Championship Show held in accordance with the Regulations governing the issue of Challenge Certificates.

2. DELEGATION OF POWERS OF THE COMMITTEE OF THE KENNEL CLUB.—The Committee may delegate all or any of their powers under these Rules to any Sub-Committee composed of Members of the Club or with the sanction of a General Meeting of the Club to any other body.

But the Committee shall not delegate to any Sub-Committee or to any other body the power to disqualify or suspend any person under Rules 16 or 17, except it be subject to a right of appeal to the Committee.

3. POWER OF THE COMMITTEE TO MAKE REGULATIONS.—The Committee shall have power from time to time to make, amend, or cancel Regulations for the following purposes :—

(a) Regulations for classification of the breeds and varieties of breeds recognised by the Kennel Club.
(b) Regulations for the Registration of Dogs, Names, Prefixes, Affixes, Pedigrees, and other registrations under Rule 7.
(c) Regulations for the license or sanction of Shows and the conditions applicable thereto.
(d) Regulations as to the preparation of dogs for exhibition.
(e) Regulations with regard to entries in the Kennel Club Stud Book.
(f) Regulations governing the issue of Challenge Certificates.
(g) Regulations for the registration and maintenance of title of Registered Associations, Clubs, and Societies.
(h) Regulations for the Definition of Classes at Shows.

4. RECOGNISED SHOWS.—Recognised Shows under Kennel Club Rules or other Regulations of the Committee are those held under licence or sanction granted by the Committee or matches permitted by the Committee.

Shows held under licence consist of :—

(a) Open Shows at which there is no restriction as to exhibitors making entries in such classes as are provided.
(b) Championship Shows which are Open Shows at which Kennel Club Challenge Certificates are offered.
(c) Shows limited to members of clubs or societies or to exhibitors within specified areas or otherwise, hereinafter referred to as Limited Shows.

5. CHAMPIONSHIPS.—A dog shall not obtain a Challenge Certificate unless it has won a prize in a class confined to its recognised breed or variety and open to all exhibitors at the Show in question.

If the Judge is not clearly of opinion the dog is worthy of the title of Champion he must withhold the Challenge Certificate and mark his judging book accordingly.

If there is more than one dog at a Show which, in the Judge's opinion, merits the award of a Challenge Certificate, it is permitted to give a Reserve Award.

The title of Champion shall attach to a dog awarded three Challenge Certificates under three different Judges, except in the case of Pointers, Setters, Sporting Spaniels, and Retrievers, when a dog must also have gained a prize or certificate of merit at a Field Trial recognised by the Kennel Club, or in lieu of such prize or certificate of merit after a dog has gained two or more Challenge Certificates, a Certificate that he has qualified for the title given at the discretion of a Judge at a recognised Field Trial, if he is of opinion that it has shown the necessary working qualifications of its breed, including in the case of Spaniels retrieving, although the Judge may not consider the dog sufficiently well broken to be worthy of a Certificate of Merit.

6. PERMISSION TO HOLD SHOWS.—The Committee shall have power to grant, withhold, or cancel permission for the holding of any Show in accordance with the Regulations for the time being in force relating to the same.

7. REGISTRATIONS.—The following registrations must be made at the Kennel Club at the times stated, on forms supplied for the purpose, and in accordance with the conditions thereon. All persons making any registration shall be considered as thereby agreeing to be bound by the Kennel Club Rules and Regulations, including, particularly, the provisions of Kennel Club Rules 16 and 17—

    (*a*) The name, etc., of a dog prior to its being first exhibited, whether for competition or not.

        Hounds from a pack or cry of beagles if exhibited at a Show must first be registered at the Kennel Club, and the name of their pack or owner must be given as part of the registered name, unless they are exempted from registration under sub-rule (*k*).

        Greyhounds already registered in the name of the exhibitor, under National Coursing Rules, must be registered at the Kennel Club under the same name and the letters " G.S.B." added afterwards.

    (*b*) Any change of the registered name of a dog prior to exhibition under its new name.

    (*c*) The last transfer of ownership of a registered dog prior to exhibition by its new owner.

    (*d*) Re-registration in rectification of any error in a previous registration if a *bona fide* mistake or misrepresentation has been made or it is proved that fraud has been committed. No re-registration to another breed or variety can be allowed without the consent of the Committee.

    (*e*) The loan of a bitch for breeding purposes.

    (*f*) A name assumed by an individual for exhibition and breeding purposes.

    (*g*) The Prefix or Affix of an individual or a partnership.

    (*h*) The Title of an Association, Club, or Society.

The Committee may decline an application for any registration or cancel any registration already made.

Dogs are exempt from registration in the following cases :—

    (*i*) (1) Dogs exhibited exclusively in Classes specially exempted by the Committee.

        (2) Classes for dogs owned by children under sixteen years of age.

        (3) Exemption Classes at Agricultural and Horticultural Shows, Fetes, and the like, for which exemption has been granted.

    (*j*) Entries in Litter Classes.

    (*k*) Hounds belonging to recognised Packs.

    (*l*) Hounds when exhibited at a recognised Hound Show.

    (*m*) Dogs in Special Classes sanctioned by the Committee.

8. SHOWS :—

    (*a*) ENTRIES AND REMOVALS.—A dog, when entered for a Show, must be solely and unconditionally the property of the exhibitor, and, except when specifically exempted, must be registered at the Kennel Club in his name, but it may be sold with its engagements and exhibited in its new owner's name subject to the transfer being registered previous to the Show with a declaration that the new owner undertakes to abide by the rules and conditions on the original entry form of the Show, except as regards the price at which it may be sold, and the right of the new owner to withdraw from classes defined by price, provided written intimation to this effect is given to the Show Secretary prior to the day of the Show.

Separate entry forms must be filled up for the exhibit of each person and must be signed by the exhibitor or his authorised agent in accordance with the provisions specified thereon.

No official may fill up any entry form except his own, or alter any entry form after the entry has been made.

Entries for a Show must close at time fixed by the Show Regulations, and in case of any violation of this Rule the Secretary or Manager of the Show or both may be dealt with under Rule 17.

Exhibits at unrecognised Shows thereupon become disqualified for entry at any Shows held under permission of the Committee.

A Show Committee may reserve the right to refuse, on reasonable grounds, any entry.

If a Show exceeds one day puppies may be finally removed at the hour of closing on the first day or on any subsequent day within half an hour prior to the opening or at the closing of the Show. An Order for this purpose must be obtained from the Secretary of the Show.

(b) ESTIMATING NUMBER OF PRIZES WON.—All wins previous to the midnight preceding the day specified in the Schedule for closing entries shall be counted when entering for any class.

Equal awards shall count as a win for each dog so placed.

(c) WITHDRAWAL FROM COMPETITION.—A dog, after admission to a Show, may not be withdrawn from competition without the written consent of the Show Committee or Secretary, except when the Judge announced in the Schedule is changed, in which case only the dog may be withdrawn before the commencement of the judging of the breed or variety of the breed, and may be removed from the Show by the owner or his accredited agent. Any dog not shown in all the classes in which it is entered may be disqualified from winning any prize at the Show.

(d) WEIGHING OF DOGS.—Every dog entered in a class limited by weight must be weighed in the presence of the Judge or of a Steward, or other official delegated by the Judge immediately before competition in any such class and in every subsequent class in which there is a change in the weight limit.

(e) JUDGE'S DECISION.—A Judge's decision shall be final, except in a case of fraud or misrepresentation or where a mistake has been made *bona fide* by the Judge. Subject to these exceptions his decision shall be deemed to be final at the termination of his judging the class.

A Judge shall be empowered to withhold any Prize or Special Prize, if, in his opinion, there is lack of sufficient merit, but he must mark on his judging slips that the award has been so withheld. When a Judge withholds a Third Prize for want of merit, the Reserve Award must also be withheld. Subject to Rule 13 the Judge is not entitled to withhold a prize for any other reason, but he must not withhold any prize in Sweepstakes Classes.

Any alteration made by a Judge must be initialled by him, and where such alteration is made the slips must bear the time and date of making such alterations endorsed upon his judging book, slips, letter, or other document.

9. CLASSIFICATION AND PRIZES.—The following are the definitions of certain Classes :—

AN OPEN CLASS, when confined to a breed, or to a variety of a breed, classified as such by the Kennel Club, is one in which all dogs of that breed or variety may compete.

A LIMIT CLASS is similar to an Open Class, save that no dog can compete which has won more than six First Prizes in Open and Limit Classes at Shows where Challenge Certificates were offered for the breed.

A GRADUATE CLASS is one for dogs that have not won more than three First Prizes confined to the breed of the value of £2.

A JUNIOR CLASS is one for dogs of six and under eighteen months of age on the first day of the Show.

A NOVICE CLASS is one in which no dog can compete which has won a First Prize in any Class (other than Puppy, Maiden, Local, Members or District), or a Challenge Certificate at an Open Show. But in a Novice Class confined to locality or district or to members, no dog can compete that has won a First Prize in any Class, other than Puppy or Maiden, at any Show whatever.

A MAIDEN CLASS is one for dogs who have never won a prize in any Class at an *Open* Show, but in a Maiden Class at a Limited Show no dog can compete that has won any prize at any Show.

The words " Novice " and " Maiden " must not be used as the name, or part of the name, in connection with any other Classes other than defined above, but they may be used in connection with Local and Members' Classes.

Dogs which have won the title of Champion under American Kennel Club Rules are not eligible for entry in a Novice or Maiden Class at a Championship or Open Show.

A PUPPY CLASS is one for dogs of six and not exceeding twelve months of age on the first day of the Show. Puppies over three months and under six months are ineligible at any Show.

A LITTER CLASS is one for puppies of one and the same litter (being not less than two in number) under three months of age on the first day of the Show. Not more than one entry can be made from one litter in the same Class.

A SWEEPSTAKE CLASS is one in which the total entry fees, subject to a deduction (if any) of not more than ten per cent. are given as the prize money, in such proportion as the Committee of the particular Show may determine.

A FIELD TRIAL CLASS is one confined to dogs that have won Prizes or Certificates of Merit in actual competition at a recognised Field Trial.

Subject to the above provisions, and any Regulations made under Rule 3, section (*h*), Show Committees may offer such Prizes and make such classification and definitions thereof as they think fit, except that—

(*a*) All Classes advertised in the Schedule of a Show must be clearly defined in the Schedule.

(*b*) When Classes or Prizes are guaranteed the names of the guarantors must be stated in the Schedule and Catalogue under such Class, Prize, or Breed.

(*c*) No Class or Prize may be offered for progeny sired by a specified dog (Specialist Club Stakes excepted), and no Prize of free service of any dog is permitted.

(*d*) No puppy shall be eligible to compete in any Class or for any Prize, Special Prize or Award, competition for which is limited to exhibits not exceeding a certain stated weight or height unless the same be confined to puppies only, but a puppy shall be eligible to compete in any Class or in any competition which is limited to exhibits exceeding a certain stated weight or height and is otherwise eligible.

(*e*) No dog shall be eligible to compete for a Special Prize (open to more than one Breed or Variety) which has been beaten in its Breed, Breed Class or Classes by another of either sex, eligible to compete for that Special Prize.

(*f*) The words Grand, Champion, or Challenge must not be used in the designation of any class or prize for which an entrance fee is charged and for which entry has to be made prior to the day of the Show.

A Show other than a Championship Show may give Sweepstakes Classes, but the fact that such Classes are offered must be prominently stated on the front page of the Schedule, and only Classes so designated in the Schedule can be offered or given at such Show.

No Classes at any Show can be amalgamated or cancelled, but a Show may be abandoned by permission of the Committee.

10. VETERINARY EXAMINATIONS.—At least one qualified Veterinary Surgeon, or some person competent to act as a substitute, if specially permitted by the Committee, must be appointed to a Show other than a Sanction Show or Match. No dog suffering from an infectious or contagious disease shall be allowed to enter or remain in a Show. The Veterinary Surgeon, or authorised substitute, shall:—

(a) Examine each dog at the entrance of the Show, and during the Show if required, and if in his opinion the dog is not fit to enter or remain in the Show he shall give his opinion in writing, stating his reasons, signed and lodged with the Secretary, as soon as possible.

(b) Examine any dog on the day it is objected to on the ground of being blind, deaf, or suffering from contagious or infectious disease, or that it has been prepared for exhibition in contravention of the Regulations made by the Committee, and give his opinion in writing, signed to the Secretary, before the Show closes. No such dog may leave the Show before such examination.

11. SALES AT SHOWS.—Any person claiming to purchase a dog exhibited at any Show must, at the time of claiming, lodge a sum at least equal to twenty per cent., and if required the whole amount of the price of the dog at the Secretary's Office in the Show, and obtain a receipt for the same. Such receipt must bear, on its face, the time the claim was made, and the dog must then be sold in accordance with the regulations of the particular Show and the Kennel Club Rules, and the remainder of the purchase money must be paid to the Secretary before the removal of the dog from the Show, or the deposit may be forfeited, in which event any such deposit must be paid over to the owner of the dog, *less* the commission (if any), which the Show is entitled to charge under their regulations on the sum deposited. Any sums deposited by anyone except the eventual purchaser of the dog, or those forfeited as before provided for, must be returned to the respective claimants, and the Committee of a Show shall see that all such deposits must be returned, and all purchase money received for a dog, sold at their Show, *less* commission (if any), must be paid to the late owner within seven days from the close of the Show.

When any dog is sold, the Secretary of a Show must see that a "Sold" card is placed over its bench as soon as possible after the completion of the sale.

A definite time shall be fixed, and announced in the Show Schedule, for the closing of applications to purchase dogs catalogued for sale. If no applications are received by this hour the first subsequent application shall be considered binding. But if more than one such application be received before the hour fixed by the Show Committee the exhibit shall be sold by the Show Committee, either by auction or by tender, within one hour of the definite time fixed for the closing of applications. The total commission, in any event, payable to the Show Committee must not exceed ten per cent. of the price paid for the exhibit. Any commission paid on the sale of a dog shall be charged to the seller.

12. OBJECTIONS.—An objection to a dog may be made by any person, except by one who is under a term of suspension by the Kennel Club.

The objection must be in writing and delivered to the Secretary at his office in the Show, or at his address as advertised in the Schedule. If the objection is made by persons other than the Show Committee or the Committee, the sum of 10s. must be deposited at the same time, which shall be returned unless the Committee deem the objection frivolous, in which case it shall be forfeited.

Where an objection is made against more than one dog a separate deposit must be lodged in the case of each dog. In the case of an objection to a Pack, Couple, Team, Brace, or Litter, one deposit only to be lodged.

The times at which an objection must be lodged are :—
  (a) If on the ground of incorrect weight—at the time of weighing, which may, in the first instance, be made verbally to the Judge (who shall make note thereof), but which must, without delay, be followed by the formal objection as above.
  (b) If on the ground of being improperly tampered with, blind, deaf, or suffering from any form of contagious or infectious disease, before the Show closes.
  (c) If on any other ground—within **twenty-one** days from the last day of the Show.

An objection shall be dealt with at a Show Committee Meeting, if possible, within fourteen days, and in no case later than twenty-eight days, of its being lodged.

A copy of the objection shall be despatched by the Secretary, within twenty-four hours of the objection being lodged, to the registered owner of the dog at his address given on the entry form, and reasonable notice of the meeting shall be sent to any persons concerned.

The decision of the Show Committee shall be communicated to parties concerned within forty-eight hours.

No objection shall be invalidated solely on the ground that any notice has not been duly given, or that any meeting has not been duly held under this Rule.

An appeal may be made to the Committee, if lodged within fourteen days of the decision.

13. DISQUALIFICATION AND FORFEIT OF PRIZES.—A dog shall be disqualified for competition :—
  (1) By the Committee, direct, or
  (2) By the Show Committee on objection, subject to appeal to the Committee, if it is proved to be—
    (a) Exhibited at an unrecognised Show.
    (b) Registered in the name of and owned by a person suspended for discreditable conduct as from the date of the charge being lodged at the Kennel Club and for the period of such suspension. (*See* Rule 17.)
    (c) Exhibited by a person disqualified or suspended under Rule 16 or 17.
    (d) Entered after the date fixed for the closing of entries.
    (e) Led into the ring or worked at a Field Trial or taken charge of at a Show or Field Trial by a person suspended under Rule 16 or 17.
    (f) Totally blind.
    (g) Totally deaf.
    (h) Castrated.
    (i) Spayed.
    (j) Prepared for exhibition in contravention of Regulations.
    (k) Suffering from an infectious or contagious disease.
    (l) Entered in a manner not complying with the classification in the Schedule.

(*m*) Exhibited for competition by a Judge of the Show.
(*n*) Bred by the judge of the breed at the Show within 12 months.
(*o*) Sold to the exhibitor by the judge of the breed at the Show within 12 months.
(*p*) Not duly registered in the Kennel Club Books before exhibition.
(*q*) Not duly transferred in the Kennel Club Books, before exhibition, where a change of ownership of a registered dog has taken place.
(*r*) Entered at a Show not in accordance with the Kennel Club Rules.
(*s*) Imported in contravention of any Regulations of the Ministry of Agriculture and Fisheries for the time being in force.
(*t*) The progeny resulting from the artificial fertilisation of a bitch, unless notification was sent to the Secretary of the Kennel Club at the time of the performance of the operation, together with a letter from the owner of the bitch stating that he had knowledge of the act, and a Certificate from a Veterinary Surgeon present at the operation.

If a dog is entered in a Class for which he is ineligible, and is not withdrawn from competition before the judging of the Class in question is begun, the dog shall be disqualified, but all such cases must be reported by the Show Secretary to the Kennel Club, and the exhibitor may be fined at the discretion of the Committee and, in addition to such penalty, the exhibitor is liable to be dealt with under Rule 17.

The owner of a dog disqualified for any of the above reasons is liable to forfeiture of all entry fees and prize money made in respect of or won by such dog at the Show or Shows in question.

The Committee shall have power to annul or remit all or any part of any disqualification under this Rule; also to inflict fines not exceeding Five Shillings, in lieu of disqualification, upon exhibitors, who shall have made errors in the entry forms, which are, in the opinion of the Committee, of a technical or clerical character.

14. **PAYMENT AND DELIVERY OF PRIZES.**—All prizes offered and won outright must be paid or delivered not earlier than twenty-one days, and not later than thirty-one days, from the close of a Show, except as otherwise provided in the Regulations. Where any money prize is offered in the Schedule it must be paid in full, without deduction except in cases where amounts are legally due to a Show Executive. Where Class Prizes are offered in kind, the value of same shall be stated in the Schedule.

Prizes awarded to dogs objected to must not be paid or delivered until the objection has been finally determined, and in the case of an appeal to, or any objection by the Committee, not until permission is granted by the Committee.

In the case of violation of this Rule the persons signing the application form upon which the licence or permission for the Show was granted shall be held primarily responsible, and may be dealt with under Rule 17. When Special Prizes are offered by a Specialist Club the Executive of such Club will be held primarily responsible.

15. **ORDER OF MERIT WHEN DOGS ARE DISQUALIFIED.**—If a prize winner be disqualified, the dogs next in consecutive order of merit, if so placed by the Judge, and awarded not less than Reserve, shall be moved into the higher places in the Prize List, and such placings shall thereupon become the awards.

16. **DISQUALIFICATION OF PERSONS OFFICIATING, ETC., AT UNRECOGNISED SHOWS.**—Any person promoting, exhibiting, judging, or in any way officiating, at an unrecognised Show shall at the discretion of the Committee be disqualified from judging, competing, winning a prize, making an objection, or taking any part at a Show or Field Trials held under the permission of the Committee.

All dogs exhibited at any such Show shall be disqualified from competition at any recognised Show.

Such disqualification shall also apply to all dogs registered in the name of, or owned by, any person disqualified under this Rule.

The Committee shall have power to remove any disqualification under this Rule.

17. SUSPENSION FOR DISCREDITABLE CONDUCT, ETC., OR DEFAULT.—The Committee shall have power to enquire into and deal with any charge which may be made against any person (whether he has made any registration at the Kennel Club or not) :—

(a) For any act or conduct in regard to a dog or any matter connected with, arising out of, or relating to, a Dog Show or these Rules or any Regulations made under same which, in the opinion of the Committee, is discreditable or injurious to those interested in canine matters.

(b) For any default or omission in regard to any matter connected with or arising out of or relating to a Dog Show, or these Rules, or any Regulations made thereunder.

The complaint may be made by the Secretary of the Club on behalf of the Committee or Show Committee, or by any person who is not suspended or disqualified. The complaint, if made by an individual, must be accompanied by a deposit of £2 (except where the complaint is against guarantors or other promoters of a Show for non-payment of a prize), which may be wholly or partly awarded, if the complaint be dismissed, to the person complained of or otherwise dealt with as the Committee shall think fit.

The Committee, if any charge is proved to their satisfaction, shall have power :—

(1) To suspend the person charged from taking part in or having any connection with or attending any Show or Field Trial.

(2) To disqualify from competition all dogs owned by him or registered in his name at the date when the charge was lodged.

(3) To disqualify him from judging at or taking any part in the management of a Show or Field Trial.

The penalties above provided may be for life or such shorter period as the Committee shall fix, and the Committee shall have power from time to time to remove or modify any suspension or disqualification.

Any persons suspended shall, during the period of such suspension, be not eligible to become or remain a member of any club or society registered at or affiliated with the Kennel Club. If any person suspended under this Rule shall attend any Show the Committee shall have power to increase the period of suspension and disqualification.

The Committee shall have power in any case under this Rule to publish the account of the same, together with the proceedings in respect thereto, in the official organ of the Kennel Club—viz., THE KENNEL GAZETTE, together with the name, description, and address, and, further, to publish the names of such disqualified or suspended persons respectively under Clauses (a) and (b) of this Rule, in two separate "Black Lists," which they shall have power to forward to any person or persons concerned, as they may think fit.

Any person who shall employ any person suspended or disqualified under this Rule in any capacity in connection with dogs will, if it is proved to the satisfaction of the Committee that he knew of such suspension or disqualification, be liable to be dealt with as an offender within the meaning of the Rule.

18. PENALTY FOR INFRINGEMENT OF KENNEL CLUB RULES BY THE COMMITTEES OR MANAGERS OF SHOWS.—The Committee shall have power to inflict a fine not exceeding £5 on the Committee, Secretary and/or Manager of a Show who may have broken Kennel Club Rules and Regulations in the conduct of the Show. In the case of non-payment of any such fine the guarantors may be held responsible.

19. FEES.—The following fees shall be payable :—

	s.	d.
Registration	2	6
Re-registration	2	6
Inquiry	2	0
Stud Book Entry	5	0
Transfer	5	0
Loan of Bitch	5	0
Cancellation of Name	10	0
Change of Name	20	0
Pedigrees—Three Generations	5	0
„ Five Generations	21	0
„ Export	10	0
List of Wins (entered in Stud Book)	10	0
Registration of Prefix	10	6
Prefix Maintenance Fee	21	0
	10	6

Holders of Prefixes paying 10s. 6d. per annum Maintenance Fee may compound on the payment of £5 5s.

	s.	d.
Prefix Maintenance Fee (for Prefixes granted prior to 1919)	5	0

Holders of Prefixes paying 5s. per annum Maintenance Fee may compound on the payment of £3 3s.

	s.	d.
Assumed Name	42	0
Registration of Title	21	0
Maintenance of Title	5	0

For Shows held under Kennel Club Rules :—

(a) Payable on application—

	s.	d.
For a Licence for a Show	15	0

(b) Payable immediately after the entries close—

	s.	d.
If the entries exceed 150 and not 250	20	0
If the entries exceed 250 and not 500	55	0
For every complete 100 entries over 500	20	0
Permission to hold Show under Kennel Club sanction	7	6
Permission to hold Matches under Kennel Club Regulations	5	0

20. THE COMMITTEE THE FINAL COURT OF APPEAL.—The Committee shall be the final Court of Appeal or Umpire in all questions or disputes of any kind whatsoever (except where such powers are delegated by the Committee) arising out of any Show held by permission of the Committee. A person attending or entering a dog for such Show shall by such act be deemed to have agreed with the Committee to refer any such question or dispute to the Committee under the provisions of the Arbitration Act, 1889, or any statutory modification thereof.

21. CONTROL OF FIELD TRIALS.—Nothing in these Rules shall affect Field Trials, which shall be governed by Kennel Club Field Trial Rules.

22. ALTERATION OF KENNEL CLUB RULES.—These Rules, which shall be known as the Kennel Club Rules, are to remain in force unless and until altered or amended by a Resolution at a General Meeting of the Club, notice to propose which has been given as required by the Constitution and Rules of the Club.

Regulations for Classification and Registration.

1. BREEDS DEFINED.—The following are the breeds of dogs recognised by the Kennel Club for the purpose of separate Registration and Stud Book entries :—

SPORTING BREEDS.
Afghan Hounds.
Basset Hounds.
Beagles.
Bloodhounds.
Borzois.
Dachshunds.
Deerhounds.
Elkhounds.
Foxhounds.
Greyhounds.
Harriers.
Irish Wolfhounds.
Otterhounds.
Salukis.
Whippets.

GUNDOGS.
English Setters.
Gordon Setters.
Irish Setters.
Pointers.
Retrievers.
Spaniels.

TERRIERS.
Airedale Terriers.
Bedlington Terriers.
Border Terriers.
Bull Terriers.
Cairn Terriers.
Dandie Dinmont Terriers.
Fox Terriers.
Irish Terriers.
Kerry Blue Terriers.
Manchester Terriers.
Scottish Terriers.
Sealyham Terriers.
Skye Terriers.
Welsh Terriers.
West Highland White Terriers.

NON-SPORTING BREEDS.
Alsatian Wolfdogs.
Bulldogs.
Chow Chows.
Collies.
Dalmatians.
French Bulldogs.
Great Danes.
Mastiffs.
Newfoundlands.
Old English Sheepdogs.
Poodles.
St. Bernards.
Samoyeds.
Schipperkes.
Shetland Sheepdogs.

TOY DOGS.
Black-and-tan Terriers (Miniature).
Griffons Bruxellois.
Italian Greyhounds.
Japanese.
King Charles Spaniels.
Maltese.
Papillons.
Pekingese.
Pomeranians.
Pugs.
Yorkshire Terriers.

2. BREED REGISTERS AND VARIETIES OF BREEDS.—A separate Register, called the Breed Register, is kept by the Kennel Club for each breed, except in the cases of the following breeds, for which a separate Register is kept for each of the varieties of the breed specified.

RETRIEVERS.	SPANIELS.
Flat-coated.	Irish Water.
Curly-coated.	Clumber.
Labrador.	Sussex.
Golden.	Field.
Interbred.	English Springer.
Crossbred.	Welsh Springer.
	Cocker.

COLLIES.	FOX TERRIERS.
Rough.	Wire.
Smooth.	Smooth.

POODLES.
Not under 15in.   Miniature, under 15in.

3. BREEDS ELIGIBLE FOR CHALLENGE CERTIFICATES.—Challenge Certificates are issued by the Kennel Club for each breed or variety of breed of which a separate Register is kept.

4. OTHER REGISTERS.—A dog which is not eligible for entry in any of the above Registers, may be entered in one of the following Registers kept by the Kennel Club :—

Any other Breed.
Interbred Dogs.
Crossbred Dogs.

5. GROUPING OF BREEDS.—For the purpose of competition between dogs of differing breeds, the grouping of breeds as shown in Regulation 1 shall be held to define Sporting and Non-Sporting Dogs, and also Gundogs, Terriers, and Toys.

6. A DOG'S BREED.—A dog is of the breed or variety of breed named in the Breed Register in which it is held to be eligible for entry.

7. BREED REGISTRATION.—A dog bred from parents of the same breed or variety of breed can be entered only in the Register of that breed. If either parent or both parents are not registered in the Breed Register, the Kennel Club may permit registration on production of such evidence as it requires.

8. CROSSBREED REGISTRATION.—A dog bred from parents of different breeds must be registered as a crossbred, and the names of the breeds making the cross must be stated.

9. INTERBRED DOGS.—A dog bred from parents of the same breed, but of different varieties, must be entered in the Register of the variety it most closely resembles, and the names of the varieties making the interbreeding must be stated, except that such a dog bred from Retriever parents must be registered as an interbred.

10. CROSSBRED RETRIEVERS.—Any Retriever ineligible for registration as a pure bred or an interbred may be registered under the heading of a Retriever (crossbred).

11. INTERBREEDS IN BREED REGISTER.—A dog bred from a parent registered as an interbred must be registered as an interbred, but provided the interbred ancestors are registered at the Kennel Club a dog can be registered in a Breed Register, if in each of the first three generations of its pedigree one of the parents making the interbreeding is eligible for entry in that Register.

12. CROSSBREEDS IN BREED REGISTER.—A dog bred from a parent registered as a crossbreed must be registered as a crossbreed, but provided the crossbred ancestors are registered at the Kennel Club a dog can be registered in a Breed Register, if in each of the first four generations of its pedigree one of the parents making the crossbreeding is eligible for entry in that Register.

13. EXCLUSIONS FROM VARIETY STAKES.—A Retriever whose pedigree is not completely known for three generations cannot be entered in a Field Trial Stake confined to dogs of one or more named varieties of the Breed.

14. DOGS WITH WHOLE OR PART PEDIGREE UNKNOWN.— A dog with part of whole of its pedigree unknown may be entered in a Breed Register by permission of the Committee.

15. OWNER.—A dog when entered for a Show (or Trial) must be solely and unconditionally the property of the Exhibitor. In case of *Partnership* the full name of every partner must be given. A dog may be sold with its engagements and exhibited by its *New Owner*, subject to previous registration of *Transfer* of ownership.

16. BREEDER.—The Breeder is (1) the Owner of a Bitch at the time of whelping; (2) the person to whom it is lent or leased for breeding purposes, provided that *prior* to the whelping a declaration of the lending or leasing signed both by him and the Owner of the Bitch has been lodged at the Kennel Club.

17. NAME.—Three names besides the one desired should be given in case the one entered in the body of the form is not available for registration. The names of notable persons, places, kennels, countries, cities, common names, colours, or of a general character should not be selected. Numbers in figures or words cannot be accepted.

A name once entered in the Stud Book cannot be again registered in the same breed.

A name once registered cannot again be registered in the same breed for ten years after the 1st of January following the last registration.

18. PREFIXES AND AFFIXES constitute part of a name. A distinguishing letter or number either in figures or words shall not be used as a prefix or affix.

19. CHANGE OF NAME.—Change of name of a registered dog may be effected, subject to the condition that if a prize winner the *old* name, *as well* as the new name, must be given when a dog is entered for exhibition, etc., till the new name has been published in *The Kennel Gazette*.

A name once entered in the Stud Book cannot be changed.

20. IMPORTED DOGS.—The name of a dog imported from, and already entered in, any country with which the Kennel Club has a reciprocal agreement, cannot be changed.

21. CANCELLATION.—If a registered dog dies before it has been exhibited or bred from, or before it has been entered in the Stud Book, the owner may cancel the name and the same shall be deemed to have been never registered.

22. NON-ACCEPTANCE OF REGISTRATIONS.—The Committee may decline an application for any registration or cancel any registration already made.

23. REGISTRATION OF DOGS WITH UNREGISTERED PARENTAGE.—The Kennel Club accepts registration of dogs whose parents are not registered, but in such cases the name of an unregistered parent is printed in italics in the official list of registrations published monthly in *The Kennel Gazette*.

24. THE ACCEPTANCE OF A REGISTRATION is not a guarantee of its accuracy.

Regulations for the Licence or Sanction of Dog Shows held under Kennel Club Rules.

LICENCE SHOWS.

1. An application for a Licence to hold a Show must be lodged with the Secretary of the Kennel Club, 84, Piccadilly, W. 1, at least thirty days previous to the Show, together with the fee of Fifteen Shillings, a draft of the Schedule, and a copy of the proposed Show Regulations.

2. A Licence Show shall commence not later than 2 p.m. and if for one breed shall provide not fewer than thirteen classes, and if for more than one breed not fewer than twenty-one classes. No Licence shall be granted for a three-day Show, except on the condition that all dogs are permitted to be removed not later than 6 p.m. on the third day. At Licence Shows the exhibits must be benched in a proper manner, but the Committee of the Kennel Club may, under special circumstances, permit such a Show to be held without benching. The Executive of any Show, wishing to be relieved from benching, must make their application for exemption when applying for their Licence and give their full reasons for exemption. No person may interfere in any way with the benching as erected by the Show Executive, and in particular the partitions as erected between one pen and another must not be removed under any circumstances.

3. UNDERTAKING BY CHAIRMAN, TREASURER, AND SECRETARY OF SHOW WHEN SENDING APPLICATION FOR LICENCE.—The application for a Licence must be signed by the Chairman of the Committee of the Show, the Treasurer of the Show, and the Secretary of the Show, on the form provided by the Kennel Club. The above officers must also give their full addresses in the space provided on the said form. The signing of the application form by such officers shall be construed as an undertaking by each of them whereby they bind themselves jointly and severally to hold and conduct the Show under and in accordance with the Rules and Regulations of the Kennel Club to guarantee the due payment of all prize moneys and to abide by and adopt any decision of the Committee of the Kennel Club, or any authority to whom the Committee of the Kennel Club may delegate its powers, dealing with or having reference to any matter or dispute arising out of or in connection with the Show, and shall be taken as an agreement by them, and each of them, that any decision given against them or any of them, under Rule 16 or 17 of the Kennel Club Rules, may be communicated by the Secretary of the Kennel Club to the Secretaries of Dog Shows, Field Trials, and Societies affiliated with the Kennel Club, and may also be published in the official organ of the Kennel Club—*The Kennel Gazette*—together with a report of the proceedings in the matter, including names, addresses, and descriptions. Any notice sent by registered post to any such officers at the addresses given by them on the said form shall be deemed full and sufficient notice on the part of the Kennel Club to them, or any of them, of any proceedings, matters, or decision of the Committee of the Kennel Club, or any authority to whom the Committee of the Kennel Club may delegate its powers, or in regard to anything arising out of the said Licence or having regard to the conduct of the said Show, or in respect of any other matter whatsoever arising out of or in connection with the said Show. The Secretary of the Show, unless a member of the Committee, will not be held responsible as a guarantor of the prize money. The Secretary, Manager, and/or Committee of a Show shall be responsible for the payment of any fines imposed (*vide* Kennel Club Rule 18).

4. The Show Committee personally or by their authorised manager must issue a Schedule which *inter alia* must contain :—

(a) On the front outside cover the names and addresses of the guarantors of the Show, except in the case of Shows where classes are provided for other exhibits as well as dogs, where the names and addresses need only be printed at the head of the dog section.

(b) A copy of Kennel Club Authorised Show Regulations.

(c) An announcement of the definite hour or hours of closing the Show, and also the hours (if any) for special early removals and the conditions under which early removals are allowed. The time of closing the Show, and the conditions for the removal of dogs on each and every day, must be included in the Regulations of every Show.

It shall be left to the Show Committee to determine the hour of closing a Show, and the hours and the conditions for the removal of dogs, on each or any day, but the conditions may not include a right to charge a fee for the removal before the hour of closing. And no exhibit, other than puppies, shall be allowed to be removed from the Show, except at the hours and on the conditions so determined, unless by and with the order of the Veterinary Surgeon, or, under very exceptional and unforeseen circumstances, of the Show Manager, which must be reported to the Kennel Club.

(d) The following notices :—

Dogs born between September 7, 1917, and January 24, 1919, " unless bred under licence of the Kennel Club," shall be allowed to be shown " not for competition " only.

In the case of a dog owned in partnership, and entered in Members' Classes or competing for Members' Specials, each member of such partnership must at the time of entry be a member of such Association, Club, or Society.

Puppies over three months and under six months are not eligible for exhibition.

(e) When any class is guaranteed the name of the guarantors must be clearly stated in the Schedule.

(f) An official entry form which must be a copy of the specimen form issued by the Kennel Club.

(g) A Registration Form.

5. The Schedule of the Show is to be treated as a contract between the Show Authorities and the public, and neither party is permitted to make any modification, except by advertisement in the canine press prior to the closing of entries. No class may be provided unless a definition of the class is given in the Schedule.

6. ENTRY FORMS.—Entries must not be accepted unless made in accordance with Kennel Club Authorised Show Regulation 6. All entry forms must be preserved by the Show Committee for at least twelve months from the last day of the Show.

7. ENTRY FOR EXHIBITION.—Entries for a Show must close at the time indicated in the Schedule, and, at the latest, five clear days before the Show opens. Entries received by post bearing the postmark of the date for closing of entries may be accepted. In case of violation of this Rule the Secretary or Manager, or both, shall be held responsible, and may be dealt with under Rule 17.

8. CATALOGUE.—The Show Committee personally or by their authorised Manager must publish a printed catalogue, which must contain similar entries to those required in the Schedule under Regulation 4 (a), (b),

(*c*), (*e*), and also full particulars of the entry of each exhibit as given on the entry form by the exhibitor, and include the names and addresses of the exhibitors.

9. DISINFECTION.—The Show Committee personally or by their authorised Manager, shall, before receiving any dog at a Show, cause all benches, pens, and utensils to be properly and efficiently disinfected, and obtain a certificate from the Benching Contractors that this has been carried out, and must see that proper disinfection is maintained during the Show. A supply of disinfectant and towels must be provided for the use of the Veterinary Surgeons of the Show.

10. EXHIBITION OF DOGS SUFFERING FROM CONTAGIOUS OR INFECTIOUS DISEASE.—No dog must be exhibited which has been exposed to the risk of any contagious or infectious disease during a period of six weeks prior to exhibition. If any dog shall be proved to be suffering at a Show from any contagious or infectious disease, the exhibitor thereof shall be liable to pay to the Kennel Club such fine not exceeding £20 as the Committee of the Kennel Club shall determine.

11. ISOLATION OF SUSPICIOUS CASES.—The Show Committee personally or by their authorised Manager of a Show shall provide a suitable place in which dogs suspected of contagious or infectious disease can be properly isolated from the rest of the Show.

12. EXCLUSION OF DOGS.—The Show Committee shall have power to exclude or remove any dog which in the opinion of the Veterinary Surgeon of the Show is, owing to disease, savage disposition, or any other cause, not in a fit state for exhibition.

13. FREE PASSES MUST BE SUPPLIED TO EXHIBITORS; EXHIBITS ONLY TO BE ALLOWED IN SHOW:—

(*a*) The Committee of a Show shall provide every exhibitor with a free pass enabling him or her to enter the Show at any time during its continuance, but in the case of a dog owned in partnership only one such free pass need be issued. Any exhibitor entering three or more dogs shall be allowed a Kennelman's Pass, free.

(*b*) No animal other than an exhibit shall be allowed within the precincts of a Dog Show during its continuance.

14. WEIGHING MACHINES.—Where any competition with a weight limit takes place, properly constructed weighing machines must be provided.

15. JUDGES. There shall not be more than three judges appointed to adjudicate for any prize or special award.

16. NECESSARY DOCUMENTS TO BE FORWARDED AND INFORMATION GIVEN TO THE SECRETARY OF THE KENNEL CLUB.—The Secretary of a Show must forward the following documents to the Secretary of the Kennel Club, 84, Piccadilly, London, W., within the time specified, as follows:—

(*a*) Within three days of publication, two Schedules of the Show, including entry form and any and all enclosures sent therewith to exhibitors.

(*b*) Immediately after the close of the Show, and by registered post, the Kennel Club's List of Suspended Persons.

(*c*) Within three days of the close of the Show, an official catalogue of the Show, containing a full and correct list of all the entries made thereat, and all the awards correctly marked thereon.

(d) Upon demand by the Secretary of the Kennel Club, any entry form, or any other documents, or any information in connection with any appeal.

(e) Not earlier than twenty-one days, and not later than thirty-one days from the close of the Show, a notification that all prize money (except such as may be in abeyance by reason of objections still under consideration) has been paid, with particulars of the exceptions.

17. No dog shall be absent from its bench except for the purpose of being judged or exercised, or by order of the Verterinary Surgeon or Show Committee. No dog shall be absent from its bench for the purpose of being exercised at any time for longer than fifteen minutes.

18. FRAUDULENT OR DISCREDITABLE CONDUCT AT SHOWS TO BE REPORTED.—The Executive of a Show must immediately report to the Committee of the Kennel Club any case of alleged fraudulent or discreditable conduct at or in connection with the Show which may come under its notice, and at the same time forward to the Secretary of the Kennel Club all documents and information in connection therewith which may be in its possession or power. Where alleged fraudulent or discreditable conduct takes place at a Show in Scotland, the Executive of the Show must make such report in the first instance to the Committee of the Scottish Kennel Club.

If evidence is placed before the Committee of the Kennel Club to its satisfaction that undue influence has been exercised by any person, or that any improper means have been adopted to obtain, or interfere with, the appointment of a Judge at any Show under Kennel Club Rules, the Committee of the Show shall produce all correspondence or evidence in connection with the case to the Committee of the Kennel Club in order that it may deal with the offenders under Kennel Club Rule 17.

CHAMPIONSHIP SHOWS.

In the event of the Committee of a Licence Show desiring to offer Challenge Certificates, provisional application to hold a Championship Show must be made at least three months before the date of the Show, and if the Show is granted the right to offer any certificate, the following additional Regulations will apply :—

19. (a) The signature of three more members of the Committee must be added to the application form. (*See* Regulation 2 above.)

(b) There must be at least four classes, including an Open Class, for each sex (with three prizes in each) provided in each breed in which Challenge Certificates are offered.

(c) The prize money must be not less than £2 for first prize in all classes at the Show, except Brace, Team, Stud Dog, Brood Bitch, Veteran, Breeders, Selling, Litter, Local, and Members'.

(d) The Show must not be on the Sweepstake principle except in Brace or Team Classes.

20. A plan of the Show Ground or Hall, with particulars of the maximum space for benching and for judging, and such other particulars as may be required by the Committee of the Kennel Club or delegated authority as to emergency exits and other accommodation, must be provided.

21. Each ring must contain at least 500 sq. ft. of clear floor space, and be not less than 16ft. in width. Each ring must have some form of enclosure and no one except the officials of the Show, a Judge, and those in charge of the dogs being judged at the time, must be allowed within the enclosure. Should the enclosure be formed by seats, those occupying the seats will not be considered to be within the enclosure, and there must be a gangway on

two sides, or seating accommodation must be provided on three sides, of each ring. Where there is a double row of benching the gangway between each row must be at least 10ft. wide, and where there is a single row of benches the gangway must be at least 7ft. wide.

22. At all Shows where judging is intended to take place in the open air particulars must be given of the arrangements which will be made, in the event of rain, for the judging of the breeds for which Challenge Certificates have been granted.

23. The Show Secretary must obtain from the Kennel Club the award card for each Challenge Certificate offered, and no other notice regarding a Challenge Certificate must be placed on the bench.

24. The Show Committee or their official assistants will be responsible for getting the signature of the Judge on the Challenge Certificate award card, and a Challenge Certificate shall not be issued until the Judge signs the award card.

25. A printed slip regarding Challenge Certificates must be obtained from the Kennel Club and be pasted into each judging book supplied to the Judges.

26. No dog can receive a Challenge Certificate unless in the Show at the time of the award is made.

27. At a Championship Show the judging of breeds in which Challenge Certificates are offered must not commence later than 11-30 a.m., and the duration of the Show shall not be less than five hours.

SANCTION SHOWS.

28. These Shows must not commence earlier than 5 p.m., except on Saturdays and the official early closing day of the district when they may commence at 3-30 p.m., and must conclude the same evening. The dogs need not be benched.

29. The fee for holding each "Sanction" Show is Seven Shillings and Sixpence.

30. Only *bona fide* members of the Association, Club, or Society holding the Show may compete.

31. A Show confined to one breed must not comprise more than twelve classes, nor a Show of various breeds more than twenty classes. A Society may hold twelve "Sanction" Shows in any one year, but not more than one in each calendar month.

32. No person disqualified under Kennel Club Rules is eligible to compete or take any part at a "Sanction" Show.

33. All dogs exhibited at these Shows must be registered at the Kennel Club in accordance with Rule 7 of the Kennel Club Rules, and must be *bona fide* the property of the persons entering them. All entries must be correctly and properly made in accordance with the registration of the particular dogs, and the exhibitors must sign a declaration on the entry form, which must be a copy of the specimen form issued by the Kennel Club, agreeing to abide by the Regulations of the Kennel Club dealing with "Sanction" Shows and those Rules of the Kennel Club applicable to the same.

34. In case of change of ownership of a registered dog, the transfer to the exhibitor of such dog must be registered at the Kennel Club, for which a fee of Seven Shillings and Sixpence will be charged, and no such dog will be eligible for exhibition at any "Sanction" Show until such transfer has been registered.

35. Definitions applicable to Sanction Shows only.—Maiden Class : A Maiden Class is one in which no dog can compete which has won any prize in any class at a Sanction Show or a Show under Kennel Club Rules.

Novice Class : " A Novice Class is one in which no dog can compete which has won a Challenge Certificate at a Show under Kennel Club Rules, or a First Prize in any class other than Puppy or Maiden, at a Sanction Show or a Show under Kennel Club Rules."

If a schedule be issued for a Sanction Show it is to be treated as a contract between the Show Authorities and the Public, and neither party is permitted to make any modification, except by advertisement in the canine press prior to the closing of entries.

36. Wins at a " Sanction " Show do not count against a dog for eligibility in classes at a Licence Show, except as provided for in Kennel Club Rules as regards Novice and Maiden Classes.

37. No dog must be exhibited which has been exposed to the risk of any contagious or infectious disease during a period of six weeks prior to exhibition. If any dog shall be proved to be suffering at a Show from any contagious or infectious disease the exhibitor thereof shall be liable to pay to the Kennel Club such fine not exceeding £20 as the Committee of the Kennel Club shall determine.

38. An objection to a dog at these Shows may be made by any person except such as are disqualified under Rule 17 of the Kennel Club Rules. Any such objection must be in writing and delivered within ten days of the Show to the Secretary of the Show, together with a deposit of Five Shillings, which is liable to be forfeited if, in the opinion of the Show Committee, the objection is frivolous. The objection must be dealt with by the Show Committee as soon as practicable after due notice to each party of the appointment, when it will be considered by the Show Committee, who, after hearing the case, are to communicate their decision to the parties concerned.

39. An appeal shall lie from the decision of a Show Committee to the Kennel Club Committee or its Delegated Authority, provided due notice is given to the Secretary of the Kennel Club or its Delegated Authority within ten days of the said decision, and a hearing fee of Ten Shillings is deposited, returnable at the discretion of the Kennel Club Committee or Delegated Authority.

40. No prize money or prize won must be paid or delivered until the expiration of twenty-one days from the close of the Show, and in the case of objection by any person or by the Kennel Club Committee or its Delegated Authority not until such objection is finally disposed of and special permission to pay is granted by the Kennel Club Committee or its Delegated Authority. Subject to the above all prize money must be paid within one month of the close of the Show.

41. Rules Nos. 7, 8 (c), 8 (e), 9 (a), 9 (b), 9 (c), 9 (d), 9 (e), 13, 14, 15, 16, 17, 18, and 20, of the Kennel Club Rules apply to " Sanction " Shows, and a copy of those Rules, as also a copy of these Regulations, both of which can be obtained from the Kennel Club, must be exhibited in a prominent position at the Show by the Secretary of the Show.

42. Dogs born between September 7, 1917, and January 24, 1919, " unless bred under licence of the Kennel Club," shall be allowed to be shown " not for competition " only.

43. In the case of a dog owned in partnership and entered in Members' Classes, or competing for Members' Specials, each member of such partnership must, at the time of entry, be a member of such Association, Club, or Society.

MATCHES.

44. A Match is one between two individual dogs.

45. Not more than twelve Matches may be held on the same evening, and no dog may be matched more than once the same evening.

46. Application for permission to hold such Matches must be made to the Secretary of the Kennel Club at least fourteen days before the date of the proposed Match.

47. No special prize shall be awarded at Matches unless permission has been obtained from the Kennel Club.

48. A fee of Five Shillings must be forwarded with each application. This fee covers a maximum number of twelve Matches, all held at the same meeting.

49. All dogs competing at Matches must be registered at the Kennel Club before the date of the Match in the name of the exhibitor.

50. A list of the names of all competing dogs with awards must be sent to the Secretary of the Kennel Club within three days of the Matches being held.

51. No dog born between September 7, 1917, and January 24, 1919, "unless bred under licence of the Kennel Club," shall be allowed to compete.

52. In the case of a dog owned in partnership and entered in Members' Classes or competing for Members' Specials, each member of such partnership must at the time of entry be a member of such Association, Club, or Society.

EXEMPTION SHOWS OR CLASSES.

53. The Committee of the Kennel Club or Delegated Authority will, under special circumstances, and, without fee, grant to Agricultural and Horticultural Shows, Fetes, and the like, under the title of Exemption Shows or Classes, permission to hold a Show of not more than four classes for dogs at their exhibitions, and the dogs exhibited at such Exemption Shows or in such classes need not be registered, but any such Shows or Classes and the exhibitors in them will be subject to Kennel Club Rules 16, 17, and 20.

Regulations as to the Preparation of Dogs for Exhibition.

A dog shall be disqualified from winning a prize or from receiving one if awarded at any Show (except as hereinafter provided) if it be proved to the Committee of the Show or the Committee of the Kennel Club, as the case may be :—

1. That any dye, colouring, darkening, bleaching, or other matter, has been in any way used for the purpose of altering or improving the colour or marking of a dog.

2. That any preparation, chemical or otherwise, has been used for the purpose of altering or improving the texture of the coat.

3. That any powder, oil, greasy or sticky substance has been used and remains in the coat during times of exhibition.

4. That any part of a dog's coat or hair has been cut, clipped, singed or rasped down by any substance, or that the new or fast coat has been removed by any means except in the following breeds :—Bedlington Terriers, Bull Terriers, Collies, Fox Terriers (Wire and Smooth), Pomeranians, Poodles, Retrievers (Curly-coated), Scottish Terriers and Yorkshire Terriers. The old or shedding coat and loose hair may be removed in all breeds.

5. That if any cutting, piercing, breaking by force, or any kind of operation or act which destroys tissues of the ears, or alters their natural formation or carriage, or shortens the tail, or alters the natural formation, or colour, of the dog, or any part thereof, has been practised, or any other thing has been done calculated in the opinion of the Committee of the Kennel Club to deceive, except in cases of necessary operation certified to the satisfaction of the Committee of the Kennel Club. Dewclaws may be removed in any breed, and shortening the tails of dogs of the following breeds will not render them liable to disqualification : Spaniels (except Irish Water), Airedale Terriers, Fox Terriers, Irish Terriers, Kerry Blue Terriers, Sealyham Terriers, Welsh Terriers, Old English Sheepdogs, Poodles, King Charles Spaniels, Yorkshire Terriers, Schipperkes, Griffons Bruxellois, and such other breeds as the Committee may from time to time determine.

6. That the lining membranes of the mouth have been cut or mutilated in any way.

PRIZE DOGS:

Their Successful Housing, Management, and Preparation for Exhibition from Puppyhood to the Show Ring (Illustrated).

BY

THEO: MARPLES, F.Z.S.
(Editor of "Our Dogs," Author of "Show Dogs," &c.).

THIS WORK IS THE

INDISPENSABLE COMPANION

TO

"SHOW DOGS"

And should be read by all Dog Owners and Exhibitors who desire success in their Kennel.

PRICE - - - 4/8 (post free)

"Our Dogs" Glossary of Technical Terms (Illustrated) Relating to Dogs.

COMPILED BY **THEO: MARPLES.**
[COPYRIGHT.]

TOPKNOT.—The hair on the top of the head, as in the Irish Water Spaniel, Dandie Dinmont, and Bedlington Terrier.
SNIPY.—Too pointed in muzzle.
FLEWS.—The lips.
HAW.—The red membrane inside the lower eyelid.
LEATHER.—The ears.
OCCIPUT.—The bony bump on the top of the head.
BURR.—The inside of the ears.
STOP.—The step or indentation between the eyes, commencing the forehead.
OVERSHOT, OVERHUNG, OR PIG-JAW.—The top jaw protruding beyond the lower jaw.
UNDERSHOT OR UNDERHUNG.—The underjaw protruding beyond the upper jaw.
DISH-FACED OR MONKEY-FACED.—The nose turned up, and the face scooped out before the eyes.
WALL-EYE.—A blue mottled eye.
CHOP.—The foreface of a Bulldog.
FROG-FACE OR DOWN-FACE.—Nose not receding. (See illustrations.)
CUSHION.—Fulness in the top lips.
LAYBACK.—Receding nose. (See illustration.)
CHEEKY.—Thick in cheeks.
DOMED SKULL.—Round skull.
ROSE EAR.
BUTTON EAR.
PRICK EAR.
SEMI-PRICK EAR.
TULIP EAR.
WRINKLE.—Loose-folding skin over the skull.
BROKEN-UP FACE.—Refers more particularly to the face of the Bulldog or King Charles Spaniel, and comprises the receding nose, or layback, deep stop, and wrinkle.
MASK.—The dark muzzle of a Mastiff or Pug.
MANE.—The profuse hair on top of neck.

FRILL.—The profuse hair under the neck.
STERN.—The tail.
PLUME.—The tail of a Pomeranian.
FLAG.—The tail of a Setter.
BRUSH.—The tail of a Collie, or any bushy tail.
KINK-TAIL.—A tail with a single break or kink in it.
TWIST.—The curled tail of a Pug.
CROOK-TAIL.—The crooked tail of a Bulldog.
RING-TAIL.—A tail curving round in circular fashion.
SICKLE-TAIL.—A tail forming a semi-circle, like a sickle.
FEATHER.—The feathering on legs, as in the Setter and Spaniel.
CULOTTE.—The feather on the thighs, as in the Schipperke and Pomeranian.
TRACE.—The dark mark down the back of a Pug.
UPRIGHT SHOULDERS.—Shoulders that are set in an upright instead of oblique position; not laid back.
OUT AT SHOULDERS.—Shoulders set on outside, as in the Bulldog.
LOINS.—That part of the anatomy of the dog between the last rib and hindquarters.
ROACH BACK OR ARCHED LOINS.—The arched or wheel formation of loin, as in a Greyhound, Dachshund, Dandie Dinmont Terrier, and Bulldog.
TUCKED-UP.—Tucked-up loin, as in the Greyhound.
BEEFY.—Big, beefy hindquarters.
LONG IN FLANK.—Long in back and loins.
SHORT-COUPLED.—Short in back and loins.
BRISKET.—Front part of chest.
DEEP IN BRISKET.—Deep in chest.
FLAT-SIDED.—Flat in ribs.
SPRING.—Round or well-sprung ribs.
SHELLY.—Narrow, shelly body.
OUT AT ELBOWS.—Elbows coming out.
PASTERNS.—The knee joints of front legs.
PAD.—The underneath portion of the foot.
HARE-FOOT.—Foot like that of the hare, long and narrow.
CAT-FOOT.—Foot like a cat's, short, round, and compact.
STIFLES.—The upper joint of hind-leg.

SECOND THIGHS.—The muscular development between stifle joint and hock.
THE HOCK.—The lower joint of hind-leg.
COW-HOCKS.—Hocks that turn in, like those of a cow.
DEW CLAWS.—The superfluous claw inside the hind just above the foot.
THUMB MARKS.—The round black spots on the foot of a Black-and-tan Terrier.
PENCILLING.—The black marks or streaks dividing tan on the toes of a Black-and-tan Terrier.
BREECHING.—The tan-coloured hairs on the back of thighs of a Black-and-tan Terrier.
VENT.—The tan-coloured hair round the anus.
CHARACTER.—A combination of points contributing the whole, and giving to a dog the desired character associated with his particular variety.
EXPRESSION.—The expression of a dog is determined by the size and placement of the eye. For instance, in a St. Bernard the eye is small, somewhat sunken, showing a little haw. This gives a soft and benevolent expression.
VARMINT EXPRESSION.—As in the eye of the Fox-terrier, which is free from haw, is not sunken, nor large and set in, in a somewhat horizontal position giving a keen varmint expression.
CORKY.—Compact and active looking.
LISTLESS.—Dull and sluggish.
CLODDY OR COBBY.—Thick-set, short-coupled, and low in stature.
RACY.—Slight in build and leggy, as in the Greyhound or Whippet.
TIMBER.—Bone.
LUMBER.—Superfluous flesh.
STYLE.—Showy and of a stylish, gay demeanour.
TRICOLOUR.—Black, tan, and white.
WHEATEN.—Pale yellowish colour.
GRIZZLE.—A bluish-grey colour.
MERLE.—A bluish-grey colour splashed with black.
HARLEQUIN.—Pied, mottled, or patchy in colour.

www.ingramcontent.com/pod-product-compliance
Lightning Source LLC
Chambersburg PA
CBHW021142160426
43194CB00007B/657